INFANTS AND TODDLERS
WITH HEARING LOSS

INFANTS AND TODDLERS WITH HEARING LOSS

Family-Centered Assessment and Intervention

Edited by
Jackson Roush and
Noel D. Matkin

York Press, Inc.
Baltimore

This book was manufactured in the United States of America. Typography by The Type Shoppe, Inc. Printing and binding by McNaughton & Gunn, Inc. Cover design by Joseph Dieter, Jr. Book design by Sheila Stoneham.

A Note regarding Terminology The terms used in reference to children and adults with hearing loss tend to change over time. Recently, some have expressed preference for the combined use of the terms "deaf" and "hard of hearing," although others consider these terms antiquated. The descriptor "hearing impaired," which was once favored over the latter terms, is now criticized by some because of the potentially negative connotation of the word "impaired." There has also been a trend in the professional literature and in recent legislation to use "people-first" terminology e.g., "a child with a disability" rather than a "disabled child." The contributors to this book were not required to adopt a particular approach in their use of terminology and some inconsistencies will be noted. The debate on preferred terminology is certain to continue and although consensus is unlikely, we view this controversy as a healthy sign of professional introspection.

Library of Congress Cataloging-In-Publication Data

Infants and toddlers with hearing loss : family-centered assessment
   and intervention / edited by Jackson Roush and Noel D. Matkin.
       p. cm.
   Includes bibliographical references and index.
   ISBN 0-912752-28-9
       1. Hearing disorders in children.   2. Hearing disorders in
infants.   3. Hearing impaired children—Family relationships.
I. Roush, Jackson.   II. Matkin, Noel D.
RF291.5.C45154   1994   94-22417
362.4'28'054—dc20   CIP

Contents

Part V. **PREPARING FOR THE FUTURE**

Contributors

Donald B. Bailey, Jr., Ph.D.
Frank Porter Graham Child
Development Center
CB #8180
University of North
Carolina–Chapel Hill
Chapel Hill, NC 27599

Barbara A. Bodner-Johnson
Department of Education
Gallaudet University
800 Florida Avenue, NE
Washington, DC 20002

Arlene Stredler Brown
Colorado Home Intervention
Program
Colorado Department of
Health
Health Care Program
4300 Cherry Creek Drive South
Denver, CO 80222

Thomas Clark, Ph.D.
SKI*HI Institute and
Department of Communica-
tion Disorders (Emeritus)
Utah State University
Logan, UT 84321

Marie-Celeste Condon, M.S.
Boys Town National Research
Hospital
555 N. 30th Street
Omaha, NE 68131

Allan O. Diefendorf, Ph.D.
Audiology and Speech/
Language Pathology
Department of Otolaryngology
Indiana University School of
Medicine
Indianapolis, IN 46202

Rebecca M. Fischer, Ph.D.
Bill Wilkerson Center
1114 19th Avenue, South
Nashville, TN 37212

Judith Gravel, Ph.D.
Albert Einstein College of
Medicine
Kennedy Center #805
1300 Morris Park Avenue
Bronx, NY 10461

Janice C. Gatty, Ed.D.
Harriet Smith Short Center
Clarke School for the Deaf
Round Hill Road
Northampton, MA 01060

Melody F. Harrison, Ph.D.
Division of Speech and
Hearing Sciences
The University of North
Carolina
Chapel Hill, NC 27599

David Luterman, Ed.D.
Division of Communication
Disorders

Emerson College
168 Beacon Street
Boston, MA 02116

Noel D. Matkin, Ph.D.
Department of Speech and
Hearing Sciences
Room 104, Speech Building
University of Arizona
Tucson, AZ 85721

Mary McGonigal, Ph.D.
1858 Mintwood Place, NW
Washington, DC 20009

Robin A. McWilliam, Ph.D.
Frank Porter Graham Child
Development Center
CB# 8180
University of North Carolina
Chapel Hill, NC 27599

Mary Pat Moeller, M.S.
Boys Town National Research
Hospital
555 N. 30th Street
Omaha, NE 68131

Jackson Roush, Ph.D.
Division of Speech and
Hearing Sciences
CB #7190
University of North Carolina
Chapel Hill, NC 27599

Nancy Rushmer, M.A.,
Preschool Family Program
Columbia Regional Program
for the Deaf and Hard of
Hearing
531 SE 14th Avenue
Portland, OR 97214

Valerie Schuyler, M.A.,
Infant Hearing Resource
Portland Center for Hearing &
Speech
3515 SW Veterans Hospital
Road
Portland, OR 97201

Marie D. Thompson, Ph.D
College of Education, Speech
and Hearing Sciences, and
Early Childhood Programs
Experimental Education Unit,
WJ-10
University of Washington
Seattle, WA 98195

Bruce A. Weber, Ph.D.
Center for Speech and Hearing
Disorders
Division of Otolaryngology
Duke University School of
Medicine
Durham, NC 27710

Pamela J. Winton, Ph.D.
Frank Porter Graham Child
Development Center
CB #8180
University of North Carolina
Chapel Hill, NC 27599

Christine Yoshinaga-Itano, Ph.D.
Department of Communica-
tion Disorders and Speech
Science
Campus Box 409
University of Colorado
Boulder, CO 80309

Foreword

Tremendous changes are occurring in the nature of the relationship between parents and professionals who work with children who have special needs. At the heart of these changes is a recognition that a child cannot be viewed apart from his or her family. Furthermore, the family is an integral member of the assessment and intervention planning team and ultimately should be "in charge" of the decisions that are made as a result of that process. Thus, the model of services is changing from one of professional as an expert who imparts information to parents and makes decisions about treatment to one of parents and professionals engaged in a collaborative process to determine what is best for both the child and the family.

The changing nature of parent-professional relationships, although widely embraced philosophically, poses a number of challenges for both professionals and families. Professionals do not usually receive training in how to work with families, and several studies have shown that most team members rate their child-centered skills as superior to their skills in working with families. Although many professionals endorse the principles of a family-centered approach, they often have substantial concerns about how this model will be implemented and how it fits with the working assumptions of their own discipline as well as other disciplines. Most families want to be seen as competent decision makers and team members, but many have had prior experiences with professionals who have not followed a family-centered approach and have come to expect a more directed model. Thus, while there is widespread enthusiasm about the theoretical assumptions underlying a family-centered approach, its implementation is fraught with many practical challenges.

Responding to these implementation challenges will require a variety of support mechanisms for both parents and professionals. Although general publications about family-centered practices are likely to be useful for all participants in the process, each discipline must develop and demonstrate ways that are uniquely applicable to the ecology in which professionals from that discipline work. The present book, edited by Jack Roush and Noel Matkin, provides an essential body of information for professionals working with young children with hearing loss and their families. The text begins with an overview of the family-centered movement, discusses its implications for assessment and intervention, and provides numerous examples of how these principles have been integrated into practice in a variety of settings.

The combination of principles, guidelines, and examples makes this text uniquely informative. Roush and Matkin have selected a competent array of contributors who reflect today's leadership in family-centered approaches to early intervention. They also have appropriately sought input from parents in this process and discuss implications for personnel preparation.

Ultimately, professionals must realize that a family-centered approach is one that is individualized on the basis of each family's resources, priorities, and concerns. No text can provide a cookbook for such individualization, because such a process requires a professional who views each interaction with families as an opportunity to learn about the family's perspective on their child and to support families as caregivers and as decision makers. Professionals who expect a text such as this to provide step-by-step guidelines for a family-centered approach will be disappointed, but such an expectation is unrealistic. What this text does provide is an invaluable framework for practitioners, as well as multiple examples of how the framework has been applied with many different families. As such, it is the springboard from which professionals working with infants and toddlers with hearing loss can begin an important journey in which they will work collaboratively with families to develop a program of services that is individualized in such a fashion as to support families and children with special needs.

Don Bailey, Director
Frank Porter Graham Child Development Center
University of North Carolina at Chapel Hill

Preface

In 1986, the U.S. Department of Education and the U.S. Bureau of Maternal and Child Health funded the Carolina Institute for Research on Infant Personnel Preparation, a five-year project designed to prepare professionals from a variety of disciplines to serve young children with special needs and their families. This book, which grew out of that Institute, seeks to explore family-centered principles as they relate to a specific population: children who are deaf or hard of hearing. Although many of the issues facing families are unrelated to a child's particular exceptionality, hearing loss presents unique challenges, particularly with regard to communication and educational placement. Many families struggle with decisions concerning the use of hearing aids, cochlear implants, signing, auditory-oral approaches, and "special" versus mainstream educational placements.

The primary goal of this book is to heighten awareness of family-centered principles and how they can be applied within our professional endeavors. We have attempted to do this without favoring any particular methodology, placement option, or service delivery setting. Indeed, it is our belief that, whenever possible, *families* should make these important decisions and professionals should encourage and support them in a decision-making role. That is not to say that professionals who believe in a particular philosophy should be expected to hide their enthusiasm or commitment. Devotion to a particular method or philosophy is often what makes it so successful! But we believe that professionals who deal with families, particularly when the diagnosis of permanent hearing loss is recent, must be able to provide a balanced and unbiased perspective. Moreover, once decisions are made regarding placement and intervention, professionals must be willing to support families who choose to modify their decisions as they become either better informed or more self-directed.

Another goal of this book is to provide information regarding clinical issues of general interest to professionals who work with this population. Information regarding identification of hearing loss and the use of hearing aids or other sensory devices is presented at a level appropriate for professionals from a variety of disciplines. A review of federal regulations is also provided with examples of how these principles may be applied to the development and implementation of an "individualized family service plan."

The practical application of a family-centered approach is illustrated through descriptions of several programs currently operating in the U.S.A. Here too we sought a balance with regard to methodology; however, it will be obvious to readers that the concepts defining a family-centered approach can be applied to many situations. Indeed, the family of today takes many forms apart from those of the traditional family unit. The demographics of hearing loss in childhood are also changing to include a growing number of children with multiple disabilities and/or milder degrees of hearing loss.

In seeking to learn more about how best to facilitate parent-professional relationships, we sought advice directly from the consumers of our professional services, the parents themselves. Through a mail survey, we solicited written comments from families with young deaf and hard-of-hearing children, asking them to share experiences that were and were not helpful. Their comments, which bring closure to this book, offer critical insights of great value to students and professionals who seek more effective parent-professional communication. Also in the final section is an examination of personnel preparation, relative to where we've been and where we must go as we educate future practitioners.

A project of this nature is possible only through the efforts of many individuals and institutions. We are especially grateful to Dr. Merle McPherson, U.S. Bureau of Maternal and Child Health, whose agency provided the resources necessary to fund Audiology and Medicine along with seven other disciplines funded by the Department of Education in the core grant of the Carolina Institute for Research on Infant Personnel Preparation. Don Bailey, director of that Institute, and Pamela Winton, a co-investigator, were particularly instrumental in providing the encouragement and freedom to pursue this project. David Luterman and Pat Roush provided support and encouragement throughout, as well as helpful comments on manuscripts in preparation. We are especially grateful for the work of our professional colleagues whose contributed chapters gave substance to the goals set forth above. Several graduate students also made important contributions to this work, both in manuscript preparation and in providing a preservice perspective on the book's content: Diana Davidson, Nikolas Klakow, Claire Goodson, Miriam Friedman, and Ann McKinley.

Finally, we are grateful for the collective contribution of the parents whose "advice for professionals" drew on the personal experiences and insights of our primary constituency: the families of young deaf and hard-of-hearing children. Our principal objective will be fulfilled if, in some measure, the book promotes and reinforces the development of healthy collaborative relationships between parents and professionals.

Jackson Roush
Chapel Hill, NC

Noel Matkin
Tucson, AZ

Infants belong intimately to their families. Entering into the lives of families as an outsider is a delicate matter. To do so when childbirth has brought unexpected outcomes requires a great deal of self-awareness and understanding of what is valued and nonintrusive for families. That understanding can only be achieved by careful, thoughtful collaboration with each family.

Linda Kjerland and Joanne Kovach
In *Interdisciplinary Assessment of Infants:*
A Guide for Early Intervention Professionals

PART • **I**

Preliminary Considerations

Chapter • 1

Family-Centered Early Intervention
Historical, Philosophical, and Legislative Issues

Jackson Roush and R. A. McWilliam

HISTORICAL PERSPECTIVES

Programs for deaf and hard-of-hearing children were among the first in this country to provide educational experiences outside a "regular" classroom environment. Although most early programs were designed to serve school-aged children, Moores (1987) recalls that early intervention programs in the United States have existed since the mid-19th century. By the late 1800s several residential schools offered programs for infants and toddlers (Craig 1983), and in the first half of the 20th century numerous preschool day programs were created for deaf children (Connery 1933). In 1940, the John Tracy Clinic established a home correspondence course for families with deaf and hard-of-hearing children.

During the past 50 years there has been considerable expansion in the number of programs for preschool-aged children. Research in the 1950s and 1960s confirmed the importance of the first few years of life on cognitive and linguistic development (e.g., Bourne 1966; Brown 1958; Brown and Bellugi 1964). This was accompanied by a growing impetus within general education to support "compensatory" preschool programs such as Head Start (Moores 1987). Improved audiologic identification procedures and hearing aid technology resulted in a growing awareness of the need for, and benefit of, early intervention for deaf and hard-of-hearing children (Knox and McConnell 1968).

These trends were well established in the mid-1960s, when a rubella epidemic dramatically increased the number of children born with hearing loss.

In the 1970s, early intervention for young children with hearing loss continued to expand and diversify, particularly regarding parent involvement (McConnell 1974; Murphy 1979). The U.S. Department of Education funded several innovative family-oriented, early intervention programs including "UNISTAPS" (Northcott 1972) and "SKI*HI" (Clark and Watkins 1978), both of which were influential nationwide in shaping other new programs. The goals of providing early home-based intervention were consistent with research findings of that period that demonstrated the importance of parent–child communication in the language acquisition of young children with hearing loss (Kretschmer and Kretschmer 1979). Even among children with normal hearing, there was growing evidence that parent involvement resulted in greater and longer lasting gains from early intervention (Bronfenbrenner 1975).

In the 1980s, research findings continued to demonstrate the importance of parent–family involvement. Moran (1985), for example, found that mothers participating in home-based programs had more positive attitudes toward their children, and Greenberg (1983) reported that a family-oriented program resulted in more developmentally mature communication, lower stress, and higher quality interaction among family members. Also in the 1980s, specialized parent-oriented curricula were developed (e.g., Schuyler et al. 1985), and there was a growing awareness of the need to address the emotional needs of parents and other family members (Luterman 1984; Moses 1985). Research in the pragmatics of communication between caregivers and young children revealed the importance of considering the social context of communication development. Fitzgerald and Fischer (1987) observed that "The gradual evolution toward an integrated, ecological perspective for family involvement results from the recognition that the hearing-impaired infant is a member of a family system and a communication network. Such an assumption dictates that intervention efforts must be directed at the systems level rather than exclusively at the child or parent level" (p. 3).

Along with the positive outcomes of family involvement, parent–professional conflicts can occur. Parents and professionals may disagree on the goals of early intervention (e.g., Cadman, Goldsmith, and Bashim 1984) or professionals may make inappropriate assumptions about parental needs (e.g., Bernstein and Barta 1988; Dunst 1985). Moreover, when parent–professional conflicts occur, parental views may not be given primary consideration (Roush, Harrison, and Palsha 1992).

Most early intervention programs for deaf and hard-of-hearing children are provided by public school districts and residential schools for the deaf (*American Annals of the Deaf*, April 1993). Although there seems to be growing support for parent and family involvement in early intervention, many programs continue to lack substantial family participation (Roush et al. 1991). Kjerland and Kovach (1990), reflecting on traditional practices in early intervention, advocate a revised perspective that abandons the image of staff at the center of the process. Instead, they argue, the task is to place families at the center and negotiate appropriate staff involvement with families. Achieving a family orientation necessitates a reconceptualization of early intervention and "parent involvement" (Foster, Berger, and McLean 1981), one that maintains a collaborative role for professionals but with families at the center of the decision-making process to the fullest extent they desire.

WHY A FAMILY-CENTERED APPROACH?

Few would argue that families are central to the "ecology" of young children. Thus, a family-centered philosophy assumes that: (1) social supports affect family functioning; (2) the child's needs are best met by meeting family needs; and (3) families have the right to retain as much control as they desire over the intervention process.

Social Systems and Social Support

Professionals working with children in the first three years of life must be sensitive to the psychological influences of family, friends, neighbors, religious community, and so forth. Also important is an understanding of formal and informal support networks as well as an awareness of the help-giver/help-seeker relationships affecting the dynamics of early intervention. Early intervention for children with special needs is increasingly being viewed from an ecological perspective (e.g., Dunst, Trivette, and Deal 1988; Turnbull and Turnbull 1986; Vincent et al. 1990). That is, intervention is seen as providing support not only to the child but also to the child's family, extended family, and community. From this standpoint, influences on children and their families may be mediated by a host of environmental and interpersonal variables that require alternatives to traditional child-centered approaches to early intervention (Dunst 1985). These alternatives include attention to the interpersonal as well as material resources of the family.

Family social networks, including formal support systems (professionals, agencies) and informal systems (extended family, neighbors, religious communities, etc.) compose a family's social support network (Dunst and Trivette 1990). For families whose young children have special needs, Dunst and colleagues found that the adequacy of social support, especially when used to meet the family's self-identified needs, improves family well-being while reducing time demands, enhancing caregiver–child interactions, reducing interfering caregiving styles, and improving parents' perceptions of their child's functioning. Also improved are child temperament and motivation (Dunst and Trivette 1990).

Family Functioning

Public Law 99-457 sought to open the door for parent–professional collaboration in a manner that facilitates the intervention outcomes desired by families. Having a child with disabilities can have a profound effect on a family's domestic roles, finances, leisure activities, and socialization (Turnbull and Turnbull 1986). Professionals must be sensitive to and accepting of families' behaviors, values, and concerns while parents and other family members make adaptations to the presence of a child with special needs.

The effects of such a child on family functioning may differ depending on the child's age and the nature of his or her special needs. For example, Hanson and Hanline (1990), using the Parenting Stress Index (PSI), reported that mothers of one-year-old children with hearing loss experienced higher stress related to child "demandingness" than did mothers of children with Down syndrome or neurologic impairments. But their findings also revealed that, by the time children reached the age of two years, there were no differences among the groups on this measure. There were, however, differences related to child "acceptability," with the least stress reported by mothers of children with hearing loss. The Hanson and Hanline study showed that parents of very young children with disabilities experience stress related to the special needs of their children, but that on the whole patterns of parental stress were similar. Interestingly, across all groups, higher stress levels were associated with less satisfaction in parenting and fewer sources of social support.

Much of the research in early intervention has been conducted with mothers. But as McLinden (1990) has shown, mothers and fathers may disagree in their perceptions of time demands, coping, and well-being. Her research also demonstrated that mothers' negative-impact scores tended to occur more frequently than fathers' for time demands and well-being, while fathers tended to use fewer positive coping strategies. An awareness of the stresses experienced by a given family as well as coping strategies it has found to be successful, can be very useful in developing a plan for early intervention. Accordingly, Public Law 99-457 and subsequent legislation include an assessment of family priorities and concerns as part of the individualized family service plan (IFSP).

Family Needs, Concerns, and Priorities. Identifying family strengths is essential when assessing the various support systems available to the child and family. According to Bailey (1989), family needs may be shelter related (e.g., food, clothing, housing); service related (e.g., medical, dental, transportation); child related (e.g., early intervention [education]); adult related (e.g., job training); or family-life related (e.g., recreational, emotional, and cultural/social). Numerous methods exist for collecting information from parents including questionnaires, naturalistic observation, and interviews (Bailey 1989). Although most families seem to prefer informal conversational methods, a study assessing parents' reaction to the Family Needs Survey (Bailey and Simeonsson 1988) revealed that 60% of fathers and 40% of mothers preferred a written questionnaire (Bailey and Blasco 1990). Because the purpose of family assessment is to discover ways to help the family identify and use resources to accomplish their goals and address their concerns, the family's preferred method of assessment should prevail (Dokecki and Heflinger 1989).

Family Systems Theory. The basic principle underlying family systems theory is that what affects one family member affects all family members (Minuchin 1974). The demands associated with early intervention, therefore, affect not only the parents but also the child's siblings and extended family. Consequently, parent education and support efforts have implications beyond those individuals directly involved in the early intervention program. Turnbull and Turnbull (1986) have conceptualized the family system as comprising family resources (characteristics of the family, of the disability, etc.), family interactions (marital, parental, etc.), family functions (economic, affection, etc.), and the family life cycle (transitions, structural change, etc.). It is within each of these components that change affecting one member affects the family as a whole. For example, money spent on hearing aids (family resources) may mean there will be less money available for recreational activities. Furthermore, a change in one component is likely to affect other components. A new sibling (family life cycle), for example, might influence the amount of time the mother has to spend with other family members (family resources), which may have an impact on the relationship between the parents or between the parents and their other children (family interactions). These changes might, in turn, affect the nature and degree of family socialization (family functions).

An extension of the family systems literature is "ecocultural theory," which acknowledges the family's viewpoint as *their* reality (Bernheimer, Gallimore, and Weisner 1990; Weisner 1984). Family systems theory and cultural diversity have a direct influence on the way early intervention is conceptualized: it is the mediation of various types of support for individuals within the family and for the family unit as a whole. The tradition of individualized intervention with children has been generalized to an approach with families that takes into account each family's preferences, values, and resources.

The extent to which social supports and family functioning are affected by the presence of a young deaf or hard-of-hearing child is not well known. For most families, however, the diagnosis of permanent hearing loss is a stressful and unfamiliar event. Considering that more than 90% of children with congenital hearing loss have normal-hearing parents (Rawlings and Jensema 1977), it is not surprising that the identification of a hearing loss is often met with shock and a profound sense of powerlessness (Luterman 1979; Schlesinger 1985). Unfortunately, contacts with professionals, instead of alleviating these feelings, may actually heighten parental feelings of inadequacy (Williams and Darbyshire 1982).

In recent years, legislation and changes in public policies have put increasing pressure on states to provide early intervention services. Although the underlying rationale is a positive one, Meadow-Orlans (1990) warns that shifting responsibility away from the family may have the undesirable side effect of fostering dependency relationships, while placing undue emphasis on cognitive and educational issues rather than social and emotional concerns. In contrast, when family-centered early intervention is achieved, there is strong evidence that better communication and more functional family relations ensue (e.g., Greenberg 1983; Moeller, Coufal, and Hixson 1990). Regrettably, effective social supports are not always available. Quittner (1990) reported that mothers of preschool-age children with severe-to-profound hearing loss had fewer support networks as well as a higher number of problematic relationships with friends and relatives. Mothers reported that many people had misconceptions that led to underestimation of their childrens' abilities, even with friends, relatives, and others likely to provide social supports.

Koester and Meadow-Orlans (1990) reported data from a nationwide survey that examined the impact of congenital hearing loss on the family. Three scales of eight items each were compiled from a pool of 39 questions related to: (1) family stress; (2) communication with the child; and (3) relationships with professionals and others outside the family. Nearly 400 questionnaires were returned, over half of which included both mothers and fathers. The children included in this survey represented a variety of educational programs and all age groups, from infancy to over 20 years. Nearly half (44%) had profound hearing loss; the remainder had lesser degrees of hearing loss. Several interesting findings were reported. First, it was noted that responses of mothers and fathers did not differ significantly on individual items; fathers, however, tended to experience less stress related to their child's hearing loss but also less satisfaction in their ability to communicate with the child. They also found that mothers and fathers of older children tended to rate their relationships with professionals less positively than did parents of younger children. Interestingly, parents of middle children reported communication to be less satisfactory than parents whose deaf and hard-of-hearing children were first-born, last-born, or only children. Among families whose children had additional handicapping conditions, they found greater stress within the family, less satisfaction regarding communication with the child, and more difficulty with relationships outside the family. Finally, a particularly interesting observation was that responses from families with profoundly deaf children were similar to those with children having lesser degrees of hearing loss.

In summary, family-centered early intervention is based on a social systems approach to working with infants and toddlers. This inevitably implies working at some level with other family members, usually the parents. But traditional "parent training," "parent involvement," or "parent support" models no longer suffice. These methods of working with families were based on models that characterized the parent as pupil, the parent as client, or the parent as patient. Some families might choose these approaches, but the options for family-centered, parent–professional collaboration must be more inclusive. Although individual differences will ultimately determine the approach selected by a family, it is incumbent upon professionals to determine a family's concerns and priorities, recognizing that the more often families can determine their own needs and preferences, the more successful those efforts are likely to be. Understanding a family's resources, interactions, functioning style, and stage of life is an enormous challenge, but when accomplished, leads to a more effective and supportive intervention process.

Implications for Program Evaluation

Program evaluation in early intervention has traditionally focused on "child-centered outcomes" (Guralnick 1988). A family-centered approach suggests that "family outcomes" should be given equal emphasis. Unfortunately, few studies have gone beyond simple parent satisfaction measures (Bailey and Simeonsson 1986; Hauser-Cram

1990). The rationale for looking at family impact is that children's development is a transactional process (Sameroff and Chandler 1975), in which both child and family characteristics contribute to the success of the intervention by their impact on one another.

Reviews of the early intervention efficacy literature reveal potential problems with internal validity (e.g., history, maturation, testing effects). Dunst (1986) argues, however, that early intervention has been conceptualized too narrowly to capture the full impact of support to families: "Early intervention is not considered to be services provided by a particular program, but rather the aggregation of sources of support by different individuals and groups" (p. 124). In assessing outcomes for young deaf and hard-of-hearing children, it is essential that we look beyond our traditional indices of child progress to include family outcomes.

Family Outcomes. What family outcomes could one use to determine whether early intervention has been effective? Commonly suggested outcomes include reduction of parenting stress, development of positive parent-child interactions and child-rearing practices, strengthening of parental and familial social support networks, promotion of healthy family functioning, enhancement of education, increase in family income and employment opportunities for parents, and promotion of positive development among siblings (Krauss and Jacobs 1990). There are literally hundreds of measurement tools for determining various aspects of family well-being (see table I for a summary of several instruments). What is *missing* from the literature is a methodology for determining how the child benefits from family-centered intervention (Vincent et al. 1990). Traditionally, special education, speech-language pathology, and audiology have all been child-centered, a fact that poses a considerable challenge when attempting to look at families in determining the success of our intervention efforts. It is essential, however, that we adopt a broader view of family outcomes, one that considers the impact on both the child and family. Cultural mores, family history, and genetics will all have an impact on the course of development, but the environment, which includes the early intervention program, will determine the relative contributions of each. If supports are in place, positive child and family outcomes are likely to occur. But if they are lacking, the child and family are apt to encounter difficulty making the adjustments necessitated by a young child with special needs.

Table I. Examples of Measurement Tools Available for Evaluating Various Aspects of Family Well-being

The Family Adaptability and Cohesion Evaluation Scales (FACES) (Olson, Portner, and Bell 1982) categorize families into one of 16 types according to measures of "cohesion and adaptability." The optimal characteristics are neither "enmeshed" nor "disengaged" (re: cohesion) and neither too rigid nor too chaotic (re: adaptability).

The Family Inventory of Life Events and Changes (FILE) (McCubbin and Patterson 1981) measures the "pile-up" of family stress (McCubbin, Patterson, and Wilson 1979). This is a 71-item self-report instrument that records the normal and abnormal life events of a family, compared to the previous year.

The Family Needs Scale (Dunst et al. 1988) This 41-item questionnaire examines nine categories of need. It was specifically designed for early intervention purposes (Dunst, Trivette, and Deal 1988).

The Family Needs Survey (Bailey and Simeonsson 1988) is a questionnaire that parents complete. It has 35 items asking how much help is needed in six major areas.

The Family Resources Scale (Dunst and Leet 1987) consists of 30 items on which families rate their satisfaction in seven domains.

The Family Support Scale (Dunst, Jenkins, and Trivette 1984) has 18 items addressing the benefit of various forms of child-rearing support.

The Home Observation for Measurement of the Environment (HOME) (Bradley and Caldwell 1984) is an observation-based measure of various issues believed to influence child development (e.g., availability of play materials, emotional climate, freedom of movement, opportunities for exploration). Although it is probably the most commonly used instrument by home-visiting programs, the HOME has been criticized because of its white, middle-class orientation and its heavy reliance on maternal report (see Krauss and Jacobs 1990).

The Parenting Stress Index (PSI) (Abidin 1983; Loyd and Abidin 1985) measures several areas of parent stress and their interpretation.

LEGISLATIVE ISSUES

Public Law 99-457, enacted in 1986, re-authorized Public Law 94-142, the Education of All Handicapped Children Act of 1975, and amended it to include mandatory special education for children aged three to five years. Resources were also provided to fund early intervention programs serving infants and toddlers with handicaps, from birth to age three, and their families. In 1990, Public Law 101-476 again authorized the Education of the Handicapped Act, changing its name to the "Individuals with Disabilities Education Act" (IDEA). Revisions to Part H of P.L. 99-457 were made in P.L. 102-119, which included changing the term "case manager" to "family service coordinator" (as one parent testified, "I'm not a *case* and I don't want to be *managed*"). The new law also employed "people first" terminology (e.g., "children with disabilities" instead of "disabled children").

Part H of Public Law 99-457 provided funding to states to develop a system of services for infants and toddlers (birth through age two) with developmental delays or disabilities, or conditions that place them "at risk" for delays or disabilities. States are not required to participate in Part H, but those electing to take part must develop and implement a statewide plan for infant-toddler services.

Part B, Section 619 of Public Law 99-457 provided for a free and appropriate public education and related services to three-, four-, and five-year-old children with disabilities. In essence, it extended the provisions existing under P.L. 94-142 to three- and four-year-olds.

Definition of Developmental Delay

Public Laws 99-457, 101-476, and 102-119 define infants and toddlers with disabilities as individuals from birth through age two who need early intervention services because they: (1) are experiencing developmental delays as measured by appropriate diagnostic measures in one or more of the following areas: cognitive development, physical development (including vision and hearing), communication development, social/emotional development, or adaptive development; or (2) have a diagnosed physical or mental condition that has a high probability of resulting in a developmental disability. When standardized assessment measures are unavailable or inappropriate, states are required to provide an "informed clinical opinion" regarding developmental status.

Legislative Requirements for Birth to Three

It is important to note that states are not *required* to provide infant-toddler services; however, at the time of this writing, all 50 states are actively participating in the planning or implementation of infant-toddler services. Key elements include the following.

Identification of Eligible Children. Each state is required to develop a comprehensive "child-find system" coordinated with existing public and private identification efforts within the state. Professionals or agencies must be alerted to refer potentially eligible children for assessment, and procedures must be established to determine eligibility for early intervention services. The regulations provide guidance for developing identification, coordination, and referral procedures. Referrals to the appropriate public agencies must be made within two working days of the child's identification, and the agency then has 45 days to assess the child and call a meeting to develop an individualized family service plan (IFSP).

Comprehensive Multidisciplinary Assessment. A comprehensive multidisciplinary assessment of the child must be provided and the family priorities and concerns must be determined as they relate to the child's development. To provide this assessment, infants and toddlers must be evaluated by a multidisciplinary team of qualified professionals. The assessment must include: (1) the child's level of functioning in the five primary developmental areas described earlier (this includes hearing), (2) the child's unique needs in these areas, (3) identification of services to meet those needs, and (4) assessment of the family's self-identified priorities and concerns related to the child's development. When extenuating circumstances prevent an assessment from occurring within the 45-day time frame, provisions are made in the law for an "interim IFSP," so that early intervention services can be initiated prior to completion of the formal assessment process. Those found eligible to receive early intervention services must be reassessed annually and their IFSP must be reviewed semi-annually.

Individualized Family Service Plan. At the heart of the early intervention program is the "individualized family service plan" (IFSP). This document is intended to draw on the multidisciplinary team to include families in developing individualized early intervention programs. Unlike the child-centered Individualized Education Plan (IEP), established under P.L. 94-142, the IFSP calls for child and family goals, when appropriate, with specific criteria for evaluating goal attainment. The legislation also calls for specification of services needed by the family and child, and the designation of a family service coordinator to ensure that the IFSP is properly implemented. A conceptual orientation and models of implementation are provided in Chapters 6 and 7 of this book.

Public Awareness. States are required to maintain a public awareness program focusing on early identification of infants and toddlers with special needs. The public awareness effort must be ongoing and involve existing state organizations. Unlike the "child-find" component, this one is aimed at the general public. States may use various media to publicize the availability of services.

Designation of Lead Agency. The governor of each state is required to designate a "lead agency" to administer, supervise, and monitor its infant-toddler programs. States have differed in their selection of a lead agency and, in some cases, more than one agency is involved in the management of early intervention services.

Directory of Services. A central directory of services, resources, experts, and demonstration sites must be maintained and updated, at least annually, and must provide information regarding resources for parent support and advocacy. The directory must be geared to families, including those in rural areas, and to people with handicaps.

Policies for Contractual Services. States must clearly establish policies for contracts with other agencies, including private service providers. Federal regulations encourage the use of existing agencies as well as new ones to serve infants, toddlers, and families. Unlike Head Start legislation, which created a single new service, the current legislative climate emphasizes collaboration (Garwood and Sheehan 1989) and use of existing resources. Lead agencies are responsible for ensuring that services provided by contracted agencies are in compliance with legal mandates.

Procedures for Funding and Reimbursement. Delays in reimbursement to service providers and agencies should not be a cause for delays in service; however, small agencies cannot operate on credit or without cash. Consequently, each state is required to establish a procedure for timely reimbursement. Furthermore, federal funding cannot be used to satisfy financial obligations that would have been covered under another program.

Procedural Safeguards. Procedural safeguards include parents' rights to examination of records, administrative complaint procedures, appointment of an impartial person to handle resolution of complaints, timelines, and other accommodations to suit parents, the right to file a civil action suit, continuation of services to the child during any such proceedings (unless parents and the state agency agree otherwise), and procedures for the assignment of surrogate parents when necessary. The congressional authors of P.L. 99-457 recognized that legal action could occur and that infants and toddlers would be especially vulnerable to delays in service resulting from such action. Therefore, agencies must also demonstrate that safeguards exist and that families are informed of these protections.

Personnel Preparation. States are required to establish policies and procedures to ensure the availability of adequately prepared and trained personnel. They are also required to develop a "comprehensive system of personnel development." In colleges and universities, the various disciplines preparing personnel to serve young children with disabilities are expected to include some infancy and family content in their preservice training programs.

THE CHALLENGE OF A FAMILY-CENTERED APPROACH

Public Law 99-457 has been widely regarded as a landmark for early intervention. Still, several areas of uncertainty remain. All 50 states have passed legislation that defines eligibility for early intervention services and establishes guidelines for their implementation. But the amount of federal money that states will receive in the coming years to support their early intervention efforts remains uncertain. Indeed, the failure of Congress to appropriate the funds authorized under past legislation has caused most states to respond cautiously to the new laws.

Another area of uncertainty for most disciplines is the new emphasis on the family and how this emphasis will affect current practices. For many professionals, moving from a child-centered to a family-oriented approach represents a philosophical leap, and one for which neither their academic training nor their professional experience has prepared them. A frank reappraisal of traditional practices is needed to determine how this critical element of the new law can be realized.

Also of concern is that in some states, resources to provide infant-toddler and preschool services are unlikely to be sufficient, even with federal support. States not already providing birth-to-three services when P.L. 99-457 was implemented felt the greatest impact. But even among those already providing infant-toddler services, considerable retooling has been needed to achieve a family-centered approach to early intervention. Still, it is important to remember that states have tremendous latitude in how they define eligibility for early intervention and to what extent they elect to provide these services. As a result, early intervention services differ significantly from one state to another.

An issue of particular relevance to professionals involved with hearing loss is that of early identification. Roush and McWilliam (1990) note that federal regulations do not require screening of every child at risk for hearing loss (or any other condition). Although some states have mandated hearing screening programs, federal regulations require only that states develop procedures to identify children *who are eligible* for early intervention services. Obviously, such a charge is open to a broad range of interpretations. For example, one state may choose to require formal screening of all infants at risk for hearing loss, while another might choose to satisfy its identification requirements by merely providing a referral mechanism when concerns regarding a child's hearing status are raised. Clearly, the two models would result in substantial differences in the average age of identification, and thus, the age at which intervention services are initiated.

Regardless of their professional discipline, the greatest challenge for all practitioners is to approach the early intervention process from an ecological perspective, incorporating the child's family, extended family, and network of other caregivers. This requires an open-mindedness toward parent-professional collaboration and a serious commitment to well-coordinated interprofessional cooperation. Matkin (1985) writes, "As the population of hearing-impaired children becomes more varied and complex, the need for interactive interdisciplinary teamwork, whether in a clinical or school setting, becomes more imperative" (p. 80). Where lacking, professionals from all disciplines will need to establish and maintain close working relationships with their colleagues on local multidisciplinary teams and with the service providers who carry out the early intervention programs.

As a result of recent federal legislation, more children will receive early intervention services in mainstream environments. Successful mainstreaming requires a spirit of professional interaction that extends beyond the usual boundaries of interdisciplinary cooperation to permit a sharing of roles, enabling primary caregivers and other professionals to carry out the recommendations of practitioners from other disciplines. Professionals will also need to play a more active and aggressive role in establishing comprehensive identification programs and well-coordinated procedures for initiating early intervention when a hearing loss is identified. Where they are lacking, policies governing the classification of hearing loss and eligibility for early intervention must be established and implemented.

There also needs to be a thoughtful re-examination of how we prepare professionals to work with young children and their families. Recent surveys in the relevant disciplines indicate that most entry-level clinicians and teachers receive minimal educational preparation to work with infants and toddlers and their families (Bailey et al. 1990; Roush, Harrison, and Palsha 1991, 1992; Oyler and Matkin 1987). Future educational preparation of specialists who will serve young deaf and hard-of-hearing children and their families must consider the multitude of special skills required. As emphasized by Sass-Lehrer and Bodner-Johnson (1989), no single discipline can provide the knowledge base required in the areas of infant and early childhood development, early communication development, family systems, counseling, and multidisciplinary team evaluation. A collaboration of professionals from several disciplines is needed within and among institutions, to adequately prepare specialists in this area.

Demographic characteristics are also changing. In recent years, the number of preschool-age children receiving services has continued to rise steadily. Schildroth, Rawlings, and Allen (1989), in a demographic analysis of deaf and hard-of-hearing children under the age of six years, showed that over a ten-year period the number of preschool-age children with hearing loss has increased significantly, with the largest growth occurring among children from ethnic minorities. White Americans, although still the largest group represented, have declined in number while those from ethnic minorities, especially Hispanic Americans, have increased. Other notable findings were a significant increase in the number of younger children, those under three years of age, and an increase in the number of hard-of-hearing children, those with hearing loss less than 70 dB HL. In addition to these trends, significant changes have occured in the composition of families. Census Bureau figures from 1990 reveal that about 1 in 4 children in the United States live with a single parent, compared to about 1 in 10 in 1960. When minorities are considered separately, the numbers are even more striking: over half of all African-American children live in single-parent households as do nearly one-third of all Hispanic-American children. Clearly, a family-centered approach to early intervention must consider these changing demographics as well as an awareness of and respect for a broad range of multicultural differences.

The rich and varied history of services to young deaf and hard-of-hearing children and current theories regarding family-centered care converge at the point of interaction between families and professionals. Whether discussing development and behavior, making recommendations for educational placement, reviewing audiologic findings, assessing the family's preferences for communication, or simply listening to the parents' concerns, the knowledge and skills required by today's infant-family specialist are greater than ever. But along with this challenge are unprecedented opportunities for parent–professional collaboration. Although the transition from a child-centered to a family-centered orientation will, for some professionals, require a fundamental reconceptualization of the parent–professional relationship, it is a transition that can and must be made, for it is in the strength of this relationship that the effectiveness of early intervention is truly measured.

REFERENCES

Abidin, R. 1983. *Parenting Stress Index*. Charlottesville, VA: Pediatric Psychology Press.

American Annals of the Deaf. Annual Reference Issue, April 1993.

Bailey, D. B. 1989. Issues and directions in preparing professionals to work with young handicapped children and their families. In *Policy Implementation and PL 99-457*, eds. J. Gallagher, P. Trohanis, and R. Clifford. Baltimore: Paul H. Brookes Publishing.

Bailey, D. B., and Blasco, P. 1990. Parents' perspectives on a written survey of family needs. *Journal of Early Intervention* 14(3):196–203.

Bailey, D., and Simeonsson, R. 1986. Design issues in family impact evaluation. In *Evaluating Early Intervention Programs for Severely Handicapped Children and Their Families*, eds. L. Brickman and D.L. Weatherford. Austin, TX: PRO-ED.

Bailey, D. B., and Simeonsson, R. J. 1988. *Family Assessment in Early Intervention*. Columbus, OH: Merrill.

Bailey, D. B., Simeonsson, R., Yoder, D., and Huntington, G. S. 1990. Infant personnel preparation across eight disciplines: An integrative analysis. *Exceptional Children* 57(1):26–35.

Bernheimer, L., Gallimore, R., and Weisner, T. 1990. Parenting a child with a disability: A longitudinal study of parental stress and adaptation. *Journal of Early Intervention* 14(3):219–33.

Bernstein, M., and Barta, L. 1988. Critical issues underlying research and intervention with families of young handicapped children. *Journal of the Division for Intervention with Young Handicapped Children* 9:27–37.

Bourne, L.E. 1966. *Human Conceptual Behavior*. Boston: Allyn and Bacon.

Bradley, R., and Caldwell, B. 1984. The relation of infants' home environment to achievement test performance in first grade: A follow-up study. *Childhood Development* 55:803–09.

Brown, R. 1958. *Words and Things*. New York: Free Press.

Brown, R., and Bellugi, U. 1964. Three processes in the child's acquisition of syntax. *Harvard Education Review* 34:133–51.

Cadman, D., Goldsmith, C., and Bashim, P. 1984. Values, preferences, and decisions in the care of children with developmental disabilities. *Developmental and Behavioral Pediatrics* 5:60–64.

Clark, T. C., and Watkins, S. 1978. *The SKI*HI Model: A Comprehensive Model for Identification, Language Facilitation, and Family Support for Hearing Handicapped Children through Home Management, Ages Birth to Six (3rd ed.).* Logan, UT: Utah State University.

Connery, J.A. 1933. A nursery school curriculum and its accomplishments. *Proceedings of the International Congress on Education of the Deaf*. Trenton, NJ.

Craig, H.B. 1983. Parent-infant education in schools for deaf children: Results of the CEASD survey. *American Annals of the Deaf* 128:82–98.

Dokecki, P., and Heflinger, C. 1989. Strengthening families of young children with handicapping conditions: Mapping backward from the "street level" pursuant to effective implementation of Public Law 99-457. In *Policy Implementation of PL 99-457: Planning for Young Children with Special Needs*, eds. J. Gallagher, R. Clifford, and P. Trohanis. Baltimore: Paul H. Brookes Publishing.

Dunst, C.J. 1985. Rethinking early intervention. *Analysis and Intervention in Developmental Disabilities* 5:165–201.

Dunst, C.J. 1986. Overview of the efficacy of early intervention programs. In *Evaluating Early Intervention Programs for Severely Handicapped Children and Their Families*, eds. L. Brickman and D.L. Weatherford. Austin, TX: PRO-ED.

Dunst, C., and Leet, H. 1987. Measuring the adequacy of resources in houses with young children. *Child: Care, Health, and Development* 13:111–25.

Dunst, C., and Trivette, C. 1990. A family systems model of early intervention. In *Parent Education and Support Programs: Consequences for Children and Families*, ed. D.P. Powell. Norwood, NJ: Ablex Publishing.

Dunst, C., Jenkins, V., and Trivette, C. 1984. Family Support Scale: Reliability and validity. *Journal of Individual, Family, and Community Wellness* 1:45–52.

Dunst, C., Leet, H., and Trivette, C. 1988. Family resources, personal well-being, and early intervention. *Journal of Special Education* 22(1):108–16.

Dunst, C., Trivette, C., and Deal, A. 1988. *Enabling and Empowering Families: Principles and Guidelines for Practice*. Cambridge, MA: Brookline Books.

Fitzgerald, M., and Fischer, R. 1987. A family involvement model for hearing impaired infants. *Topics in Language Disorders* 7(3):1–18.

Foster, M., Berger, M., and McLean, M. 1981. Rethinking a good idea: A re-assessment of parent involvement. *Topics in Early Childhood Special Education* 1(3):55–65.

Garwood, S. G., and Sheehan, R. 1989. *Designing a Comprehensive Early Intervention System: The Challenge of Public Law 99-457.* Austin, TX: PRO-ED.

Greenberg, M.T. 1983. Family stress and child competence: The effects of early intervention for families of deaf infants. *American Annals of the Deaf* 128(3): 407–17.

Guralnick, M. 1988. Effective research in early childhood intervention programs. In *Early Intervention for Infants and Children with Handicaps,* eds. S. Odom and M. Karnes. Baltimore: Paul H. Brookes Publishing.

Hanson, M., and Hanline, M. 1990. Mothers' and fathers' reports of the effects of a young child with special needs on the family. *Journal of Early Intervention* 14(3):249–59.

Hauser-Cram, P. 1990. Designing meaningful evaluations of early intervention services. In *Handbook of Early Childhood Intervention,* eds. S. Meisels and J. Shonkoff. Cambridge, MA: Cambridge University Press.

Kjerland, L., and Kovach, J. 1990. Family-staff collaboration for tailored infant assessment. In *Interdisciplinary Assessment of Infants: A Guide for Early Intervention Professionals,* eds. E. Gibbs and D. Teti. Baltimore: Paul H. Brookes Publishing.

Knox, L.L., and McConnell, F. 1968. Helping parents to help deaf infants. *Children* 15:183–87.

Koester, L., and Meadow-Orlans, K. 1990. Parenting a deaf child: Stress, strength, and support. In *Educational and Developmental Aspects of Deafness,* eds. D. Moores and K. Meadow-Orlans. Washington, DC: Gallaudet University Press.

Krauss, M., and Jacobs, F. 1990. Family assessment: Purposes and techniques. In *Handbook of Early Childhood Intervention,* eds. S. Meisels and J. Shonkoff. Cambridge, MA: Cambridge University Press.

Kretschmer, R., and Kretschmer, L. 1979. The acquisition of linguistic and communicative competence: Parent-child interactions. *Volta Review* 81:306–322.

Loyd, B., and Abidin, R. 1985. Revision of the Parenting Stress Index. *Journal of Pediatric Psychology* 10:169–77.

Luterman, D. 1979. *Counseling Parents of Hearing-Impaired Children.* Boston: Little-Brown.

Luterman, D. 1984. *Counseling the Communicatively Disordered and their Families.* Boston: Little-Brown.

Matkin, N. 1985. Effective communication: Interactive interdisciplinary teamwork. In *Hearing Impaired Children and Youth with Developmental Disabilities,* ed. E. Cherow. Washington, DC: Gallaudet College Press.

McConnell, F.E. 1974. The parent teaching home: An early intervention program for hearing-impaired children. *Peabody Journal of Education* 51:162–70.

McCubbin, H., and Patterson, J. 1981. *Systematic Assessment of Family Stress, Resources and Coping: Tools for Research, Education and Clinical Intervention.* St. Paul: Family Social Science.

McLinden, S. E. 1990. Mothers' and Fathers' reports of the effects of a young child with special needs on the family. *Journal of Early Intervention* 14:249–59.

Meadow-Orlans, K. 1990. The impact of childhood hearing loss on the family. In *Educational and Developmental Aspects of Deafness,* eds. D. Moores and K. Meadow-Orlans. Washington, DC: Gallaudet University Press.

Minuchin, S. 1974. *Families and Family Therapy*. Cambridge: Harvard University Press.

Moeller, M.P., Coufal, K., and Hixson, P. 1990. The efficacy of speech-language pathology intervention: Hearing impaired children. *Seminars in Speech and Language* 2(4):227–41.

Moores, D. 1987. *Educating the Deaf: Psychology, Principles, and Practices*. Boston: Houghton Mifflin.

Moran, M. 1985. Families in early intervention: Effects of program variables. *Zero to Three* 5(5):11–14.

Moses, K.L. 1985. Dynamic intervention with families. In *Hearing-Impaired Children and Youth with Developmental Disabilities: An Interdisciplinary Foundation for Service*. Washington, DC: Gallaudet College Press.

Murphy, A. 1979. The families of hearing-impaired children. *Volta Review* 81(5).

Northcott, W.H. 1972. *Curriculum Guide: Hearing-Impaired Children-Birth to Three Years, and Their Parents*. Washington, DC: Alexander Graham Bell Association for the Deaf.

Olson, D., Portner, J., and Bell, R. 1982. *FACES II: Family Adaptability and Cohesion Evaluation Scales*. St. Paul: Family Social Science, University of Minnesota.

Oyler, R., and Matkin, N. 1987. National survey of educational preparation in pediatric audiology. *Asha* 29(1):27–33.

Quittner, A.L. 1990. Coping with a hearing-impaired child: A model of adjustment to chronic stress. In *Advances in Child Health Psychology: Proceedings of the First Florida Conference*, eds. J.H. Johnson and S.B. Johnson. Gainesville, FL: University Press of Florida.

Rawlings, B., and Jensema, C. 1977. Two studies of the families of hearing impaired children. Series R, No. 5. Washington, DC: Gallaudet University, Office of Demographic Studies.

Roush, J. and McWilliam, R. 1990. A new challenge for pediatric audiology: Public Law 99-457. *Journal of the American Academy of Audiology* 1:196–208.

Roush, J., Harrison, M., and Palsha, S. 1991. Family-centered early intervention: The perceptions of professionals. *American Annals of the Deaf* 136(4):360–66.

Roush, J., Harrison, M., and Palsha, S., and Davidson, D. 1992. A national survey of educational preparation programs for early intervention specialists. *American Annals of the Deaf* 137(5):425–30.

Sameroff, A., and Chandler, M. 1975. Reproductive risk and the continuum of caretaking casualty. In *Review of Child Development Research* (Vol. 4). Chicago: University of Chicago Press.

Sass-Lehrer, M., and B. Bodner-Johnson. 1989. Public Law 99-457: A new challenge to early intervention. *American Annals of the Deaf* 134:71–77.

Schildroth, A., Rawlings, B., and Allen, T. 1989. Hearing-impaired children under age 6: A demographic analysis. *American Annals of the Deaf* 63–69.

Schlesinger, H. 1985. Deafness, mental health, and language. In *Education of the Hearing Impaired Child*, eds. F. Powell, T. Finitzo-Hieber, S. Friel-Patti, and D. Henderson. San Diego: College-Hill Press.

Schuyler, V., Rushmer, N., Arpan, R., Melum, A., Sowers, J., and Kennedy, N. 1985. *Parent-Infant Communication* (3rd ed.). Portland, OR: Infant Hearing Resource.

Turnbull, A., and Turnbull, H. 1986. *Families, Professionals, and Exceptionality: A Special Partnership*. Columbus, OH: Merrill Publishing.

Vincent, L., Salisbury, Strain, P., McCormick, C., and Tessier, A. 1990. A behavioral-ecological approach to early intervention. In *Handbook of Early Childhood Intervention*, eds. S. Meisels and J. Shonkoff. Cambridge, MA: Cambridge University Press.

Weisner, T.S. 1984. Ecocultural niches of middle childhood: A cross-cultural perspective. In *Development During Middle Childhood: The Years from Six to Twelve*, ed. W.A. Collins. Washington, DC: National Academy of Sciences Press.

Williams, D. and Darbyshire, J. 1982. Diagnosis of deafness: A study of family response and needs. *Volta Review* 84:24–30.

Chapter • 2

Becoming Family Centered
Strategies for Self-Examination

Pamela J. Winton and Donald B. Bailey, Jr.

Historically, early intervention for children with disabilities has been justified as a means for enhancing optimal child development and preventing or reducing the magnitude of either pervasive or specific delays. In the case of children with hearing loss, the rationale for early intervention generally focuses on preventing delays in oral communication, cognition, and social skills that may result from reduced or impaired auditory stimulation. Intervention typically consists of a combined use of instructional strategies, therapeutic activities, and sensory aids. Although more research is needed and controversies exist regarding the most appropriate models for treatment, the efficacy and importance of early intervention for children with hearing loss is widely recognized.

The presence of or suspicion of a hearing loss initiates an ongoing series of interactions with professionals from multiple disciplines. The child is both the stimulus and focus of these interactions and the nature and degree of hearing loss often determines the nature of the services needed. Thus, early identification and treatment of hearing loss historically has been a very child-focused endeavor.

In recent years it has been argued that in addition to serving children, a primary mission of early intervention is to provide family support. In early intervention, numerous labels have been applied to the family support movement, including parent empowerment (Dunst, Trivette, and Deal 1988), family-focused intervention (Bailey et al.

1986), and family-centered care (Shelton, Jeppson, and Johnson 1987). Although these models differ in some respects, each emphasizes (1) the importance of support of the family as a primary goal of early intervention, and (2) the expectation that families should be able to choose their level of involvement in program planning, decision making, and service delivery. Brewer (1989) describes family-centered care as follows:

> Family-centered care is the focus of philosophy of care in which the pivotal role of the family is recognized and respected in the lives of children with special health needs. Within this philosophy is the idea that families should be supported in their natural care-giving and decision-making roles by building on their unique strengths as people and families. In this philosophy, patterns of living at home and in the community are promoted; parents and professionals are seen as equals in a partnership committed to the development of optimal quality in the delivery of all levels of health care. To achieve this, elements of family-centered care and community-based care must be carefully interwoven into a full and effective coordination of the care of all children with special needs (p. 1055).

Being family centered is reflected in the willingness of an agency or a program to develop a collaborative relationship with each family and to provide services in accordance with family values and priorities.

The passage of Public Law 99-457 and its requirement for an Individualized Family Service Plan firmly establishes not only a philosophical but also a functional basis for being family centered. The regulations accompanying this law emphasize the role of parents as decision makers in determining the extent to which they accept or decline services. The importance of family choice, consent, and involvement is reflected throughout the regulations. The requirement for an Individualized Family Service Plan (IFSP) is the most visible and often-discussed aspect of the legislation with respect to a family focus. The IFSP must include, in addition to the child components required in the Individualized Education Plan (IEP), a documentation of family strengths and needs, a specification of major family outcomes, a description of services to be provided for the family, and the name of a family service coordinator who is to assist the family in implementing the plan and coordinating services with other agencies and persons. Clearly, however, a family-centered approach is broader than the IFSP. Also, it is clear that the way the law is implemented will vary widely across states and communities. Local planning and decision making are important.

Despite the obvious importance of being family centered, implementation of P.L. 99-457 has proved to be a challenging task, for a number of reasons. First, most professionals involved in early intervention for children with hearing loss enter their fields out of a desire to work with children, and their training is almost exclusively child focused (Bailey et al. 1990; Roush, Harrison, and Palsha 1991). Thus, many have neither the skills nor expectation to work with families. Second, a family-centered philosophy challenges the long-held view of the professional as the primary decision maker in the management of young children with disabilities, because a fundamental tenet of the family support movement is family choice and a responsiveness to family priorities (Bailey 1987). Relinquishing control of decisions about the nature and extent of early intervention services is likely to be viewed as threatening by many professionals. Third, professionals work in service delivery systems designed to provide child-based services. A recent study found that systems barriers were mentioned by professionals as one of the major reasons they were not more family centered in their services (Bailey, Buysse, Edmondson, and Smith 1992). Furthermore, the data indicate that many professionals feel that families have neither the interest nor the skills needed to participate fully in program planning and decision making. Finally, each of these factors is exacerbated by the uncertainty surrounding the actual implementation of a family-centered approach and the specific requirements to be followed. Many states have yet to develop guidelines for the IFSP or to provide comprehensive training for professionals with regard to either the guidelines, skills, or procedures needed to implement the law (Harbin, Gallagher, and Lillie 1989).

Given this information, it is safe to assume that there is considerable variability in the extent to which programs for young children with hearing loss are meeting the philosophical intent and basic requirements of Public Law 99-457 related to providing family support. Indeed, there is probably uncertainty and some confusion about what it means to be family centered. One of the first steps in changing practices related to such an innovation is to identify recommended practices in a concrete way and determine how they are different from or similar to those employed currently.

This chapter presents information that might be used by individuals or programs in order to identify concrete dimensions related to providing support to families of children with hearing loss, and assess whether their current practices are in keeping with recommended practices. This information is provided to enable professionals to become more family centered in their work. Four key areas of practice are presented: (1) developing a philosophy about work with families; (2) involving families in child assessment; (3) identifying family needs and resources; and (4) developing intervention plans in collaboration with families. Within each of these key areas, specific questions are raised to provide examples of how a family-centered approach might be put into operation. These questions provide an opportunity to consider current practices in light of family-centered assumptions.

DEVELOPING A PHILOSOPHY ABOUT WORK WITH FAMILIES

The literature on how institutions respond to change suggests that innovations are more likely to be implemented when they are compatible with the staff's existing values, attitudes, and philosophy (Havelock and Havelock 1973; Glaser, Abelson, and Garrison 1983). As mentioned earlier, the assumptions underlying current definitions of family-centered intervention challenge many traditional practices and beliefs related to working with families and young children with hearing loss. This suggests that the first step toward becoming more family centered is for staff members to compare their current program philosophy with the philosophical assumptions underlying family-centered intervention. Assumptions about family-centered operations that might be used for comparison purposes have been described in a number of publications (Shelton, Jeppson, and Johnson 1987; Dunst, Trivette, and Deal 1988; Johnson, McGonigel, and Kaufmann 1991). The following represents a compilation of the key points underlying the assumptions mentioned above:

Family centered   We recognize that the family is the constant in the child's life, whereas the service systems and personnel within those systems may be involved only episodically.

Ecologically based   In our work with families, we need to consider the interrelatedness of the various contexts that surround the child and family.

Individualized   Because the needs of each child and each family differ, services should be individualized to meet those unique needs.

Culturally sensitive   Families come from different culture and ethnic groups. Families reflect their diversity in their views and expectations of themselves, or their children, and of professionals. Services should be provided in ways that are sensitive to these variations and consistent with family values and beliefs.

Enabling and empowering   Services should foster a family's independence, skills, and sense of competence and worth.

Needs based   A "needs-based" philosophy starts with a family's expressed needs and attempts to help families identify and obtain services according to their priorities.

Coordinated service delivery   Families should be assisted in gaining access to and coordinating resources from a variety of informal and formal sources as needs indicate.

Normalized   Programs work to promote the integration of the child
      and the family within the community.
Collaborative   Early intervention services should be planned, imple-
      mented and evaluated through collaboration between parents
      and professionals.

Developing a set of beliefs, shared by staff members at all levels, provides a framework for decisions about policies and practices. Proceeding without consensus on basic philosophy is likely to result in conflict and disagreement about more specific practices.

One of the underlying assumptions of the family-centered approach is that families should be given opportunities and choices to be involved at all levels of service delivery including policy formulation, *if they so desire*. As mentioned earlier, data from a recent study indicated that professionals felt that families had neither the interest or skill to participate fully in program planning and decision making (Bailey, Buysse, Edmondson, and Smith 1992). This is clearly an area in which existing professional assumptions may be in conflict with the family-centered assumptions.

Recently we engaged in an in-service training experience that provided us with evidence that parents are willing and able to collaborate with professionals in the area of policy formulation (Bailey, Buysse, Smith-Bonahue, and Elam 1992). Data from several sources were used to assess the effects and perceptions of parent participation in a workshop designed to help professionals become more family centered in their work. Results indicated that the presence of parents influenced the extent to which professionals perceived a need for change in program practice. Both parents and professionals were positive about the experience; furthermore, professionals who attended a workshop where no parents were present felt strongly that parents should have been there.

Questions for Self-Assessment

The following questions (Bailey, McWilliam, Winton, and Simeonsson 1992) provide an opportunity for examining current practices related to policy formulation in light of the family-centered assumptions.

Is a family focus central to our program philosophy and shared by all
      team members?
Have families of young children with hearing loss been invited to col-
      laborate in the development of our program philosophy?
Do we attempt to implement our program philosophy in all areas of
      contact with families?

INVOLVING FAMILIES IN CHILD ASSESSMENT

Traditionally, responsibility for planning and conducting assessments of young children with hearing loss has been in the hands of professionals. The two primary reasons for conducting assessments are to determine a diagnosis and/or eligibility and to plan intervention. In order to accomplish these goals, professionals have relied on formal tests administered under standardized conditions. The results of such testing are scores or labels used to identify deficits that are to be remediated through intervention or therapy. The limitations to such an approach have been described in the literature and include the following: the focus is on deficits rather than strengths; the goals identified may not be functional; parents may feel incompetent and left out of the assessment process; and parents may not be committed to working on goals identified in this fashion (Sheehan 1988). Research from the medical field has indicated that families are less likely to comply with professional recommendations when they do not value or understand what is being recommended (Cadman et al. 1984). This suggests the importance of conducting assessments of children in ways that facilitate consensus among families and professionals on the following questions: (1) What is the diagnosis?; (2) Is intervention needed?; and (3) What type of intervention would work best? Too often professionals may make recommendations related to intervention when families are still questioning the diagnosis. A family-centered approach would suggest that involving families from the beginning in the diagnostic procedure makes it more likely that consensus on that and the subsequent intervention questions will develop.

The first step in involving families in child assessment is to develop a clear picture of how the family understands the child's disability and what they hope to learn from an assessment. In some cases families may have already undergone several assessments with different and conflicting outcomes. Perhaps another assessment is not needed. A group meeting including family members with the other professionals who have been involved with the family in the past might better serve the family's need for clarity and understanding of their child's condition instead of or prior to conducting further evaluations.

The following types of questions, phrased in ways unique to the understanding of individual families, may be helpful in eliciting from families their preferences regarding the purpose of child assessment:

What information have you been given about your child's hearing loss?
How does that information fit with what you know and believe about
    your child?
What kinds of advice have you been given and by whom?
How has that advice been helpful or not helpful?

What more would you like to find out about your child?
What ideas do you have about how we might find out those things?

A commitment to a family-centered approach would suggest that the format for child assessment would be influenced by what parents want to find out about their children and, more specifically, by what parents may think are the best ways of acquiring this information. Few parents know about specific procedures or tests for conducting assessments, but many parents appreciate finding out about the various options for gathering information and being provided with an explanation for why a professional might recommend certain strategies. Parents may then be able to consider what options they think would work best with their children.

When considering possible assessment formats, the role that family members might play in assessments is an important and related issue. The following represents six possible roles that families might play in the child assessment process (Bailey, McWilliam, Winton, and Simeonsson 1992): (1) receivers of information; (2) observers of professional assessment; (3) informants about specific behaviors and developmental milestones; (4) describers of parent-generated child skills and competencies; (5) interpreters of child's strengths and needs; and (6) participants in gathering data. Simply stating these roles and asking parents how they might want to be involved would probably leave most parents staring blankly. However, providing parents with specific examples of how they might work with professionals in gathering certain information that they have indicated they believe to be important gives them the opportunity to be informed decision makers. For example, if family members indicate that they believe that their hearing-impaired child may be developmentally delayed as well as hearing impaired, they might be given the option of participating in the development of a profile of their child's functioning across several developmental domains.

Involving parents in decisions about the time and place for assessments is another way of implementing a family-centered approach. Several issues related to time and place are of concern to families. Ensuring that assessments are conducted at a place and time that will optimize their children's performance is one such concern. Planning assessments for times and places convenient to all relevant family members is another, especially if working parents and siblings are involved. Project Dakota (Kjerland and Kovach 1990) has developed a Preassessment Planning Form, designed to elicit preferences from families in this regard (table I).

The implications for giving families choices is that their preferences will be considered and respected when possible. This may entail changing policies regarding hours of operation and staff schedules.

Table I.   Pre-assessment Planning

1. What questions or concerns do others have (e.g., babysitter, clinic, preschool)?
2. Are there other places where we should observe your child?
   Place:
   Contact Person:
   What to Observe:
3. How does your child do around other children?
4. Where would you like the assessment to take place?
5. What time of day? (The best time is when your child is alert and when working parents can be present.)
6. Are there others who should be there in addition to parents and staff?
7. What are your child's favorite toys or activities that help the child become focused, motivated, and comfortable?
8. Which roles would you find comfortable during assessment?
   _____ a. Sit beside your child
   _____ b. Help with activities to explore the child's abilities
   _____ c. Offer comfort and support to your child
   _____ d. Exchange ideas with the facilitator
   _____ e. Carry out activities to explore your child's abilities
   _____ f. Prefer facilitator to handle and carry out activities with your child
   _____ g. Other

Source: Project Dakota Outreach, Dakota, Inc., Eagan, MN.

Adapted from Kjerland and Kovach 1990, table 2. Reprinted with permission from Paul H. Brookes Publishing. L. Kjerland and J. Kovach. Family-staff collaboration for tailored infant assessment. In *Interdisciplinary Assessment of Infants*, eds. E. Gibbs and D. Teti. Baltimore, MD: Paul H. Brookes Publishing, PO Box 10624, Baltimore, MD 21285-0624.

Questions for Self-Assessment

The following questions (Bailey, McWilliam, Winton and Simeonsson 1992) provide an opportunity for professionals to consider current child assessment practices in light of some family-centered assumptions.

Are we complying with all P.L. 99-457 regulations regarding child assessment?

Do we try to determine family preferences about the purpose and format of child assessment, as well as their desire to become involved?

Do we convey assessment information in a sensitive and jargon-free fashion?

Does the family's perception of their child's needs determine the focus of child assessment?

Do we listen to families' preferences in determining settings, times, and parental roles in assessment of the child?

Do we address children's strengths in the assessment process?

IDENTIFYING FAMILY RESOURCES, CONCERNS, AND PRIORITIES

Traditionally, family-related information has been gathered for three reasons: (1) to further an understanding of the child; (2) to help design an appropriate intervention plan; and (3) to assess the family's abilities to carry out intervention plans. Gathering family information has received increasing attention as an area of practice as professionals attempt to become more family centered. For instance, the federal regulations for P.L. 99-457 specify that an Individualized Family Service Plan must be developed for every infant and toddler served in early intervention, and that this plan must include a statement about family resources, concerns, and priorities. Although this is a positive development, from many perspectives, there are some, including family members, who are apprehensive and uncertain as to what the emphasis on assessment of the family might mean.

The term *assessment* may be equated with *evaluation* and *judgment* by some parents, as illustrated in the following quote by Jeannette Behr in testimony to Congress.

> A family rated as "strong" may in fact fall apart because it is subsequently not given support. Even worse, a family rated as "weak" may be prevented from growing and coping by the perceptions of professionals. A poor rating may follow a family for years, and most likely, become self-fulfilling. To illustrate, I am not particularly interested in cleaning my house. It is not a priority with three small children who so quickly and utterly mess it up. Yet I still clean my house if any of the professionals involved in our lives are coming over. I am not willing to be judged by some, perhaps unconscious, standard.

An alternative interpretation of what is meant by family assessment might be derived from models and theories related to how families cope with crises (Hill 1958; Olson et al. 1983). These theories emphasize that an important part of understanding each families' unique way of coping, or the strengths they bring to bear on a situation, is to consider how a family defines both the crisis and the resources available to them. It is quite possible that simply identifying how families are defining and coping with events related to raising their children might best meet the intent of the law related to needs and strengths, rather than conducting lengthy and perhaps intrusive assessments. The further comments of Jeannette Behr support this interpretation.

> Finally, it is critical that professionals understand the real intent of P.L. 99-457 is to strengthen families. [It is] not to provide a certain level of service, not [to] do a certain assessment, but [to] understand a family's values and philosophy without judging and then [to] ask the family how it would like to build support. The constant concern heard now, which I share, is that professionals need multi-cultural awareness. But I

maintain that every family is a culture unto itself. States must address the training of professionals in view of a family-centered law, not an agency-centered law. To illustrate, I compare parenting any child to a dance; sometimes it is exhilarating and joyful, sometimes exhausting. Adding all the professionals can be most confusing unless we remember that parents pick the music and professionals help us with the steps we don't already know.

We suggest the following definition of family assessment: the process by which professionals gather information in order to determine family priorities for goals and services (Bailey, McWilliam, Winton, and Simeonsson 1992). This definition suggests that our purpose for gathering family information has changed. Rather than gathering information so that professionals can determine what is best for the child, the purpose is to gather information to determine what the family thinks is best for themselves and the child. Knowing what the family views as important provides a starting point for sharing information and professional expertise.

There are a variety of ways for gathering information from families, including standardized forms, questionnaires, checklists, and interviews. Examples are available in Bailey and Simeonsson (1988), Dunst, Trivette, and Deal (1988) and Johnson, McGonigel, and Kaufmann (1991). Research with parents provides some guidance when considering approaches. Bailey and Blasco (1990) reported that parents feel it is important to be given choices about how they might share information about their needs related to early intervention. Research by Summers et al. (1990) indicated that parents preferred face-to-face conversations for imparting information on needs and strengths.

The information on strategies for collecting family information leads to another issue for consideration, that of communication skills related to eliciting information effectively on resources, concerns, and priorities during family conversations. Is it as simple as saying, "Tell me your strengths"? If not, can therapists and teachers trained to work with children be expected to have or to develop the skills necessary to gather information from families effectively through conversations? Traditionally, social workers and psychologists have been viewed as the professional staff persons responsible for dealing with family issues. However, if one accepts the family-centered assumption that family-professional collaboration is the key to planning and implementing intervention, then it is implied that any and all interventionists, speech-language pathologists, audiologists, and teachers of deaf and hard-of-hearing children must be able to engage in on-going conversations with families about resources, concerns, and priorities. Is this a realistic expectation? And, if not, what can programs do to help staff members achieve competence in family communication?

Several articles addressing the skills needed to communicate with families in early intervention settings (Winton 1988; Andrews and Andrews 1990; Murphy 1990) and strategies and activities for staff development (Winton and Bailey 1993) have appeared in the literature. One strategy suggested for staff development has been to use team members with expertise in family communication, such as social workers, to help other staff members develop those skills (Winton 1990). This implies an acceptance of the assumption that all staff members should have skills in family communication and should participate in family assessment; therefore, consensus on this question is important before pursuing this staff development goal.

Questions for Self-Assessment

The following questions (Bailey, McWilliam, Winton, and Simeonsson 1992) provide an opportunity to consider current practices related to family assessment in light of the family-centered assumptions.

Are we complying with all P.L. 99-457 regulations regarding family assessment?

Do parents know that we are responsive to family needs?

Do we try to determine family preferences regarding family assessment?

Have we agreed on a flexible model and alternative procedures for assessing family resources, concerns, and priorities?

Is family assessment recognized as part of each team member's role?

Does each team member have the skills needed to communicate effectively with families?

DEVELOPING INTERVENTION PLANS IN COLLABORATION WITH FAMILIES

Traditionally, information about the family and child is gathered, taken back to staff meetings, used to develop an intervention plan, and presented to families for their approval. Getting this approval has been the usual way of involving families in planning. We often say, "We want your feedback or suggestions," when, in fact, our plan already may be neatly typed and our meeting time nearly depleted. Obviously, such an approach is not in keeping with the family-centered assumptions of equality, partnerships, building on strengths, and providing families with choices. Sensitively and accurately developing a picture of what a family needs and wants is an important step in the planning process. It is critical to continue working with the family in developing ideas about how to address those needs in an intervention plan.

A strategy for achieving these goals is to provide family members with the opportunity to be involved in all discussions related to the child and family (Kjerland and Kovach 1990; Johnson et al. 1989). Kjerland and Kovach (1990) have described how this strategy is implemented into the Arena Assessment process used at Project Dakota. Underlying this approach is the belief that talking about and identifying resources, concerns, and priorities naturally leads to discussion about strategies for meeting those needs. Conceptualizing assessment and intervention planning as two separate activities that occur at two different times, as is often done in practice and in the literature, sets up a false dichotomy that does not reflect the reality of how family conversations occur. In talking with families about their interests and concerns, information about how they might accomplish what they want emerges naturally.

The following types of questions, phrased in ways suited to each individual family, may help to direct conversations toward identifying needs, goals, and strategies for reaching goals.

If you were to focus your energies on one thing for (child's name), what would it be?

What would help you the most at home with (child's name)?

If you could change one thing about (event of importance), what would that be?

What are some ways of getting to where you want to go? Who would need to be involved in getting done what you want to do?

What would each of you need to do in order to accomplish what you want?

How will you know when you've done what you want to do?

How will you know when (child's name) has made progress in the ways you described?

How long do you think it will take to get to where you want to go?

Another issue related to collaborative goal setting is how to resolve disagreements about appropriate goals. The traditional approach to intervention planning often ignored conflict by not allowing it to emerge. For example, research by Brinckerhoff and Vincent (1986) on Individualized Education Programs (IEPs) indicated that the majority of IEPs were written and presented to parents for their signatures, this being the extent of parental input. Implementing the family-centered approach of eliciting and attending to family perspectives about goals may increase the possibility of conflict if those perspectives are different from professional ones. This presents a significant challenge to our beliefs about who is in charge of intervention. It also caused us to consider what happens when we do impose our beliefs and opinions on a family about what it should do. We are usually frustrated by a family's lack of follow through or involvement in carrying out our plans.

The ability to share professional knowledge and expertise without imposing our opinions on families is a delicate art. It takes time and trust to build a relationship in which all participants feel comfortable sharing and disagreeing about strongly held beliefs. In building that kind of relationship with families, being able to listen and accept families' perspectives on intervention plans, even when the plan is one that, in your opinion, will not work or is inadvisable, is critical. Equally important is our honest perspective about what we as professionals would do in the parents' shoes. How that perspective is conveyed is important in building the relationship. If you honestly agree with the family-centered assumption that families are the ultimate decision makers in regard to their children's services (unless, of course, it represents an extreme situation in which child abuse or neglect is involved), then letting parents know you are willing to support them even though you may disagree with the decision, is important. In this way "the door is still open" to reconsideration of the plan, and you may have the opportunity to be part of that reconsideration. Most families come to professionals for expert opinions; yet most parents find it necessary to sift and sort to find the kernels of "wisdom" that fit with what they know and believe. This suggests that intervention planning is an on-going sharing of information in interactive ways that allow professionals and parents to react and respond to each other. If this process works well, it is likely that the intervention plan has a higher probability for success than if professionals or parents engaged in planning on their own. The professional is able to provide current information about effective strategies and technologies; the family is able to identify how those might fit within its already existing routine and enhance the naturally occurring resources and strategies that it is already using. Research by Gallimore et al. (1989) suggested that no matter how brilliantly conceived an intervention plan might be in terms of level of stimulation for enhancing the child's outcome, its ultimate success rests on the extent to which the plan can be incorporated into the daily routine of the family. It takes input from the family to be able to make that match.

Questions for Self-Assessment

The following questions (Bailey, McWilliam, Winton, and Simeonsson 1992) are meant to provide an opportunity for professionals to examine ways that interventions are planned in light of the family-centered assumptions.

Are we complying with all P.L. 99-457 regulations regarding the team and family's participation on it?

Do we try to determine family preferences regarding its role on the team?
Do families determine team membership?
Do we employ strategies to make sure that families feel comfortable participating in team meetings?
Do we function as a team or as individual specialists?
Do we hold our meetings in settings and at times convenient to the family?
Do we respect parents' decisions, even if professionals disagree?

SUMMARY

Implementing a family-centered approach in programs for young children with hearing loss is apt to be a long and challenging process. In providing information that might be helpful in identifying how family-centered assumptions might be put into practice we have posed a number of questions to elicit comparison of current practices with those reflective of a family-centered approach. Our hope is that this process will inspire further exploration of the gap between current practices and desired changes. As programs and individuals engage in this process, there are a number of training materials that might prove helpful.

For example, an in-service curriculum on becoming family centered in early intervention, on a team-based, decision-making model of training, has recently been developed, field tested and evaluated (Bailey, McWilliam, Winton, and Simeonsson 1992; Bailey, McWilliam, and Winton 1992; Winton et al. 1992). This curriculum is founded on the proposition that change is a gradual process, best facilitated by ongoing staff development that includes entire teams or agencies rather than isolated individuals. Therefore, the curriculum provides a series of activities to help teams decide what changes they want to make and how to make them. The activities are designed so that family members may take active roles in the process.

Checklists or rating scales designed to help agencies or programs assess the extent to which they are family centered have also been recently developed. For example, a 15-item checklist, entitled *Where Does Your Program Stand?*, has been developed by Pip Campbell (1989) as a means for programs to assess current services and the extent to which they are family centered. The *FOCAS: Family Orientation to Community and Agency Services* (Bailey 1990) is an instrument designed to help professionals rate current and desired levels of 12 family related aspects of early intervention. This instrument has been used as part of the team-based, decision-making IFSP inservice curriculum developed by Bailey and his colleagues (Bailey et al. 1991). *BRASS TACKS: Part I & II* (McWilliam and Winton 1990) are instruments designed to help programs and individuals focus on specific practices within four areas of practice, identify areas in which change is desired, and develop a specific plan.

As professionals serving young children with hearing loss and their families continue to explore the concept of family-centered intervention and its meaning in terms of day-to-day practices, new techniques and training strategies will undoubtedly emerge. The subsequent chapters of this book provide specific information on diverse and effective programs and practices for making the desired changes.

REFERENCES

Andrews, J. R., and Andrews, M. A. 1990. *Family Based Treatment in Communicative Disorders: A Systemic Approach.* Sandwich, IL: Janelle Publications, Inc.

Bailey, D. 1990. *FOCAS: Family Orientation to Community and Agency Services.* Chapel Hill, NC: Carolina Institute for Research on Infant Personnel Preparation.

Bailey, D. B. 1987. Collaborative goal-setting with families: Resolving differences in values and priorities for services. *Topics in Early Childhood Special Education* 7(2):57–71.

Bailey, D. B., and Blasco, P. M. 1990. Parents' perspectives on a written survey of family needs. *Journal of Early Intervention* 14(3):196–203.

Bailey, D. B., Buysse, V., Edmondson, R., and Smith, T. M. 1992. Creating a family focus on early intervention: Professionals' perceptions of typical practices, ideal practices, and barriers to change. *Exceptional Children* 58(4):298–309.

Bailey, D., and Simeonsson, R. 1988. *Family Assessment in Early Intervention.* Columbus, OH: Charles Merrill.

Bailey, D., McWilliam, P., Winton, P., and Simeonsson, R. 1992. *Implementing Family-centered Services in Early Intervention: A Team Based Model of Change.* Cambridge, MA: Brookline Books.

Bailey, D. B., McWilliam, P. J., and Winton, P. J. 1992. Building family-centered practices in early intervention: A team-based model of change. *Infants and Young Children* 5(1):73–82.

Bailey, D. B., Simeonsson, R. J., Winton, P. J., Huntington, G. S., Comfort, M., Isbell, P., O'Donnell, K. J., and Helm, J. M. 1986. Family-focused intervention: A functional model for planning, implementing, and evaluating individualized family services in early intervention. *Journal of the Division for Early Childhood* 10:156–71.

Bailey, D. B., Simeonsson, R. J., Yoder, D. E., and Huntington, G. S. 1990. Preparing professionals to serve infants and toddlers with handicaps and their families: An integrative analysis across eight disciplines. *Exceptional Children* 57:26–35.

Bailey, D. B., Buysse, V., Smith-Bonahue, T., and Elam, J. 1992. *Evaluation and Program Planning* 15:23–32.

Behr, J. 1991. Testimony to the Senate Subcommittee on Disability Policy, March, 1991, Washington, DC.

Brewer, E. J., McPherson, M., Magrab, P. R., and Hutchins, V. L. 1989. Family-centered, community-based, coordinated care for children with special health care needs. *Pediatrics* 83:1055–1060.

Brinckerhoff, J., and Vincent, L. 1986. Increasing parental decision-making at the individualized educational program meeting. *Journal of the Division for Early Childhood* 11(1):46–58.

Cadman, D., Shurvell, B., Davies, P., and Bradfield, S. 1984. Compliance in the community with consultants' recommendations for developmentally handicapped children. *Developmental Medicine and Child Neurology* 26:40–46.

Campbell, P. 1989. A program checklist for families and staff. *The Networker* 2(3). Washington, DC: United Cerebral Palsy Associations.

Dunst, C. J., Trivette, C. M., and Deal, A. G. 1988. *Enabling and Empowering Families: Principles and Guidelines for Practice.* Cambridge, MA: Brookline Books.

Gallimore, R., Weisner, T., Kaufman, S., and Bernheimer, L. 1989. The social construction of ecocultural niches: Family accommodation of developmentally delayed children. *American Journal on Mental Retardation* 94(3):216–30.

Glaser, E. M., Abelson, H. H., and Garrison, K. N. 1983. *Putting Knowledge to use: Facilitating the Diffusion of Knowledge and the Implementation of Planned Change.* San Francisco, CA: Jossey-Bass Publishers.

Harbin, G., Gallagher, J. J., and Lillie, T. 1989. *States' Progress Related to Fourteen Components of P.L. 99-457,* Part H. Carolina Policy Studies Program, Frank Porter Graham Child Development Center, University of North Carolina at Chapel Hill, NC.

Havelock, R., and Havelock, M. 1973. *Training for Change Agents.* Ann Arbor, MI: University of Michigan Press.

Hill, R. 1958. Social stresses on the family. *Social Casework* 39:139–50.

Johnson, B. H., McGonigel, M. J., and Kaufman, R. K. 1991. *Guidelines and Recommended Practices for the Individualized Family Service Plan.* 2nd Ed. Washington, DC: Association for the Care of Children's Health.

Kjerland, L., and Kovach, J. 1990. Family-staff collaboration for tailored infant assessment. In *Interdisciplinary Assessment of Infants,* eds. E. Gibbs and D. Teti. Baltimore: Paul H. Brookes Publishing.

McGonigel, M. J., Kaufmann, R. K., and Johnson, B. H. (eds.) 1991. *Guidelines and Recommended Practices for the Individualized Family Service Plan,* 2nd Ed. Bethesda, MD: Association for the Care of Children's Health.

McWilliam, P., and Winton, P. 1990. *BRASS TACKS: Part I & II.* Chapel Hill, NC: Frank Porter Graham Child Development Center Carolina Institute for Research on Infant Personnel Preparation.

Murphy, A. 1990. Communicating assessment findings to parents. In *Interdisciplinary Assessment of Infants,* eds. E. Gibbs and D. Teti. Baltimore: Paul H. Brookes Publishing.

Olson, D., McCubbin, H., Barnes, H., Larsen, H., Muxen, M., and Wilson, M. 1983. *Families: What Makes Them Work.* Beverly Hills, CA: Sage.

Roush, J., Harrison, M., and Palsha, S. 1991. Family-centered early intervention: The perceptions of professionals. *American Annals of the Deaf* 136(4): 360–66.

Sheehan, R. 1988. Involvement of parents in early childhood assessment. In *Assessment of Young Developmentally Disabled Children,* eds. T. D. Wachs and R. Sheehan. New York: Plenum Press.

Shelton, T. L., Jeppson, E. S., and Johnson B. H. 1987. *Family-centered Care for Children with Special Health Care Needs.* Washington, DC: Association for the Care of Children's Health.

Summers, J. A., Dell'Oliver, C., Turnbull, A. P., Benson, H. A., Santelli, E., Campbell, M., and Siegal-Causey, E. 1990. Examining the IFSP process: What are family and practitioner preferences? *Topics in Early Childhood Special Education* 10(1):78–99.

Winton, P. J. 1990. A systemic approach for planning inservice training related to Public Law 99-457. *Infants and Young Children* 3(1):51–60.

Winton, P. J. 1988. Effective communication between parents and professionals. In *Family Assessment in Early Intervention*, eds. D. B. Bailey and R. J. Simeonsson. Columbus, OH: Charles Merrill.

Winton, P., and Bailey, D. 1993. Communicating with families: Examining practices and facilitating change. In *Children with Special Needs: Family, Culture and Society* (2nd Ed.), eds. J. Paul and R. Simeonsson. Fort Worth, TX: Harcourt, Brace, Jovanovich.

Winton, P. J., McWilliam, P. J., Harrison, T., Owens, A. M., and Bailey, D. B. 1992. Lessons learned from implementing a team-based model of change. *Infants and Young Children* 5(1):49–57.

PART • II

Identification and Audiologic Management

Chapter • 3

Identification of Hearing Loss
Programmatic and Procedural Considerations

Allan O. Diefendorf and Bruce A. Weber

Identification of a child's hearing loss at an early age is the first step in a comprehensive plan that allows for early medical management, consideration of acoustic amplification, and placement in an early intervention program. Early identification and intervention have been shown to increase the child's readiness for school while reducing the long-term need for special services (Downs 1986).

In 1982, and again in 1990, the Joint Committee on Infant Hearing recommended that, whenever possible, diagnostic testing should be completed and habilitation begun by the time an infant with a congenital hearing impairment reaches the age of six months. Unfortunately, for nearly all hearing-impaired infants, the age of diagnosis and the resulting enrollment in a habilitation program far exceeds the Joint Committee's recommendations. This is reflected in the findings of Stein, Clark, and Kraus (1983) who conducted a three-year retrospective study of 88 hearing-impaired infants enrolled in a hospital-based parent-infant program. They found that graduates of a neonatal intensive care unit (NICU) were not enrolled until a median age of 18.0 months. For well-nursery graduates, the enrollment date was somewhat later, 22.0 months. The same authors (Stein et al. 1990) conducted a six-year follow-up study, which they completed in 1988. The results of the second study showed little improvement in the early management of hearing impairment. Of the 107 hearing-impaired infants identified, the median enrollment date was 20.0 months for

NICU graduates and 19.6 months for well-nursery babies. Craig (1983) found the average age of referral to programs for hearing-impaired children was 25.5 months. More recently, Elssmann, Matkin, and Sabo (1987) reported similar results. As these findings indicate, young infants with hearing losses are frequently lost to follow-up and consequently, intervention plans are not initiated at an early age. Although the difficulties involved in tracking and initiating follow-up services for an infant with impaired hearing must be acknowledged, it is clear that the initial step is the early identification of hearing loss.

There is a growing response to the need for early detection of hearing loss as evidenced by the passage of Public Law 99-457 (The Education of the Handicapped Act Amendments of 1986). In part, this law is a discretionary program that addresses the needs of neonatal to three-year-old children with special needs. Public Law 99-457 and subsequent legislation offer individual states an opportunity to develop or improve their statewide public awareness programs for early identification and referral.

Currently, a number of states have created the legislation needed to permit establishment of programs for early identification of hearing loss. Blake and Hall (1990) provided the most recent survey of state-wide policies for neonatal hearing screening. According to their report, 14 states had legislative mandates for newborn hearing screening. Twelve others had no legislative mandate, but have addressed the issue at the state level. The remaining 24 states had no mandate and have not addressed the issue at the state level. Of the 14 mandated state-wide programs, 10 have implemented state-run programs, two programs are administered privately, and the remaining two states are in the process of developing programs. The 14 mandated states are: Arizona, California, Connecticut, Florida, Georgia, Kentucky, Maryland, Massachusetts, Mississippi, New Jersey, Ohio, Oklahoma, Rhode Island, and Virginia. In addition, the Canadian provinces of British Columbia and Nova Scotia have provincial-wide neonatal hearing screening programs.

It is unlikely that statewide neonatal hearing screening programs will be established in every state in the near future. Therefore, to address the problem of early detection of hearing loss, some form of early identification program will need to be developed in individual locales. A logical focus is on those hospitals with newborn nurseries. Brooks (1990) surveyed 553 hospitals known to have a NICU and found that 81% reported some form of hearing screening program. Although screening procedures differed markedly among hospitals, the results of the survey indicated that many hospitals have made a serious commitment to newborn hearing screening.

IDENTIFYING THE NEWBORN WITH HEARING IMPAIRMENT

Regardless of specific screening procedures, the principal objective of any newborn hearing screening program is to correctly identify hearing loss in those infants who are truly hearing impaired. The focus of screening is not to specify the infant's hearing sensitivity, but rather to determine whether or not a hearing loss exists.

Principles of Screening

For any hearing screening test, there are four possible outcomes. An infant with a hearing loss can fail the test (true-positive) and a normally hearing infant can pass the test (true-negative). Conversely, an infant with a hearing impairment can pass the test (false-negative) and a normally hearing infant can fail (false-positive). *Sensitivity* is the frequency with which persons who have the disorder test positive. *Specificity* is the frequency with which persons who do not have the disorder test negative (Thorner 1981). The ideal screening test would have both 100% sensitivity and specificity, but in practice this is not achieved. In the administration of a screening program, the examiner has some control over the likelihood of the potential outcomes described above. For example, making the criterion for passing the screening test more stringent (e.g., screening at a lower stimulus intensity level) will result in more infants failing the test. This more stringent criterion will increase the likelihood that a hearing-impaired infant will fail the screening; thus, sensitivity is raised. However, this more stringent screening criterion will also increase the probability that normal-hearing infants will fail the test, so specificity is reduced. No hearing screening test can be perfectly designed to avoid error and there will always remain a group that is incorrectly classified. Because the most serious error is missing a hearing-impaired infant, the goal is to keep this group as small as possible, without an excessive number of normal-hearing infants requiring follow-up.

Selecting Infants for Screening

In 1969 a Joint Committee on Infant Hearing (JCIH), composed of representatives from otolaryngology, pediatrics, nursing, and audiology, was established and charged with the responsibility of making recommendations concerning newborn screening programs. The JCIH recognized the problems associated with universal screening and did not support the concept of mass hearing screening for all newborns. Instead, the committee endorsed the concept of a high-risk register for selecting babies who should receive hearing screening. Initially, five factors were identified as placing an infant at increased risk for hearing loss. In 1983, and more recently in 1990, the Joint Committee revised and expanded the high-risk criteria to include the ten risk factors for neonates as shown in table I. Since that time the high-risk register has been reviewed, and recommendations in the areas of ototoxic medications, severe depression, prolonged mechanical ventilation, and conductive hearing loss are being considered. It is anticipated that revisions will be made in the future as the causes of congenital hearing loss are understood better and as technological innovations permit new and improved methods of hearing screening.

Hearing Screening Techniques

There are two broad categories of hearing screening procedures: behavioral and electrophysiologic. Within these two categories, testing techniques can be divided further into those that are automated and those in which the test protocol is under the control of the examiner. Of the numerous testing procedures used in newborn hearing screening, five deserve special mention.

Behavioral Testing. Behavioral Observation Audiometry (BOA) is an approach to hearing screening in which a high intensity (e.g., 90 dBA) narrow band of noise is presented by a hand-held instrument

Table I. The Joint Committee on Infant Screening (1990) *Risk Criteria:* Neonates (Birth–28 days)

1. Family history of congenital or delayed onset childhood sensorineural impairment
2. Congenital infection known or suspected to be associated with sensorineural hearing impairment, such as toxoplasmosis, syphilis, rubella, cytomegalovirus, and herpes
3. Craniofacial anomalies including morphologic abnormalities of the pinna and ear canal, absent philtrum, low hairline, etc.
4. Birth weight less than 1500 grams—3.3 lbs
5. Hyperbilirubemia at a level exceeding indication for exchange transfusion
6. Ototoxic medications including, but not limited to, the aminoglycosides used for more than five days (e.g., gentamicin, tobramycin, kanamycin, streptomycin) and loop diuretics used in combination with aminoglycosides
7. Bacterial meningitis
8. Severe depression at birth, which may include infants with Apgar scores of 0–3 at 5 minutes, or those who fail to initiate spontaneous respiration by 10 minutes, or those with hypotonia persisting to two hours of age
9. Prolonged mechanical ventilation for a duration equal to or greater than 10 days (e.g., persistent pulmonary hypertension)
10. Stigmata or other findings associated with a syndrome known to include sensorineural hearing loss (e.g., Waardenburg or Usher's Syndrome)

positioned near the infant. The expected response includes cessation of activity, eye widening, subtle changes in facial expression, crying, and gross startle response. The determination of whether a response has occurred is highly subjective and can often be difficult, even for experienced observers. As a result, there are serious concerns about the effectiveness of BOA for screening. Using BOA, Plotnick and Leppler (1986) identified only two severely hearing-impaired infants among 356 newborns screened in the NICU. Assuming a very conservative two percent prevalence of significant sensorineural hearing loss in the NICU at least three times as many hearing-impaired infants should have been identified in the group tested. Because of the high stimulus intensity used, BOA is likely to miss an infant with a mild-to-moderate bilateral hearing loss, as well as those with a unilateral impairment. False-negative rates of 40%–86% have been reported for BOA (Alberti et al. 1983; Durieux-Smith et al. 1985; Jacobson and Morehouse 1984) meaning that a large number of infants with significant hearing loss pass behavioral screening and are thus lost to immediate intervention. Although BOA is no longer viewed as an effective screening procedure, there are still some proponents of the technique, as evidenced by a small hand-held screener currently being marketed as a convenient and inexpensive alternative to more elaborate and costly instrumentation. Because of its poor sensitivity and specificity, however, BOA cannot be recommended for neonatal hearing screening.

Automated Behavioral Testing. The Crib-O-Gram (COG) hearing screening device uses motion sensitive detectors under the baby's mattress to detect changes produced by the test stimulus. A microprocessor determines when the infant is sufficiently quiet; it then presents a high-intensity stimulus (a 92 dB SPL band of noise centered at 3000 Hz). The COG apparatus records the responses and indicates whether the infant has met the passing criteria. Responses range from subtle changes in respiratory patterns to startle reflexes. An advantage of the COG is its automation, so less examiner time is required (McFarland, Simmons, and Jones 1980). However, as with BOA, high stimulus intensities are needed to elicit a detectable behavioral response. As a result, the COG also may miss infants with mild-to-moderate bilateral hearing losses or unilateral impairment. In addition, COG results are unreliable. Durieux-Smith et al. (1985) found that 32% of the infants tested with COG shifted from pass to fail, or vice versa, when they were retested within 48 hours. Because of these serious limitations and its poor cost effectiveness (Markowitz 1990), there has been a significant reduction in the use of the COG technique in recent years.

Conventional Auditory Brainstem Response Screening. The Auditory Brainstem Response (ABR) or the Brainstem Auditory

Evoked Response (BAER), as it is commonly referred to in pediatric and neonatology literature, was first used in a neonatal intensive care unit by Schulman-Galambos and Galambos (1975). Unlike behavioral screening procedures, ABR audiometry is based on synchronous neural firings within the auditory nerve and brainstem. The stability of the ABR permits recording of detectable responses at varying stimulus intensity levels.

As a hearing screening measure, the ABR has two major limitations: (1) the acoustic click routinely used in neonatal screening elicits responses predominately in the 2000 Hz to 4000 Hz range, consequently, hearing sensitivity at other frequencies is not evaluated; and (2) because the ABR reflects synchronous neural firing to the level of the brainstem only, its presence is not evidence of a conscious response at the cortical level. Therefore, the rare infant with a purely cortical auditory impairment would not be detected with ABR screening. Despite these limitations, the ABR with infants is highly accurate in detecting sensorineural hearing loss in excess of 30 dBHL (Hyde, Riko, and Malizia 1990). Although the instrumentation is costly, the ABR is now the most commonly used technique in newborn hearing screening programs.

Automated Auditory Brainstem Response Testing. The most common automated ABR screener, the ALGO-1 Plus, is a battery-operated microprocessor dedicated solely to newborn ABR screening (Kileny 1988). After the examiner has positioned recording electrodes on the baby's scalp, the ALGO is activated and the unit automatically presents 35 dBnHL click stimuli whenever electrode impedance, ambient noise level, and movement artifacts are within acceptable limits. As the stimuli are presented, the ALGO is comparing the infant's accumulated response in memory with an internal template of the typical neonatal ABR. When the likelihood of a response reaches a predetermined criterion level, the test stimuli automatically cease and a display panel indicates whether the baby has passed the screening test. If the likelihood of response is not sufficiently high at the end of 15,000 sweeps, testing is automatically halted and the display panel indicates that the infant should be referred for further testing (Kileny 1988).

A major advantage of an automated screening device such as the ALGO is that it does not require the presence of a sophisticated examiner. Furthermore, an ABR screener is relatively inexpensive compared with the cost of diagnostic ABR test units. A significant disadvantage, however, is the stringent recording requirements for electrode impedance, background noise levels, and muscle artifacts. Automated screening may be precluded in some NICU environments where recording conditions are poor.

Otoacoustic Emission Testing (OAE). A promising new technique for newborn hearing screening is the measurement of otoacoustic emissions (OAEs), first described by Kemp in 1978. As sound enters the ear canal, it moves through the middle ear into the cochlea, where thousands of hair cells vibrate to transmit the signal through the VIIIth cranial nerve to the brain. Kemp's work showed that if the tiny hair cells within the cochlea are functioning normally, these cells simultaneously emit sound or an "echo" back through the middle ear. This echo, or OAE, can be recorded in the external ear canal by a small, sensitive microphone connected to a specially equipped microcomputer.

OAEs can be obtained objectively and quickly. They test a wide range of frequencies simultaneously, yet tend not to be measurable in ears with greater than 25–30 dB of peripheral hearing loss. These features suggest obvious utility in the screening for peripheral auditory dysfunction, especially in infants; however, certain technical and procedural variables have been reported to influence the sensitivity and specificity of OAE measures applied to infants. Jacobson and Jacobson (1991), for example, reported that effects of ambient acoustic and physiologic noise compromised OAE detection in their investigation, which was conducted at crib side in well-baby and special care nurseries. Additionally, there is some indication that infants tested within 24 hours of birth have lower pass rates than those tested 2–4 days after birth. Because most healthy babies leave the hospital within 48 hours of birth, the window of opportunity for this screening may be limited.

It is likely that OAEs will be used in conjunction with other tests to provide a more complete diagnosis of hearing loss. OAEs are a measure of cochlear functioning, and as a "first pass" they are an efficient, sensitive tool to detect even mild degrees of hearing loss. Therefore, if used in conjunction with ABR, a complete, objective picture of peripheral and brainstem functioning can be obtained.

Although there is evidence to suggest that OAEs have excellent potential as a screening tool for detecting hearing loss in neonates, continued research in this area is needed before the optimal test parameters are determined, and sensitivity and specificity for detection of hearing loss are established.

Financial Considerations

Most hospital administrators acknowledge the importance of early detection of hearing loss; however, few welcome the initiation of a screening program if it is likely to create a significant financial deficit. The most logical source of financial support for hearing screening is through fees added directly to the hospital bill. Unfortunately, the matter is not as straightforward as it may seem. As a result of a nationwide prospective payment system (PPS) initiated in 1983, billing for services within most hospitals in the United States has changed dramatically. Under the PPS system, prior to actual treatment, the hospital receives a set dollar amount based on the patient's admitting diagnosis. Thus, unless the diagnosis is changed based on later complications, the payment to the hospital is predetermined by the patient's diagnosis related group (DRG) regardless of the actual cost of the services provided (Shakno 1984). The system devised originally for Medicare patients has now been adopted by other state and federal agencies that assume responsibility for the hospital costs of many of the babies in the newborn nurseries. Commonly, over half of the babies in a nursery are covered by one of the prospective payment systems.

The PPS approach to payment was designed to motivate hospitals to monitor closely and limit patient services. If hospital costs are kept low, the hospital makes money on a PPS patient. Conversely, if expensive services are provided during the patient's hospital stay, the hospital may lose money because it will receive no additional compensation for those services. Not surprisingly, this approach to health care financing motivates hospitals to reduce the use of procedures that are not central to the primary health problems of their patients. Thus, there are pressures on the medical staff to refrain from ordering elective procedures that do not generate additional revenue for the hospital. One such procedure is newborn hearing screening. Because of these financial constraints, it is unlikely that the entire cost of a hearing screening program can be supported through direct patient billing. Although some infants will be covered by insurance, which can be billed directly, a sizable portion of the screening costs may need support from other sources. Likely alternative sources are local service organizations such as Sertoma or Lions clubs.

Services to Low-Risk Newborns

The prevalence of significant hearing loss is approximately 10 to 20 times higher in the neonatal intensive care unit than in the full-term nursery (FTN). This figure can be misleading, however, because only a small percentage of newborns will ever spend time in the NICU. Stein et al. (1990) estimate that only one-third of hearing-impaired newborns manifest perinatal conditions requiring the specialized care of the NICU. Thus, as many as two-thirds of hearing-impaired infants may be missed if hearing screening is confined to the NICU. It is clear, therefore, that every screening program must have some strategy for serving low-risk infants. Because of the expenses involved, it is not cost effective to carry out ABR screening on all newborns (Hosford-Dunn et al. 1987). Nevertheless, the focus on high-risk infants should not result in a failure to address the identification of hearing-impaired babies in the low-risk group through the use of the high-risk register. Continued development of otoacoustic emissions may eventually lead to a cost-effective method of conducting universal hearing screening.

Even when financial and staffing considerations restrict routine hearing screening to NICU infants and selected babies in the FTN, cost effective ways have been devised to serve the low-risk population. Increased parent awareness is an inexpensive approach to increase the likelihood of detecting a hearing-impaired baby who exhibits none of the known risk factors. This can be accomplished by means of a simple hearing checklist card like the one shown in figure 1. This particular checklist is included in the free packet (containing formula, diapers, etc.) that a mother receives when a baby is discharged from the FTN at Duke University Medical Center. One side of the card explains the importance of early identification of hearing loss and provides information on who to call regarding questions about the baby's hearing.

CAN YOUR BABY HEAR?

CONGRATULATIONS ON YOUR NEW BABY! We are sure that you will receive great pride and pleasure as you watch your baby grow and mature. The Friendly City Sertoma Club of Durham hopes that you will use this card to track your child's development in one important area: hearing.

A large part of what your baby learns will be through hearing. Your child will learn that different sounds have different meanings and this will serve as the foundation for talking. Speech and language, however, will only occur if your baby can hear other people talk. A child with a significant hearing loss can be permanently delayed in many areas of development. Therefore, it is very important to detect a hearing loss as soon as possible to permit early treatment and training to minimize the damage it can cause.

You can help your baby using the information on the other side of this card. Check your child's responses to sound with what is expected for a child of the same age (be sure to reduce your child's age if your baby was premature). If you find that your child falls behind what is expected call the number shown below for information on where your child's hearing can be tested. The Friendly City Sertoma Club wants you to know that no child is too young to have their hearing tested, so don't wait if you have concerns about hearing.

HEARING CHECKLIST

BY 3 MONTHS
Startle or cry when there are loud noises.
Show signs of waking up to loud sounds.

BY 6 MONTHS
Stop playing when there is an interesting sound.
Enjoy toys that make noise.

BY 9 MONTHS
Understand words like "NO" and "BYE BYE."
Show signs of responding to soft sounds.
Turn head to find source of interesting sounds.

BY 12 MONTHS
Try to imitate the speech sounds you make.
Can point to familiar objects when asked.

BY 15 MONTHS
Follow simple spoken instructions.
Speak simple words.

If your baby does not appear to be responding normally to sound or if you just have some questions call the staff at BEGINNINGS and they will tell you where your baby's hearing can be tested. Call toll free: 1-800-541-HEAR (in Durham please use 286-9797)

Figure 1.   Example of a hearing checklist.

The information also describes how to arrange to have the baby's hearing tested. The other side of the card contains developmental milestones that allow the parents to gauge whether their child is responding normally to sound. Parents are urged to place this card in a prominent place as a frequent reminder to consider the child's auditory responsiveness.

Counseling the Family Regarding Test Results

When properly administered, ABR or OAE screening can provide useful information regarding newborn hearing status. It is important, however, that a screening test be interpreted as such, and not considered "diagnostic" for the confirmation of permanent hearing loss. Therefore, test results must be interpreted clearly in the infant's medical record and appropriately conveyed to the parents. Obviously parents should not be told that their child has a permanent hearing loss on the basis of a failed screening test; rather, a screening failure should be viewed as reason for concern about hearing impairment. This concern dictates that further testing be carried out to define the infant's hearing status better. At a time when parents may have numerous concerns regarding their baby's health status, care is taken to stress the importance of additional testing without adding to their level of anxiety.

PROBLEMS IN FOLLOWING SCREENING FAILURES

When an infant fails an ABR or OAE screen and a hearing loss is suspected prior to his or her discharge, follow-up procedures are of primary concern. Aside from financial considerations, failure to achieve compliance with follow-up appointments is the weakest element in newborn hearing screening programs. Clinical reports have shown that 25% to 80% of NICU graduates will be lost to follow up unless intense recruitment efforts are made. Patient attrition is a particular concern for children with mild hearing losses when the parents' impressions of hearing status are not consistent with screening test findings. Shimizu et al. (1990) put forth considerable effort to increase the likelihood of returns for follow-up evaluation. Testing was performed free of charge, there was no fee for parking, transportation was provided, and the family was kept well informed through frequent phone calls and written reminders. Despite these efforts, 26% of the babies who failed the intensive care nursery (ICN) screening did not return for their follow-up appointments. Minimizing the number of infants who fail to return for their follow-up evaluation remains one of the greatest challenges in any newborn hearing screening program.

Improving Follow up

A follow-up network, dedicated to tracking all infants who fail the initial screen as well as selected infants who pass, is required in order to ensure that all infants with hearing impairment are identified. Financial planning for such a system must be given the same importance as the hearing screening itself. Advanced computer networks offer promise in making statewide tracking possible, provided that concerns regarding confidentiality can be overcome. In addition, the following steps are recommended to maximize the likelihood that infants who have failed the newborn screening will return for follow up: (1) coordinate multiple appointments for the same day, making scheduling easier for parents, particularly those with transportation problems; (2) counsel the parents, whenever possible, at the time of the original screening, emphasizing the importance of additional testing; (3) send the family a follow-up letter explaining the nature and significance of the test results; (4) send a letter to the primary-care physician, social worker, or local health department (primary-care provider), enlisting their support in facilitating follow-up testing.

Program success depends upon aggressive plans for follow up and dedication to the philosophy that hearing screening is an on-going process in all children. Service delivery systems (birth-related, primary care-related, and school-related) must dovetail with each other to maximize the follow-through process; and most importantly, administration and implementation of these systems must recognize the key role of parents in understanding why hearing health care systems exist and how they work. Unfortunately, some infants will be lost to follow up despite all efforts. Reasons may include changes of address, transportation problems, or in some cases, parental neglect. Although no program will be completely successful, screening is of little or no value without proper follow up. Every reasonable effort must be made to minimize the number of babies lost to follow up due to inadequate program administration and coordination.

Until recently, follow-up services were routinely provided only to those infants who failed the initial hearing screening. Now there is increasing evidence of delayed onset or progressive hearing loss in the high-risk newborn population (Naulty, Weiss, and Herer 1986); Hendricks-Munoz and Walton 1988; Allen and Schubert-Sudia 1990). As a result, screening programs are now extending their follow up to selected infants who pass initial screening. Decisions regarding the most appropriate form of follow up are based on ABR or OAE screening results, the nature and degree of the baby's medical problems, and family history. If a child passes the ABR or OAE screening and the history is nonsignificant for progressive hearing loss, follow-up testing is not routinely scheduled. Ideally, school-related hearing screening programs will identify children with undetected progressive, unilateral, or mild hearing losses. In contrast, if a child passes the NICU screening but has a history that suggests increased risk of delayed onset or progressive hearing loss, the child should be followed after hospital discharge.

Converging Systems in Follow up

School-related, birth-related, and primary-care approaches must be viewed as complementary to the hearing screening and follow-up process. How these approaches are integrated into a single system should be considered prior to establishing a hearing screening program. Furthermore, the development of a single system requires a team approach with parents as active participants.

Considering the importance of the early years on speech and language acquisition, as well as social and cognitive development, the detection of congenital hearing loss cannot wait until school entry. The detrimental effects of prolonged sensory deprivation and the importance of early parent-child interaction to later language learning are well documented. Kuhl et al. (1992) reported that normal hearing is critical for speech and oral language development as early as the first 6 months of life. Therefore early detection of congenital hearing loss requires birth-related, primary-care-related, or statewide school approaches applicable to children and beginning at birth. Given that birth registration comes closer to universal access than does a school-based approach, the linkage of hearing screening to the newborn period is highly desirable.

In response to the need for a well-coordinated service delivery system, P.L. 99-457 and subsequent legislation provide guidelines for identification and early intervention for children with impaired hearing. Professionals or agencies must be alerted to refer potentially eligible children for assessment and procedures must be established to determine eligibility for early intervention services. Computerized statewide support networks can integrate a neonatal screening program with an educational program, to form a complementary and integrated identification system with good accessibility and follow up.

The advantage of an effective statewide system with a school focus is that there is an opportunity to identify both congenital and acquired hearing losses. Furthermore, if the risk criteria for infants (table II) are applied throughout a child's developmental years, earlier identification of acquired hearing loss can be facilitated. In cases where the hearing impairment has a delayed onset, a comprehensive school-based screening program can be crucial to both early identification and appropriate management. Individuals who encounter institutional barriers can point to state and federal guidelines in their efforts to promote expanded identification and intervention services. Central to the success of this approach is effective communication among relevant agencies at the state level. As Blake and Hall (1990) note, those engaged in hearing screening must share their experiences, not only with others in audiology, but with colleagues in education, medicine, and public health. Without a broad base of interdisciplinary support and a team approach, successful implementation of a comprehensive statewide hearing screening program is unlikely to occur.

The effectiveness of primary-care physicians in eliciting patient compliance with various health-related requirements is well established. Additionally, the primary-care physician can greatly facilitate the audiologic rehabilitative effort. Conversely, failure of the physician to seek timely and appropriate referral can contribute to significant delays in identification and intervention. Shah, Chandler, and Dale (1978) surveyed the parents of 200 hearing-impaired children and found that the major obstacle to follow up of early suspicions of hearing loss reported by parents was an unwillingness of physicians to accept parents' views regarding hearing status, or to refer children for evaluation. These authors also reported, however, that when early detection occurred, it was the result of joint cooperation between parents and physician. Kenworthy et al. (1985) surveyed 474 primary-care physicians regarding referral of children for speech, language, and hearing services. Their findings suggest that primary-care physicians

Table II. The Joint Committee on Infant Hearing (1990) *Risk Criteria:* Infants (29 days–2 years)

1. Parent/caregiver concern regarding hearing, speech, language, and/or developmental delay
2. Bacterial meningitis
3. Neonatal risk factors that may be associated with progressive sensorineural hearing loss (e.g., cytomegalovirus, prolonged mechanical ventilation and inherited disorders)
4. Head trauma, especially with either longitudinal or transverse fracture of the temporal bone
5. Stigmata or other findings associated with syndromes known to include sensorineural hearing loss (e.g., Waardenburg or Usher's Syndrome)
6. Ototoxic medications including, but not limited to, the aminoglycosides used for more than 5 days (e.g., gentamicin, tobramycin, kanamycin, streptomycin) and loop diuretics, used in combination with aminoglycosides
7. Children with neurodegenerative disorders, such as neurofibromatosis, myoclonic epilepsy, Werdnig-Hoffmann disease, Tay-Sachs disease, infantile Gaucher disease, Niemann-Pick disease, any metachromatic leukodystrophy, or any infantile demyelinating neuropathy
8. Childhood infectious diseases known to be associated with sensorineural hearing loss (e.g., mumps, measles)

play important roles in either facilitating or impeding early identification. Thus, it seems that incorporating primary-care physicians in the identification process enhances accessibility and continuity of service.

Because the intent of an infant hearing screening program is to facilitate identification and habilitation, programs must maintain strict protocols following the identification of a suspected hearing loss in an infant. With sufficient effort, significant time lags between the suspicion of hearing loss and confirmation and intervention (e.g., Bergstrom 1984; Jones and Simmons 1977; Stein, Clark, and Kraus 1983; and Stein et al. 1990) can be reduced. For example, with a systematic and aggressive approach to tracking, data from the University of Colorado Medical Center for the years 1976–1979 show the average suspected age of hearing loss to be 2.1 months, with the age of confirmation of hearing loss at 5 months (Northern and Downs 1984).

DIAGNOSIS FOR INFANTS FAILING SCREENING

The diagnostic evaluation of an infant requires the sophistication and specialization of the otologic-audiologic team. The otologic exam includes a general physical examination and history including: (1) examination of the head and neck; (2) otoscopy and otomicroscopy; (3) identification of relevant physical abnormalities; and, (4) laboratory tests such as urinalysis, creatinine, thyroid, EKG, and STORCH (syphilis, toxoplasmosis, rubella, cytomegalovirus, herpes).

A comprehensive audiologic evaluation is required to establish degree, type, symmetry, stability, and configuration of the child's hearing status. For infants less than six months, the diagnostic test of choice is the ABR. The ABR is recommended by the American Speech-Language-Hearing Association in its *Guidelines for the Identification of Hearing Impairment in At-Risk Infants Age Birth to 6 Months* (ASHA 1988). Diagnostically, however, the ABR does not easily provide the frequency specific information necessary for a complete description of hearing loss. Although establishing degree, type, symmetry, and configuration of hearing loss is desirable prior to recommending acoustic amplification, it is not prerequisite to initiating a habilitation plan. The Joint Committee's position statement on infant hearing (1990) asserts that habilitation of the hearing-impaired child may (and should) begin while the audiologic portion of the diagnostic evaluation is in process. Medical evaluation and intervention for conductive hearing loss should also be initiated, particularly given the high prevalence of middle ear effusion in newborns. Moreover, when sensorineural hearing loss is identified, counseling, education, and guidance should be initiated, as well as preliminary strategies for fitting of hearing aids.

Limitations of Behavioral Audiometry in Diagnosis of Hearing Loss—Less than Six Months

Behavioral Observation Audiometry (BOA) lacks precision in determining the degree and configuration of hearing loss. In BOA, a stimulus may elicit a reflexive response, but without reinforcement, infants' responses to sound habituate rapidly and may not occur at low intensity levels. Because of the reflexive nature of the newborn's responses, the utility of behavioral observation audiometry (BOA) in the diagnostic process is limited.

Certainly much can be done to address the technicalities of response definition and observer-related variables through training of audiologists and/or automation of these procedures. The fact remains, however, that neither well-trained observers nor an automated system can compensate for the high signal presentation levels (approximately 70-90 dB SPL) required for newborns and infants younger than three months to elicit a response. Additionally, subject variability in BOA shows a wide range in normals. For 24 to 30-month-old children Thompson and Weber (1974) reported a range of 24 dB. An even greater range, approximately 65 dB, was observed for 3- to 5-month-old children. Others have reported similar variability, a fact that makes interpretation of test results difficult for all but severe losses.

The restrictions on validity and reliability imposed by stimulus and response factors when using BOA with infants and young children are clear: suprathreshold stimulation is required to elicit reflexive responses, and the probability of obtaining a response is dependent upon the nature of the stimulus, the activity state of the child, examiner bias, and the noise levels in the test environment. Accordingly, such methods are limited to the detection of hearing losses greater than 50 dBHL. These parameters are not acceptable when considering the importance of the diagnosis of mild and mild-to-moderate hearing loss in young children.

Application of Behavioral Audiometry in Diagnosis of Hearing Loss—Greater than Six Months

Once an infant has achieved a developmental age of five to six months, audiometric information can be obtained efficiently using a behavioral technique based on the principles of operant conditioning. Visual reinforcement audiometry is a behavioral test method that capitalizes on the natural interests and developmental abilities of children.

Visual Reinforcement Audiometry. Visual Reinforcement Audiometry (VRA) has emerged as a successful evaluation procedure for infants and young children, five and one-half months through two years of age. In VRA, an infant responds to stimuli that allow accurate interpretation of hearing status. The VRA procedure capitalizes on the child's natural inclination to turn toward a sound source. The success of VRA is related to the fact that the response (head-turn) and reinforcer (i.e., animated toy) are well suited to the developmental level of children within this age range. The data obtained from infants tested with VRA are impressive. Normally developing infants respond to a variety of signals at low sensation levels as reliably as adults, often allowing for detection of even slight impairments of hearing sensitivity.

Visual reinforcement audiometry is based on the premise that the discrimination of a change in the child's auditory environment (detection of the presence of sound from no sound) results in reinforcement. Through operant conditioning, the child learns that a head-turn toward a reinforcer following the detection or discrimination of a change results in reinforcement (see figure 2). Once the child is under stimulus control, he or she will continue to respond at low sensation levels long enough to provide an estimate of threshold (also called minimum response level). In contrast to BOA, some investigators have found that infants during VRA respond as well to pure tones as to noise (Wilson and Moore 1978). Others have demonstrated that the bandwidth of the signal affects neither threshold nor the number of responses required to reach threshold, once conditioning is established (Thompson and Folsom 1985).

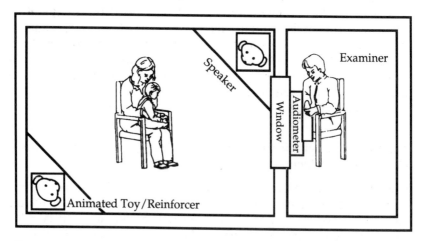

Figure 2. Visual reinforcement audiometry (VRA). Infant sits on mother's lap and is observed by examiner, who presents an auditory stimulus through a loud speaker to right or left of child. The infant's response, a head-turn toward the auditory stimulus is reinforced by activation and illumination of the animated toy housed in a smoked plexiglass enclosure.

The validity of results obtained with VRA is well documented. Numerous studies have shown that infant responses differ only slightly from those of adults (e.g., Wilson, Moore, and Thompson 1976; Thehub, Schneider, and Endman 1980; Nozza and Wilson 1984). A variety of acoustic signals can be used successfully either in sound field or under earphones. Because there is minimal variability, mild hearing losses, such as those accompanying otitis media with effusion can be defined accurately. Generally, as long as the child is under stimulus control, VRA provides audiometric information useful for making diagnostic and management decisions (Diefendorf 1988).

Recent advances in perinatal care have led to significant improvement in the survival rate of low birth weight (LBW) infants and others considered to be at risk for developing hearing impairments. Prematurity and other health-related factors affecting development must be considered in the follow-up process.

Several studies (Greenberg et al. 1978; Thompson, Wilson, and Moore 1979) have reported the use of VRA with children having Down syndrome and other developmental disabilities, suggesting that developmental age may be a determining factor in VRA success. Widen (1990) evaluated VRA as a function of developmental age in high-risk babies. Clearly, the more developmentally mature babies were more often tested successfully. VRA was successful for most by five to six months corrected age. Infants' ability to perform the VRA task was then compared with their mental age score on the Bayley Scales of Infant Development (BSID). When test outcome in VRA was compared to developmental age in a subset of infants, success was achieved approximately 90% of the time in infants with a developmental age of five and one-half months to six and one-half months of age. Therefore, clinical applications of VRA in diagnostic follow up must consider: corrected age adjusted for prematurity rather than chronological age; or developmental age when disparities exist between corrected age and the child's developmental status.

Program Considerations

The philosophy underlying any screening program is determined largely by the goals and rationale for the screening program and the age at which children are to be screened. A program aimed at identifying severe sensorineural hearing loss would be approached differently than a program geared toward detecting milder hearing losses or the presence of middle ear disease and conductive hearing loss. Moreover, selecting those learning-disabled children who need to be screened for the possibility of auditory processing problems would be approached in a different manner. Age is of crucial importance in determining program goals. For example, expectations regarding screening efficiency are different in a program designed to identify hearing loss and/or ear disease in a neonatal population than they are in a program designed to identify hearing loss and/or ear disease in the school-age population. The high prevalence of middle ear effusion in newborns, combined with spontaneous resolution in many cases, can easily lead to an overload of any neonatal screening program. Thus, it is of utmost importance to establish clearly the intent of any hearing screening program. At a minimum, the following steps should be included in planning a screening program: (1) Define the purpose of the program and set program goals; (2) Choose the test(s) or procedure(s) to be used in screening; (3) Determine the population to be screened; (4) Arrange for diagnostic follow up; (5) Arrange for treatment/intervention; (6) Select and train screening personnel; and, (7) Monitor the outcome(s) of the screening program.

As noted previously, identification of hearing loss may be accomplished by behavioral and electrophysiologic approaches; however, the detection of middle ear disease (otitis media with effusion) or other otic pathology, as well as central auditory disorders cannot be accomplished by screening hearing sensitivity alone. The issues of mass screening for middle ear disease and selected screening for central auditory disorders will continue to be debated. In part, these debates stem from contradictions between the natural history of otitis media with effusion, the etiology of central auditory disorders, and the potential impact of either disorder on learning and development. Nonetheless, the importance of specifying the intent of a screening program cannot be overstated.

Identification of latent or progressive hearing loss is not possible in a neonatal hearing screening program. While children at risk of developing such losses may be suspected at birth, confirmation of hearing loss will occur only when systematic referral and tracking of children are accomplished.

Although school-based screening and intervention programs have not been fully implemented across the country, federal and state legislative mandates have increased the likelihood of proper follow up. With the implementation of P. L. 99-457 every state must develop specific procedures to identify children who qualify for early intervention services. States may elect to include hearing screening as part of their statewide "child-find" effort (Roush and McWilliam 1990).

A potential disadvantage of the primary-care provider approach is that it relies heavily on the physician's sensitivity to early signs of hearing loss. If primary-care providers do not appreciate a child's need for hearing testing, their attitudes may allay parental concerns, creating a false sense of security regarding the child's hearing status. In the primary-care approach, it is important to focus on the goal of screening for developmental delay, not just hearing or speech and language disorders per se. Obviously, children with mild sensorineural hearing losses or losses associated with otitis media with effusion will not be detected by this approach unless they also manifest a significant speech-language delay. Consequently, any parental concern about hearing status or speech-language delay or any history of recurrent otitis media with effusion should prompt further referral and evaluation, regardless of the developmental screening outcome. As shown in table II, any concern on the part of parent or caregiver regarding hearing, speech-language, and/or developmental delay is considered a risk criterion, thus parents must persist in obtaining appropriate information and services.

Combined with neonatal and school-based approaches, a primary-care approach might address several weak links in the identification network. Because of the improvement in continuity of services, timely diagnosis and intervention, as well as transfer of information, would present less of a concern. The incorporation of the primary-care provider in the process should substantially improve follow up.

Unfortunately, a comprehensive system that optimizes the contribution of birth-related, school-related, and primary-care approaches does not ensure that appropriate habilitative services and facilities will be available. Without early intervention programs, the benefits of early identification are lost. In accordance with the objectives for Healthy People 2000, hearing professionals, along with parents, must continue to focus on lowering the age of identification and intervention of hearing loss. Professionals must advocate for a broad range of habilitative service models, so that families can choose an early intervention program best suited to their needs.

REFERENCES

Alberti, P. W., Hyde, M. L., Riko, K., Corgin, H., and Abramovich, S. 1983. An evaluation of BERA for hearing screening in high-risk neonates. *Laryngoscope* 93:1115–1121.

Allen, M. C., and Schubert-Sudia, S. E. 1990. Prevention of prelingual hearing impairment. *Seminars in Hearing* 11:134–49.

American Speech-Language-Hearing Association 1988. Guidelines for the identification of hearing impairment in at-risk infants age birth to 6 months. *Asha* 30:61–64.

Bayley, N. 1969. *Bayley Scores of Infant Development.* New York: Psychological Corp.

Bergstrom, L. 1984. Congenital deafness. In *Hearing Disorders*, 2nd Ed., ed. J. L. Northern. Boston: Little, Brown and Co.

Blake, P. E., and Hall, J. W. 1990. The status of statewide policies for neonatal hearing screening. *Journal of the American Academy of Audiology* 1:67–74.

Brooks, W. S. 1990. Status of nationwide neonatal hearing screening programs and procedures. Poster presentation at annual meeting of the American Academy of Audiology, New Orleans, LA.

Craig, H. 1983. Parent-infant education in schools for deaf children: Results of CEASD survey. *American Annals of the Deaf* 128:82–98.

Diefendorf, A. O. 1988. Behavioral evaluation of hearing-impaired children. In *Hearing Impairment in Children*, ed. F. H. Bess. Parkton, MD: York Press, Inc.

Downs, M. P. 1986. The rationale for neonatal hearing screening. In *Neonatal Hearing Screening*, ed. E. Swigart. San Diego: College-Hill Press.

Durieux-Smith, A., Picton, T., Edwards, C., Goodman, J. T., and MacMurray, B. 1985. The Crib-O-Gram in the NICU: An evaluation based on brain stem electric response audiometry. *Ear and Hearing* 6:20–24.

Elssman, S., Matkin, N., and Sabo, M. 1987. Early identification of congenital sensorineural hearing impairment. *Hearing Journal*, September:13–17.

Greenberg, D. B., Wilson, W. R., Moore, J. M., and Thompson, G. 1978. Visual reinforcement audiometry (VRA) with young Down syndrome children. *Journal of Speech and Hearing Disorders* 43:448–58.

Hendricks-Munoz, K. D., and Walton, J. P. 1988. Hearing loss in infants with persistent fetal circulation. *Pediatrics* 81:650–56.

Hosford-Dunn, H., Johnson, S., Simmons, F. B., Malachowski, N., and Low, K. 1987. Infant hearing screening: Program implementation and validation. *Ear and Hearing* 8:12–20.

Hyde, M. L., Riko, K., and Malizia, K. 1990. Audiometric accuracy of the click ABR in infants at risk for hearing loss. *Journal of the American Academy of Audiology* 1:59–66.

Jacobson, J. T., and Jacobson, C. A. 1991. EOAE infant screening: A caveat. Poster presentation at the third annual convention of the American Academy of Audiology, Denver, CO.

Jacobson, J. T., and Morehouse, C. R. 1984. A comparison of auditory brain-stem response and behavioral screening in high risk and normal newborn infants. *Ear and Hearing* 5:247–53.

Joint Committee on Infant Hearing. 1991. 1990 Position Statement. *Asha* 33 (Suppl. 5):3–6.

Joint Committee on Infant Hearing Screening Position Statement 1982. 1983. *Ear and Hearing* 4:3–4.

Jones, F. R., and Simons, F. B. 1977. Early identification of significant hearing loss; the Crib-O-Gram. *Hearing Instruments* 28:8–10.

Kemp, D. T. 1978. Stimulated acoustic emissions from within the human auditory system. *Journal of the Acoustical Society of America* 64:1386–1391.

Kenworthy, O. T., Triggs, E., Perrin, J., and Bess, F. 1985. Current screening practices of primary care physicians. Paper presented at the Conference on Otitis Media and Development: Screening, Referral and Treatment. Vanderbilt University, Nashville, TN.

Kenworthy, O. T., Bess, F. H., Stahlman, M. T., and Lindstrom, D. P. 1987. Hearing, speech, and language outcome in infants with extreme immaturity. *The American Journal of Otology* 8:419–25.

Kileny, P. 1988. New insights on infant ABR hearing screening. *Scandinavian Audiology Supplement* 30:81–88.

Kuhl, P. K., Williams, K. A., Lacerda, F., Stephens, K. N., and Lindblom, B. 1992. Linguistic experience alters phonetics perception in infants by six months of age. *Science* 225:606–8.

Markowitz, R. K. 1990. Cost-effectiveness comparison of hearing screening in the neonatal intensive care unit. *Seminars in Hearing* 11:161–65.

McFarland, W. H., Simmons, F. B., and Jones, F. R. 1980. An automated hearing screening technique for newborns. *Journal of Speech and Hearing Disorders* 45:495–503.

Menuyk, P. 1977. Effects of hearing loss on language acquisition in the babbling stage. In *Hearing Loss in Children*, ed. B. F. Jaffe. Baltimore: University Park Press.

Naulty, C. M., Weiss, I. P., and Herer, G. R. 1986. Progressive sensorineural hearing loss in survivors of persistent fetal circulation. *Ear and Hearing* 7: 74–77.

Northern, J., and Downs, M. 1984. *Hearing in Children* (3rd ed.). Baltimore: Williams and Wilkins.

Nozza, R. J., and Wilson, W. R. 1984.. Masked and unmasked pure-tone thresholds of infants and adults: Development of auditory frequency selectivity and sensitivity. *Journal of Speech and Hearing Research* 27: 613–22.

Plotnick, C. H., and Leppler, J. G. 1986. Infant hearing assessment: A program for identification and habilitation within four months of age. *The Hearing Journal* 39:23–25.

Roush, J., and McWilliam, R. A., 1990. A new challenge for pediatric audiology: Public Law 99-457. *Journal of the American Academy of Audiology* 1:196–208.

Schulman-Galambos, C., and Galambos, R. 1975. Brain stem auditory-evoked responses in premature infants. *Journal of Speech and Hearing Research* 18:456–65.

Shah, C., Chandler, D., and Dale, R. 1978. Delay in referral of children with impaired hearing. *Volta Review* 80:207.

Shakno, R. J. 1984. *Physician's Guide to DRGs*. Chicago: Pluribus Press.

Shimizu, H., Walters, R. J., Proctor, L. R., Kennedy, D. W., Allen, M. C., and Markowitz, R. K. 1990. Identification of hearing impairment in the neonatal intensive care unit population: Outcome of a five year project at the Johns Hopkins Hospital. *Seminars in Hearing* 11:150–60.

Stein, L., Clark, S., and Kraus, N. 1983. The hearing-impaired infant: Patterns of identification and habilitation. *Ear and Hearing* 4:232–36.

Stein, L., Jabaley, T., Spitz, R., Stoakley, D., and McGee, T. 1990. The hearing impaired infant: Patterns of identification and habilitation revised. *Ear and Hearing* 11:201–05.

Thompson, G., and Folsom, R. C. 1985. Reinforced and unreinforced head-turn responses of infants as a function of stimulus bandwidth. *Ear and Hearing* 6:125–29.

Thompson, G., and Weber, B. A. 1974. Responses of infants and young children to behavioral observation audiometry (BOA). *Journal of Speech and Hearing Disorders* 39:140–47.

Thompson, G., Wilson, W. R., and Moore, J. M. 1979. Application of visual reinforcement audiometry (VRA) to low-functioning children. *Journal of Speech and Hearing Disorders* 44:80–90.

Thorner, R. M. 1981. Screening and early detection of disease. In *Preventive and Community Medicine*, eds. D. Clark and B. MacMahon. Boston: Little, Brown and Co.

Trehub, S. E., Schneider, B. A., and Endman, M. 1980. Developmental changes in infant's sensitivity to octave-band noises. *Journal of Experimental Psychology* 29:282–93.

Widen, J. E. 1990. Behavioral screening of high-risk infants using visual reinforcement audiometry. *Seminars in Hearing* 11:4:342–56.

Wilson, W. R., Moore, J. M., and Thompson, G. 1976. Sound-field auditory thresholds of infants utilizing visual reinforcement audiometry (VRA). Paper presented at the American Speech and Hearing Association Convention, Houston.

Wilson, W. R., and Moore, J. M. 1978. Pure-tone earphone thresholds of infants utilizing visual reinforcement audiometry (VRA). Paper presented at the American Speech and Hearing Association Convention, San Francisco.

Chapter • 4

Acoustic Amplification and Sensory Aids for Infants and Toddlers

Jackson Roush and Judith Gravel

Most young children with hearing loss can learn to use their residual hearing effectively, often as the primary channel for the acquisition of language and speech. In fact, the vast majority derive substantial benefit from conventional hearing aids or from alternative sensory devices. The amount of benefit is determined by a complex interaction of many variables including the type, degree, and configuration of hearing loss, as well as the qualitative aspects of the child's peripheral and central auditory function. The length of time and the consistency with which a device has been used are also important variables. In addition, there are influential factors of an even more individual nature such as a family's acknowledgment of the need for these devices and their readiness to assume responsibility for their maintenance and operation. Finally, the degree to which these devices are incorporated into routine use by early intervention programs has a substantial impact on the benefits derived. This chapter explores a variety of options for acoustic amplification and sensory aids appropriate for infants and toddlers. Interdisciplinary issues are also considered.

OPTIONS FOR ACOUSTIC AMPLIFICATION

The most critical function of hearing aids is to make sound, in particular speech, audible to the young listener. The goal is to provide sufficient acoustic amplification to make detectable as many of the sounds in speech as possible without exceeding the child's range of comfortable listening. When infants and toddlers with hearing loss can hear speech, they can frequently acquire language through the auditory channel in a manner similar to that of children with normal hearing. Even infants with severe and profound hearing losses can benefit from amplified speech signals.

Delivery of amplified sound to the ear is most frequently provided through conventional hearing aids. For infants and toddlers, the most practical options for acoustic amplification are either ear-level (behind-the-ear) or body-worn instruments (see figures 1a and 1b). The principal advantage of a behind-the-ear (BTE) hearing aid fitting is improved "binaural" (two-eared) hearing. Because hearing aid microphones can be located at ear level, true stereophonic reception can be achieved, as well as an enhancement of high-frequency energy. Other BTE advantages include elimination of clothing noise (a common problem when body-worn microphones are covered by clothing or rub against it), ease of maintenance, and cosmetic appeal. But the potential advantages of an ear-level fitting are of little consequence if acoustic feedback (whistling) from the hearing aid prohibits delivery of the amplification needed. Stated differently, when the volume control on a BTE hearing aid is turned down to eliminate acoustic feedback, all sounds delivered through the hearing aid are reduced. Thus, the pros and cons of an initial ear-level fitting must be carefully

a
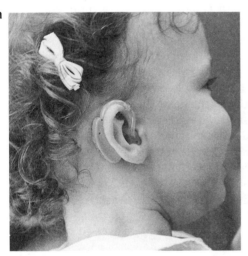
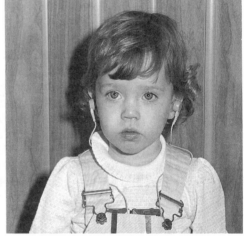
b

Figure 1.   (a) Behind-the-ear and (b) body-worn hearing aids are the types most commonly used with infants and young children. (Photo from Roush, J. 1990. Acoustic amplification for hearing-impaired infants and toddlers. *Infants and Young Children* 2(4):59–71, with permission.)

weighed, especially in young infants with severe-to-profound hearing loss.

When an initial ear-level fitting is deemed unfeasible, body worn instruments or "body aids" may be recommended. Because the hearing aid's microphone, located within the case of the instrument is spatially separated by a cord from the hearing aid's receiver/earmold, the output of the hearing aid may be increased without the problem of acoustic feedback. Typically, body-worn instruments are employed on a temporary basis (on loan) until adequate ear-level amplification becomes practical (Ross and Madell 1988).

FM Systems

Another important option for infants and children is the radio frequency FM system, or "auditory trainer." In the past, FM systems have been used primarily in educational settings; however, their suitability for use in a variety of listening situations is becoming increasingly evident. Once considered only for those with severe or profound hearing loss, the flexibility and current range of fitting options makes FM worthy of consideration for virtually any degree and configuration of hearing loss.

The primary components of an FM system consist of a microphone/transmitter, one or more receiver units, and an antenna for each. The person talking (e.g., parent/caregiver or teacher) wears the microphone/transmitter while the child wears the receiver. In effect, a miniaturized FM radio station, which transmits and receives on a specific restricted FM frequency band, is established between the talker and listener(s). The microphone of the FM transmitter, generally clipped to the speaker's lapel, is attached to a small transmitter worn on a belt clip. The effective transmission range of an FM system may vary from 100 to 300 yards depending on the unit and may be used indoors or outdoors. The advantage of an FM system is that when the child is within the FM broadcast and reception range, amplified sounds are delivered to the ear as if he or she were within a few inches of the person talking. Stated differently, regardless of the physical distance between the speaker and listener, signals arriving at the ear are the same as if the child were consistently in close proximity to the person talking (or other sound source). The child using an FM system receives the speaker's voice or primary signal at a level well above any background noise competition, resulting in a highly favorable signal-to-noise (S/N) condition. Thus, FM systems significantly reduce the problems of background noise, speaker-listener proximity, and room echo or reverberation, all factors known to degrade the speech understanding abilities of children with hearing losses (e.g., Finitzo-Hieber 1981).

Presently, various options are available for coupling the FM signal to the child's ear. Especially for young children, it is important that the receiver provide the dual role of both FM system and conventional hearing aid. It is essential, therefore, that the FM unit include standard microphones through which environmental sounds may be amplified and received. This is particularly important for infants and young children still developing language and speech because the "environmental" microphones allow the child to monitor his or her own vocal output as well as the speech of others in the immediate vicinity.

The environmental microphone (EM) is often contained within the case of the FM receiver. In this option, the EM signals are amplified by the receiver and delivered either with or without the FM signal to the child's ears, via cords, to either button receivers (snapped to personal earmolds), headsets, or "Walkman"-type earphones. In another option, EMs may be located in behind-the-ear instruments; one at each ear. Although similar in appearance to conventional BTE hearing aids, these devices contain only the EMs and are attached via cords to the body-worn receivers. An advantage of locating the EMs at ear level is enhancement of amplification and elimination of clothing noise. By having EMs activated, self-monitoring and reception of environmental signals are provided while simultaneously receiving FM transmission (EM + FM option). In addition, the receiver may serve as a conventional hearing aid if FM transmission ceases or should the child's personal hearing aids be nonfunctional or unavailable. Thus, when both FM and EM options are available on the receiver, the options for signal reception are multiple: FM signal only, EM signal only, or a combination of both the FM and EM signals, adjusted to deliver the FM signal at a relatively higher level.

A current fitting option on some FM systems allows a body-worn FM receiver to be coupled directly to a child's personal ear-level hearing aids. In this arrangement (termed direct audio input), conventional microphones within the child's own hearing aids remain active. An FM signal is delivered from a receiver through a cord to the hearing aid, coupled via a "boot" or plug-in connection. Thus, the FM signal and the environmental input from conventional microphones are processed through the child's individually fitted hearing aids. An advantage of this arrangement is that electroacoustic characteristics of the signal delivered to the child's ear are similar when using either an FM or a personal hearing aid.

In another arrangement, coupling of an FM signal from a receiver to a child's personal hearing aid is accomplished inductively via a "T" or telecoil option on a personal hearing aid. A loop worn around the neck and attached to an FM receiver transforms the FM signal into an electromagnetic field. When a child's hearing aids are switched to the telecoil position, the FM signal is delivered to the hearing aid's telecoil. The limitation of this coupling arrangement is that in order to hear environmental sounds, either the receiver must have active EMs or the hearing aid must have an M-T (microphone-telecoil position) option. Without such provisions, the only signal heard is the FM, thus precluding reception of one's own voice or that of others in the vicinity.

Obviously, there are myriad factors that must be considered: determination of optimal FM/EM ratios, compatibility of various manufacturer's equipment, and the changes in electroacoustic response that may occur during each type of coupling (Ross, Brackett, and Maxon 1991). Recently, a new FM system has become available, the receiver unit being completely contained in an ear-level instrument (see figure 2). This behind-the-ear FM receiver offers FM, EM, and FM-EM listening combinations without the necessity of a body-worn receiver, inductive coupling, or cords. As shown, an antenna is still a critical feature for FM reception. A single amplification unit that offers both conventional and FM options enhances flexibility and fitting options; however, the larger size of this instrument, compared to standard BTE hearing aids, makes fitting to infants and very young children a greater challenge. Still, an ear-level FM device represents an important innovation worthy of consideration for a variety of pediatric hearing aid fittings (Ross 1992; Ross, Brackett, and Maxon 1991). Regardless of which FM system is chosen, teachers and parents must be aware of good FM technique. That is, the FM transmitter should always be located near the source of the desired primary input signal (teacher's/ parent's lips, another child or sibling, television, tape player etc.). When a message is not relevant for the child, it is important to

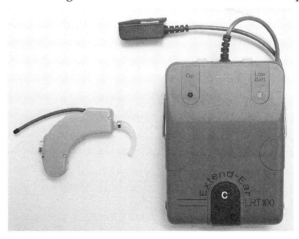

Figure 2. An ear-level FM receiver (left) and transmitter (right). (Photo courtesy of Sonovation.)

turn off the FM transmitter to preclude unwanted, extraneous (or confidential!) input. For an excellent review of FM selection and fitting techniques, see Ross (1992).

An innovative use of FM technology is also available for children with milder forms of hearing loss and/or those with normal hearing who are having difficulty listening (attending) in a noisy classroom environment. One approach is through the use of a low-output personal FM unit. This smaller FM device has no EMs, offers only a volume control, and is usually coupled to the child's ears via non-occluding "Walkman"-type earphones or miniature receivers known as ear buds. This arrangement allows the child to self-monitor while hearing surrounding environmental sounds "normally." An FM signal serves to enhance the primary message over the background competition.

Another use of FM technology is the "soundfield" listening system. In this arrangement, a teacher wears a microphone/transmitter. An FM signal is transmitted to a receiver/amplifier, which delivers the amplified signal to one or more loudspeakers. The loudspeakers are located at various points within the classroom (if two loudspeakers are utilized, they are usually located at the back of the room). The teacher's amplified voice is broadcast through the loudspeakers enabling him or her to move freely around the room. Because a microphone is placed close to the sound source, the primary signal (the teacher's voice) is heard at nearly equal levels throughout the classroom. Thus, children at some distance from the teacher still receive a favorable signal-to-noise ratio. Although children with mild forms of hearing loss (either stable sensorineural or fluctuating conductive hearing loss) seem to benefit from this arrangement, anecdotal reports indicate that even children with normal hearing gain a noticeable listening advantage. Moreover, the teacher's need for vocal effort is significantly reduced (Ray 1987; Ray, Sarff, and Glassford 1984).

In summary, current FM technology is benefiting infants and young children at home and in the preschool setting. As a result, the use of FM is becoming more popular for children with all types, degrees, and configurations of hearing loss.

SELECTION OF ACOUSTIC AMPLIFICATION

Once there is sufficient audiologic data to proceed with hearing aid fitting, decisions must be made regarding selection of the instrument's electroacoustic characteristics. In recent years, a new clinical electroacoustic assessment procedure has emerged that offers the audiologist greater control over the initial selection and subsequent adjustment of hearing aids for young children. Known as "probe tube microphone" or "real-ear" measurements, these procedures permit an objective assessment of a hearing aid's amplification characteristics as they exist in an individual listener's ear canal. Because there are significant individual differences in size and shape of the external ear of infants and toddlers relative to older children and adults, real-ear measures obtained using probe microphone instrumentation are useful in determining the actual sound pressure levels being delivered to a child's ear as a function of frequency. Figure 3 illustrates probe microphone measurements being obtained in the ear of an infant. To examine the hearing aid's maximum output, a test stimulus is presented at a high level, providing a "real-ear saturation response." Due to the relatively small volume of the ear canal in young children, hearing aid output levels measured in the child's ear tend to be higher than one would expect from the manufacturer's technical description of the instrument, which is based on measurements made in a standard hard-walled coupler. Coupler measurements are useful for monitoring the functional status of a hearing aid or for determining whether it conforms to technical specifications, but the resulting output is likely to differ signifi-

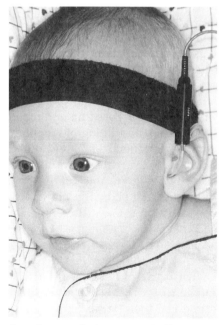

Figure 3.   Probe microphone techniques permit direct measurement of the amplified sound pressure levels in the ear canal. To obtain these measurements, a small probe tube is placed in the ear canal and the earmold is inserted over it. (Photo from Roush, J. 1990. Acoustic amplification for hearing-impaired infants and toddlers. *Infants and Young Children* 2(4):59–71, with permission.)

cantly from the real-ear response, especially in children (Feigin et al. 1989). Because sound levels tend to increase as the ear canal volume decreases, infants may be inadvertently "over-fitted."

Careful and complete measurements of a hearing aid's output characteristics are critical to the successful fitting of amplification in young children. Too much amplification may cause the child to reject hearing aid use due to discomfort associated with the sound being "too loud." Over-amplification can also damage the ear, potentially jeopardizing already decreased hearing sensitivity. Conversely, an overly conservative approach leading to underamplification results in output levels too low for sufficient auditory stimulation. For a more technical description of probe tube microphone measures and their clinical application to young children, the interested reader is referred to Hawkins and Northern (1992).

Although probe tube microphone measures are useful in determining actual sound pressure levels in the ear canal, they cannot specify the electroacoustic characteristics that are truly optimal for a given individual. Furthermore, they cannot provide an indication of what a child actually perceives. Probe tube microphone measurements can, however, guide the audiologist in the selection of a safe and appropriate initial fitting that can be modified, as needed, over time. They are most useful when used in conjunction with a well-defined protocol for pediatric hearing aid selection.

Recently, Seewald and colleagues (1991) described a computer-assisted approach to hearing aid selection specifically designed for use with young preverbal children.[1] Based on audiometric thresholds, the program guides the selection and fitting of amplification by providing estimates of the required frequency-gain and output-limiting characteristics, as defined for both the real ear and the standard 2cc coupler. The program also provides a graphic representation of aided and unaided results, similar to that shown in figure 4, which is useful for orientation and counseling purposes. Presented in this manner, it is clear to parents and others that the purpose of a hearing aid is not to "correct" for a hearing loss, but rather to increase the intensity of speech, thus allowing access to the widest possible frequency range, at intensity levels within the child's range of loudness tolerance (Seewald, Ross, and Spiro1985; Seewald and Ross 1988). Verification of an appropriate fitting can then be carried out using behavioral and probe tube microphone measures.

---

[1]Information regarding the D. S. L. computer program developed by Seewald and colleagues can be obtained from the Child Amplification Laboratory, Hearing Health Care Research Unit, University of Western Ontario, London, Ontario, Canada N6G 1H1.

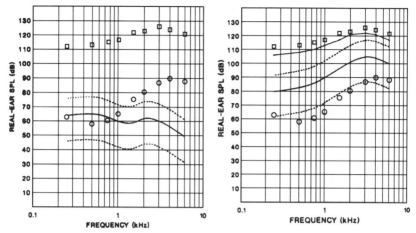

Figure 4.   (a) Pure tone air conduction thresholds (◯) and loudness discomfort levels (☐) expressed in dB SPL. Also shown are one-third octave band levels for average conversational speech (——) with an average range of intensities (– – –) across frequencies. (b) electroacoustic outcome of the hearing aid selection and fitting process, based on the Desired Sensation Level (DSL) method. Note that the amplified speech spectrum is now within the child's dynamic range of hearing. (From Seewald and Moodie. 1992. Electroacoustic considerations. In *Auditory Training Systems: Characteristics, Selection, and Use*, ed. M. Ross. Timonium, MD: York Press.)

ALTERNATIVES TO CONVENTIONAL AMPLIFICATION

Bone Conduction Hearing Devices

Most permanent hearing losses in children are due to abnormal *inner* ear function (i.e., sensorineural impairment). There are congenital conditions, however, that result in a significant hearing loss due to middle and/or external ear anomalies. These losses are often associated with *normal* inner ear function. When the use of a standard earmold and hearing aid is precluded by an external ear anomaly, a "bone conduction" device may be recommended. By converting the amplified sound to a vibrotactile stimulus, the signal is conveyed directly to the inner ear by a bone vibrator worn on the head. In figure 5, an infant is shown wearing a bone conduction transducer fitted to an elastic head band. Although somewhat cumbersome, this arrangement can provide useful stimulation for purposes of speech/language acquisition and development. In recent years, a surgically implantable bone conduction device (coupled to the head by way of transcutaneous magnetic coupling) has been developed for older children and adults (Hough, Himelick, and Johnson 1986). Although its usefulness with young children has not been systematically investigated, problems with magnetic retention are likely to limit its feasibility with this population.

Figure 5. An infant using a bone conduction transducer fitted to an elastic head band. All components are self-contained within the head-worn device.

Vibrotactile Aids

For children with little or no usable hearing, an alternative mode of input may be used to supplement visual information available on the speaker's face and lips. Known as "tactile aids," these devices present acoustic information that is decoded tactually on the skin's surface. Unlike a bone conduction hearing aid, which presents a vibratory signal to the intact inner ear, tactile stimulation is presented to either the wrist, forearm, stomach, back, leg or sternum, depending on the design of the device (Roeser 1988, 1989; Lynch, Oller, and Eilers 1989). Although these devices are recommended far less frequently than conventional hearing aids or FM systems, there is evidence that profoundly deaf children can use them to derive information for purposes of speech reception (Roeser 1988, 1989; Lynch, Eilers, and Oller 1989).

Tactile aids may "code" the speech signal in simple or elaborate ways. In the simplest case (a single channel), a child may obtain critical information about presence or absence of sound as well as rhythm and voicing information in the speech signal. With more complex devices (that use more than one channel processing), frequency information contained in the speech signal may be available. Frequency information is coded by place of stimulation on the skin's surface (Roeser 1988, 1989; Lynch, Eilers, and Oller 1989). Like conventional hearing aids, tactile aid microphones can pick up extraneous sounds in noisy environments, which can be confusing to the child. One-to-one therapy with the device is generally the procedure of choice.

Cochlear Implants

Technology is now available to provide an alternative to acoustic amplification. Before becoming a candidate for a cochlear implant, a child must be at least 24 months of age; have a profound sensorineural hearing loss in both ears; receive little or no benefit from conventional hearing instruments; and have no medical contraindications for surgical implantation. It is also generally recommended that the child be enrolled in an educational program that emphasizes development of auditory skills and that the family be highly motivated but properly oriented with regard to appropriate expectations.

At the present time, the only device approved for use in children is the Nucleus 22 electrode cochlear implant manufactured by Cochlear Corporation. The cochlear implant, which consists of a magnet, a receiver-stimulator, and a banded array of 22 electrodes, is surgically implanted in the child's mastoid bone just behind the ear. The externally worn portion of the implant consists of a microphone, similar in appearance to a small BTE hearing aid, which connects, via cable, to a speech processor (see figure 6a and b). Slightly larger than a body hearing aid, the speech processor is worn in a harness or attached to a waist band. A transmitting coil containing a small magnet is attracted to a second magnet located within the internal receiver/stimulator. The device is held in place by magnetic attraction across the skin.

There are controls on the body-worn unit that turn the device on and off and regulate its sensitivity. The microphone worn at ear level picks up an audio signal and sends it to the speech-processor. The "processed" electrical signal, which is then delivered to the implanted electrode array, is the representation of speech that the child must learn to decode. Thresholds and comfort levels are set for each electrode with a computer, a procedure known as mapping. A child's "map" is individually determined and may be redone frequently until optimum settings are determined. In general, mapping is carried out at the center where the device was implanted.

Pediatric cochlear implant users receive varying degrees of benefit from their devices. According to Cochlear Corporation, manufacturer of the Nucleus device, nearly all children who participated in the FDA clinical trials achieved greater awareness of conversational speech and environmental sounds at comfortable loudness levels. After training and experience, one-third to one-half could identify everyday sounds such as car horns and doorbells from a closed set of alternatives; identify speech in context; and exhibit improved speechreading. Over half could distinguish among different speech patterns and demonstrate improvements in speech production and loudness control. Up to one-third could understand speech without context. Because cochlear implantation in children has only had FDA approval since 1990, their long-term implications and benefits are as yet unknown.

INTERDISCIPLINARY ISSUES

Conventional Amplification

In most cases, sensorineural hearing loss in children cannot be treated medically and the audiologist assumes responsibility for the selection

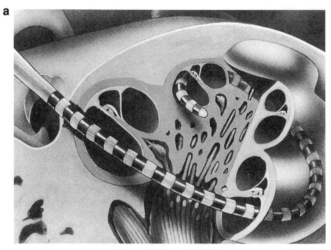

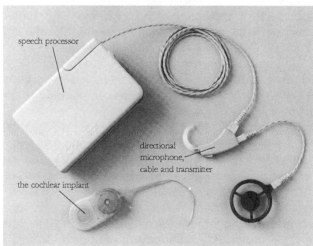

Figure 6.   (a) Components of the Nucleus Mini System 22. (b) Multichannel electrode array after insertion in the inner ear.

and fitting of amplification. Once the hearing aid fitting has been completed, however, the child's habilitative management involves a variety of professionals and family members, all of whom play key roles in maximizing the child's use of residual hearing. It is important to emphasize that optimizing a hearing aid fitting is a continuous process. Changes in the electroacoustic parameters, for example, may be made as the child develops and as observations from parents and professionals are considered. Because the audiologist is most likely to see a child in a clinical environment, family members and specialists from other disciplines are generally in the best position to observe the benefits of amplification in various listening situations. Moreover, it is the responsibility of those who see a child outside an audiologic setting to ensure that the devices are worn, that the earmolds are properly inserted, that external controls are at the prescribed settings, and that batteries are functional. In reality, these goals are not easily accomplished. Audiology literature is replete with surveys from the 1960s to the 1980s, showing that at any given time, approximately half the hearing aids being worn by children are functioning inappropriately (e.g., Robinson and Sterling 1980). Only through effective parent/caretaker orientation and interdisciplinary cooperation can this unfortunate state of affairs be ameliorated. A dialogue between audiologist, family, and other professionals working with the family needs to be established to ensure proper orientation to the care and use of hearing aids and to implement a mechanism for providing information to the audiologist regarding the child's progress. Children with multiple handicaps, in particular, require careful long-term observation to judge the benefits of amplification.

Cochlear Implants

Family members and professionals are encouraged to share their observations with the cochlear implant team. Input from parents, preschool teachers, speech-language pathologists, and others who interact frequently with the child can be invaluable to the process of determining implant candidacy or in assessing performance with the device after implantation. If a child has or is scheduled to receive a cochlear implant, the cochlear implant center must remain in close contact with family members and early intervention personnel. In-service presentations should be provided so that these individuals feel comfortable with the use and maintenance of the device as well as any specific therapeutic techniques that may be beneficial. Problems related to mechanical breakdown (broken cords, damaged microphones, etc.) can occur with cochlear implants, just as they do with the more conventional instruments worn by young children. Thus, frequent equipment checks are important for children with cochlear implants to ensure that the device is turned on and functioning properly. If professionals involved in early education programs feel uncomfortable or uninformed about the cochlear implant, they are advised to contact the cochlear implant center directly to request further information. When the center is located some distance from the child's home, it is imperative that regular contacts be established by telephone or other communication. For more information on cochlear implants in children, interested readers are directed to Owens and Kessler (1989) or Staller, Beiter, and Brimacombe (1991). Audiologic issues are reviewed by Tyler (1992) and an informative guide for parents has been prepared by Tye-Murray (1992).

Acoustic Environment

Of equal importance to the devices themselves is a critical examination of the auditory environment where they are used. It is well known that children with hearing loss are more detrimentally effected by adverse listening conditions (the interactions of noise, distance, and room reverberation) than are children with normal hearing (e.g., Finitzo-Hieber 1981). Even the best efforts to achieve optimal fitting of hearing aids can be defeated by a poor acoustic environment. The audiologist must consult with family members and professionals involved with the children to evaluate the listening environment and make whatever acoustic modifications are feasible.

Final Considerations

Regardless of educational philosophy or communication modality, there can be no doubt that reception of spoken language is facilitated for nearly all children by hearing aids or other sensory devices. But the management of these devices requires a serious commitment to interdisciplinary coordination and a sharing of professional roles. With proper fitting and orientation accompanied by a close working relationship with the audiologist, family members and professionals who interact with the child on a daily basis can assume primary responsibility for the day-to-day management of hearing aids or other assistive devices, as well as the acoustic environment in which they are used. Successful parent-professional collaboration ensures each child the opportunity to use his or her sensory capacities to their fullest advantage.

REFERENCES

Feigin, J., Kopun, J., Stelmachowicz, P., and Gorga, M. 1989. Probe tube microphone measures of ear canal sound pressure levels in infants and children. *Ear and Hearing* 10:254–58.

Finitzo-Hieber, T. 1981. Classroom acoustics. In *Auditory Disorders in School Children*, eds. R. Roeser and M. Downs. New York: Thieme-Stratton.

Hawkins, D., and Northern, J. 1992. Probe microphone measurements with children. In *Probe Microphone Measurements: Hearing Aid Selection and Assessment*, eds. G. Mueller, D. Hawkins, and J. Northern. San Diego: Singular Publishing Group.

Hough J., Himelick T., Johnson, B. 1986. Implantable bone conduction hearing device. *Annals of Otology Rhinology and Laryngology* 95:498–504.

Lynch, M., Eilers, R., and Oller, D. K. 1989. Profoundly hearing impaired subjects: Use of tactile aids in speech perception tasks. *Volta Review* 91:(5):113–26.

Owens, D., and Kessler, D. 1989. *Cochlear Implants in Young Deaf Children*. Boston: College-Hill.

Ray, H. 1987. Put a microphone on the teacher: A simple solution for the difficult problem of mild hearing loss. *The Clinical Connection* 14–15.

Ray, H., Sarff, L., and Glassford, J. 1984. Sound field amplification: An innovative educational intervention for mainstreamed learning disabled students. *The Directive Teacher* 18–20.

Robinson, D., and Sterling, G. 1980. Hearing aids and children in school: A follow-up study. *Volta Review* 82:229.

Roeser, R. J. 1989. Tactile aids: Development issues and current status. In *Cochlear Implants in Young Deaf Children*, eds. E. Owens and D. K. Kessler. Boston: Little, Brown and Company.

Roeser, R. J. 1988. Cochlear implants and tactile aids for the profoundly deaf student. In *Auditory Disorders in School Children* (2nd ed.), eds. R. Roeser and M. Downs. New York: Thieme Medical Publishers.

Ross, M. 1992. *FM Auditory Training Systems: Characteristics, Selection, and Use*. Timonium, MD: York Press.

Ross, M., and Madell, J. 1988. The premature demise of body-worn hearing aids. *Asha* November: 29–30.

Ross, M., Brackett, D., and Maxon, A. 1991. *Assessment and Management of Hearing Impaired Children: Principles and Practices*. Austin TX: PRO-ED.

Roush, J. 1990. Acoustic amplification for hearing impaired infants and toddlers. *Infants and Young Children* 2(4):59–71.

Seewald, R., and Ross, M. 1988. Amplification for young hearing impaired children. In *Amplification for the Hearing Impaired*, ed. M. Pollack. Orlando: Grune and Stratton.

Seewald, R., Ross, M., and Spiro, M. 1985. Selecting amplification characteristics for young hearing-impaired children. *Ear and Hearing* 6:48–53.

Seewald, R., Zelisko, D., Ramji, K., and Jamieson, D. 1991. *DSL 3.0 User's Manual*. London, Ontario, Canada: University of Western Ontario.

Staller, S., Beiter, A., and Brimacombe, J. 1991. Children and multichannel cochlear implants. In *Cochlear Implants—A Practical Guide*, ed. H. Cooper. London: Whurr Publishers.

Tye-Murray, N. 1992. *Cochlear Implants and Children: A Handbook for Parents, Teachers, and Speech and Hearing Professionals*. Washington, DC: A. G. Bell Association for the Deaf.

Tyler, R. 1992. *Cochlear Implants: Audiologic Applications*. San Diego: Singular Publishing Group.

PART • III

Multidisciplinary Team Evaluation and the Individualized Family Service Plan (IFSP)

Chapter • 5

Strategies for Enhancing Interdisciplinary Collaboration

Noel D. Matkin

A belief widely held in the professional community is that hearing-impaired children and their families represent a homogeneous group with similar needs. This assumption, although unfounded, can prevent young children, especially those with significant hearing impairment and additional developmental disabilities (HI-DD), from reaching their full potential. The use of such terms as *the deaf child* or *the hard-of-hearing child* subtly implies that youngsters, once categorized by degree of hearing loss, are more alike than different. As a consequence, routine assessments and traditional intervention programs are implemented without first considering each child's unique profile of strengths, limitations, and special needs. In the past, comprehensive resources were mobilized in many instances only after a child's development reached a plateau, most often in the areas of communication, language learning, and academic achievement. In other words, we unintentionally continued to support a failure-based rather than a pro-active or prevention model.

Many years ago, Myklebust (1953) stressed that a cooperative effort among specialists was essential if the needs of hearing-impaired children, especially those with multiple disabilities, were to be met. He prophetically stated that only through a team endeavor would knowledge continue to accumulate relative to individual differences and their developmental implications. Over two decades later this premise was integrated into the federal mandate Public Law (P.L.) 94-

142, designed to ensure a free and appropriate education for all school-age children with special needs.

In 1973, the Rand Corporation, under contract to the Department of Health, Education, and Welfare, published a study relative to the delivery of services to children with special needs, including those with hearing impairment (Brewer and Kakalik 1973). This study concluded that special services were often poorly coordinated and fragmented. Various professionals and agencies often provided only one or a limited range of services. As a consequence, each single service met only one aspect of a child's total needs. In concluding, the report noted that service delivery systems tended to be specialty oriented, when they needed to be child oriented. Professionals who dealt with special-needs children were urged to work together and to view each child as a total human being.

In recent years with the refinement of neonatal intensive care, the development of an array of antibiotics and vaccines, and improved general pediatric care, an increasing number of children survive high-risk pregnancies, traumatic births, or serious childhood illnesses that would have been fatal in previous decades. As a result, many youngsters with complicated prenatal and perinatal histories have multiple developmental disabilities, including hearing impairment. Thus, teamwork has become even more imperative. To explain, a national survey of approximately 52,000 hearing-impaired students indicated the prevalence of one or more additional handicapping conditions in as many as one out of every three hearing-impaired children (Karchmer 1985). Such multiple disabilities were more commonly encountered among males, children of color, and those youngsters whose congenital hearing losses were exogenous rather than genetically based.

The issue of fragmented services and reactive rather than proactive evaluations was addressed with the passage of the Education for All Handicapped Children Act, Public Law 94-142. Recall that the Individualized Education Program (IEP) is to be based on findings from a team evaluation so that a current developmental status of each child is ascertained before program placement is determined. Although the rules and regulations of P.L. 94-142 represented a major step forward, it seems in many instances that evaluation teams are limited in both the developmental areas evaluated and the number of professional specialties represented by the primary team.

With the more recent passage of Public Law 99-457, a multidisciplinary team approach is no longer an option. Under Part H, the new law requires, rather than recommends, that a team process be used to provide three services: assessment, development of an Individualized Family Service Plan (IFSP), and case management. Furthermore, families must be viewed as essential members of the collaborative group that forms the team. In this chapter the primary focus is placed upon collaboration among professionals. Winton and Bailey in Chapter 4 (this volume) highlight the unique and critical role that families play in all phases of service delivery.

EFFECTIVE COMMUNICATION

The issue of effective communication among professionals is a primary consideration in the context of teamwork. Six major deterrents consistently impair interactions among professionals during service delivery and, consequently, limit the effectiveness of teamwork. These problem areas are:

1. The trend toward specialty rather than interdisciplinary training is reflected both by current accreditation standards for training programs and by certification requirements for individual professionals. As a result, professional studies often incorporate an extensive curriculum exclusively within a single specialty area. Students graduating from such programs appreciate neither the broad scope of the research literature in child development nor the competencies of specialists from related professionals. Such naiveté can serve as a barrier to planning both comprehensive diagnostic and intervention strategies.

2. There is a lack of common terminology among various professionals who work with children having developmental disabilities. In other words, each professional discipline tends to develop its own lexicon. Consequently, both oral and written evaluation reports may communicate effectively only within one's colleagial group, rather than with other specialists, educators or importantly, parents.

3. Many professional training programs include neither classroom instruction nor clinical experience in interactive teamwork. As a consequence, territorial defensiveness and paranoia may develop as we provide professional services in the context of a multidisciplinary team. As noted by Holm and McCartin (1978), bringing together a group of child development specialists does not automatically create a functional team. Fortunately, several publications have suggested key issues that need to be addressed, as well as potential training models, for education in interactive teamwork (Gray, Coleman, and Gotts 1981; Brill 1976; Crisler 1979; Golin and Ducanis 1981; Lyon and Lyon 1980; Pfeiffer 1980; Yoshida 1980).

4. There tends to be a professional pecking order among the various pediatric specialties. Unfortunately, the physician, who may spend the least amount of time with the child and family, often has the most clout when a diagnosis and recommendations for intervention are finalized. In other words, there is a *tier* rather than a *peer* model of service delivery.

5.   The escalating costs of early assessment and intervention provide an impetus for streamlining teamwork so that fewer professional hours are needed for assessment and staffing. Participation of family members in assessment is one less costly alternative; another is the involvement of professionals with transdisciplinary training and experience (Sheehan 1988).

Too often personality differences create tensions among team members, which results in strained communication and uncooperative behaviors, thereby limiting the effectiveness of an interdisciplinary team approach.

A tool used in corporations, service industries, and consulting firms that merits consideration is the Myers-Briggs Type Indicator (MBTI). The MBTI provides a useful measure of personality type by looking at eight preferences, divided into four bipolar scales that individuals use in their daily life, including at work (Myers and Myers 1983). It is important to understand that the MBTI was not designed to identify pathology or to indicate that one preference is right while another is wrong. Rather, the tool can be used to indicate preferences among team members, thereby helping people understand themselves and their behaviors as well as appreciating others in order to make constructive use of individual differences. Research conducted over a forty-year period indicates that use of the tool can promote communication among professional workers, improve teamwork, and facilitate conflict resolution. Studies reveal further that by understanding each colleague's typology, it is possible to understand better varying leadership and work styles, as well as the contribution that each person may make to a team. As a simple example, an extrovert who tends to like variety and action often develops ideas by discussion and then acts quickly. In sharp contrast, an introvert who often develops ideas by reflection prefers to think at length before acting. Obviously, neither workstyle is right or wrong. Unless recognized and appreciated, such differences among team members can create disharmony. For teams whose members are likely to interact frequently, a worthwhile activity would be to engage an experienced consultant to administer, interpret, and discuss the result of the MBTI as a means of improving interactive teamwork and, in the long run, to save valuable time.

6.   With the passage of P.L. 99-457 requiring the development of an Individualized Family Service Plan, there has been heated discussion among various specialists as to the preferred strategy for involving parents in the assessment process. Traditionally, assessments of infants and toddlers have been focused on the child with parents, at best, being passive observers of the process and, at worst, being excluded from the evaluation entirely. One strategy for ensuring that parents perceive their role as important and that they serve as equal

status collaborators in a developmental team evaluation is to involve them in developmental screening. A number of developmental questionnaires, such as the Minnesota Child Development Inventory, are designed to solicit parent input. My experience in using this particular screening instrument with hearing-impaired toddlers and preschoolers for the past decade has been positive in that the resulting developmental profile of current strengths and limitations assists the team in individualizing an assessment plan, while providing parents with visual feedback about their child's strengths and needs.

It has been argued that parents' developmental estimates are inconsistent and thus do not serve a useful purpose; yet an extensive review of the literature suggests that when only those instruments specifically designed for parental use are considered, parental and professional assessment data show a remarkably high degree of consistency. For further consideration of this important issue, the reader is referred to Sheehan (1988).

Clearly, one potential barrier to effective teamwork is the variety of opinions one may encounter in any group of professionals relative to the extent and type of parent involvement that is desirable during assessments. Consensus on this issue within any team is essential for effective collaboration and to ensure that parents are in partnership with the assessment team. Again, such issues are described in depth by Winton and Bailey in Chapter 4 of this text.

Despite the problem areas described, there is an increased probability of developing a more effective partnership with the parents when an interdisciplinary team evaluation, rather than a series of unrelated specialty assessments, is undertaken. By including parents in the evaluation and by having coordinated feedback, there is a much higher probability of parents feeling a sense of unity and, thus, following through on recommendations for medical, educational, and related clinical support services.

Another obvious benefit of a team evaluation is that a pro-active, rather than a reactive approach is taken to program modification. In other words, one benefit of teamwork is that the child being evaluated is monitored over time, with team members having the opportunity to assess the validity of their initial recommendations as the child matures and develops. If it becomes apparent that a child is not making adequate progress, it is then possible to reconvene the team and establish a new set of short- and long-range objectives.

Finally, in this writer's experience, one of the major advantages of participating as a member of a functional child development team—and an issue that is rarely mentioned—is the professional stimulation and growth that accrue over time. In listening to each specialist present his or her findings, by discussing the evaluation procedures employed, and in generating recommendations for future management, each member of the team develops a heightened sensitivity to the various domains of child development and the impact that various disabilities can have on development. In short, effective teamwork is informative and stimulating, and furthermore represents one form of continuing education. As a consequence, it is my perception that professional burnout becomes less of an issue among members of an interactive interdisciplinary team.

VARIABLES INFLUENCING TEAMWORK

Having served on three different evaluation teams over the past 20 years, it has been my experience that several major issues must be addressed when formulating a child study team to serve hearing-impaired children and their families. Each of these six considerations directly influences the efficiency of interactive teamwork.

The first is adoption of a philosophy regarding the manner in which the team functions and the role of various team members. The second is recognition of the broad spectrum of children who fall into the generic classification of "hearing impaired." Adoption of a developmental screening procedure that ensures that only those children are selected who need such a concerted (and expensive) approach to evaluation is a third consideration. Fourth, the development of a routine schedule of activities is necessary if interactive teamwork is to become a reality. Fifth, the adoption of a structure to guide the sequence of the team's composition regarding members of the primary team versus consultants to the team. Finally, adoption of a developmental model that will be used both to guide various aspects of the team evaluation and to determine referrals for additional specialty assessments is essential.

Philosophy

With respect to adopting a philosophy to guide the team's function, Brill (1976), in *Teamwork: Working Together in the Human Services*, notes that there are essentially two philosophies that underlie and influence the manner in which any team will function. The first is a *leadership team* where one member of the team serves as the chair and directs the team's activities. Each team member works independently, serving as a consultant to the team leader who makes final decisions regarding the need for further evaluations and strategies for management. In medical settings, this role is often assumed by the primary physician.

In contrast, a psychologist often fills the leadership role in an educational setting. While time-efficient, such a team structure can reinforce the traditional professional pecking order and result in team members feeling subordinate to the team leader. Furthermore, the leadership team often uses a medical model. Such a model yields a diagnosis but provides limited input relative to development of a comprehensive intervention plan.

The alternative is a *fraternal team*, or peer rather than tier model. With this structure, the basic philosophy is that each member assumes equal responsibility for assessment and has equal input into the diagnostic process. Moreover, the generation and setting of priorities of the final recommendations are guided by group decisions. This team structure has been found most beneficial if the goal is interdisciplinary or transdisciplinary teamwork. Rossetti (1990) has developed excellent visual models to supplement descriptions and comparisons of multidisciplinary, interdisciplinary, and transdisciplinary teamwork. The fraternal team, while more time consuming, tends to minimize territorial defensiveness and to facilitate interactive professional communication. In either case, it is essential that team members agree at the outset upon the philosophy that will guide the function of the team. Otherwise, each member may view his or her potential role somewhat differently, and inevitably conflict will develop.

Spectrum of Children Served

Second, it must be recognized that children identified and referred for evaluation will represent a broad spectrum of individual needs. This is particularly important when making critical decisions about the selection of a battery of test instruments and evaluation procedures. The bulk of clinical investigations and research efforts in past decades have focused on the so-called deaf child; that is, the child with a severe or profound bilateral sensorineural hearing loss. Yet, current surveys indicate that five or six youngsters with mild-to-moderate impairment exist for every child with a severe-to-profound loss (Berg and Fletcher 1970). In other words, it must be anticipated that the preponderance of referrals will be hard-of-hearing, not deaf children. As Davis (1977) has pointed out, hard-of-hearing youngsters often represent our "forgotten children" in terms of diagnostic and educational services.

One further issue relative to the nature of hearing loss in young children merits careful consideration. That is, the largest group of children will be those with a history of otitis media and a fluctuating conductive hearing loss that may be either unilateral or bilateral. At present there is disagreement within the professional community as to the short- and long-range effects of such transient impairments. On one hand, it has been suggested that such hearing loss will have minimal impact on language learning in most children (Stickler 1984). In contrast, other investigators have concluded that the impact may be pervasive in many cases, with long-term speech, language, and subsequent academic difficulties as the end results (Padden, Matthies, and Novak 1989). The adverse effects of recurrent otitis media upon language and learning among children with additional handicapping conditions has not been addressed adequately. This is a topic that merits longitudinal study because the prevalence of middle ear dysfunction is relatively high among infants and toddlers, as well as among multi-handicapped youngsters (Klein 1986; Todd 1986). In recent years, a fourth group of youngsters with permanent hearing loss have been targeted for identification and support services. Clinical investigations of young children with permanent unilateral impairments have revealed that a substantial portion of this population encounters academic learning difficulties once they reach school age (Bess, Klee, and Culbertson 1986; Oyler, Oyler, and Matkin 1988). Those at greatest risk seem to be children with a severe-to-profound loss, especially when the hearing impairment is in the right ear.

Developmental Screening Procedures

Third, the time and effort—not to mention the cost—involved in each evaluation by a child study team are substantial. A rigorous admissions procedure, therefore, should be established to ascertain whether or not each child referred needs a comprehensive team evaluation or whether a transdisciplinary assessment by a limited number of specialists is sufficient. Obviously, there is no single tool that will serve as an adequate admission screening strategy. As a minimum, a comprehensive parent questionnaire should provide three types of information: (1) the parents' chief concerns; (2) the child's developmental history across the areas of motor, cognitive, communication, and social/emotional development; and (3) a medical history covering the pre-, peri-, and postnatal periods. Some parents, especially those with limited educational backgrounds or those for whom English is a second language, may require assistance in completing the parent questionnaire. Furthermore, with preschoolers, the completion of the Minnesota Child Development Inventory (Ireton and Thwing 1974) has proved to be fruitful for establishing a profile of strengths and limitations as perceived by the primary caregiver. If the child is older and enrolled in an educational program, a teacher's report in conjunction with the Myklebust Pupil Rating Scale (Myklebust 1981) or the SIFTER (Anderson 1989) can contribute additional key information. Input from an educator serves as a cross-check of the parent's perceptions about the child's level of function and profile of strengths and special needs. Obviously, copies of all previous medical, audiologic, speech-language, and psychoeducational reports should be obtained and carefully reviewed, otherwise, the same tests and measures may inadvertently be re-administered. Not only should such duplication be avoided for financial reasons, but the test results on repeat measures may be of questionable validity due to the learning effect.

Finally, if supported by the family, making a home visit to collect observational data on both the child's behavior and interaction within the family is invaluable. If the family lives in the vicinity of the team's base of operation, it is best for the family service coordinator to complete the home visit. Otherwise, a community health nurse often will cooperate with the team if the family lives at a distance. Use of the Home Observation for Measurement of the Environment (HOME) scale (Caldwell and Robert 1970) in such instances will ensure that observations are collected in a systematic manner. This scale, which is easy to interpret, facilitates communication within the team while limiting the need for the home observer to prepare a detailed written report.

Schedule of Activities

The efficiency of a team's function is enhanced further if a routine schedule of activities is developed and maintained. As a minimum, it is essential that a brief staff meeting be scheduled before initiating each evaluation. Otherwise, a good deal of duplication in testing may be encountered among the various team members. Another pitfall is that critical areas inadvertently may not be assessed, because each member may assume that someone else on the team will complete such evaluation.

Without adoption and adherence to a few basic procedural guidelines, such a meeting can become time consuming. To facilitate discussion during the meeting, a case summary should be developed and distributed to all team members prior to the meeting. The task of preparing and distributing this key document may be assigned to a caseworker or may be completed by various members of the team on a rotating basis. This summary should be concise, yet contain the highlights from previous evaluations, all pertinent medical and developmental history, and a clear statement of the parents' and/or referring agency's concerns. A review of the case summary allows each team member to generate specific questions and concerns, as well as a basic assessment plan, *before* rather than *during* the meeting. With such preparation, an overall plan for evaluation, including the need for outside consultation, often can be agreed upon within 15 to 20 minutes.

It is ideal if the day and time for both the pre- and post-staffing meetings are mutually agreed upon and maintained over time. Otherwise, coordinating the work schedules of different individuals on the team becomes a major barrier. Of equal importance is the development of a plan for conducting post-staffing meetings. Such a meeting should be conducted before sharing findings with the family or representatives from the referring agency, to ensure that an integrated and comprehensive plan of action has been developed. Again, lack of preparation can result in long, verbose, and relatively nonproductive staff meetings. Ideally, each team member will come to the post-staffing meeting with a succinct summary of the child's strengths and needs.

Although each team member should come to the meeting with a plan of action, recommendations for further assessment or for intervention should remain tentative until the family's views and the findings from all members of the team have been presented. For example, a child may seem to be substantially delayed in language development if only the results from such testing are considered. However, a comparison of the child's mental and language ages may reveal no difference between the two areas of development. Certainly, such a finding will substantially alter the type of recommendation that is made relative to specific language intervention.

Prior to termination of the post-staffing meeting, each team member should finalize his or her recommendations, and the list of strengths, needs, and recommendations should be given to a family service coordinator. Such lists from the various specialists on the team are invaluable during feedback to the parents and later, when a master evaluation summary is prepared.

A strategy must be selected that communicates effectively the findings from the various team specialists in a printed format that facilitates use of diagnostic information by clinicians, teachers, and program administrators. It is not uncommon for each specialist to prepare a report of three to five pages describing test procedures, findings, and recommendations. If the referring agency receives five to eight such specialty reports from the team without a unifying cover document, it is unlikely that the various reports will ever be read in their entirety. Two strategies have been found useful to overcome this potential breakdown in communication. First, plotting all objective scores from the various tests on a profile yields a graphic display of the child's strengths and limitations. The profile can be organized either with a bell curve as the reference and the various scores converted to percentiles thereon, or the child's chronological age can serve as a reference with all test results converted to developmental age scores. In my experience, developmental age scores are more easily interpreted with preschoolers. Second, the various specialty reports should be preceded by a cover document in which all findings and recommendations are succinctly summarized in a page or so under the headings: *strengths, current limitations,* and *key recommendations.* With this master summary and the attached profile, a coordinated overview of the child's present developmental status and needs is provided to anyone who receives the team's report. Each speciality report then serves to expand, to provide details, and to clarify the statements in the master summary.

Team Structure

The composition of the interdisciplinary team is a fifth consideration. Ideally, the developmental model discussed in the following section will influence the inclusion of certain specialists as primary team members. Obviously, the setting in which the team is working will dictate the availability of various specialists to serve on the team. Nevertheless, my experience in working with a broad spectrum of hearing-impaired children suggests that the primary evaluation team ideally will consist of:

A pediatrician with a strong developmental orientation

A social worker or pediatric nurse with skills in evaluating the home
environment and family dynamics

A psychologist experienced in the administration of performance measures and sensitive to the difficulties in achieving a valid assessment of children with limited communication and language
delay

An audiologist with clinical competencies in administering a pediatric
battery of behavioral and/or electrophysiologic measures of
hearing

A speech-language pathologist familiar with the preferred procedures
and special precautions to be observed with hearing-impaired
children in test administration

An occupational therapist familiar with the motor skills needed to
communicate effectively through the use of signing and finger-
spelling

A physical therapist with a developmental orientation

A special educator with competency in assessing young hearing-
impaired children

The child's primary caregiver

In addition to the primary team, other key individuals should be identified and be available readily as consultants to the team when deemed appropriate. The specialists most frequently needed for consultation include:

A pediatric ophthalmologist skilled in eye examinations with children
  having limited communication skills
A pediatric neurologist
A geneticist familiar with the various etiologies and syndromes related
  to sensorineural hearing losses
A child psychiatrist with diagnostic skills as well as experience in
  developing behavioral management programs for home and
  preschool implementation
An otolaryngologist to determine the nature of the hearing loss and to
  treat any subsequent middle ear disorders

Ideally, the primary team members as well as the consultants will have basic manual communication skills so that children from Total Communication programs are evaluated appropriately. Recognizing that this is rarely the case, utilization of the child's parent or early interventionist as an interpreter during the various evaluations can be highly effective. The obvious advantage of this strategy is that the child will be at ease with a familiar caregiver who knows the manual communication system used. Both factors, familiarity with the child and his or her communication system, serve to improve the reliability and validity of findings from the various evaluations. Another advantage of this approach is that including a parent or teacher in the evaluation process provides an opportunity to compare "clinical behaviors" with those encountered in the home or preschool classroom. For example, it is not unusual to find that some hearing-impaired children function relatively well in a structured one-to-one learning environment. Yet, these same children may find it difficult to maintain their attention when placed in a setting where there are multiple activities and visual as well as auditory distractions. Finally, including the primary caregiver as an active participant in the evaluation process makes it more likely that recommendations of the team will be implemented. Without such implementation, one must question whether the theoretical advantages of a team evaluation over a more traditional series of uncoordinated specialties assessments offer any real benefits to the child, the family, or the intervention program.

Developmental Model

Another issue, the sixth and final one that merits consideration during the organization of a team, is the adoption of a developmental model. A variety of developmental models, some quite elaborate, have been proposed for diagnostic use. In my experience, a simple model proposed by Myklebust (1954) has been found adequate and comprehensive. He suggests that four major developmental areas be the points of focus while taking a case history, during clinical observations, and during formal testing. Those areas are motor development, cognitive development, language development, and social/emotional development. Obviously, each of these developmental areas can be subdivided into as many component parts as deemed necessary for the child under study.

Knowledge of each child's visual and auditory status must be established before formal assessment in the various areas outlined above is undertaken. If the goal of the evaluation is to establish optimal performance in various developmental areas, vision should be corrected and hearing appropriately aided. One persistent problem that illustrates this point is the use of oral intelligence scales with young children who have an undetected hearing loss. Obviously, a child's inability to follow oral instructions and the language delay associated with hearing loss interact to invalidate the score obtained on an oral measure. The same problem may be encountered if pencil and paper tests are administered to a child with uncorrected vision.

Finally, understanding a child's physical status and related health problems, as well as environmental influences, are important before attempting to interpret test findings. For example, language scores must be interpreted cautiously if a child is ill or is relatively noncompliant during testing, or if a youngster comes from a bilingual home. Thus, completion of both a pediatrician's examination and a home visit should be given priority as the evaluation schedule is finalized. Furthermore, hearing and vision testing must be scheduled early so that appropriate modifications can be made in the selection of tests and procedures during the subsequent developmental assessments if an impairment in either sensory domain is identified.

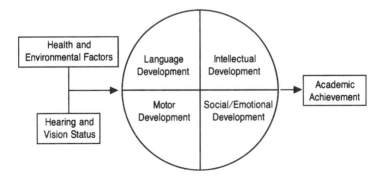

Figure 1.   Developmental model for interdisciplinary collaboration.

In short, one can visualize the preceding points by reviewing figure 1. The child's current level of daily function is best understood if each of the components of the model is considered.

SUMMARY

In summary, the need for effective communication among various professions has been highlighted and identified as the basic consideration in teamwork. Implicit is the belief that as the population of hearing-impaired children becomes more varied and complex, the need for interactive interdisciplinary teamwork, whether in a clinical or early intervention setting, becomes more imperative. To assume that hearing-impaired children are a homogeneous group with similar strengths and needs will lead to a substantial number of youngsters who fail to reach their optimal level of function across the various developmental areas.

Six deterrents to effective teamwork were discussed and six considerations for improving the function of any team, regardless of setting, were presented. Although there are numerous advantages in coordinating the services of various specialists, there are pitfalls that must be recognized and avoided. Otherwise, fragmented service delivery and conflicting recommendations from various specialists will undermine the development of a comprehensive service delivery model. Finally, and most importantly, interactive interdisciplinary teamwork should not be viewed as relevant to evaluation clinics or medical centers only. The key to improving services to all hearing-impaired children and their families is the development of effective parent-professional communication and teamwork among the various team specialists during such activities as IFSP meetings and semi-annual progress reviews.

REFERENCES

Anderson, K. L. 1989. *S.I.F.T.E.R.: Screening Instrument for Targeting Educational Risk*. Danville, IL: The Interstate Printers and Publishers, Inc.

Berg, F., and Fletcher, S. 1970. *The Hard of Hearing Child*. New York: Grune and Stratton.

Bess, F. H., Klee, T., and Culbertson, J. W. 1986. Identification, assessment and management of children with unilateral sensorineural hearing loss. *Ear and Hearing* 7:43–51.

Brewer, G., and Kakalik, J. 1973. *Improving Services to Handicapped Children (R-1420, HEW)*. Santa Monica: Rand Corporation.

Brill, N. 1976. *Teamwork: Working Together in the Human Services*. Philadelphia: Lippincott.

Caldwell, B. M., and Robert, H. B. 1970. *Home Observation for Measurement of the Environment (HOME)*. Little Rock: University of Arkansas Center for Child Development and Education.

Crisler, J. R. 1979. Utilization of a team approach in implementing Public Law 94-142. *Journal of Research and Development in Education* 12:101–08.

Davis, J. 1977. *Our Forgotten Children: Hard of Hearing Pupils in the Schools*. Minneapolis: University of Minnesota, Audio Visual Library Service.

Golin, A. K., and Ducanis, A. J. 1981. *The Interdisciplinary Team: A Handbook for the Education of Exceptional Children*. Rockville, MD: Aspen Systems.

Gray, N. M., Coleman, J. M., and Gotts, E. A. 1981. The interdisciplinary team: Challenges to effective functioning. *Teacher Education and Special Education* 4(1):45–49.

Holm, V. A., and McCartin, R. E. 1978. Interdisciplinary child development team: Team issues and training in interdisciplinariness. In *Early Intervention-A Team Approach*, eds. K. E. Allen, V. A. Holm, and R. L. Schiefelbusch. Baltimore: University Park Press.

Ireton, H., and Thwing, E. 1974. *Minnesota Child Development Inventory*. Minneapolis: Behavioral Science Systems.

Karchmer, M. A. 1985. A demographic perspective. *Hearing Impaired Children & Youth with Developmental Disabilities*, ed. E. Chernow. Washington, DC: Gallaudet College Press.

Klein, J. O. 1986. Risk factors for otitis media in children. *Otitis Media and Child Development*, ed. J. F. Kavanagh. Parkton, MD: York Press.

Lyon, S., and Lyon, G. 1980. Team functioning and staff development: A role release approach to providing integrated educational services for severely handicapped students. *Journal of the Association for the Severely Handicapped* 5:250–63.

Myers, I. B., and Myers, P. B. 1983. *Gifts Differing*. Palo Alto, CA: Consulting Psychologists Press, Inc.

Myklebust, H. 1953. Toward a new understanding of the deaf child. *American Annals of the Deaf* 98:496–99.

Myklebust, H. 1954. *Auditory Disorders in Children*. New York: Grune & Stratton.

Myklebust, H. 1981. *The Pupil Rating Scale Revised*. New York: Grune & Stratton.

Oyler, R. F., Oyler, A. L., and Matkin, N. D. 1988. Unilateral hearing loss: Demographics and educational impact. *Language, Speech and Hearing Services in Schools* 19:201–10.

Padden, E. P., Matthies, M. L., and Novak, M. A. 1989. Recovering from OME-related phonologic delay following tube placement. *Journal of Speech and Hearing Disorders* 54:94–100.

Pfeiffer, S. I. 1980. The school based interprofessional team: Recurring problems and some possible solutions. *Journal of School Psychology* 18:388–94.

Rossetti, L. M. 1990. General and specific assessment considerations. *Infant-Toddler Assessment: An Interdisciplinary Approach*. Boston: College Hill Press.

Sheehan, R. 1988. *Involvement of Parents in Early Childhood Assessment of Young Developmentally Disabled Children*, eds. R. Sheehan and T. Wachs. New York: Plenum Press.

Stickler, G. B. 1984. The attack on the tympanic membrane. *Pediatrics* 74:291–92.

Todd, N. W. 1986. High risk populations for Otitis media. *Otitis Media and Child Development*, ed. J. R. Kavanagh. Parkton, MD: York Press.

Yosha, R. K. 1980. Multidisciplinary decision making in special education: A review of the issues. *School Psychology Review* 9:221–27.

Chapter • 6

The Individualized Family Service Plan
Philosophy and Conceptual Framework

Mary J. McGonigel

The Individualized Family Service Plan (IFSP) is at the heart of new family-centered approaches to early intervention. From the beginning, the IFSP, with its explicit promotion of the pivotal role of the family, was seen as a radical departure from the often professionally directed and child-centered Individualized Education Program (IEP). The IFSP is only one of 14 components of the statewide program of early intervention services for infants and toddlers with disabilities and their families supported by Part H of P.L. 99-457 (now Part H of IDEA—the Individuals with Disabilities Education Act). However, this one component is frequently held to be the aspect of Part H that has the most potential to result in truly family-centered early intervention services.

This chapter explores a family-centered philosophy and conceptual framework for the IFSP and outlines the content of the IFSP required by Part H—as recently reauthorized by P.L. 102-119—and current regulations. The chapter is based on the consensus document, *Guidelines and Recommended Practices for the Individualized Family Service Plan* (McGonigel, Kaufmann, and Johnson 1991b), which itself is based on the work of an "Expert Team" and Task Force appointed by the National Early Childhood Technical Assistance System (NEC*TAS), at the University of North Carolina at Chapel Hill, and the Office of Special Education Programs, U.S. Department of Education. Readers who are interested in a more complete discussion of a family-centered philosophy and approach to the IFSP are referred to this document.

PROMISE AND CHALLENGE

The IFSP embodies a promise to children and families—"a promise that their strengths will be recognized and built on, that their beliefs and values will be respected, that their choices will be honored, and that their hopes and aspirations will be encouraged and enabled" (McGonigel and Johnson 1991, p. 1). The purpose of the IFSP has been defined in a variety of ways in the early intervention literature and in practice. There is clear agreement, however, that the IFSP's primary purpose and opportunity is to create a means for families and professionals, working together as a team, to help families reach their chosen goals for their children and themselves (Campbell 1990; DiVenere 1988; Hunt et al. 1990; McGonigel and Johnson 1991).

In contrast to the IEP and other traditional service plans, in which great emphasis has been placed on the written plan, the written IFSP product itself has been called "possibly the least important aspect of the entire IFSP process. Far more important are the interaction, collaboration, and partnerships between families and professionals that are necessary to develop and implement the IFSP" (McGonigel and Johnson 1991, p. 1). The centrality of the process, rather than the document, is a hallmark of family-centered approaches to the IFSP (Dunst and Deal 1990; Elsayed, in press). In the absence of a family-centered process, the Individualized Family Service Plan becomes "just another program plan" (McGonigel, Kaufmann, and Johnson 1991a, p. 48).

A family-centered approach to the IFSP process challenges professionals to transcend the narrow boundaries of their own disciplines or agencies and to reach out to others who are also supporting young children and their families. Professionals and families also are challenged to work together in new ways. Both groups are meeting this challenge by examining and refining past practices and approaches in light of newly emerging family-centered philosophies, models, and program practices that support children and families in their neighborhoods and communities.

Enabling and Empowering

One result of this re-examination has been the increased acceptance of the concepts of *enabling* and *empowering* as best practice in family-centered early intervention. These terms embody both the spirit and the heart of a family-centered approach to the IFSP. *Empowering* means interacting with families in ways so that they keep or develop a sense of control over their family lives and attribute positive changes to their own strengths, abilities, and actions. *Enabling* means creating opportunities and ways for families to use the abilities and competencies they already have and to learn new ones as needed to meet child and family needs (Dunst, Trivette, and Deal 1988).

The application of these concepts to early intervention is most closely associated with the work of Carl Dunst and his former colleagues at the Family, Infant and Preschool Program in Morganton, North Carolina (Deal, Dunst, and Trivette 1989; Dunst 1992; Dunst and Trivette 1987). For the single best source of information on the philosophy, principles, and research underlying family-centered early intervention, see *Enabling and Empowering Families: Principles and Guidelines for Practice* (Dunst, Trivette, and Deal 1988).

PRINCIPLES UNDERLYING THE IFSP PROCESS

The principles articulated in *Guidelines and Recommended Practices for the IFSP* (see table I) have been used in many states as a foundation for their IFSP work—in Part H and Interagency Coordinating Council mission statements, in state and local IFSP task forces, in university training programs, in family advocacy efforts, and in local early intervention programs. In fact, several states have directly incorporated the principles into their own IFSP policies and procedures (McGonigel, Kaufmann, and Johnson 1991a). Such wide acceptance of these principles mirrors the experience of the IFSP Expert Team and Task Force. Despite the diversity of disciplines, regions, and perspectives represented on the Expert Team and Task Force, there was a remarkable consensus on the principles that underlie a family-centered IFSP process. These IFSP principles are rooted in the belief that family-centered early intervention seeks to build on and promote the strengths and competencies present in all families. Taken together, they form a conceptual framework for early intervention planners and providers, other practitioners, and families seeking to translate family-centered philosophies into IFSP practices.

Infant and Toddler Dependence

Infants and toddlers are uniquely dependent on their families for their survival and nurturance. This dependence necessitates a family-centered approach to early intervention. An infant or toddler with special needs is part of a family system, which in turn is part of a larger network of informal and formal support systems. For this reason, the IFSP sup-

Table I. Principles Underlying Family-Centered Early Intervention

- Infants and toddlers are uniquely dependent on their families for their survival and nurturance. This dependence necessitates a family-centered approach to early intervention.
- States and programs should define "family" in a way that reflects the diversity of family patterns and structures.
- Each family has its own structure, roles, values, beliefs, and coping styles. Respect for and acceptance of this diversity is a cornerstone of family-centered early intervention.
- Early intervention systems and strategies must honor the racial, ethnic, cultural, and socioeconomic diversity of families.
- Respect for family autonomy, independence, and decision making means that families must be able to choose the level and nature of early intervention's involvement in their lives.
- Family/professional collaboration and partnerships are the keys to family-centered early intervention.
- An enabling approach to working with families requires that professionals reexamine their traditional roles and practices and develop new practices when necessary—practices that promote mutual respect and partnerships.
- Early intervention services should be flexible, accessible, and responsive to family-identified needs.
- Early intervention services should be provided according to the normalization principle—that is, families should have access to services that are provided in as normal a fashion and environment as possible and that promote the integration of the child and family within the community.
- No one agency or discipline can meet the diverse and complex needs of infants and toddlers with special needs and their families. Therefore, a team approach is necessary for family-centered early intervention.

From McGonigel, M. J. 1991. Philosophy and conceptual framework. In *Guidelines and Recommended Practices for the Individualized Family Service Plan* (2nd ed.), eds. M. J. McGonigel, R. K. Kaufmann, and B. H. Johnson. Bethesda, MD: Association for the Care of Children's Health.

ports young children within the context of their families, neighborhoods, and communities. A family-centered systems approach to the IFSP acknowledges the importance of family direction in all aspects of service delivery.

Definition of "Family"

States and programs should define "family" in a way that reflects the diversity of family patterns and structures. Because IFSPs are family service plans, the definition of who is considered to be "family" determines who is eligible for early intervention services. Inclusive definitions of family transcend traditional, legal definitions to encompass primary caregivers and others who assume major, long-term roles in a child's daily life. Adopting such inclusive definitions makes it possible for a family to choose which of its members will take part in the IFSP process. This choice makes it possible for families to use the strengths and resources already present in their support network—whether that be grandparents, cousins who live in the same house, a trusted neighbor who becomes an "aunt," or a highly valued, long-time child caregiver. Inclusive definitions also acknowledge the new reality for the majority of American families.

Respect for Diversity of Families

Each family has its own structure, roles, values, beliefs, and coping styles. Respect for and acceptance of this diversity is a cornerstone of family-centered early intervention. Respect for family diversity means that the IFSP process is supportive of each family's efforts to care for its infant or toddler with special needs, while at the same time attending to the needs of the entire family. Respecting and accepting family diversity means acknowledging that there are strengths, competencies, and resources present in *all* families. Early intervention professionals are learning to recognize and build upon these positives as part of their work with families.

Early Intervention vis à vis Diversity of Families

Early intervention systems and strategies must honor the racial, ethnic, cultural, and socioeconomic diversity of families. Increasingly, American society is made up of people of many colors, cultures, ethnic origins, religions, and beliefs. The past 20 years have seen a profound change in the racial and ethnic makeup of the United States (Jones 1991). This change is accelerating. According to Felicity Barringer, writing in 1991 in *The New York Times*, "The racial and ethnic complexion of the American population changed more dramatically in the past decade than at any time in the 20th century, with nearly one in every four Americans claiming African, Asian, Hispanic or American Indian ancestry" (p. A1).

Early intervention services generally, and the IFSP particularly, must reflect and respect this diversity. When translated into action, this principle is known as "cultural competence," a concept that transcends traditional, more passive notions such as cultural relevance and cultural sensitivity. Cross (1988) defines cultural competence as "a set of congruent behaviors, attitudes and policies that come together in a system, agency or professional [practitioner] and enable that system, agency or professional [practitioner] to work effectively in cross-cultural situations" (p. 1), a definition that captures the pro-active nature of this powerful concept. Table II lists fundamentals of cultural competence as described by the Institute for Family-Centered Care in Bethesda, Maryland and the Institute on Cultural Dynamics and Social Change in Madison, Wisconsin.

Table II.   Fundamentals of Cultural Competence

Honoring the cultural diversity of families—racial, ethnic, religious, and socioeconomic—by:

- Recognizing the power of culture in shaping values, beliefs, and experiences.
- Examining one's personal and cultural makeup, and learning how they affect interactions with others.
- Learning about the cultural norms of the communities with which one engages, and about the extent to which individual families share these norms.
- Approaching each family on its own terms, with no judgments or preconceptions, and enabling each family to define its own needs.
- Helping families navigate the health, education, and social service systems of the dominant culture.
- Acknowledging that many families and communities have experienced racism and other forms of exclusion and disempowerment, experiences that are likely to affect their interactions with service providers and service systems.
- Eliminating institutional policies and practices that exclude families from services because of race, ethnicity, sexual orientation, beliefs, or practices.
- Building on the strengths and resources of each child, family, and community.

M. J. McGonigel, Institute for Family-Centered Care, Bethesda, Maryland, and D. A. Jones, The Institute on Cultural Dynamics and Social Change, Madison, Wisconsin.

Cultural competence was made a mandatory aspect of each state's early intervention system in 1991, as one of several amendments to the enabling legislation for Part H. In a culturally competent early intervention system, policies and practices "promote meaningful participation by low-income, minority, rural and other under-represented families and ensure local access to culturally competent services" (Mental Health Law Project 1992, p. 5). At the local program level, culturally competent programs offer services and supports that match a family's language, culture, and spiritual beliefs. Paraprofessionals from families' own communities (Vincent 1992) and family-to-family support and networking are powerful resources in providing culturally competent services and supports to families.

Recent initiatives through the federal Maternal and Child Health Bureau are providing a similar focus for statewide systems of health care for children with special needs and their families (Maternal and Child Health Bureau 1991). For an essential resource on cultural competence in early intervention, see *Developing Cross Cultural Competence: A Guide for Working with Young Children and Their Families* (Lynch and Hanson 1992).

Respect for Family Autonomy, Independence, and Decision Making

Respect for family autonomy, independence, and decision making means that families must be able to choose the level and nature of early intervention's involvement in their lives. Families must be able to choose how early intervention will be involved in their lives—a choice based on their values and beliefs, their hopes, and their dreams. This choice has been called a family's "agenda." This agenda shapes the entire IFSP process for that family. In a family-centered IFSP process, there are no predetermined roles for families, no absolute sequences of events, and no preset service configurations—a pronounced departure from accepted practice in early intervention only a few years ago.

Family/Professional Collaboration

Family/professional collaboration and partnerships are the keys to family-centered early intervention and to a successful IFSP process. Collaboration and partnerships are essential to a family-centered IFSP process. Learning to collaborate with families requires new attitudes and new skills on the part of many early intervention providers. Families also learn new skills as they assume more collaborative roles in their interactions with professionals. Therapists and teachers working with preschoolers and older children and their families are encountering a new generation of families, experienced in a family-centered IFSP process and expecting to establish the same kinds of family/professional partnerships throughout their children's lives. Many such professionals are seeking to meet the challenge of these new expectations by creating more opportunities for true collaboration within the IEP process.

An enabling approach to working with families requires that professionals reexamine their traditional roles and practices and develop new practices when necessary—practices that promote mutual respect and partnerships. The move toward family-centered early intervention represents a profound shift of perspective for many professionals whose training and practice equipped them to work primarily with children and whose role with families has been primarily an instructive one (Bailey 1991). Dunst and his colleagues (1988) identified eight professional roles encompassed by family-centered early intervention: empathetic listener, teacher/therapist, consultant, resource, enabler, mobilizer, mediator, and advocate. Therapists, special education teachers, and other primarily child-oriented professionals may find these role descriptors helpful as they examine their own interactions with families.

Leviton and her colleagues (1992) at the Kennedy Krieger Institute in Baltimore suggest a consultation model as a framework for reconceptualizing family/professional relationships. Professionals view their roles as consultants to families; families are the decision makers, determining for themselves how they will use the information and perspectives shared by professionals. Such a consultant model can help professionals seeking to make the transition from professionally directed to family-centered early intervention services.

Several federally funded personnel preparation projects across the country also are challenging professionals to re-examine and reconceptualize their traditional roles. The Family-Centered Institute, a joint program of Parent to Parent of Vermont and the Center for Developmental Disabilities at the University of Vermont, is one such project. The Institute is reaching professionals-in-training by creating an opportunity for the faculty who teach them to explore the best practices in family-centered services and family/professional partnerships.

Early intervention services should be flexible, accessible, and responsive to family-identified needs. Family-centered early intervention requires that services be developed with family individuality in mind. Rather than asking families to adjust to program needs and policies, and available services, early intervention programs must adapt their policies and services to the concerns, priorities, and resources of individual families. The IFSP, particularly, must reflect this responsiveness; words most often used to describe the ideal IFSP include fluid, flexible, dynamic, and alive (DiVenere 1988; Dunst 1991; Kramer, McGonigel, and Kaufmann 1991). For this reason, a family-centered process for the IFSP cannot be conceptualized as a step-by-step progression: "Rather than the linear progression from component to component that has been typical in early intervention and true also of the Individualized Educational Program (IEP) process, each family moves through this dynamic process as befits its circumstances (McGonigel, Kaufmann, and Johnson 1991b, p. 15). Family choices shape the IFSP process from beginning to end.

Responding to family-identified needs as part of the IFSP process means being open and honest with families about professional limitations and withholding judgments based on one's own biases. Lisbeth Vincent (1988) beautifully captured this imperative:

> We sometimes think that parents are asking us to teach things that cannot be taught or that are not good for the child. Instead, we may be reacting to the fact that we don't know how to teach the things parents want their children to learn. We need to be frank about the limits of our knowledge. (p. 3)

Early intervention services should be provided according to the normalization principle—that is, families should have access to services that are provided in as normal a fashion and environment as possible and that promote the integration of the child and family within the community. Many parents of young children with special needs say that they feel isolated from their neighborhood and community when the only activities in which their children participate are those designed specifically for children with special needs. IFSP outcomes and strategies that include typical community activities help promote interdependence and a sense of belonging. The 1991 reauthorization of Part H, Public Law 102-119, reflected the importance of this principle to families by adding a new IFSP requirement—all IFSPs must now address the provision of services in the "natural environments, including the home, and community settings in which children without disabilities participate" (U.S.C.§ 1472(2)(G) and 1477(d)). This requirement codifies what families have long known. Children live in neighborhoods and communities, not in early intervention programs, and they won't be infants and toddlers forever.

The importance to families of taking the long view—of keeping their child with special needs in focus as part of the entire family, the neighborhood, and the community—has long been emphasized by families, advocates, and key researchers. One implication of this priority, in the words of one professional, has been that parents'

> . . . ideas on proper goals may be quite different from ours. We are likely to think in terms of achieving skills that will lead to the next developmental milestone. Parents often take a longer view. In my experience, parents define their goals for their children in terms of the quality of life their children will have as they get older. They speak of wanting their children to be happy and have friends, to make a contribution to the world they live in, even if it is not through a regular paying job, and to live in the community like other people. (Vincent 1988, p. 3)

The most successful IFSPs will be those that reflect this reality. The work of Linda Kjerland, Shirley Kramer, and their colleagues at Project Dakota in Egan, Minnesota has illustrated many neighborhood- and community-based options for early intervention that can help professionals envision how IFSPs can meet this challenge.

No one agency or discipline can meet the diverse and complex needs of infants and toddlers with special needs and their families. Therefore, a team approach to planning and implementing the IFSP is necessary. A team approach, in fact, has been a required part of the IFSP process since 1986, when Part H and the IFSP component were first established. Although Part H does not provide guidance concerning specific roles and relationships among IFSP team members, creative redesign by families and professionals of traditional team models is strengthening family role choices and options.

In addition to teams operating within an early intervention program, multi-agency teams are a critical aspect of comprehensive early intervention and a necessary resource for family-centered, community-based IFSPs. Such a multi-agency, family-centered approach is proving especially critical for many of today's most vulnerable children and families—those affected by HIV or prenatal exposure to alcohol, cocaine, or other drugs (Jeppson, in press; Panel on Women, Adolescents, and Children with HIV Infection and AIDS 1991; Schmitt and Sanford, in press; Woodruff et al. 1990).

CONTENT OF THE IFSP

Section 1477 of Part H specifies the content of the IFSP and certain requirements for participation and implementation. The current regulations—
Federal Register, Department of Education, 34 CFR, Part 303—elaborate
on the IFSP requirements as specified in the law itself. Proposed new
regulations for implementing the 1991 amendments to Part H were
recently published in the Federal Register; final regulations are expected
sometime in late 1992. For an analysis of these new regulations once
they appear in their final form, see the Mental Health Law Project publi-
cation *Early Intervention Advocacy Network NOTEBOOK.*

The current and proposed regulations include requirements for
every aspect of the IFSP component of the Part H statewide programs
of early intervention. Among these are evaluation and assessment;
lead agency responsibilities; definition of early intervention services;
general roles of service providers; time frames for IFSP development,
implementation, and review; provisions for procedural safeguards;
participants in and conduct of the IFSP meeting; service coordination;
and early provision of services. It is beyond the scope of this chapter
to discuss the many regulations governing the IFSP. Readers are
referred directly to the current regulations, published in the Federal
Register for June 22, 1989, and the proposed regulations for the 1991
amendments, published in the Federal Register for May 1, 1992.

The contents of the IFSP, as outlined in the statute, Part H Section 1477(d), and some clarifying information from the regulations are
described below:

> The IFSP must be a written plan developed by a multidisciplinary team,
> including the parent(s) or guardian(s), that contains the following:
>
>> a statement of the infant's or toddler's present levels of development
>> in these developmental areas: cognitive, physical, communication,
>> social or emotional, and adaptive;
>
> (Regulations specify vision, hearing, and health status as aspects of
> physical development that must be included in the statement of the
> child's present level of development. {303.344(a)})
>
>> a statement of the family's concerns, priorities, and resources related to
>> enhancing the development of the infant or toddler with a disability;
>
> (Regulations clarify that this activity should be directed by the family,
> based on information provided by the family, and strictly voluntary on
> the part of the family. {303.322(d)})
>
>> a statement of the major outcomes expected to be achieved for the
>> child and family; the criteria, procedures, and timeliness to be used
>> to measure progress toward achieving the outcomes;
>
>> a statement of specific early intervention services necessary to meet
>> the unique needs of the infant or toddler and family, including the
>> frequency, intensity, and method of delivering services;

(Regulations specify that "payment arrangements, if any" must be included in the IFSP. [303.344(d)] Regulations also require a statement of the location where a service is provided, for example, at home, at a center, in a hospital, or in other settings as appropriate.)

(These same regulations further clarify that, to the extent possible, "other services" must be included in the IFSP, as well as, if necessary, the steps that will be taken to secure those services from public or private sources. Among these services are non-routine medical and other services that a child needs, but that are not required by Part H. Routine medical services such as "well-baby care" and immunizations should be included when a child needs such services and they are not provided or are not otherwise available. {303.344(e)})

> a statement of the natural environments in which early intervention services shall appropriately be provided;
>
> the projected dates for initiation of services and the anticipated duration of the services;
>
> the name of the service coordinator (from the professional most immediately relevant to the child's or family's needs, or who is otherwise qualified to carry out these responsibilities) who will be responsible for implementing the plan and coordinating with other agencies and persons; and

(Regulations clarify that service coordination can be considered a "profession" {303.344(g)}; the House report on the 1991 amendments to Part H adds that "a parent may become qualified to perform all of the service functions carried out by a service coordinator and provide the service coordination service for another family if the parent obtains appropriate training by qualified persons." The report also clarifies that a state may, if it chooses, "as a matter of State policy or practice, pay a parent to be his or her own service coordinator or reimburse a parent for carrying out certain tasks.")

> the steps to be taken supporting the child's transition to Part B preschool services, if appropriate.

(Regulations clarify that the child's transition to other available services should be addressed, and require that transition support include discussion with and training of parents about transition issues, including future placements, and preparation of the child for changes in service delivery, including steps to help the child adjust to and function in a new setting. {303.344(h)})

Some of the above provisions are much like those that have been addressed in traditional early intervention service plans. Other provisions, particularly those related to family self-identification of concerns, priorities, and resources and the collaborative development of outcomes, services, and supports in "natural" environments that will help families achieve their chosen outcomes, are recent requirements for most early intervention programs.

What are the best ways to identify family concerns, priorities, and resources? How will programs and agencies choose the early intervention services and supports they offer? What should an IFSP team do when a family identifies needs and asks for help that a program is neither able to provide nor help arrange for the family? What happens when staff and families disagree on priorities for services? These are questions that families, Part H planners, and early intervention providers are struggling to answer as they work together to develop IFSP policies and practices.

Despite some of the differences surfacing among these participants in the IFSP process, all of these stakeholders agree that a family-centered philosophy and conceptual framework is essential if the promise of the IFSP is to be met. In her keynote address to the Division of Early Childhood annual conference in St. Louis, Lisbeth Vincent (1992) proposed a "next step" strategy for implementing all of the components of Part H, including the IFSP:

> We can join with families in our local communities, in our programs, and reach for a common dream—comprehensive, coordinated services which support and empower families to be as competent as they can be as they raise their child with special needs. We can do this by developing relationships with individual families that are family-centered. We can share dreams with families about the lives of their children. We can learn to see the world hand-in-hand with them, through their eyes. They will help us keep perspective on the process that is early intervention. While none of us is indispensable to our programs or systems, all of us can make an incredible difference. Let's join together in a collaborative partnership with families, across agencies on the local level. Let's make dreams come true. (p. 172)

REFERENCES

Bailey, D. B. 1991. Building positive relationships between professionals and families. In *Guidelines and Recommended Practices for the Individualized Family Service Plan* (2nd ed.), eds. M. J. McGonigel, R. K. Kaufmann, and B. H. Johnson. Bethesda, MD: Association for the Care of Children's Health (ACCH).

Barringer, F. 1991, March 11. Census shows profound change in racial make-up of the nation. *The New York Times* B8, pp. A1, B8.

Campbell, P. 1990. *The Individual Family Service Plan: A Guide for Families and Early Intervention Professionals*. Akron, OH: Children's Hospital Medical Center. (Available from Family Child Learning Center, 90 West Overdale Dr., Tallmadge, OH 44278.)

Cross, T. L. 1988. Cultural competence continuum. *Focal Point* 3(1):1–4. (Focal Point is available from Research and Training Center on Family Support and Children's Mental Health, Regional Research Institute for Human Services, Portland State University, Box 751, Portland, OR 97207, [503] 725-4040.)

Deal, A. G., Dunst, C. J., and Trivette, C. M. 1989. A flexible and functional approach to developing Individualized Family Support Plans. *Infants and Young Children* 1(4):32–43.

DiVenere, N. J. 1988. The development and management of Individualized

Family Service Plans: The family perspective. Paper presented at the American Academy of Pediatrics Meeting on P. L. 99-457, Washington, DC, November.

Dunst, C. J. 1991. Implementation of the Individualized Family Service Plan. In *Guidelines and Recommended Practices for the Individualized Family Service Plan* (2nd ed.), eds. M. J. McGonigel, R. K. Kaufmann, and B. H. Johnson. Bethesda, MD: ACCH.

Dunst, C. J. 1992. What do we mean by enablement and empowerment? *Family Enablement Project MESSENGER* 4(2):1–2. (Available from Family, Infant and Preschool Program, Western Carolina Center, 300 Enola Rd., Morganton, NC 28655, [704] 433-2661.)

Dunst, C. J., and Deal, A. G. 1990. Individualized family support plans: Model, methods, and strategies. *Family Systems Intervention Monograph*, No. 2,1. Morganton, NC: Family, Infant and Preschool Program.

Dunst, C. J., and Trivette, C. M. 1987. Enabling and empowering families: Conceptual and intervention issues. *School Psychology Review* 16(4):443–56.

Dunst, C. J., Trivette, C. M., and Deal, A. G. 1988. *Enabling and Empowering Families: Principles and Guidelines for Practice.* Cambridge, MA: Brookline Books.

Elsayed, S. S., with L. Edelman, M. McGonigel, and D. Van Rembro. 1993. *Maryland's IFSP: A Facilitator's Guide.* Baltimore: Kennedy Krieger Institute.

Hunt, M., Cornelius, P., Leventhal, P., Miller, P., Murray, T., and Stoner, G. 1990. *Into Our Lives.* Akron, OH: Children's Hospital Medical Center. (Available from Family Child Learning Center, 90 West Overdale Dr., Tallmadge, OH 44278.)

Jeppson, E. S. In press. Family-centered care for children and families affected by prenatal drug exposure. In *Babies and Cocaine: A Resource Handbook*, eds. M. J. McGonigel, and B. H. McCabe. San Diego, CA: Singular Publishing.

Jones, D. 1991. A question of diversity. *ACCH NETWORK* 9(3):1, 10–11.

Kramer, S., McGonigel, M. J., and Kaufmann, R. K. 1991. Developing the IFSP: Outcomes, strategies, activities, and services. In *Guidelines and Recommended Practices for the Individualized Family Service Plan* (2nd ed.), eds. M. J. McGonigel, R. K. Kaufmann, and B. H. Johnson. Bethesda, MD: ACCH.

Leviton, A., Mueller, M., and Kauffman, C. 1992. The family-centered consultation model: Practical applications for professionals. *Infants and Young Children* 4(3):1–8.

Lynch, E. W., and Hanson, M. J. 1992. *Developing Cross-Cultural Competence: A Guide for Working with Young Children and Their Families.* Baltimore: Paul H. Brookes Publishing.

Maternal and Child Health Bureau, Division of Services for Children with Special Health Needs. 1991. *Improving Services for Culturally Diverse Populations.* St. Paul, MN: Pathfinder Resources, Inc.

McGonigel, M. J. 1991. Philosophy and conceptual framework. In *Guidelines and Recommended Practices for the Individualized Family Service Plan* (2nd ed.), eds. M. J. McGonigel, R. K. Kaufmann, and B. H. Johnson. Bethesda, MD: ACCH.

McGonigel, M. J., and Johnson, B. H. 1991. An overview. In *Guidelines and Recommended Practices for the Individualized Family Service Plan* (2nd ed.), eds. M. J. McGonigel, R. K. Kaufmann, and B. H. Johnson. Bethesda, MD: ACCH.

McGonigel, M. J., Kaufmann, R. K., and Johnson B. H. 1991a. A family-centered process for the Individualized Family Service Plan. *Journal of Early Intervention* 15(1):46–56.

McGonigel, M. J., Kaufmann, R. K., and Johnson, B. H. 1991b. *Guidelines and Recommended Practices for the Individualized Family Service Plan* (2nd ed.). Bethesda, MD: ACCH.

Mental Health Law Project. 1992. New Guide to the Part H law and regulations. *Early Intervention Advocacy Network NOTEBOOK.* Washington, DC: Author.

Panel on Women, Adolescents, and Children with HIV Infection and AIDS. 1991. *Family-centered Comprehensive Care for Children with HIV Infection.* Washington, DC: Public Health Service, U.S. Department of Health and Human Services.

Schmitt, C., and Sanford, L. D. In press. Model programs and approaches. In *Babies and Cocaine: A Resource Handbook*, eds. M. J. McGonigel, and B. H. McCabe. San Diego: Singular Publishing.

Vincent, L. J. 1988. What we have learned from families. *OSERS News in Print* 1(4):3, 12.

Vincent, L. J. 1992. Families and early intervention: Diversity and competence. *Journal of Early Intervention* 16(2):166–72.

Woodruff, G., Hanson, C. R., McGonigel, M., and Sterzin, E. D. 1990. *Community-Based Services for Children with HIV Infection and their Families: A Manual for Planners, Service Providers, Families and Advocates.* Brighton, MA: South Shore Mental Health Center.

Chapter • 7

Preparing the Individualized Family Service Plan
An Illustrative Case

Melody F. Harrison

Public Law 99-457, and subsequent legislation, directed states to develop and implement a statewide, comprehensive, coordinated, multidisciplinary, interagency program of early intervention services for infants and toddlers with special needs and their families (Brown 1990).

This chapter describes the family of an infant with a hearing impairment and presents the Individualized Family Service Plan (IFSP) developed to match the concerns, priorities, strengths, and resources of that particular family. Central to the philosophy of Part H is recognition and respect for the pivotal role that families of children with special needs have in every aspect of the development of their children. Also inherent in this philosophy is an appreciation of the values that a family holds, as well as the values of the community in which a family lives.

To create an IFSP document that reflects the philosophical perspective of the law, parents and professionals are seen as equal partners in determining the concerns, priorities, strengths, and resources of both child and family. Services that are then selected by the IFSP team ideally complement not only the needs but also the strengths of each particular family. Because the priorities and needs of a child and family can change rapidly as an infant grows and develops, an IFSP should be as fluid and as flexible as possible. Ongoing review of the plan can accommodate a child's development as well as the unique and dynamic interaction that occurs between parents and professionals.

Federal guidelines are specific in requiring that an IFSP be written. By extension, many professionals expect specificity regarding the format that an IFSP should follow. Contrast between the clear requirement that the document exist, and the paucity of information about the form it is to take, has caused confusion for many.

Although several states have created one IFSP form to be used by all programs that exist under Part H guidelines, others have left the development of the IFSP form to professionals at local levels. Some early intervention professionals are comfortable with this charge; however, many others have voiced the desire for a uniform IFSP form. Although there is not a federally mandated form that must be used, Section 1477(d) of Part H outlines the contents that are required in the IFSP. The following summary highlights the required components of the IFSP; as found in the *Early Intervention Advocacy Network Notebook* (1992).

A multidisciplinary team including parent(s) or guardian(s) must develop a written Individualized Family Service Plan that contains:

- a statement of an infant's or toddler's present levels of physical development, cognitive development, language and speech development, psychosocial development, and self-help skills, based on acceptable objective criteria;
- a statement of the family's strengths and needs related to enhancing development of their infant or toddler with a disability;
- a statement of major outcomes that are expected to be achieved for the child and family;
- criteria, procedures, and timeliness used to determine the degree to which progress is being made, and whether revisions are necessary;
- a statement of specific early intervention services necessary to meet the unique needs of infant or toddler and family, including information about frequency, intensity, and method of delivering services;
- projected dates for initiation of services and anticipated duration of the services;
- name of the service coordinator who will be responsible for implementing the plan and coordinating with other agencies and individuals;
- steps to be taken supporting the child's transition to Part B preschool services, if appropriate.

The concern expressed by many agencies and individuals regarding the IFSP and the form that it should take is understandable; however, it is crucial to remember that neither Public Law 101-476 nor forms generated to satisfy the law are sufficient to achieve a goal of meaningful collaboration between families and professionals. The process that occurs in creation of the document is as important as the document itself.

In a study of family and professional preferences in the IFSP process, Summers et al. (1990) found that parents uniformly stressed the importance of informality on the part of professionals in gathering information required to develop the IFSP. Family members expressed a strong preference for open-ended conversations and informal approaches. The nature of the relationship that can develop in an informal atmosphere, and information that is exchanged in that relationship is likely to be different from that created by formal, structured assessment.

At the heart of the IFSP process is identification of the family's concerns, priorities, and resources, as well as strategies and activities that fit naturally into a family's daily life. Although a number of instruments to assess needs are available (Bailey and Simeonsson 1990; Dunst, Trivette, and Deal 1988; Seligman and Darling 1989), the tone that is set during the initial meetings between family members and professionals will likely determine to what degree a family will elect to have professional involvement in their lives. In identifying family concerns, priorities, values, and resources, Turnbull and her colleagues (1991) have identified "pointers for listening" that can be used as guidelines by all professionals.

a. Listen for cultural and family values that are important to the family.
b. Listen for the names of family friends and professionals who are already in the support network and whose support has been particularly valued.
c. Listen for interests, needs, and strengths that might link the child and the family with a wider network of supporters.
d. Listen for the coping strategies that the family uses and any expressed desire for expanding coping strategies.
e. Listen for the things the family would like to do to help their child and to help themselves.
f. Listen for how the family has typically approached problem-solving in the past.
g. Listen for the concerns, hopes, and plans that the families have concerning transitional issues.
h. Listen for the kinds of evaluations that have been conducted in the past and the evaluation questions they would like to have addressed.
i. Listen for and acknowledge the specific strengths the family has shown in adjusting to their child's disability in meeting the child's needs. (p. 2).

Identifying concerns, priorities, and resources of child and family is an interactive, dynamic, and evolving process. There is no discrete endpoint in the process of developing an IFSP; rather, it should be viewed as a work in progress that evolves and changes throughout the period in which services are provided (McGonigel, Kaufmann, and Johnson 1991). The process of developing an IFSP begins as soon as the family comes into contact with the many professionals who provide services for young children with hearing impairments. Referrals for early intervention services come from a number of sources including neonatal intensive care units, public health nurses, pediatricians, well-baby clinics, audiologists, and teachers of hearing-impaired children. For the family described below, the initial contact was a speech-language pathologist at a university hospital.

The IFSP presented in this chapter was developed to illustrate one approach to meeting concerns, priorities, resources, and services that can be incorporated into an IFSP document. There is no single approach that can capture the dynamics that occur in the process of developing an Individualized Family Service Plan. We have attempted to demonstrate only one of the many possibilities that exists in the wide array of options in developing the IFSP. An excellent document with extensive discussion of the IFSP process and a variety of IFSP models is: *Guidelines and Recommended Practices for the Individualized Family Service Plan*, available through the National Early Childhood Technical Assistance System (NEC*TAS).[1]

The IFSP format used below was developed by the North Carolina Department of Human Resources, Division of Mental Health/Developmental Disabilities/Substance Abuse, in conjunction with the North Carolina Interagency Coordinating Council. The North Carolina IFSP form is divided into six sections.

Section I, **Identification**, includes information about the child, names of the parents and service coordinator, and dates during which the IFSP is in effect.

Section II is a **Needs Assessment** of both family and child. Included in it are:

1. a statement of Initial Family Concerns summarizing the parents' or other family members' concerns about themselves, the child, or circumstances that impact upon the child;
2. a section about the family summarizing the parents or other family members' statements about characteristics or resources that contribute to the growth and development of the child and family; as

---

[1]NEC*TAS, Frank Porter Graham Child Develpment Center, 137 E. Franklin Street, Suite 500 Nations Bank Plaza, Chapel Hill, NC 27514.

well as a summary of statements about areas they would like help addressing;

3. a section about the child summarizing parents', other family members', caregivers', and professionals' statements about the child's characteristics that contribute to his or her growth and development; as well as those areas in the child's growth and development for which help is wanted.

Section III is the **Child Assessment** in which the child's medical status, fine motor development, gross motor development, cognitive development, speech and language development, psychosocial development, self-help skills, and sensory development are reported.

Long-Range Child and Family Outcomes can be described in Section IV. This section is optional and the family can elect not to complete it at the time the IFSP is developed.

All team members who participate in writing the IFSP sign it in Section V.

Section VI comprises the **IFSP Service Delivery Plan**. In it the type of service and type of provider are listed, as are the frequency/intensity and location of the service. Dates at which each are to be initiated and terminated are indicated. Estimated costs to the family and payment arrangement (insurance, self-payment, Medicaid) for each service are listed. Also indicated in the plan is whether the service is optional or required (as per the North Carolina Interagency agreement). Finally, the parents are asked to initial each of the services specified in the plan.

Section VII is the **Goal Plan**. In this section child and family goals and criteria, along with methods and procedures for meeting those goals, are listed. The parties responsible for carrying out methods or procedures are recorded. The goal type (transition, service coordination, or other) is identified. Start date, target date, and date achieved are all to be recorded. Finally, there is space to indicate current status of the goal and the date on which that status was noted.

Section VIII is a **Review Section** in which each goal is to be reviewed at a specified time in the future.

The following family vignette and the accompanying IFSP were developed to illustrate the concepts presented in this chapter. The family vignette represents a composite of several families, and the names used are fictitious. The IFSP format is one of many that can be used and is in no way meant to indicate a preference for this particular IFSP design.

FAMILY VIGNETTE: THE BENNETT FAMILY

Denise and Doug Bennett and their two children, four-year-old Mike and three-month-old Jason, live in a small town in North Carolina, 25

miles from an urban center. Doug and Denise were high school sweet-
hearts who married after Doug finished two years of college. Both of
their families live in the town. Doug's family owns a local restaurant
that he manages. The restaurant is open for breakfast, lunch, and dinner and keeps Doug, his mother, and father busy many hours of each
day. The three of them work well as a team and are close to one another.
Denise has been employed as a bookkeeper at a small business in the
town for the past 7 years. Denise's father is a manager at a textile mill
and her mother is a homemaker. Denise's mother is unwilling to be
left alone with Jason or even to hold him because of his special needs.
Her religious beliefs are such that she has stated that Jason must have
been born with disabilities because of something that Denise had done
in the past. Denise's younger sister Charlene, still lives at home and
she and Denise have a supportive relationship.

Although Denise experienced an uneventful pregnancy and a
normal delivery with Jason, at birth he was hypotonic and generally
unresponsive. A few days after Jason's birth, it was determined that
during pregnancy, cytomegalovirus (CMV) had crossed the placenta
and infected his neurological system. Because of the CMV, he was
transferred from the community hospital where he was born to a large
hospital with a neonatal intensive care unit (NICU) an hour's drive
from their home.

There, a number of tests were initiated. Auditory brainstem
responses (ABR) were consistent with a severe, bilateral hearing loss
in the frequencies from 1,000 to 4,000 Hz. Using frequency-specific
stimuli (low-frequency tone bursts), a moderate-to-severe hearing loss
was suspected. Jason continued to be hypotonic and was identified in
the NICU as having feeding/swallowing problems related to the
hypotonicity.

The speech-language pathologist in the NICU provided the
Bennetts with information about Jason's feeding/swallowing problems and demonstrated the position in which he was most efficiently
fed. She also referred the Bennetts to the early intervention program in
their community.

Denise Bennett returned to work when Jason was 6-weeks old.
Both of the children are cared for by a sitter, Janice Levy. Janice, who
has a small child herself, has taken care of Mike since he was 6-weeks
old and is important to the family. She and Denise have developed a
friendship over the past three years and Janice is sympathetic to
Jason's disabilities. Though she is willing to do what she can to help,
she is unsure of what she should do.

Jason continues to be difficult to feed and this has caused the
mornings and evenings to be stressful for the Bennett family. Jason
requires a long time for each feeding. Although Denise usually spends

an hour feeding Jason, Doug and Denise feel that he is not getting enough nourishment. In fact, Jason is at the bottom of the growth charts for weight.

Jason is a visually alert child who is comforted by being held and rocked. He seems to enjoy interacting with his parents and brother and smiles and coos in response to their attention. They all enjoy holding and talking to him.

The other concerns that the Bennetts have involve Jason's hearing loss and his need for physical therapy. Doug is worried that Jason might have other problems that have not yet been noticed. He specifically asked if Jason might be mentally retarded. Both parents are anxious about what the future holds for Jason and for them. They have expressed anxiety about caring for a child with impaired hearing and neuromotor problems, especially when he is older and larger. They are also concerned that the demands of Jason's care are affecting the amount of time and attention that is available for Mike, and fear that he may become jealous of his brother.

Doug would like to be able to be more helpful with the children, especially at breakfast and dinner times, but doesn't see how this is possible because those are busy times at the restaurant. Several times during the initial meeting with the early intervention team he mentioned that he is concerned about Denise and wishes he had more time to help her at home.

The IFSP that follows was developed to reflect the concerns and needs of Jason's family while at the same time acknowledging and reinforcing those areas where the Bennetts feel they have resources and strengths.

NORTH CAROLINA INTERAGENCY
INDIVIDUALIZED FAMILY SERVICE PLAN

I. IDENTIFICATION

Jason Robert Bennett	04 | 22 | 93	BENJ042293
1. Child's Name	2. Date of Birth	3. Unique ID #

Doug and Denise Bennett	67-5305
4. Parent or Guardian	5. Agency Case #

Amanda Jackson, M.S.	Educational Audiologist
6. Service Coordinator	7. Job Title

Infant Parent Program	07 | 30 | 93	01 | 30 | 94
8. Agency	9. IFSP Start Date	10. Anticipated End Date

Atypical Development	12. ☐ Interim IFSP
11. Eligibility Category (Optional)	

II. NEEDS ASSESSMENT

Initial Family Concerns

Family

A. Family Strengths Doug and Denise Bennett are willing to do whatever is necessary to help in Jason's development. The child care provider the family has for Mike and Jason is supportive and willing to learn whatever is necessary to help with Jason's care during the day. Denise's sister, Charlene, provides emotional support for Denise and assistance with the children when Denise asks for it.

B. Family Needs The family identified several specific needs. They would like assistance and information from a nutritionist about preparing nutritious feedings for Jason. Though they feel that the speech-language pathologist at the hospital taught them to feed Jason more effectively, they are very concerned about his low weight. The family is also concerned and confused about what the future holds for Jason.

They want information about children like Jason who are older. They would also like to gather information about the types of programs available for Jason when he is preschool age.

They feel that they need help for Denise in feeding Jason at breakfast and at dinner. They also expressed a need for respite care, so that Doug and Denise can spend some time with Mike.

PARENT ACKNOWLEDGEMENT: **Sign after IFSP forms are completed.**

☑ I have had the opportunity to participate in the development of this IFSP.
☑ I have been informed about all of the available services and their costs.

COMMENTS: _____

_____

_____

_____

Michel H. Bennett   7 | 29 | 93
Parent/Guardian Signature   Date

Denise B. Bennett   7 | 29 | 93
Parent/Guardian Signature   Date

| Child |

A. Child Strengths

Jason likes to be held and talked to. He is responsive to his brother, parents, and babysitter and he vocalizes when he is being held and played with. He can be calmed by being held closely and having his back rubbed.

B. Child Needs

Jason's needs include physical therapy with a P. T. who has a strong neurodevelopmental background. Speech-language intervention with emphasis on auditory stimulation and language development should begin immediately. Additionally, Jason needs to be monitored on an ongoing basis by an audiologist. His feeding difficulties need to be managed so that he receives enough nutrition to grow normally.

III. CHILD ASSESSMENT

Jason Bennett
_____
Child's Name

A. Medical Status
Date Administered   06 | 20 | 93

Neurological Status of the Preterm and Full-Term Newborn Infant
Assessment Procedure

Melissa Hamilton, M.D.   Pediatrician
Conducted By   Job Title

Remarks: Jason is a 3 month old who is below the growth chart for weight for babies of his height and age. His general muscle tone is hypotonic, although when he is distressed he becomes rigid. His responses to visual and tactile stimuli are characterized by lability, moving rapidly from a positive to a distressed response. When distressed, Jason is difficult to console. Slight nystagmus was noted. Hand grasp was not found on the right, with a weak grasp on the left.

B. Fine Motor Development
Date Administered   ____ | ____ |

_____
Assessment Procedure

_____   _____
Conducted By   Job Title

Remarks: Fine motor development was not asssessed at this time due to the age of the child.

BENJ 042293
Unique ID #

67-5305
Agency Case #

C. Gross Motor Development

Date Administered 05 | 23 | 93

Hawaii Early Learning Profile
Assessment Procedure

Sharon Ballard, M.S.
Conducted By

Physical Therapist
Job Title

Remarks: Jason has almost no head control. At the present time, he is unable to lift his chin from his chest or to turn his head from side to side. Though head control is not a fine motor skill it (as well as vision and trunk control) is a foundation for development of fine motor skills. Grasp reflex in the right hand was not noted, though a weak and inconsistent grasp was noted in the left. Two motor behaviors that normally develop in the first 4 months were not observed. An asymmetrical tonic neck reflex is not yet present. The neck righting reaction, which is the rotation of the body toward the side to which the infant's head is turned, was not observed.

D. Cognitive Development

Date Administered 06 | 14 | 93

Adaptive Performance Instrument
Assessment Procedure

Robert McDonald, Ph.D.
Conducted By

Developmental Psychologist
Job Title

Remarks: Jason responds to light and to air with eye blinks and startles at unanticipated touches and sights. As expected, he does not startle to sound. In an assisted position he is able to suck to take in nourishment. His suck reflex is weak due to global hypotonicity.

III. CHILD ASSESSMENT (CONTINUED)

Jason Bennett
Child's Name

E. Speech and Language Development   Date Administered   05 | 21 | 93

Parent interview and administered the *Receptive-Expressive Emergent Language Scale*
Assessment Procedure

Paula Porter, M.S. CCC-SP   Speech-language Pathologist
Conducted By   **Job Title**

Remarks: Denise says that Jason is interested in people and that he tries to make eye contact. He likes to be held so that he can see the face of the person holding him. In this position he will respond to his mother's vocalizations. She believes that when they are playing this way he tries to continue the play by making small facial gestures himself. He cries to gain attention and his mother reports that she is able to tell if he is hungry by his cry. He does not alert to sounds or startle to loud noises.

F. Psychosocial Development   Date Administered   06 | 15 | 93

Observation
Assessment Procedure

Robert McDonald, Ph.D.   Developmental Psychologist
Conducted By   **Job Title**

Remarks: Jason responds positively to being held by either of his parents. He focuses intently on their faces and appears to be attempting to respond to facial movements, demonstrating some social reciprocity. He responded in a similar manner with the speech-language pathologist for about three minutes. He moves rapidly from being comfortable to being distressed. When he is distressed, he is not easily consoled, although he does respond to being held and having his back stroked. He does not seem to like being rocked.

BENJ 042293
Unique ID #

67-5305
Agency Case #

G. Self-Help Skills

Date Administered _____ | _____ | _____

Not completed at this time
Assessment Procedure

_____   _____
Conducted By   **Job Title**

Remarks: Self-help skills were not assessed at this time because of the age of the child.

H. Sensory Development (Vision, Hearing, Other)

Clinical Behavioral Assessment   07 | 22 | 93
Vision Assessment Procedure   Date Administered

Virginia Grant, M.D.   Opthalmologist
Conducted By   **Job Title**

Remarks: Jason has a normal pupillary response to light. He can track to midline and his eyes move together. These behaviors are consistent with normal development of vision. Refraction was within limits for normal vision.

Auditory Evoked Potential   04 | 26 | 93
Hearing Assessment Procedure   Date Administered

Tom Rabinowitz, M.S.   Audiologist
Conducted By   **Job Title**

Remarks: Auditory Brainstem Responses were consistent with a severe, bilateral hearing loss in the frequencies from 1,000 to 4,000 Hz. Use of low-frequency tone bursts indicates a probable moderate-to-severe loss in the frequencies below 1,000 Hz. ABR was repeated at 12 weeks of age and was in good agreement with initial results. Earmold impressions were made for fitting of amplification.

_____ | _____ | _____

_____   _____ | _____ | _____
Other Sensory Development Assessment Procedure   Date Administered

_____   _____
Conducted By   **Job Title**

Remarks:

IV. OUTCOMES

Jason Bennett
_____
Child's Name

IV. Long Range Child and Family Outcomes   **This Section Is Optional**

Check and initial if applicable:

☐ Family elects not to complete at this time.   **Parent/Guardian Initials**

The Bennetts would like to be certain that they have done all that is possible to aid in Jason's physical development. They especially want him to develop better control of his head by the time he is 1 year old. They have expressed the wish that he be able to reach for and hold lightweight objects.

The Bennetts have also said they would like Jason to learn to use his hearing as much as possible. They feel that sign language will make him even more different from other children. Because his motor control is a major concern, they are also worried that he may not be able to sign, even if it is necessary. They understand that his motor skills may prevent him from being able to speak well; however, they want to develop his ability to hear as much as possible. They would like to learn about the options that are available for communicating with a child who has Jason's hearing and motor impairments.

They would also like Jason to be above the 10 percentile in weight for his age by the age of 1 year.

Another goal is to work together as a team to find some support for Denise, especially at meal times.

V. TEAM SIGNATURES

BENJ 042293		67-5305
Unique ID #		Agency Case #

| V. Team Signatures | | | |

Michel H Bennett   7/29/93
Signature of Parent/Guardian   **Initials**   **Date**

Dessie B. Bennett   7/29/93
Signature of Parent/Guardian   **Initials**   **Date**

Amanda Jackson   7/29/93
Signature of Service Coordinator   **Initials**   **Date**

Educational Audiologist
Job Title   **Agency**

Signature of Family Member   **Initials**   **Date**

Relationship to Child

Sharon Ballard   7/29/93
Signature of Provider   **Initials**   **Date**

Physical Therapist   Triangle Physical Therapists
Job Title   **Agency**

Paula Porter   7/29/93
Signature of Provider   **Initials**   **Date**

Speech/Language Pathologist
Job Title   **Agency**

Signature of Provider   **Initials**   **Date**

Job Title   **Agency**

Signature of Provider   **Initials**   **Date**

Job Title   **Agency**

Jason Bennett
Child's Name

VI. IFSP SERVICE DELIVERY PLAN

BenJ042293
Unique ID #

67-5305
Agency Case #

Service	Provider	Start Date	Location*	Frequency/ Intensity	Optional/ Required	Payment Arrangement	Estimated Cost to Family	Parent Initials	Date Ended
Nutritional Consultation	Guilford Co. Health Dept.	7/30	Bennett's Home	Six-one hour sessions 1per/ week.	0	NA	NA		
Physical Therapy	PACT Team	7/30	Levy Home Bennett Home	1 session per week w/Jamie Levy who has volunteered to be involved in Jason's PT 1 session per week w/Denise					
Speech-lang. Therapy Auditory Training	NC School for the Deaf Parent Infant Program	8/1	Bennett Home	1 hr/wk	R	NA	NA		
Ongoing Audiological Evaluation	NC School for the Deaf Comprehensive Evaluation Clinic	8/17	Central NC School for the Deaf Greensboro NC	2Xs	R	NA	NA		
Consultation/Inform. meeting w/dev. psych at Sch for Deaf	NC School for the Deaf Comprehen Evaluation Clinic	8/17	Central NC School for the Deaf Greensboro	2Xs per /week	R	NA	NA		
Consultation/Information meeting w/physical therapist at the Developmental Eval. Center (DEC)	Developmental Evaluation Center	8/24	Tri-County Dec.	2 Xs per /yr	R	NA	NA		
		1993							

Jason Bennett
Child's Name

VII. IFSP GOAL PLAN

BENJ042293
Unique ID #

67-5305
Agency Case #

Service Coordinator

Start Date	Goal #	Type*	Child and Family Goals and Criteria	Methods and Procedures	Responsible Parties	Target Date	Date Achvd.	Goal** Status	Date Rated
7/30	1	SC	Nutritional Consultant to help plan meals for Jason	Contact nutritionist of Orange Co. Health Dept.	Claire Roberts RNT	8/30/93			
7/30	2	0	Physical therapy for improved head control and develop. of upper body strength	Refer to Guilford PACT (parents & children together) team for physical therapy	Sharon Ballard PT	6/30/94			
7/30	3	0	Speech language therapy and aud. training. J. B. will wear hearing aids when awake. Jason will show awareness of 6 environmental sounds. Child will show awareness of voice	Central North Carolina Sch. for) the Deaf (parent/infant program	Paula Poiter CCCSP	3/30/94			
8/17	4	0	Audiologic evaluation & monitoring	Central NC School for the Deaf	Taylor Freeman CCC A	6/30/94			
8/17	5	SC	To gather information which will help the Bennetts predict what Jason's needs and abilities as a preschooler might be	Arrange for informational meetings w/the developmental psych at Sch. for the Deaf & with physical therapist	Sharon Ballard Robert McDonald	8/18/93			
7/15	6	0	Respite care so Doug & Denise can spend time w/Mike	Arrange with Charlene Bennett a regular time each Sunday afternoon	Denise & Doug Bennett	On-going			
6/30	7	SC	To obtain assistance for Denise at mealtimes	The family has come up with several strategies. 1) Doug will bring dinner home for the family 3Xs per week and once on the weekend. 2) Janice Levy has offered to feed Jason just before Denise picks up the children. Doug wants to be more available in the mornings and is going to be taking Mike to the restaurant several mornings a week. He will then take him to the babysitter.				

*GOAL TYPE
T transition   O Other
SC Service Coordination

**GOAL STATUS SCALE
0 - No longer a goal
1 - Goal cannot be reached

2 - No change but still a goal
3 - Goal partially reached

4 - Goal partially reached but not to the family's satisfaction
5 - Goal reached to the family's satisfaction; is ongoing
6 - goal reached to the family's satisfaction

IFSP FORM — PAGE 6

5/91

VIII. IFSP REVIEW

Jason Bennett
Child's Name

Modifications/Revisions	
Goal #	(To be completed at time of review—01/30/94)

Review Date _____   <u>BENJ04229</u>   <u>67-5305</u>
                            Unique ID #   Agency Case #

| Summary Comments |

(IFSP will be reviewed by 01/30/94)

Review Cycle   **Target Date**
☐ 6-month   ☐ 12-month   ☐ other _____   for Next Review __|__|__

_____
Parent/Guardian Signature   Date

_____
Parent/Guardian Signature   Date

_____
Service Coordinator Signature   Date

_____
Family Member Signature   Date

_____
Service Provider Signature   Date

_____
Service Provider Signature   Date

_____
Service Provider Signature   Date

_____
Service Provider Signature   Date

_____
Service Provider Signature   Date

REFERENCES

Bailey, D., and Simeonsson, R. 1990. *Family Needs Survey, Revised Edition.* Chapel Hill, NC: Frank Porter Graham Child Development Center.

Brown, W. 1990. *Early Intervention Regulation: Annotation and Analysis of Part H.* Horsham, PA: LRP Publications.

Dunst, T., Trivette, C., and Deal, A. 1988. *Enabling and Empowering Families: Principles and Guidelines for Practice.* Cambridge, MA: Brookline Books.

Early Intervention Advocacy Network Notebook. 1992. Washington, DC: Mental Health Law Project.

McGonigel, M., Kaufmann, R., and Johnson, B., eds. 1991. *Guidelines and Recommended Practices for the Individualized Family Service Plan.* Bethesda, MD: Association for Children's Health.

Seligman, M., and Darling, R. 1989. *Ordinary Families, Special Children: A Systems Approach to Childhood Disability.* New York: Guilford Press.

Summers, J., Dell'Oliver, C., Turnbull, A., Benson, H., Santelli, E., Campbell, M., and Seigal-Causey, E. 1990. Examining the individualized family service process: What are family and practitioner preferences? *Topics in Early Childhood Special Education* 10(1):78–79.

Turnbull, A., Lee, I., and Turbiville, V. 1991. IFSP process model. In *Guidelines and Recommended Practices for the Individualized Family Service Plan*, eds. M. McGonigel, R. Kaufmann, and B. Johnson. Bethesda, MD: Association for Children's Health.

Chapter • **8**

F.A.M.I.L.Y. Assessment
A Multidisciplinary Evaluation Tool

*Arlene Stredler Brown and
Christine Yoshinaga-Itano*

HISTORICAL BACKGROUND AND
INTERVENTION PROGRAM

There are many approaches to consider when working with hard-of-hearing and deaf infants. Dunst (1988) has clearly defined the characteristics of child-centered, family-centered and family-focused therapy. Each approach has reasonable justification. Frequently, a combination of therapeutic approaches works best to meet the needs of a hearing-impaired child and the family. In Colorado, family-focused intervention is offered through the Colorado Home Intervention Program (CHIP) under the auspices of the Colorado Department of Health.

Family-centered Intervention

The philosophy of the Home Intervention Program is that parents are the best facilitators for a child. Through their active participation in the early process, they become empowered and consequently develop

The authors gratefully acknowledge the contributions made to facilitate the development of this project and to support ongoing research. Funding was received from the Colorado Department of Health, the University of Colorado, the Colorado Department of Education, Colorado School for the Deaf and Blind, Children's Hospital of Denver, and several local school districts and community center boards.

an optimal interactive match (Bailey and Simeonsson 1988) with their child. We believe this approach is critical in meeting the needs of children with special challenges.

Population Served

The Home Intervention Program operates statewide, serving 80 to 120 families of infants and toddlers who are deaf or hard of hearing. The program was initially established to serve families of low socioeconomic status. Because of increased requests from middle and upper income level families, the program is now available to those families as well, although they do not receive financial assistance. In 1991, 33% of the families had no income, 33% had some income but were still at poverty levels, and 33% had middle or higher income levels. With the advent of Public Law 99-457, coordination of services through interagency collaboration, specifically the State Department of Education, the State Department of Health, and the Outreach Program of the Colorado School for the Deaf and Blind has begun.

Due in part to Colorado's historically aggressive approach to early identification of hearing loss (Northern and Downs 1984): (1) 39% of our children are identified before 12 months of age; (2) 43% are identified between 13 and 24 months; and (3) an additional 15% are identified by their third birthday (Yoshinaga-Itano 1987). Forty-one percent of the population has been identified as multiply handicapped; 8% of the children have mild hearing losses, 35% have moderate losses, 22% have severe losses, and 34% have profound hearing losses.

Parent Facilitators

There are approximately eighty-five parent facilitators providing services to families with infants with hearing loss. The facilitators are from a variety of professional backgrounds including speech/language pathology (approximately 25%), audiology (approximately 30%), deaf education (approximately 40%), and early childhood special education (approximately 5%). In most cases, graduate training of these professionals is in some aspect of child-centered care. Parent facilitators participate in a three-day workshop when they enter the program. They also travel to Denver for semi-annual, two-day workshops to update skills, to present case studies, to provide mutual support, and to participate in group problem-solving of difficult cases. The administrative staff includes a consulting family psychologist who provides in-service training in topics such as: (1) the grieving process (Moses 1983); (2) family systems (Minuchin 1979); (3) "joining" the family (Haley 1976); (4) instructional techniques (Hersey and

Blanchard 1977); and (5) resources available within the program and the community to further support the family (see figure 1). Because of the significant growth of the program, the state has been divided into nine regions. Regional supervisors, who are parent facilitators with extensive experience in the program, coordinate training and services for parent facilitators and families within their geographic regions. Parent facilitators have regular telephone contact and meetings with their regional supervisors.

The same principles espoused in the CHIP philosophy of family-centered intervention, are applied to the development of parent facilitators and overall program development. Parent facilitators must feel equal with program supervisors so that they have a sense of owner-ship in the program and its development. Program supervisors believe

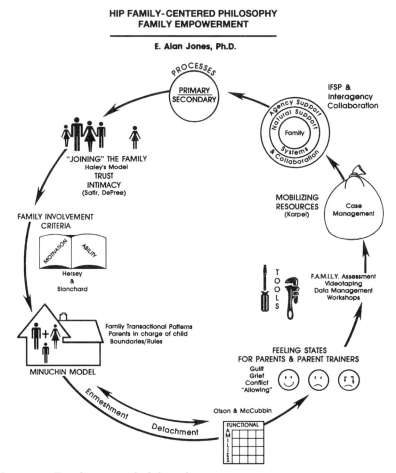

Figure 1.   Family-centered philosophy.

that the best way to instill this is to "practice what you preach" at all levels of the program. Thus, the program described here is the cumulative product of our 85 parent facilitators who have collaborated over a period of several years.

The facilitators' role is a complex one. Because weekly intervention occurs in a family's home, facilitators often find themselves in an intimate and trusting relationship with family members. Many questions about normal child development and the effects of the hearing loss on the child are discussed.

A facilitator may serve as a case manager, providing assistance to a family in obtaining appropriate services and facilitating interagency and interprofessional collaboration. These services may include additional diagnostic information or additional intervention services such as child-centered speech and language therapy, occupational therapy, physical therapy, or mental health services. Most important is identification of the parents as major participants in the team process. In most cases, parents participating in CHIP have chosen the parent facilitator initially as the case manager. Many parents share the role of case manager prior to the end of their program with CHIP.

A parent facilitator may assume a counseling role with specific goals related to establishing parent-professional partnerships; empowering parents to make decisions, setting goals and obtaining direct services for their family and child; and assisting families through the grieving process.

A parent facilitator may also serve in a transdisciplinary role (Hart 1977; Lyon and Lyon 1980; Golightly 1987). A transdisciplinary model of intervention is an integral part of the CHIP process. Parent facilitators are primary service providers but they receive consultation from individuals who specialize in psychology, audiology, speech/language pathology, education of the deaf, occupational therapy, and physical therapy, requiring considerable interagency and interprofessional collaboration. A parent facilitator may provide counsel to a family after consulting with a clinical psychologist, or may provide information about occupational or physical therapy techniques with the help of an occupational or physical therapist.

A parent facilitator may serve an instructional role, providing families with specific content information. Another important task of a facilitator is to assist parents in the acquisition of skills needed to integrate therapeutic techniques into a child's daily routine. The techniques chosen for instruction meet the needs of a particular child and are in direct response to the concerns of those parents. The content may include the development of auditory skills, speech skills, communication abilities, play skills, and behavior management. During each home visit, one or two techniques are emphasized.

The Content/Strategies Component

When enrolled, each family is introduced to a Home Intervention Program Facilitator, who makes weekly visits to the family's home. Programming starts at the time of identification, often before acoustic amplification has been fitted. This is justified because family members often need information and support at the time of identification when their expectations for a "normal" child have been shaken (Moses 1985).

During a home visit, specific techniques are conveyed to the parents through a carefully designed five-step program. First, the specific technique is discussed so parents can understand the theoretical underpinnings of the technique and its relevance to the child's habilitation needs. Second, the facilitator demonstrates the technique while interacting with a child. The third step is very important: evaluating the effectiveness of the technique in context of a child's behavior. This step is accomplished through a parent-facilitator partnership. It is important to take notice of a child's behavior and any effect the technique has had. Parental input is essential because of extensive experience with their child. Their perspectives should blend with the facilitator's account of the child's behavior during implementation of the targeted therapeutic strategy. The fourth and fifth steps shift the focus to the parents as they are asked to implement the technique. Then, they join the facilitator in evaluating the effects of intervention. They also have the opportunity, at this time, to discuss how comfortable they feel implementing the technique. It is at this point that the program fulfills its family-centered premise.

Decision-making Process

How are these techniques chosen? Who decides the order of presentation? When only two skills are emphasized during a session, how can the needs of child and parents be prioritized? And, what method of intervention will be used? All these questions are posed to each facilitator, to the family, and to other members of the intervention team.

Goal Setting

The ultimate objective is for parents to choose their own goals and objectives. A parent facilitator's role is to provide a menu of topics that are important to the development of the child and family. A parent facilitator also provides a non-judgmental presentation of methodology and programming issues as well as information available on the topic. This does not, however, prevent a parent facilitator from offering his or her own professional opinions and viewpoints when asked by parents to provide this information. If a parent facilitator has successfully "joined the family" (Haley 1976), both parents and facilitators should feel comfortable, whether or not they agree on a specific course of action. The goal of a parent facilitator is to be able to express a differing opinion without having parents feel that they are being judged. A parent facilitator continues to reiterate that ultimate decision-making lies with the parents.

Response to Program Needs

The "FAMILY Assessment" was designed to respond to specific needs of CHIP. In order to justify and obtain continued funding, the program needed to demonstrate that progress was being made. The needs of the program dictated that the assessment process be time efficient and cost effective. Families were seen in their homes for 90 minutes each week and most families were too far from centers to participate in traditional multidisciplinary assessments. Even if families could participate, the allocation for programming was not sufficient to pay for hours of diagnostic services by numerous professionals. There was agreement that a standard assessment protocol should be used with all families and children in the program. It was felt that the assessment should be designed to provide information regarding changes in parents' knowledge-base, changes in the communicative interaction between parent and child, and changes in the child's development. The information obtained from the assessment needed to provide guidelines for specific intervention. Additionally, the parent facilitators wanted (1) to monitor the family and child's development over time, (2) to compare this information with families and children who did not have the challenge of hearing impairment, and (3) to compare the characteristics of the child/family to others with similar ages, hearing impairments, additional handicapping conditions, ethnicity, etiology, or communication methods.

ASSESSMENT PROCESS

FAMILY Assessment has been used successfully for the past eight years by the Home Intervention Program. First, FAMILY Assessment can identify present levels at which a child is functioning, as well as the strengths, needs, and concerns of family members as they relate to the child. Results quantify the present skill-level of a child in areas of communication, language, audition, speech, cognition, play, social/emotional, gross and fine motor, and general development. Second, characteristics of parent-child interactions are quantified. The third component elicits from parents their concerns, questions, and needs as they relate to their child. FAMILY Assessment offers parents an array of choices for the focus of intervention.

Using the FAMILY Assessment

FAMILY Assessment is a naturalistic assessment, incorporating videotape analysis and inventories completed by the parents. Information is
obtained from videotapes of parents playing with their child, parent
reports, and parent interviews. An hour to two hours of the parents'
time is required to fill out the developmental inventories. In addition,
the videotaped interaction takes a half hour. Home visits are scheduled at times when participation is most convenient for both mother
and father. The first videotape is made after the parents become familiar with their facilitator and are comfortable with the program and
then at six-month intervals. The first videotape session usually occurs
within three to six months after enrollment in the program. Before the
first videotape is made, an emphasis is placed upon establishing trust,
answering questions about technical information, and providing contact with other agencies that are, or will be, involved in providing services to the child and family.

When families feel comfortable with the evaluation procedure,
the facilitator arranges a time to videotape the parent/child interactions. Using specific guidelines, the facilitator operates a video camera
and obtains a 30-minute interaction sample. The parent then decides
whether the taped interaction represented a normal interaction. If not,
another taping session is arranged. The videotape is then sent to the
University of Colorado–Department of Communication Disorders and
Speech Science for analysis. Graduate students in speech/language
pathology and audiology, who have undergone fifteen weeks of
instruction, as well as coordinated instruction throughout their graduate curriculum, learn to code the video samples in four areas: phonology, language, communication, and parent-child interaction. Coding
reliability is established during the 15-week training period.

While the videotape is being coded at the University, a set of
questionnaires and developmental inventories is sent to the facilitator.
These are taken to the child's home and together the parents and facilitator decide which questionnaires/protocols they want to complete.
Areas that can be evaluated include: play; auditory skills; gross and
fine motor skills; and environmental and family needs (see figure 2).

Thirteen different questionnaires/protocols are offered and the
facilitator and parents select which protocols they want to complete at
that time. Family involvement in this process is essential. It is important that parents feel they are working collaboratively with professionals in assessing their child's skills. Parents frequently see skills that a
facilitator and other therapists do not observe in their relatively brief
encounters with a child. In addition to the belief that parents are the
best facilitators of their child's development, the assessment is based

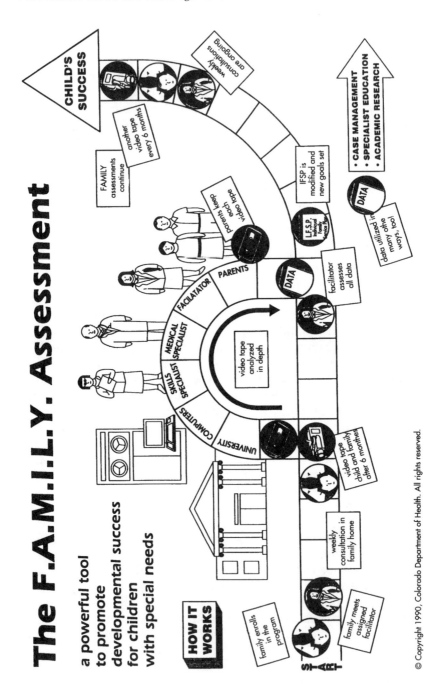

Figure 2.　F.A.M.I.L.Y. Assessment Model.

on the assumption that parents are also the best informants regarding their child's abilities. Therefore, the assessment does not include any professional/ child elicitation tasks. Upon completion of these questionnaires and protocols, the parent facilitator sends the information to the university for analysis.

The protocols used in our assessment procedure can be divided into three categories: (1) protocols designed to evaluate a child's language, communication, play, cognition, and motor skills; (2) protocols designed to evaluate the parent-child interactive match; and (3) protocols intended to focus on parent needs. The assessment tools used to evaluate these three areas are listed in table I.

Table I. A List of the Diagnostic Instruments by Category, and Type of Evaluation Procedure

Area Evaluated	Instrument	Videotape Analysis	Questionnaire
Child Skills	Communicative Intention Inventory (Coggins and Carpenter 1981)	X	
	Systematic Analysis of Language (SALT) (Miller and Chapman 1985)	X	
	Ling Phonologic Level Speech Evaluation (Ling 1978)	X	
	Speech Intelligibility Checklist (Yoshinaga-Itano and Ruberry 1988)	X	X
	Developmental Approach to Successful Listening (DASL) (adapted) (Stout and Windle 1986)		X
	Play Assessment Questionnaire (Calhoun 1987)		X
	MacArthur Communicative Development Inventory 1989		X
	Minnesota Child Development Inventory (Ireton and Thwing 1972)		X
	Gross and Fine Motor Screening (James 1988)		X
Parent-Child Interaction	Caregiver-Child Interactive Behavior Analysis (Cole and St. Clair-Stokes 1984)	X	
	Systematic Analysis of Language (SALT) (Miller and Chapman 1985)	X	
Parent Needs	Family Needs Survey (Bailey and Simeonsson 1985)		X
	HOME Inventory (Caldwell and Bradley 1984)		X
	Parenting Events (Crnic and Greenberg 1990)		X

EVALUATING THE CHILD'S SKILLS

Communication and Language

All our assessment procedures and intervention techniques recognize that every area of language must be considered: pragmatics (child and parent communicative intent and parent-child interaction styles), semantics (receptive and expressive vocabulary and parts of speech), and syntax (grammatical forms, sentence structures, and mean length of utterance). Because communication and language are always affected by a hearing loss, programming must carefully analyze the onset of communication and the progress a child makes over time. Taking test results into consideration, as well as recommendations from ongoing team meetings, parents may decide to alter the communication method when adequate progress is not recorded.

Pragmatics. The Communicative Intention Inventory (Coggins and Carpenter 1981) is used to determine which pragmatic categories a child is using. It also looks at the quality of a child's utterances. Each communicative bid can be coded as gestural, vocal, spoken, or signed. The total number of communicative bids is tallied. This information is obtained when the 30-minute videotape is analyzed at the university.

There are several guidelines to consider when interpreting the results. First, there is a general trend in the normally hearing population to increase the number of pragmatic categories used as a child becomes older (Olswang et al. 1987). Also, an increase in the total number of communicative bids within the 30-minute sample is expected as the child gets older (Olswang et al. 1987). Third, there is typically a shift from nonverbal (gestural and/or vocal) utterances, which may occur as early as nine-months of age to predominantly verbal (spoken and/or signed) utterances (Carpenter, Mastergeorge, and Coggins 1983).

The facilitator shares the results with the parents and the intervention team. The child's existing communication patterns are explained and goals are established to promote more developmentally advanced patterns. The SKI*HI Home Visit Curriculum (Clark and Watkins 1985) is used as a guide in teaching appropriate communication strategies. The Hanen Curriculum (Girolametto, Greenberg, and Manolson 1986) also provides examples of activities that can be used to help promote a parent's understanding of communication intention. The Transactional Intervention Program by Mahoney and Powell (1986) is also available to parent facilitators.

Semantics. The MacArthur Communicative Development Inventory (1989) is completed by the parents. This inventory provides us with an estimate of the number of words a child understands, the number of words a child produces, and the types of words a child has in his or her lexicon. Parents look at a long list of approximately 400 vocabulary words and indicate which items their children have in their receptive or expressive repertoire. Because vocabulary development has been shown to be a strong predictor of later reading skills in both the normally hearing (Anderson and Freebody 1979, 1981) and the hearing-impaired populations (Davis et al. 1981, 1986; Osberger 1986; Geers and Moog 1989), vocabulary development is considered crucial.

Syntax.   When the child has at least 10 or more verbal utterances, a language sample analysis (Miller and Chapman 1985) is obtained. The analysis identifies the mean length of utterance (MLU), the parts of speech used, and the sentence structures observed in the sample. The assessment helps identify linguistic competencies. The parent facilitators then follow normal developmental progressions to assist parents in their use of techniques to stimulate their children's English language development. Strategies employed come from the SKI*HI Curriculum (Clark and Watkins 1985) and INREAL approaches to language development (Weiss 1981). Parents become skilled observers of their child's communication. They also learn appropriate strategies to reinforce the child's communication. Parents become highly skilled at creating opportunities for communication.

Phonology.   The Phonologic Level Speech Evaluation is used to measure speech development of a child (Ling 1976). Coders (graduate students) at the University of Colorado transcribe each vocalization made by a child during a 30-minute videotape. All vocalizations are noted including short syllables, reduplicated and nonreduplicated babbling, jargon, and words. From this information we obtain a total number of vocalizations, a mean length of syllables per utterance, and a phonemic repertoire of all sounds produced.

To measure progress, we look for an increase in the total number of vocalizations made in the 30-minute period. Parent facilitators also look for an increase in the mean length of syllables per utterance as a child learns more sophisticated and lengthy patterns of babbling, jargon, and word strings. An increase in the diversity of phonemic repertoire is another indication of change.

Intervention techniques in speech and audition are elicited from phonologic information. Parents learn strategies for consistently reinforcing their child's vocalizations. They may need help in becoming better observers of vocal utterances of the child. They can learn to imitate the child's utterances as an effective method of reinforcement. Parents can learn how to set higher standards for the child by expecting him or her to vocalize and by providing more opportunities for vocalizations to occur.

Auditory Skills. An informal checklist of auditory skills is completed by the parents. It incorporates elements of the Developmental Approach to Successful Listening (DASL) (Stout and Windle 1991) as well as other measures (Clark and Watkins 1985; Northcott 1977, 1978; Alpiner and Amon 1974; Erber 1982; Office of the Los Angeles County Superintendent of Schools 1979). Items on the checklist follow a traditional hierarchy of auditory skill development starting at a reflexive level and moving through awareness, searching, localization, and discrimination. Hearing aid use is also monitored.

It is essential that development of auditory functions be monitored (Pollack 1985; Ling 1976) because the level of auditory skill development directly affects speech, language, cognitive, and social-emotional development. There is also justification to make changes in acoustic amplification if progress in auditory skill development and speech development are not seen.

Teaching parents about hearing aid management and auditory training is rewarding but challenging. This is an area that requires practice and use of specialized techniques. Therefore, parents need to be carefully instructed in the rationale for auditory training. Each discrete skill is modeled until the child reaches an 80% success rate. The effect of visual distractions and visual cues is explained and monitored, and parents learn how to incorporate active listening into their daily routines.

Critical to the success of any program of auditory skill development is the consistent use and management of a child's personal amplification. For parents, hearing aids are a concrete reminder of a child's hearing impairment, and counseling may be needed to facilitate their acceptance.

Cognition and Language

It is important to obtain a measure of developmental achievement that is not affected by a child's hearing loss. To accomplish this, a questionnaire is used to measure a child's symbolic play behaviors. The underlying assumption for use of this questionnaire is that symbolic play is a nonverbal representation of prelinguistic and linguistic development (Bates and Snyder 1987; Bates, Bretherton, and Snyder 1988; Casby 1980; McCune-Nicolich and Carroll 1981; McCune-Nicolich 1981; Casby and McCormack 1985; Darbyshire 1977; McCune-Nicolich and Brusken 1982). We are assuming that the way children interact with toys and people in their environment is an indication of their developmental achievement. Two different questionnaires are used. The Play Assessment Questionnaire adaptation (Calhoun 1987) of the Play Assessment Scale (Fewell 1984) is a 45-item questionnaire to be completed by a parent with the help of a parent facilitator. Each question is answered "yes," "no," or "yes, in imitation." The raw score is then converted to a "symbolic play age." For children older than 30 months, the Symbolic Play Scale Checklist (Westby 1981, 1988) is used. Here, too, parents and a CHIP facilitator work together to complete the checklist. Answers are based on observations of a child's play. These play skills do not need to be observed directly during a testing session.

Based on play behaviors identified in the checklist, the facilitator designs a program to expand a child's repertoire of play skills. Parents are taught to become reliable observers of their child's play and learn to join in. Both play scales have the skills listed in hierarchical order, which offers the parents a convenient guide to follow as they demonstrate more sophisticated play routines. Parents often need encouragement and assistance from the facilitator in choosing appropriate and stimulating materials to elicit play. Most parents benefit from information that shows the relationship between play and language development.

Mahoney and Powell's *Transactional Intervention Program* (1986) provides guidelines about a child's inherent ability to accommodate. It is important to appreciate the level at which a child is functioning and to ascertain how sophisticated the adult's model can be. We want to encourage development of more advanced play skills while appreciating that each child can only strive a certain distance beyond his or her present skill level. Some children have limited ability to accommodate to an adult model. Others can observe and successfully imitate a significantly more difficult play skill. A facilitator, in collaboration with parents, develops an individualized plan for the advancement of play routines.

Overall Development

The FAMILY Assessment offers a standardized measure of child development in a checklist format that can be used to obtain age equivalents in the areas of fine motor, gross motor, personal-social, self-help, receptive language, and expressive language. The *Minnesota Child Development Inventory* (Ireton and Thwing 1972) is completed by parents with the help of a parent facilitator. The primary advantages of this questionnaire are to obtain a standardized profile of a child's skills and to have a profile of skills in six developmental areas. There are also disadvantages in using a developmental profile that compares a hearing-impaired child's skills to his or her normally developing peers. Parents may focus more on a child's deficit areas than on his or her competencies, particularly in those cases where overall development is very slow possibly due to multiple handicapping conditions. This can be discouraging to parents and may impede progress. Therefore, discretionary use of this checklist is suggested. A facilitator, the parents, and an intervention team decide when this developmental information is needed. In contrast, items on the videotape analysis allow parents to focus on quantitative gains without focusing on developmental comparison with normally developing infants and toddlers.

Motor Developmental Screening. Many children with hearing impairments are at risk for gross and fine motor delays. The incidence of sensory integration dysfunction also increases when there is a sensorineural hearing loss (Barrett 1979; Finocchiaro 1982; Jirgal 1982; Pennella 1979; Poizner, Battison, and Lane 1979; Ingalls et al. 1979). Therefore, it is important to screen for dysfunction in these areas. Parents are asked to complete two developmental progressions (James 1988). These questionnaires are designed to elicit information regarding gross and fine motor development. If delays appear to exist, a referral for a complete diagnostic evaluation is recommended.

Describing Parent-Child Interactions

Caregiver-Child Interaction Analysis. Cole and St. Claire-Stokes (1984) developed a system to evaluate the dynamic interaction between the parent and child objectively. This sophisticated procedure was adapted by Georgitis (1987) who uses a three-minute transcription of the videotape to obtain objective and quantifiable information about the communicative interchange. It is possible to examine the number of turn-taking episodes, topic maintenance, attention-getting techniques, gaze behavior, parents' pragmatics, and the modality of each partner's input (e.g., vocal, gestural, oral words, signed words).

In theory, an optimal interaction would be one in which the child takes at least half the turns (Kaye and Charney 1981). By dominating the interaction, the child acquires greater competence in communication. We suggest that parents respond to the child rather than dominate a conversation with questions and commands. The Home Intervention program uses many "reactive" techniques (Weiss 1981) such as expansion, self-talk, parallel-talk, imitation, and appropriate pause time. We monitor gaze behaviors because visual attention is essential for optimal learning to occur in the young child. We also look at the modality in which a child communicates, and make suggestions to parents as to how they can "match" their child's style. Successful attention-getting strategies used by both members of the dyad are quantified so parents can learn to identify the most effective techniques.

Pragmatic intentions of the parents are quantified. Effective techniques to develop speech and language in a young child are expansions of the child's preceding turn, imitation of the child's preceding turn, and repetition of the caregiver's own utterance (Weiss 1981; Clark and Watson 1985; Mahoney and Powell 1986; Manolson 1985). Imitation and expansion place the focus of the interaction on the child, offering reinforcement for his or her actions. When a parent self-repeats, it offers a child the redundancy needed to learn language, particularly when that child has a significant hearing loss. In general, the less a child can accommodate, the more important it is for a parent to use these optimal pragmatic intentions.

The mode of communication used by each partner to establish an optimal interactive match (Bailey and Simeonsson 1988) is also analyzed. The premise here is that a child's mode of communicating will influence the characteristics of the parent. The parent, in turn is encouraged to interpret the child's modality, and to imitate the child in order to reinforce his or her communication. The parent then learns to give the child a model that encourages more advanced communication. Each child is encouraged to extend his or her communication efforts according to his or her inherent ability to accommodate.

Another area of coded parent-child interaction involves attention-getting behaviors of both child and parent. There are two reasons to evaluate this area. First, it is important for parents to recognize how a child attempts to get an adults' attention. Often, a child's attention-getting behavior is not obvious. If a child tries to get an adult's attention by making a gesture and this attempt is not recognized, the behavior will often cease. Second, it helps parents to know just how they can successfully get their child's attention. Many parents habitually call a child's name to get his or her attention. This method is not always the most useful with hearing-impaired children. Therefore, we want to give parents strategies for getting their child's attention so that this convenient and effective method can be employed when needed.

Because our population is hearing-impaired, gaze behaviors are considered essential to effective communication. Gaze behaviors can be scored in two ways. Mutual gaze is when both partners in the dyad are looking at one another. Joint attention is when both partners are looking at a common referent such as a toy. We have found that either type of gaze pattern is acceptable. Many infants are more likely to demonstrate mutual gaze because the parent's face is of great interest. Toddlers are often more interested in a toy and, therefore, exhibit joint attention more frequently.

Parent Syntax Characteristics. A parent narrative of at least 100 consecutive utterances is compiled. The narrative is evaluated for mean length of utterance, semantic, and syntactic structure, using the *Systematic Analysis of Language* software program (Miller and Chapman 1985). Parents are encouraged to communicate by using language patterns at or slightly above the child's language level. For example, if a child is at a holophrastic stage, we encourage use of a 2 to 4 word level, depending on the child's ability to accommodate (Mahoney and Powell 1986).

If a total communication approach is being used, videotaped language samples of simultaneous spoken and signed utterances are obtained so parents can observe how their signed utterances compare to their oral utterances. Our research indicates that parents' oral language is generally much more elaborate than their signed production (Yoshinaga-Itano and Stredler Brown 1990) because parents frequently do not use a true speech-to-sign correspondence. Examination of videotaped samples helps parents evaluate their simultaneous communication skills and this often motivates them to seek more sign language instruction in classes or during home visits.

Parents are also provided with information about the grammar and syntax they are using in their everyday conversations. Mean length of utterance is also calculated. Our research indicates that many parents become accustomed to short simple sentences (Yoshinaga-Itano and Stredler Brown 1990) and that they frequently decrease their mean length of utterance, as well as the variety of sentence structures and parts of speech.

This analysis is not done for families whose primary language system is not English, (e.g., American Sign Language, Spanish, or Vietnamese).

IDENTIFYING PARENTAL NEEDS

When asking parents about their concerns and perceived needs, we are careful to respect their privacy. Some parents find questions of this sort to be intrusive. We always give them the option of answering questions about themselves or of foregoing these protocols entirely. The benefit of obtaining the information is to assist a family in identifying their strengths and needs. The questions relate to the family's perceived needs in light of their child with special needs.

Family Needs

Bailey and Simeonsson's *Family Needs Survey* (1985) is administered when the videotape is made. Parents identify areas in which they have adequate resources and specify areas for which they are requesting information or support. These areas may include child development, the effect of a challenging condition on development, support systems, financial assistance, child care services, and community resources.

This protocol is especially helpful to the facilitator in planning intervention because the parents are clearly stating their needs. Many parents take responsibility for managing their own affairs without knowing that the intervention team can support them. Several families enrolled in the Home Intervention Program participated in a study to determine the usefulness of parent surveys (Moore, Conroy, and Yoshinaga-Itano 1991). Preliminary results suggest that surveys may provide important information to some families; however, some choose not to share this information with the early intervention team. The appropriateness of using family needs surveys must be determined on an individual basis.

Family Environment

A second questionnaire, the HOME Inventory for Measurement of the Environment (Caldwell and Bradley 1984), may be used to supplement information about a child's environment, a parents' involvement with a child and some aspects of behavior management. This questionnaire, which is administered through an interview, was chosen because of its practicality. If a family chooses to share this information, the results offer parents and the intervention team insight into areas that are working well and issues with which the family desires assistance.

In summary, families must be viewed as part of a collaborative team that is designed to meet their self-identified child and family needs. They make decisions about when an assessment is most helpful, what instruments they want to include, whether they want to share the information with parent facilitators, and when they want to take an active role in decision making related to intervention techniques and goal setting.

CASE STUDY: MARK

The child in this study (Mark) was videotaped four times. The result of the selected evaluations are presented in each table. An interpretation of the information is provided followed by a discussion of the goals and objectives derived from the data.

Mark was diagnosed at birth with Treacher Collins Syndrome. He had multiple anomalies including a maximum conductive hearing loss secondary to bilateral microtia and atresia, and a cleft palate that was repaired at approximately ten months of age. At four months of age he was fitted with a bone conduction hearing aid which he tolerated well. Mark was enrolled in the Home Intervention Program at five months of age. He was videotaped a total of four times at the ages of six months, 14 months, 20 months, and 27 months.

Communication and Language

Pragmatics. The Communication Intention Inventory (Coggins and Carpenter 1981) was administered starting at 14 months of age because children are not expected to demonstrate communicative intentions at six months of age when Mark was videotaped for the first time. Mark's first communicative behaviors were vocal and/or gestural (see table II). He used six different pragmatic intents including: comment on object, comment on action, request for object, request for information, answers, and acknowledgments. On the fourth videotape, he was using all eight pragmatic categories. The other trend was an increase in the total number of communicative bids. This increased from 47 communicative bids at 14 months of age to 76 bids at 27 months of age. An important change in the quality of Mark's communicative bids was monitored; he gradually included more verbal communication and reduced the number of non-verbal bids (see table III). This is a developmental pattern commonly observed in normally hearing children.

Table II. The Development of Mark's Pragmatic Language through Nonverbal Communicative Intentions Coded at 6, 14, 20, and 27 Months of Age

	VT #1 6 Months	VT #2 14 Months	VT #3 20 Months	VT #4 27 Months
Comment on Object	0	26	24	27
Comment on Action	0	1	16	5
Request for Object	0	11	29	6
Request for Action	0	0	6	0
Request for Information	0	2	0	2
Answers	0	1	2	8
Acknowledgment	0	6	4	3
Protests	0	0	11	2
Total Nonverbal	0	47	92	53

Table III. The Development of Mark's Pragmatic Language through Verbal Communicative Intentions Coded at 6, 14, 20, and 27 Months of Age

	VT #1 6 Months	VT #2 14 Months	VT #3 20 Months	VT #4 27 Months
Comment on Object	0	0	0	1
Comment on Action	0	0	0	0
Request for Object	0	0	0	0
Request for Action	0	0	0	6
Request for Information	0	0	0	0
Answers	0	0	0	3
Acknowledgment	0	0	0	10
Protest	0	0	0	2
Total Verbal	0	0	0	23

Semantics.   *The MacArthur Communicative Development Inventory for Infants* (1989) was first used when Mark was 27 months of age. At this time, he demonstrated semantic skills at the 21 month level, as reported by his parents. This measure was adopted as part of the FAMILY Assessment in 1990 and is now being used longitudinally with all infants and toddlers.

Syntax.   Because of the paucity of Mark's expressive language, a language sample analysis could not be obtained until the fourth video-tape. At that time, 100 utterances were recorded. Mark used 12 parts of speech and four different sentence patterns. He had a mean length of 1.26 words and 1.32 morphemes per utterance, and he was using only the present tense (see table IV).

Phonology.   Mark's phonologic development was slow until the fourth videotape (see table V). The number of vowels in his phonemic repertoire was limited to two sounds at six months of age and improved slowly during the next fourteen months. On the fourth video-tape, he showed a significant improvement, using 18 different vowels during the 30-minute sample. A slow progression in his use of consonants was noted as well. On the first videotape, no consonants were used. Only one consonant was used when he was 14 months of age on videotape number two. By the fourth videotape, Mark had made a significant improvement; 19 consonants were being used including six stops (Ling 1976).

Table IV.   A Description of the Child's Use of Syntax and Grammar through the Systematic Analysis of Language (SALT) Coded when Mark was 27 Months of Age

	VT #4—27 Months
	Child
Type Token Ratio	.45
# Forms	12/81
# Structures	4/32
MLU—Words	1.26
MLU—Morphemes	1.32
# Verb Tenses	1/12

Table V.   A Description of Mark's Phonetic/Phonologic Development at 6, 14, 20, and 27 Months of Age

CA	VT #1 6 Months	VT #2 14 Months	VT #3 20 Months	VT #4 27 Months
Vowels	2	6	11	18
Consonants	0	1	4	19
Mean Length of Syllable				
Per Utterance	1.0	1.2	2.0	2.4
Total # of Utterances	25	23	68	114

Mark demonstrated minimal use of vocalizations. On the first videotape he only vocalized 25 times. Compared to our database (Yoshinaga-Itano 1990) of 92 hearing-impaired children on the Home Intervention Program, Mark falls well below the mean for the total number of utterances made in 30-minutes time. This pattern continues until the fourth videotape when a significant increase in the number of speech utterances is observed. At this time there are 114 utterances in the same 30 minutes.

Mark used only single syllable vocalizations at six months of age. By 27 months of age he was using a mean length of 2.4 syllables per utterance, supporting his use of 2 to 4 word phrases.

The CHIP facilitator was concerned about Mark's limited vocalization, the limited phonemic repertoire, and the short length of his utterances. Certainly, his cleft palate would be expected to have a direct impact on speech production. A speech-language pathologist at the local hospital's Cleft Palate Clinic was consulted. A program for oral motor stimulation was jointly prepared and implemented by a speech/language pathologist and the CHIP facilitator. In addition, added emphasis was placed on appropriate hearing aid use and the development of Mark's residual hearing. Mark received a screening of gross and fine motor skills to evaluate the possibility that low muscle tone was affecting respiratory support for speech production. As a result, the parents were instructed in techniques and strategies to enhance vocal play. Another result of this investigation was the discovery that Mark's bone conduction aid was not functioning optimally. It was repaired several times.

The CHIP facilitator and parents were very pleased with the changes in Mark's communication. Although the facilitator was concerned about the slow development of speech, the parents were satisfied and at no time did they want to consider a change in the oral/aural approach they had adopted.

Play. Mark's play age always presented at or slightly above age level according to the Play Assessment Questionnaire (Calhoun 1987) (see table VI). We considered this an encouraging profile. As noted earlier, this questionnaire is completed by the parents with input from the facilitator, as suggested by Calhoun (1987) to ensure reliability. Mark was able to advance his performance in imitation of the adults' model.

Table VI. The Results of the Play Assessment Questionnaire Administered when Mark was 6, 14, 20, and 27 Months of Age

	VT #1	VT #2	VT #3	VT #4
Age in Months	6 Months	14 Months	20 Months	27 Months
Play Age	7 Months	17 Months	24 Months	27 Months

Parent-Child Interactive Match

The analysis of Caregiver-Child Interactive Behaviors (Cole and St. Claire-Stokes 1984) was completed for a three-minute videotape sample.

Turn-Taking. On the tally of turns, Mark's mother started out clearly dominating the interaction by taking 65% of the turns on the first videotape. (An optimal interaction has the parent taking less than half of the turns, according to Kaye and Charney [1981.]) The number of turns the mother took reduced to 57%, 55%, and 56% respectively after intervention. This mother, therefore, was encouraged to let Mark take the leading role in their interaction, thus allowing him to dominate the interaction and receive the benefit of practice and involvement.

Gaze Behaviors. In Mark's first videotape, mutual gaze was established 66% of the time and joint attention was observed 24% of the time. This pattern changed over time (see table VII). On the third tape, mutual gaze was established 50% of the time and joint attention occurred 38% of the time. These patterns are optimal. They demonstrate effective gaze behaviors during more than 85% of the interactions.

Parent Syntax. Mother's use of syntax was also charted. Mark's mother used 28 and 25 parts of speech of the 81 identified on the language sample analysis during the first two videotape sessions. She increased the use of forms to 34 out of 81 in videotape session three and in videotape session four. She did not necessarily use the same 34 forms in both sessions.

Mark's mother used 8 to 11 sentence structures. This increase in the number of structures used reflects the longer mean length of utterance (MLU). Her MLU increased from 2.88 words per utterance to 3.36, from the first to the fourth videotape. She also increased the use of her verb tenses from 3 out of 12 to 4 out of 12 by the fourth videotape session. The changes in the number of forms, structures, verb tenses, and mean length of utterance are appropriate considering Mark's language development. When he started to use verbal language on the fourth tape, the mother increased the complexity of her utterances in order to provide an appropriate model. (See table VIII.)

Table VII. A Description of Parent-Child Interaction Characteristics, Mutual Gaze and Joint Attention, Coded when Mark was 6, 14, 20, and 27 Months of Age

	VT #1–6 Months	VT #2–14 Months	VT #3–20 Months	VT #4–27 Months
	Mother & MC	Mother & MC	Mother & MC	Mother & MC
Mutual Gaze	66%	23%	50%	73%
Joint Attention	24%	12%	38%	7%

Table VIII.   A Description of the Mother's Use of Syntax and Grammar through the Lingquest Language Analysis Coded when Mark was 6, 14, 20, and 27 Months of Age

	VT #1–6 Months	VT #2–14 Months	VT #3–20 Months	VT #4–27 Months
	Mother	Mother	Mother	Mother
Type Token Ratio	.34	.31	.35	.37
# Forms	28/81	25/81	34/81	34/81
# Structures	8/32	9/32	11/32	9/32
MLU—Words	2.88	3.08	3.67	3.36
Uninflected Single Words	29	6	13	19
# Verb Tenses	3/12	2/12	4/12	4/12

SUMMARY

The typical sequence of events of a habilitation program for infants, toddlers, and their families on the Home Intervention Program follows. Collaboration with family members begins shortly after the initial diagnosis. The facilitator meets with the family on a weekly basis, providing information and support. Together they make plans for therapeutic intervention. Curricular areas are designed to address the child, the family, and the interactional patterns between the child and the caregivers. The FAMILY Assessment is used as a method of securing baseline data, monitoring changes in performance, and providing choices regarding method of intervention. Diagnostic information gathered from the FAMILY Assessment is conveyed by the facilitators to team members, including the family. The information is most frequently presented in a criterion-reference fashion.

Information from 150 infants and toddlers has been compiled into a database that can be used to compare a child and his or her interactions to those of other infants and toddlers with hearing loss. Many of the protocols used are standardized on the hearing population and can provide age equivalencies as well. Parents usually report a desire to see how the child has changed over time as opposed to developmental age equivalents.

A diagnostic teaching approach is used to provide parents with the information they need to make methodology decisions, and they learn to apply communication strategies basic to good communication, regardless of the method chosen. Because intervention begins as soon after diagnosis as possible, the most frequent requests for information center around the hearing test, amplification issues, and auditory training. When families use American Sign Language as their primary mode of communication and, in addition, do not consider hearing aid use or the development of audition, the parent facilitator responds to the wishes and directions of the family. These are usually deaf children whose parents are also deaf. For hearing parents, families' needs at the beginning of intervention often center around issues of grief and mourning. These issues must be addressed in conjunction with early intervention.

Methodology Decisions

As soon as the family expresses interest in acquiring information about instructional and communication methods, the parent facilitator begins to provide this information. This presupposes a basic understanding of the relationship between communication, language development, speech development, auditory development, cognitive development, and social-emotional development. Because most of our families have children whose hearing impairments are identified in the first year of life, the program operates under the principle that decisions related to methodology should be made at a time when family members feel comfortable that they understand the numerous variables that enter into this decision-making process. Acceptance of methodology decisions has, in our experience, been greatly facilitated when families do not feel pressured or rushed into a decision. It is also our philosophy that each method has pros and cons that differ according to each family and each child. We believe that it is important to encourage families to evaluate the appropriateness of any instructional decisions continually and to feel that they have the right and the option to change any decision when they feel it is in the best interests of the child or family.

Parents have also indicated that they want to have as much objective data as possible, so they can make informed decisions. Those parents who choose a simultaneous communication method often want to know not only about progress in semantics and syntax, but in auditory skill development and speech development. Those parents who choose an auditory-verbal method want to know not only about auditory and speech skills, but about language development with respect to semantics and syntax and how they compare to other normally hearing and hearing-impaired children of the same age.

Until recently, American Sign Language was not offered as an option to our families. This occurred for several reasons. First, none of the parent facilitators was fluent in American Sign Language. Second, choice of American Sign Language, by its nature, precludes the use of spoken English. In 1992, however, a group of deaf professionals and children of deaf adults with training in either education or counseling were prepared to serve as parent facilitators. These individuals provided all families with the option of pursuing American Sign Language as a primary method of communication and instruction. We have also expanded the number of parent facilitators fluent in Spanish and have learned a Spanish version of simultaneous communication to provide appropriate services to those families who communicate in Spanish.

The parent facilitator monitors progress in weekly session plans and reports, in staff meetings, and through the results obtained on the FAMILY Assessment. When limited progress is seen in an area, the concerns are taken to the team to explore alternative intervention strategies.

Approximately 50% of the children in the Colorado Home Intervention Program use a simultaneous communication approach by the time they "graduate" at three years of age. All changes in methods are made by the team in collaboration with the parents. The Home Intervention Program is eclectic in its approach to intervention and does not have a philosophical bias toward any particular method. The Home Intervention Program also supports the philosophy that unless a child with a hearing impairment has an additional cognitive disorder, he or she has the potential to function at age levels in the areas of language, communication, and social-emotional development. In addition, there is a strong philosophical belief that successful development of language and social-emotional skills can be obtained without sacrificing development in either area. Finally, program staff believe that the key to successful development in both of these areas is to provide family-centered habilitation services aimed at preventing a discrepancy between chronological age and language/social-emotional age. Our experience has taught us that it is much more difficult to close such a gap than it is to prevent one from occurring.

The publicly funded CHIP program has identified several components that make replication of the early intervention program possible. These components were identified during a replication study through the Colorado Department of Education using Part H funds. Through this two-year study, an effort was made to replicate the project in three distinct geographic areas throughout the State with children with special needs who did not exhibit a hearing loss. There are eight critical components that need to be considered when replicating this family-centered intervention program.

1.   A public agency, such as a state department of health, state department of education, or state school for the deaf and blind, must be willing to hire a coordinator to administer and develop the program.

2.   The number of infants and toddlers with hearing impairments must be determined.

3.   A funding allocation, per child, must be determined. At this time, the infant program in Colorado operates on half the average allocation of school-aged children with hearing impairments. Funding for

the program comes from a combination of sources including: The Colorado State Department of Health Care Program, grant funds for services delivered to deaf/blind children, infant/toddler grant funds from the Colorado Department of Education, Medicaid payments, private insurance payments, Community Center Board funding for children with developmental disabilities, and occasional private payments by individual families.

4.   Key individuals, preferably with experience and education in the area of hearing impairment, must be identified. An effort should be made to identify at least one key person in each geographic location so that any child with an identified hearing impairment can be seen by a professional residing in the community.

5.   An ongoing inservice training program should be set up to educate the professionals to provide family-centered intervention to families having children with hearing impairments. Occasionally, intensive ongoing inservice training of professionals in related areas is required. In order to meet this challenge adequately, Colorado has recently divided the state into nine regions. A master parent facilitator has been identified as the primary provider of inservice training to all other parent facilitators in a specific region. This ensures that expert professional support is available to all families and parent facilitators throughout the state.

6.   The identified specialists, together with the supervisor, must convey the philosophical beliefs of the program and program goals. Each family and each parent facilitator must feel vital to the development and growth of the program.

7.   The intervention model must be consistent with the philosophical bases of the program.

8.   An assessment must be developed that measures the goals of the program.

CHIP and the FAMILY Assessment project can be described as a system that is continuously evaluating goals, strategies, and outcomes. As a result of this self-evaluation, the program continues to be in a dynamic system of change. The delivery service model is now being evaluated and adapted to provide services to families with preschool-aged, children with hearing loss. The role of infant behavior and personality in the development of communication is being studied. Parents have posed specific questions about communication that we are attempting to answer. Do specific communication styles facilitate specific developmental areas? Is the optimal communication style for the enhancement of audition and speech different from the enhancement of conversational dialogue skills, vocabulary development, or the development of syntax and morphology? Should adult communication styles change according to the communication skills of the child? These challenging questions serve as an impetus to gain more knowledge in order to improve the quality of our intervention. We encourage other states to share the excitement and enthusiasm we have experienced in working collaboratively toward the goal of developing the best services possible for children with hearing loss and their families.

REFERENCES

Anderson, R., and Freebody, P. 1979. *Vocabulary Knowledge* (Tech. Rep. No. 136). Urbana, IL: University of Illinois, Center for the Study of Reading. (ERIC Document Reproduction Service No. ED 177 480).

Anderson, R., and Freebody, P. 1981. Vocabulary knowledge. In *Comprehension and Teaching: Research Reviews*, ed. J. Guthrie. Newark, DE: International Reading Association.

Alpiner, J., and Amon, C. 1974. *Project Parent-Child*. University of Denver, Department of Speech Pathology and Audiology. Office of Education, Training Grant Report.

Bailey, D., and Simeonsson, R. 1985. *Family Needs Survey* Frank Porter Graham Child Development Center. Chapel Hill, NC: University of North Carolina.

Bailey, D., and Simeonsson, R. 1988. *Family Assessment in Early Intervention*. Columbus: Merrill.

Barrett, S. S. 1979. Assessment of vision in the program for the deaf. *American Annals of the Deaf* 124:745–52.

Bates, E., and Snyder, L. 1987. The Cognitive Hypothesis in language development. In *Research with Scales of Psychological Development in Infancy*, eds. I. Uzgiris and McV. Hunt. Champaign-Urbana: University of Illinois Press.

Bates, E., Bretherton, I., and Snyder, L. 1988. *From First Words to Grammar*. New York: Cambridge University Press.

Caldwell, B. M., and Bradley, R. H. 1984. *HOME Observation for Measurement of the Environment (Revised)*. Little Rock, AR: University of Arkansas.

Calhoun, D. 1987. A comparison of two methods of evaluating play in toddlers. Unpublished Master's Thesis, Ft. Collins, CO: Colorado State University.

Carpenter, R., Mastergeorge, A., and Coggins, T. 1983. The acquisition of communicative intention in infants eight to fifteen months of age. *Language and Speech* 26:101–16.

Casby, M. W. 1980. Symbolic functioning of normal and developmentally delayed children. Ph.D. diss., University of Kansas, Lawrence, KS.

Casby, M. W., and McCormack, S. M. 1985. Symbolic play and early communication development in hearing-impaired children. *Journal of Communication Disorders* 18:67–78.

Coggins, T., and Carpenter, R. 1981. The communicative intention inventory. *Applied Psycholinguistics* 2:235–51.

Cole, E., and St. Clair-Stokes, J. 1984. Caregiver-child interactive behaviors: A videotape analysis procedure. *The Volta Review* 86:200–16.

Crnic, K. A., and Greenberg, M. T. 1990. Minor parenting stresses with young children. *Child Development* 61(5): 1628–37.

Darbyshire, O. 1977. Play patterns in young children with impaired hearing. *Volta Review* 79:19–26.

Davis, J. M., Elfenbein, J., Schum, R., and Bentler, R. A. 1986. Effect of mild and moderate hearing impairments on language, educational and psychosocial behavior of children. *Journal of Speech and Hearing Disorders* 51(1):53–62.

Davis, J. M., Shepard, N. T., Stelmachowicz, P. G., and Gorga, M. P. 1981. Characteristics of hearing-impaired children in the public schools: Part II. Psychoeducational data. *Journal of Speech and Hearing Disorders* 46:130–37.

Dunst, C. 1988. Supporting and strengthening families: New visions, new directions. *Family Resource Coalition Report No. 2.* Morganton, NC: Center for Family Studies.

Erber, N. 1982. *Auditory Training.* Washington, DC: A. G. Bell Association for the Deaf.

Fewell, R. 1984. *Play Assessment Scale.* Seattle, WA: University of Washington.

Finocchiaro, A. C. 1982. Sensory integration: Considerations for programing for deaf school children. *Sensory Integration Special Interest Section Newsletter* 5:2.

Geers, A., and Moog, J. 1989. Factors predictive of the development of literacy in profoundly hearing-impaired adolescents. *The Volta Review* 91(2):69–86.

Georgitis, B. 1987. Reliability study of the adaptation of the Cole and St. Clair-Stokes caregiver interaction analysis for use with the Colorado Home Intervention Program. Denver, CO.

Girolametto, L. E., Greenberg, J., and Manolson, H. A. 1986. Developing dialogue skills: The Hanen early language parent program. *Seminars in Speech and Language* 7(4).

Golightly, C. J. 1987. Transdisciplinary training: A step forward in special education teacher preparation. *Teacher Education and Special Education* 10: 126–30.

Haley, J. 1976. *Problem Solving Therapy.* New York: Harper Colomon Books.

Hart, V. 1977. The use of many disciplines with the severely and profoundly handicapped. In *Educational Programming for the Severely and Profoundly Handicapped*, eds. E. Sontag, J. Smith and N. Certo. Reston, VA: The Council for Exceptional Children, Division on Mental Retardation.

Hersey, P., and Blanchard, K. H. 1977. *Management of Organizational Behavior (3rd Ed.)* Englewood Cliffs, NJ: Prentice Hall.

Ingalls, F. M., Holderbaum, M. A., Ritz, S., Hassanein, K. M., and Goetzinger, C. P. 1979. A study of otoneurologic and balance tests with deaf children. *American Annals of the Deaf* 124:753–59.

James, J. 1988. Screening Inventories for fine motor and gross motor skills. Informal assessment developed for the Home Intervention Program. Denver, CO: Colorado Department of Health.

Jirgal, D. 1982. Sensory integration and the hearing impaired child. *Sensory Integration Special Interest Section Newsletter* 5:2.

Kaye, K., and Charney, R. 1981. Conversational asymmetry between mothers and children. *Journal of Child Language* 8:35–49.

Ling, D. 1976. *Speech and the Hearing-Impaired Child: Theory and Practice.* Washington, DC: A. G. Bell Association for the Deaf.

Lyon, S., and Lyon, G. 1980. Team functioning and staff development: A role release approach to providing integrated educational services for severely handicapped students. *Journal of the Association for the Severely Handicapped* 5:250–63.

The MacArthur Communicative Development Inventory: Infants. 1989. San Diego, CA: Center for Research in Language, UCSD C-006.

The MacArthur Communicative Development Inventory: Toddlers. 1989. San Diego, CA: Center for Research in Language, UCSD C-006.

Mahoney, G., and Powell, A. 1986. *Transactional Intervention Program.* Farmington, CT: University of Connecticut School of Medicine.

Manolson, A. 1985. *It Takes Two to Talk—Hanen Early Language Parent Guidebook.* Toronto: Hanen Resource Centre.

McCune-Nicolich, L. 1981. Toward symbolic functioning: Structure of early pretend games and potential parallels with language. *Child Development* 52:386–88.

McCune-Nicolich, L., and Bruskin, C. 1982. Combinatorial competency in symbolic play and language. In *The Play of Children: Current Theory and Research,* eds. D. H. Pepler and K. Rubin. New York: Karger.

McCune-Nicolich, L., and Carroll, S. 1981. Development of symbolic play: Implications for the language specialist. *Topics in Language Disorders* December: 1–15.

Miller, J., and Chapman, R. 1985. *Systematic Analysis of Language Transcripts.* Madison, WI: University of Wisconsin.

Minuchin, S. 1979. *Families and Family Therapy.* Cambridge, MA: Harvard Press.

Moore, S., Conroy, E., and Yoshinaga-Itano, C. 1991. Parent needs surveys: Parent, professional and student attitudes. Paper presented at the Convention of the Colorado Speech/Language/Hearing Association, Breckenridge, CO.

Moses, K. 1985. Infant deafness and parental grief: Psychosocial early intervention. In *Education of the Hearing Impaired Child,* eds. F. Powell, T. Finitzo-Hieber, S. Friel-Patti, and D. Henderson. San Diego, CA: College-Hill Press.

Moses, K. 1983. The impact of initial diagnosis: Mobilizing family resources. In *Parent-Professional Partnerships in Developmental Disability Services,* eds. J. A. Mulick and S. M. Pueschell. Cambridge, MA: Academic Guild Publishers.

Northern, J. L., and Downs, M. P. 1984. *Hearing in Children, 3rd Ed.* Baltimore, MD: Williams and Wilkins.

Northcott, W. 1977. *Curriculum Guide: Hearing Impaired Children and their Parents (0–3 years),* Washington, DC: A. G. Bell Association for the Deaf.

Northcott, W. 1978. *I Heard That: A Developmental Sequence of Listening Activities for the Young Child.* Washington, DC: A. G. Bell Association for the Deaf.

Office of the Los Angeles County Superintendent of Schools. 1979. *Auditory Skills Curriculum.* North Hollywood, CA: Foreworks.

Osberger, M. J. (Ed.) 1986. *Language and Learning Skills of Hearing-impaired Students.* ASHA Monograph Number 23, Rockville, MD: American Speech-Language-Hearing Association.

Pennella, I. 1979. Motor ability and the deaf: Research implications. *American Annals of the Deaf* 124:366–72.

Poizner, H., Battison, R., and Lane, H. 1979. Cerebral asymmetry for American Sign Language: The effects of moving stimuli. *Brain and Language* 7:351–62.

Pollack, D. 1985. *Education Audiology for the Limited-Hearing Infant and Preschooler, 2nd Ed.* Springfield, IL: Charles C Thomas.

Stout, G., and Windle, J. 1991. *Developmental Approach to Successful Listening.* Englewood, CO: Cochlear Corp.

Westby, C. 1981. *Assessment of Cognitive and Language Abilities Through Play.* Albuquerque, NM: University of New Mexico.

Westby, C. 1988. Children's play: Reflections of social competence. *Seminars in Speech and Language* 9(1):1–14.

Weiss, R. S. 1981. INREAL intervention for language handicapped and bilingual children. *Journal of the Division for Early Childhood* 4:40–51.

Yoshinaga-Itano, C. 1987. Aural habilitation: A key to the acquisition of knowledge, language and speech. *Seminars in Hearing* 8(2):169–74.

Yoshinaga-Itano, C., and Stredler Brown, A. 1990. Parent-child interaction: Characteristics of the parents' language. Training workshop for the Home Intervention Program.

Yoshinaga-Itano, C., and Ruberry, J. 1988. *Speech Intelligibility Checklist.* Denver, CO: Colorado Department of Education.

Chapter • **9**

D. E. I. P.

A Collaborative Problem-Solving Approach to Early Intervention

Mary Pat Moeller and
Marie-Celeste Condon

INTRODUCTION

The Diagnostic Early Intervention Program (DEIP) (Moeller, Coufal, and Hixson 1990) uses the tools of parent-professional partnership, transdisciplinary collaboration, and discovery-oriented diagnostic teaching to formulate a family-oriented intervention plan. The program is initiated immediately after the identification of hearing impairment and is designed to support families in their exploration of intervention needs and options.

A father of a hearing-impaired infant shared the following story, which reflects on the purposes of the Diagnostic Early Intervention Program.

> My daughter recently survived meningitis. Our family was elated by her recovery from a frightening illness. We were a little worried about residual problems the doctors had warned us about, but our daughter was alive and that was all that mattered. Suddenly we were told she was deaf, and that it was imperative that we sign to her in the hospital. We were being taught how to interact with our baby—it made us feel like she was now a stranger. Unwilling to accept the professional advice, we spent over $500 calling experts around the nation. They lined up on two sides of a fence—some saying "you must sign" others saying "you must *not.*" We were confused and angry. It was too soon to even face such a decision. We decided to participate in the Diagnostic Early Intervention Project because the attitude conveyed was, "we will work together with you to discover over time what methods seem most successful for your family and your daughter."

Bailey (1987) describes how professionals' values can conflict with family values or needs. The description above illustrates several points of potential family-professional conflict. The professionals strove to provide immediate intervention (a well-intentioned goal); the parents were focused on the miracle of their daughter's survival. The professionals attempted to provide "expert" guidance. In so doing, they eliminated options and removed the parents' opportunities to participate in decision making on a critical issue that would have significant impact on family interaction. The parents' protest that it was "too soon" to face such a decision highlights another area where professional and parental values may conflict. The DEIP approach addresses these potential pitfalls by allowing families to face such decisions over a period of time, as they observe successes and discover what approaches allow them to interact with their child in a manner they find comfortable.

In 1981 the Omaha Public Schools (OPS) requested that Boys Town National Research Hospital (BTNRH) collaborate in developing a new management model for hearing-impaired infants. The OPS district completed a longitudinal review of decision-making patterns and discovered that placements were often made on the basis of preliminary audiological data, and that parents and school district personnel were minimally involved in the decision-making process. Their conclusion was that a failure-based model was in effect, and that placements, rather than child and family needs, were determining approaches. In response to these concerns, OPS and BTNRH collaborated to initiate a diagnostically oriented intervention program in which children's and families' needs could be determined and efficacious approaches could be identified objectively. A transdisciplinary team evolved to support primary interventionists, and collaborative decision-making models were established to guide practices (Moeller, Coufal, and Hixson 1990).

In its early stages, DEIP functioned much like a multidisciplinary team following a medical model. Various "expert" opinions were gathered across developmental domains, and objective data were presented to the parents relative to the best options for their child. Early efforts to assess family needs were often intrusive or ineffective. Initial attempts to make predictions about a child's needs were unsuccessful, usually because they lacked an ecological perspective. The team has struggled over the past eight years to evolve a family-centered model, in which family members participate as team collaborators. The DEIP team continues to modify procedures by scrutinizing its own areas of difficulty and by interviewing families about their experiences in the program. The following describes the DEIP process and some of what has been learned from families during the ongoing evolutionary process.

A child and his or her family enter the Diagnostic Early Intervention Project at BTNRH for a period of at least six months, following identification of the hearing loss. A DEIP advocate (a parent/infant specialist), who functions similarly to an Individualized Family Service Plan (IFSP) service coordinator, is assigned to provide intervention services twice weekly and to coordinate the efforts of other team collaborators. Family members have regular opportunities to participate in support groups, if they desire. Team members (including the family) monitor intervention outcome through ethnographic measures, parental reports, and pre- and post-data. Through the objective monitoring program, family members participate in a discovery process (c.f. Schuyler and Rushmer 1987). The advocate and parents collaboratively set and implement goals and examine the child and family system responses to the approaches and outcome. Families also participate in observing and exploring each of the potential available placements in the community and consider these placements in light of what they have discovered about their child. The process ultimately culminates in the selection of a formal educational placement and collaborative revision of the Individualized Family Service Plan (IFSP).

Specific objectives of the Diagnostic Early Intervention Project are as follows:

1. To support the parent and family in understanding and coping with a child's hearing impairment.
2. To guide the family in the stimulation of their child's language, auditory, and speech development, while helping them understand and cope with the impact of hearing impairment.
3. To assist the family in developing an objective information base to support decision-making and goal-selection processes.
4. To gain a comprehensive understanding of the family's and child's needs, through diagnostic teaching/discovery and transdisciplinary evaluation.
5. To provide a mechanism within the school district for longitudinal monitoring of the decision-making process and its efficacy.

THEORETICAL MOTIVATION: BASIC PREMISES

The theoretical basis for the Diagnostic Early Intervention Project practices is based on the following fundamental statements. These premises are founded on professional beliefs, program experiences, and concepts families have taught the DEIP team through their candid feedback. The diagnostic approach, inherent in DEIP, applies not only to child/family management, but to the team process itself. In this, there has been discovery, leading to the formation of guiding premises.

Premise One: *Hearing-impaired children represent a heterogeneous group, requiring individualized management. Intervention methods need to be tailored to the individual family and need to be supported by objective evidence of their success.*

This premise embodies the belief that hearing-impaired children require options by virtue of the heterogeneous nature of this group of individuals. Adherence to one philosophical approach or option fails to respect this heterogeneity. The premise also incorporates the team's efforts to evolve from a failure-based approach (where a method is tried until it is proven ineffective) to a success-oriented approach (where an active discovery process is implemented to search for efficacious approaches).

Professionals serving hearing-impaired children do not necessarily agree on how to define "success." Perhaps this is because professional definitions are tied to long-term needs of a child (i.e., need to interact with the hearing world; need to affiliate with the deaf community). These well-intentioned concerns about success, however, may interfere with professionals' ability to examine how families view success in the "here and now." In a success-oriented approach, professionals actively attend to what families perceive as progress. What small successes lead a family to feel hopeful about their child? What techniques will promote the family's feelings that they can be successful in interacting with their child and in bringing about positive change?

Premise Two: *An ecological approach to evaluation of needs is essential.*

Early interventionists (Sparks 1989; Trout and Foley 1989; Fitzgerald and Fischer 1987; Ensher 1989; Simmons-Martin and Rossi 1990) have stressed the importance of viewing a child within the ecological system of the family. Such a viewpoint respects the central role that relationships play in development. An "ecologically valid evaluation system" from the authors' perspective involves at least the following components: (1) family members' report and perspective; (2) naturalistic contexts for evaluation; (3) measures that evaluate the child within the family system; (4) focus on strengths, not just limitations; (5) focus on caregivers/family members and child interactions, not just child variables.

The DEIP team has made discoveries in their search for ecologically valid measurement strategies. The team originally intended to develop prediction formulas, such as the Deafness Management Quotient (Downs 1974) or the Prediction of Spoken Language Acquisition (Geers and Moog 1987). Formulas that rely on discrete, single time measures, however, failed to respect the dynamic interplay between the child's development and environmental factors. Furthermore, the team discovered time and again that children and families are often resilient in response to crises, and early predictions can be unnecessarily negative. The team learned to avoid long-term predictions, to view parenting as a developmental process, and to view child development as inseparable from environmental/familial influences. The team continues to struggle to reduce the tendency to make both positive and negative judgments about these influences.

> **Premise Three:** *Families need to have opportunities to develop balanced partnerships with professionals.*

Clearly, this premise represents the spirit and the challenge of P.L. 99-457. Many authors discuss the need for balanced collaboration with parents, and acknowledge that this is a difficult relationship to bring about (Bailey 1987; Dunst 1985; Cadman, Goldsmith, and Bashim 1984; Winton 1990). Imbalance in roles can result from parents feeling a lack of power in a situation (Luterman 1991).

One of the authors distinctly recalls bringing home her first child from the hospital, and gradually gaining some confidence in handling him in those first few days. On the fourth day, grandmother arrived. She was entirely competent in soothing the baby and anticipating its every need. Each time the baby cried, the grandmother (unlike the mother) could quiet the baby quickly. These events left the mother feeling insecure and uncomfortable with her own skills. How often does a similar event occur when the parent/infant teacher enters a home? If the parents are in the early stages of signing, and in walks a person entirely competent at communicating with their child, how is the parent left feeling? One DEIP parent reported, "It was hard to see the professional be so capable of communicating with my child, when I couldn't." Strategies that support feelings of empowerment need to be identified and implemented.

Parent/infant curricula often stress the many strategies that parents need to develop so that they can interact with a hearing-impaired child. How might they instead stress techniques for recognizing what parents bring to the process that will contribute to the intervention? One DEIP mother remarked that she felt uncomfortable being taught to interact with her daughter. This mother's feelings changed once she felt that her knowledge base about her child was respected. This was a result of the clinician showing by her actions that she desired and needed regular input from the mother about how to elicit responses from the child. The mother reported that this allowed her to move forward and trust the information she was given.

Trout and Foley (1989) stress that a family-centered approach respects the decision-making rights and autonomy of each family. The DEIP team has attempted to address this goal by involving families in a discovery process. Schuyler and Rushmer (1987) define diagnostic teaching as "a way of working with the child in which questions about the child's abilities and the meaning of his behaviors are posed and tested out during virtually every interaction with that child" (p. 261). Inherent in their definition is an attitude of discovery, in which parents and clinician have a notion of how the child may respond, but are objectively open to the possibility that the child may surprise them. Through this type of discovery process, families identify what strategies work for them, what choices they have, and what strengths and skills they have to work with. The team has had to resist the temptation to enforce decisions, and instead must allow the family the right to grow into their own decisions in their own time. This has required the professional to resist the role of giving "expert advice" and to learn to take on new and flexible roles with the family.

> **Premise Four:** *Development is a dynamic, multidimensional process. Multiple dimensions must be considered in a comprehensive evaluation of children's and family's needs.*

Singular focus on a child's hearing impairment can result in imbalanced intervention approaches. Belief in this premise has led the team to monitor 14 aspects of a child's development in relation to his or her family system. This allows the team to focus on a child from a holistic, child development perspective in relation to the family system. A listing of evaluation tools used to assess families and monitor objectives of the program is contained in Appendix A. These protocols are not static, but are continually revised as new techniques become available, or as the team discovers more efficacious approaches.

PROBLEMS WITH TRADITIONAL APPROACHES

Traditional approaches had to be modified to implement the DEIP process. All too often, programs and professionals have described their approaches to parent/infant intervention as "diagnostic and family-centered." Unfortunately, parents involved in early intervention have frequently experienced myriad deficit-focused conversations, and endured hundreds of hours of professional modelling. They have often believed their children's progress to be a result of "good schooling," feared that their children's failures were consequences of their own failures, and struggled to cope with the unvoiced grief that results from becoming a parent of a child with a disability. What would be the ramifications of an early intervention program dedicated to enabling parents and children to get on with being parents and children much as they would have had disability not intruded into their lives? Thoughtful, respectful, empowering, productive, family-focused early intervention has been the goal of the collaborative problem-solving approach.

Furthermore, some professionals responded to the need to serve infants by "watering down" traditional preschool curriculum materials, which resulted in developmentally inappropriate approaches. Other professionals were accustomed to being dominant in the decision-making process. Consequently, professional staff training was necessary to evolve a family-centered model with developmentally appropriate approaches executed *through* family members, rather than *for* them.

In addition, the longstanding controversy over oral versus Total Communication methods had to be addressed. The DEIP team re-analyzed the methods controversy from a family system's perspective. Team members asked, "What impact does lack of professional consensus have on families?" The DEIP team identified several potential effects that have led to the selection of a "pro-choice" attitude. Professionals may guide the family to choose a particular method because of its historic success with hearing-impaired children. This requires that the family have faith in the professional's expert judgment and opinion. This may promote an imbalance in the parent/professional relationship, with the parents reliant on professional advice.

Parents are often faced with the need to confront this choice early in their intervention experience. The decision process may focus a great deal of energy on academic/content issues at a time when parents are needing emotional support and time to heal the family. Confrontation with this issue puts pressure on the family to face lifelong choices with few facts; a situation that leaves many feeling powerless and willing to turn the decision over to "experts." What happens when the expert's choice is not successful for the child and family? As Bailey (1987, p. 64) stresses, "problem-solving is an important skill in any professional, yet it can be counterproductive if applied too early in a goal-setting endeavor, especially if done for the clients rather than with them." S. Doctors (Schwartz 1987) advises parents that the most important choice they will make in the long run is the decision to believe that their child is capable of learning.

In a day when methodological and sign language/sign systems controversies abound, families are sometimes confronted with lack of support for their choices or direct contradiction of their choices. What is the impact of these forces on the family system?

These perspectives and problems have led the DEIP team to adopt a pro-choice or pro-options stances. Choices are based on joint decisions, not professional bias or prediction. Efforts are made to determine the family agenda and how that agenda may be addressed in intervention. The team has observed that many parents have narrow boundaries relative to their hopes for the child. The continual process of observing the child's successes objectively often allows families to dare to have more hope. The challenge to professionals is to have an ever-expanding and flexible bag of tricks, not bound by methodological bias, or judgments about "what makes a good parent."

In the next section, we discuss specific strategies for establishing the discovery process and for involving parents in a balanced partnership from the beginning.

JOINING WITH FAMILIES: DEVELOPING BALANCED PARTNERSHIPS

In a success-oriented approach there is a balance maintained between:

the amount of time and energy spent on the child's disability and the whole child;

the amount of time spent imparting information and skills to parents and the amount of time spent listening and learning from parents;

the focus on child development and the focus on parent development;

assessment and teaching so that learning opportunities are both diagnostic and stimulating;

the amount of time and energy spent on cognitive and affective areas; and

parental and professional agendas.

A basis of the collaborative relationship is that the professional's impact on the young disabled child is minimal in even the best and most intensive child-focused early intervention programs. Whether or not parents want to be or feel prepared enough, they are their child's teachers with profound life-long consequences for them both. Collaborative, family-focused early intervention affords both parents and professionals with the best chance of effecting a powerful, positive impact on the lives of the child, parents, and other family members as well as ameliorating the potentially devastating effect of childhood hearing loss.

Several skilled providers of family-focused early intervention services have described strategies for ensuring collaborative professional and parental involvement in the habilitative process (Schuyler and Rushmer 1987; Trout and Foley 1989; Bailey 1987; Winton 1990; Dunst, Trivette, and Deal 1988; Andrews and Andrews 1986). These authors emphasize the importance of acknowledging and respecting parental expertise and role in decision making, and discuss the importance of establishing an effective and empowering working relationship between parents and professionals. But the task of establishing this relationship is difficult to describe and to quantify. It often seems tied to personality styles. A collaborative approach that seeks to empower parents requires great flexibility on the part of the professional when assuming his or her role with families of diverse backgrounds. Role flexibility and commitment to empowering parents requires ongoing self-examination.

There are many functional family systems quite different from the professionals' own families or their ideal image of acceptable family structures. Family differences must be assessed and appreciated so that intensive intervention services are modified on every level. Highly desirable outcomes can be achieved without violating family systems. Appreciation for unique family characteristics is fundamental to the establishment of balanced partnerships.

INITIAL CONTACTS: KICKING OFF THE PARTNERSHIP

The initial contact with a family sets the tone for the subsequent parent/professional relationship. The professional must strike a balance between forming first impressions on "objective" information gathered by experts *outside* the family versus information provided by the experts *within* the family. During the initial interviews, conversations, and play times together, a focus on the child can be set aside for the time being, with care and attention directed to the parents themselves. An important goal is to establish a quality relationship between the parent and the professional, while being sensitive to the fact that the parents are still reeling from the impact of identification of hearing impairment and the incredible consequences and challenges they face.

A tone of shared expertise between parent and professional should be established in place of the familiar power differential experienced in most parent/professional relationships. This can result in a great relief for both parties, understanding that the pain is the parents' alone to integrate. The need to share responsibility also makes sense given the fact that parents and professional will be seeing one another more frequently than they see many of their own friends and extended family. In addition, at their first meeting the parents and the professional can be assured that the professional will know the parents' agenda—a gratification typically delayed when conversation focuses on the child, who seems to be the reason for coming together in the first place.

Siegel (1975) described the best evaluation instrument as a sensitive, informed clinician who applies current theoretical knowledge to analysis of behaviors and modification of established procedures. The professional will develop open-ended questions that will serve as a framework for building knowledge he or she will need to serve as the family's advocate. Helpful questions are outlined in table I.

In our experience, professionals who are most helpful in the shortest time talk little and listen attentively and skillfully (Simons

Table I.   Questions Used in Initial Contacts to Promote Collaboration

1. What are your concerns?
2. What type of product or outcome are you hoping for from our time together today?
3. How do you know what your child wants? Needs? Thinks?
4. How does your child like to play with you, Dad? Mom?
5. What have you been told so far about your child's communication abilities?
6. What have you been told so far about your child's learning ability?
7. How does that compare with what you have discovered yourselves?
8. What have you, Mom, and you, Dad, found works to engage your child in conversations with you?
9. What are your frustrations and worries as a consequence of the disability?
10. What do you expect will forevermore be different in your lives now as a result of having discovered your child's handicap?
11. What are your hopes for your child and for yourselves, say six months down the road?
12. Who are the other important people in your child's life?
13. Who are the people on your "support staff?"
14. What intervention are you currently seeking? Getting?
15. In our efforts to provide productive, collaborative intervention services, who would you like to include on your team?
16. What should our plan for action include?

1987). Synthesizing statements, nonjudgmental observations that convey a sense of warmth and respect, and statements that bring and keep both parents and the professional on task are essential. Judgmental observations can reinforce the professional's role as an evaluator and expert. Both criticism and praise are forms of judgment that should be used judiciously. Praise needs to be specific and concrete. Professional observations need to be believable, valid descriptions of readily apparent, noteworthy behaviors. Developing a list of shared concerns, as well as noted strengths, is more helpful to the intervention process than voiced or unvoiced implicit criticism. Such lists serve to expand the parents' and professionals' database.

PARTNERS IN EVALUATION

Early sessions should include both conversation and play time during which the parents' interactions with their child at play and during routines can be unobtrusively observed. Parents will come to recognize that they can expediently help the professional obtain a baseline on their child's communication and learning strengths and needs by eliciting and demonstrating typical play and conversational interactions. Later, assessment using parental reports, interviews, and checklists can be completed. Much later in a comfortable, familiar environment with the family present, when the child is well-acquainted with the professional, assessment of elicited child behaviors can be completed to enhance the information already known about the child's development and communication competency.

Adequate time must be given for the parent and child to get involved in their activity, for conversation to develop and for the fun to begin. It is difficult, but essential, for clinicians to force themselves to avoid interrupting, to avoid becoming a direct communication partner with the child, and to support the parents' interaction. After a while, the professional can serve as an "eye witness" reporter focusing on apparent cause and effect relationships by making nonjudgmental observations during parent-child interactions. As the parents and professional share their observations, synthesizing statements such as, "It seems to me that ———"; "Please tell me more about ———"; "How typical is ———?" are helpful. Before the session ends, the professional should help the parents appreciate concrete contributions they have made that day to the intervention process and to the professional. The professional can summarize discoveries made during parent/child interactions and strategies used by the parent that effectively enhanced the child's skills. The professional can reflect aloud on the insights into parenting, play, or communication gained as a consequence of being privileged to share in the parents' interaction with their child. He or she can emphasize what parts of the session were particularly enjoyable and remark on anticipated events for the next session. By reviewing the notes of the session and listing significant outcomes, the professional demonstrates the parents' important role in successful, responsive intervention and in shaping future lessons.

Once a family has enrolled in DEIP, a variety of professionals become involved in contributing to information about the child and the family. The goal is to gain a holistic and integrated perspective through collaborative consultation. Idol, Paolucci-Whitcomb, and Nevin (1986, p. 9) define the approach as follows: "Collaborative consultation is an interactive process that enables teams of people with diverse expertise to generate creative solutions to mutually defined problems. The outcome is enhanced and altered from original solutions that any team member would produce independently." The collaborative DEIP team combines the resources of an educational system with a clinical and medical setting.

In addition to the family members, DEIP team members may include: an educator of the hearing impaired, speech/language pathologist, or educational audiologist; family counselor/social worker; pediatric audiologists and human sensory physiologists; developmental psychologists; medical staff (e.g., ENT, pediatrics, neurology, ophthalmology, neonatology); geneticists (including dysmorphologist);

occupational and physical therapists; educational specialists (e.g., educator of the visually handicapped).

Team members are selected for a specific case by the intervention team, depending on needs of the individual. Specialty evaluations are completed as necessary during the six-month diagnostic teaching process. Ancillary team members provide regular input to the clinical and public school team from "behind the scenes," through regular meetings, held for the purpose of interpreting and integrating the incoming information. The decision-making process followed by the team is described in detail in Moeller, Coufal, and Hixson (1990).

One of the most useful sources of data for decision making has been the close monitoring of intervention outcomes by the family and advocates. Diagnostic questions are posed and outcomes are continually evaluated, based on the children's and family's responses. Outcome measures include pre- and post intervention comparisons, coding of response patterns across intervention sessions, and naturalistic observations of family/infant interactions. Through the monitoring of multiple developmental domains and family needs, an integrated, ecologically valid perspective of intervention priorities is developed by the team.

PARTNERS IN DISCOVERY

The DEIP approach advocates that parents and professionals collaboratively set up a series of experiments designed to gather desired information, develop or strengthen desired behaviors, or resolve problems. Together the parents and professional describe the hypothesis they want to test, select or set up an activity including agreeing on what each participant will do and watch for, and consider their expectations of the child. Often, the professional is then able to withdraw from the parent-child interaction and facilitate desired behaviors by prompting, expanding, and supporting the parents' skills, knowledge, and discoveries. Together the parents and professional can describe their observations, evaluate the outcomes, and plan for both the next step in the discovery process and opportunities to apply and generalize the skill in other situations. Schuyler and Rushmer (1987) describe a similar process in their parent involvement method (PIM) as does Kilburg (1990) in her approach to family language skills assessment and intervention using videotape analysis at each session.

Parental self esteem is enhanced by the balance maintained in the parent/professional relationship, the reward inherent in successfully eliciting desired behaviors from the child, the lack of professional intrusion into a precious, sometimes fragile parent/child relationship, as well as the productivity and fun of the sessions. Jointly developed realistic challenges and plans for follow-up can be developed instead of professionally assigned "home" work. Assigned homework can generate feelings of guilt and anxiety as parents wonder whether the professional will notice evidence of the time and energy spent working on the assignment. Other parents worry about how they have measured up to professional expectations, or attempt to "fake it" when asked to perform during the parent/infant session.

To illustrate the discovery-oriented process, three case studies are presented in table II. The primary diagnostic questions facing the team are described along with results and the modified plan or outcome. These particular cases were selected to illustrate how a clinician joins with family and diagnostic team to solve a problem.

Facilitating parents' roles in the decision-making process is critical to the DEIP process. One former DEIP parent commented, "DEIP was vital to our family in beginning to accept and live with hearing loss. The key was unbiased, complete information and then the opportunity to observe our child's strengths and weaknesses along with skilled teachers who were able to focus on those aspects with us." Another said, "I could suggest something and it was always followed through." Another said, "The staff turned to me for my opinion. I was given choices and was able to pick what I wanted." Obviously, diagnostic, family-centered problem solving is not a plateau to be reached but an on-going, growing process. Reduced stress, the ability to communicate effectively and a new vision of themselves and their children were important outcomes for the families described above. Based on experience as well as theory, the DEIP team can trust the concept that empowering families results in desired outcomes for children, even in complicated cases. Hence, parents and professionals are able to attend to and integrate diverse areas of need while maintaining a focus on the whole child within the family. Intervention is adjusted to meet changing family needs, abilities, and priorities. Recommendations are made and courses of action chosen in consideration of the potential impact on family balance and relationships as well as apparent child intervention needs.

PARTNERSHIP IN INTERVENTION

In order to bring about a shared responsibility for problem solving, it is critical to devote discussion time to parent/professional relationships, roles, and the habilitative process itself. It cannot be assumed that a cursory explanation of the frequency, intensity, and focus of services will mean to parents what it has come to mean to a professional.

Table II.   Case Studies Illustrating the DEIP Process

Case One: M.

Presenting Issue: M. was served by a rural school district in an aural/oral approach for three years prior to her enrollment in DEIP. M. was profoundly hearing impaired and four years old at the time of her entry in the program. M.'s teacher spoke glowingly about the child's progress, yet the parents were skeptical and anxious. They reported being unable to understand her speech and added that she understood little of what they said to her. Yet, they knew no other deaf children, and did not know how to gauge "success." The parents desired an oral approach, but wondered if progress was supposed to be so slow.

Diagnostic Questions	Findings	Plan or Outcome
At what level is M. currently functioning in her communication skills?	At age four, M.'s receptive and expressive language skills fell below an 18 month level. Learning rate data showed minimal progress over last two years. Family strongly desired oral approach.	Discuss concerns for slow learning rate with the family. Establish "discovery" approach, beginning with oral option.
If the family selects specific target goals that are meaningful to them and work steadily toward these few goals, what will the outcome be?	Following six months of aggressive exposure to five family-selected goals, M. has made little measurable progress.	Confer with family regarding their observations, feelings, and concerns. Collaborate with family to select next phase of discovery process.
If the family learns a limited set of signs to support their implementation of the same five goals, what will the outcome be?	Goals were all achieved in less than one month.	Family expressed feelings of success and satisfaction, but feared that their daughter would lose her oral skills.
Can the TC approach be implemented in a way to support continued oral growth?	Family and advocates design plan that includes regular auditory/oral teaching and prompting within M.'s TC program.	Expand repertoire of signs and goals the family will implement. Monitor efficacy.
Is TC approach having a negative effect on M.'s oral communication?	Initially M. had to be prompted to use voice with sign. Within one month, M. adjusted to speaking and signing simultaneously.	Parents choose a TC option with a strong aural/oral component. Family members enroll in Family Sign Program.

Diagnostic Questions	Findings	Plan or Outcome
	Parents enthusiastic about the positive shift in M.'s learning rate and in her increasing ability to participate as a communicating member of the family.	

Case Two: J.

Presenting Issues: J. was one month old when he was referred to DEIP from the neonatal intensive care unit. Born six weeks prematurely, J. required supplemental oxygen and presented with multiple medical needs. ABR results indicated profound hearing loss. However, during the first five months of diagnostic observation, J. demonstrated consistent responses to verbal and environmental stimuli. Regression in motor skills was observed over time. (Note: Due to his young entry age, J. remained in DEIP for 12 months.)

Diagnostic Questions	Findings	Plan or Outcome
Does J. have more residual hearing than predicted by ABR?	Early audiological sessions were equivocal. Even after nine months, J. was unable to turn for VRA.	Collect data on hearing responses at home. DEIP advocate collaborated with audiology to determine facilitative responses.
Are motor skills interfering with localization attempts?	PT confirms regression in motor behaviors and referral made to neurology.	Advocate and PT collaborate to train J. to shift eye gaze and turn in response to sound.
Will repositioning facilitate responding?	Neurology evaluation at six months is inconclusive. At ten months, repositioning yields latent responses to VRA.	OT/PT services given.
What do therapy observations reveal about motor and auditory skills?	At ten months, J. has difficulty lifting his head; is unable to sit; trunk and arm control limited.	Obtain second neurological consultation.
	J. demonstrates anticipatory laughter to "daddy's coming," puckers to "no-no," shifts eye gaze to kitchen at "time to eat" (all auditory-only).	
Is J. orthopedically handicapped?	Second neurological evaluation results in diagnosis of spastic quadriplegia.	Shift program emphasis to orthopedically handicapped.

Diagnostic Questions	Findings	Plan or Outcome
	Adaptive positioning is successful in audiology and results in borderline normal-hearing thresholds.	Involve augmentative communication decision-making team.
	At 12 months of age, receptive language skills (judged by selective eye gaze) approximate chronological age.	Continue OT/PT and audiological monitoring.
Family concerned with need to adjust to a new colloquial of professionals.	Put family in contact with other parents of children with ortho-handicaps for mutual support. DEIP advocate participates in transdisciplinary services for one month to facilitate transfer of strategies to new instructors. Discovery approach initiated with augmentative communication team. Professionals' sessions "bundled" and coordinated to reduce number of sessions and assignments.	Communication Board begins to yield successful interactions; J.'s frustration reduced.
Facing mistrust due to issues of misdiagnosis, stressed by financial and service provider demands.		Parent support options are helpful to family.
How can transition be streamlined to support family?		Placement in orthopedically handicapped program recommended.

Case Three: A.

Presenting Issues: For six months after identification of her severe/profound hearing loss, in addition to overall developmental delay, A. and her family received weekly home based early intervention services with an early childhood developmental specialist through her local school district. Hearing aid use, attendance, and family participation were very poor and progress was negligible, so the DEIP team reconsidered case. The chaotic family situation seemed chronic.. Developmental delay in all areas was so severe that the DEIP team questioned whether hearing loss was A.'s primary handicap. The goals of placement in DEIP included addressing family issues, gathering missing data about the impact of multiple disabilities, establishing consistent participation in intervention, identifying learning strengths and needs, and evaluating communication modalities.

Diagnostic Questions	Findings	Plan or Outcome
What are the family issues?	A.'s father was incarcerated for abuse, then paroled and involved in rehab-	Ongoing counseling became a regular part of P/I sessions.

Diagnostic Questions	Findings	Plan or Outcome
	ilitation. A.'s mother was overwhelmed with personal, family, and financial issues in addition to A.'s disabilities, needs, and care. A.'s mother was on verge of abandoning her. A.'s mother's sister, A.'s primary caregiver, was overwhelmed with A.'s care.	Family assessment results were discussed with the family.
What is the family system like?	Family assessment was done. Family satisfaction fell below the first percentile. Family was continually in crisis and primary caregivers were in constant conflict and stress was overwhelming. Social Services were not collaborating nor cooperating as each attending to its "part" of family problem. Case workers changed frequently so no consistent professional contact was maintained.	Family members heard and voiced priorities, needs, goals, strengths, and frustrations for the first time to one another and to professionals. Mother began counseling and entered a shelter. Primary caregiver became less negative and judgmental toward A.'s mother and more capable of caring for A.
How can we build on family strengths?	Through P/I intervention, the family learned new ways of interacting with A., (that nurtured rather than threatened A.'s development) while developing their spoken/signed conversational competencies.	Intervention was adjusted, despite risk of loss of follow-up, to minimize chaotic tendencies and to support family movement toward flexible, connected, balanced relationships. The family felt themselves to be capable, important decision-makers.
How can we tailor intervention goals and process to family system, needs, and priorities?	Collective family goals included: (1) Continuing consistent participation in A.'s intervention program; (2) Safely rejoining Mom and A.— while empowering Mom to resume	Family was presented with data and encouraged and helped to make own decisions. The family developed and continued to monitor for themselves plans of action to achieve mutually desired family goals.

Diagnostic Questions	Findings	Plan or Outcome
	care and parenting role; (3) Total Communication; and (4) Stress management.	Family's understanding of scope of A.'s needs and strengths grew. Counseling focused on grief and guilt issues. Additional mental health services were secured by the family.
What is the extent of A.'s disabilities?	CMV etiology. Spastic diplegia. Petit mal seizures. Performance on intellectual assessment in the average to low average range of ability (higher than previous results).	P/I, OT, and PT intervention sessions were integrated, provided at one location, and coordinated to reduce the number of sessions, trips around town, and assignments. Family was helped to focus on whole child.
What services and follow-up are needed?	Intervention needs to include routine follow-up with audiology, neurology, and ophthalmology, as well as OT, PT, mental health services, and P/I intervention.	Family participation and home follow-up increased as they saw A.'s progress to be a result of their abilities and efforts.
How can we get consistent attendance so A. is able to participate in all necessary evaluations and intervention?	"Dual" P/I and OT or PT sessions once a week at one location relieved some family stress. Intervention was focused on integrating strategies to enhance A.'s development during daily routines.	Attendance improved dramatically from mostly "lost to follow-up" to punctual, routine attendance with total family involvement and follow-up on all recommendations from evaluations.
Can family commit to and implement Total Communication?	Family was "hooked" on positive impact of their involvement in intervention and became committed to Total Communication.	Immediate and extended family routinely participated in the family sign program.
What would be A.'s potential if full-time hearing aid use could be established and maintained?	Family saw demonstrated listening and vocal behaviors with consistent hearing aid and FM system use. A.'s communicative use of voice increased.	Full-time hearing aid use was established. A. began developing awareness, discrimination, and auditory feedback mechanism behaviors.

Diagnostic Questions	Findings	Plan or Outcome
How do developmental delays and (initially apparently limited) cognitive ability have an impact on communication developments?	New (previously hidden) learning strengths emerged. Motor deficits improved dramatically with consistent intensive intervention.	Family appreciates A.'s auditory-oral potential and limitations and effectively promotes her auditory-vocal as well as sign communication. Discussed implications of findings with family in light of the progress made in communication. Family was relieved. A. can/is learning. Adaptive devices and braces are routinely used now.
What would be the change in A.'s rate of learning with Total Communications emphasis?	After six months, dramatic increase in receptive and expressive language as well as social, cognitive, and perceptual motor skills was documented. (Minimum of six months gain in four months time in every area of development.) "A. was like a new child as soon as she started to sign," remarked the family, "That took a lot of pressure off of us." Family frequently and enthusiastically described their new vision of A. and themselves.	Steady improvement in A.'s rate of language learning continued one year later. A.'s parents have begun slowly to resume their child's care with lots of professional and family support.

Discussion must center around the parents' selection of players on their team and on their strategies for team management and coaching. It is helpful to talk about what is happening to them as parents and as a family as a result of the child's special needs and the consequent intrusion by a large group of professionals. What was family life like and what would it be like without numerous professionals involved? It is essential to talk with parents about how they and other family members feel and to react with understanding and acceptance but without a need to change feelings or speed up the adjustment process.

A former DEIP parent commented that one of the most helpful outcomes of DEIP for their family was the comfort they felt with where they were in the "growing process." It was useful to talk about help, success, hopes, disappointments, fears, fantasies, and realizations. Professionals must discuss with families the kinds of help and intervention services that would be tolerable, palatable, and desirable, demonstrating to them that each family has a strong say in the matter. Families need to be able to mobilize their resources and build on their strengths even before there are firm answers (Segal 1988). Healy, Keesee, and Smith (1985) discuss parent/professional transactions in terms of redefining professional competence, the nature of parent/ professional relationships and interactions, differing perceptions of "success," problem families, and shared problem-solving techniques.

IEP/IFSP PARTNERSHIP

During the early years of DEIP, Individual Education Programs (IEPs) that contained primarily child objectives were developed. More recently IFSPs are being developed that include both the child-centered components of IEPs as well as family strengths, areas of need, priorities assessment input, goals, specific objectives, and perspective on the necessary outcomes of service during DEIP. A brainstorming session with the family and professional is held to examine issues such as those listed in table III. This yields the essential fabric or framework of the IFSP. Questions that guide this discussion are included in table III.

If parents are involved in the assessment and discovery process, joint parent/professional review of criterion-referenced assessments will yield selection of appropriate IFSP objectives that reflect parents' realistic priorities for themselves and their child (Roush and McWilliam in press). The professional's open sharing of his or her task analysis in breaking desired outcomes into manageable, achievable steps empowers parents with knowledge and skill in decision making. It also helps parents realistically adjust expectations they hold for themselves, for their child, and for intervention, while paring down some fear of the unknown that lies ahead.

Table III.   Questions Used in the Brainstorming Session to Facilitate Family Involvement in IFSP Development

1.   Imagining your child six months from now, what do you expect or hope he or she will be doing that he or she is not doing (or just beginning to do) now?
2.   What would you like to know and be able to do six months from now that you don't now?
3.   What improvements would you hope for in your interactions/relationship with your child? With your child and other family members?
4.   In what ways would you hope/expect that daily and weekly routines would be easier or at least as "back-to normal" as possible?
5.   What concerns are your greatest priority now?
6.   What ramifications of your child's diagnosis concern you most? What "unknowns" do you feel we need to be sure to address?
7.   Who are the people you want to be sure are included on your "team?"
8.   What can we do to be sure "team players" work together without an overwhelming number of appointments or efforts to strike out in different directions?

TRANSITION PROCESS

Because DEIP is by definition a relatively short-term diagnostic placement, care and attention to transition is necessary from the beginning. The closeness and importance of the family's relationship with their first parent/infant specialist is well recognized. Parents need help to realize that the working partnership established with their DEIP advocate, however critical, is a short-term one dedicated to discovering the "most appropriate" communication system and intervention program for their family. When focus is maintained on empowering the family with knowledge and skills while data necessary for decision making are gathered, the family's first intervention experience can become a positive prototype from which they can continue to develop necessary advocacy and coping skills. Parent and professional staff meetings, visitations, and even joint intervention sessions with staff of the subsequent intervention program is time well spent in ensuring that the transition process is a smooth one. The DEIP advocate strives to ensure the transfer of all the information necessary for the next professional to step into the habilitation process without a missed beat.

FAMILY SUPPORT PROGRAMS

Providing support for families who are adjusting to the impact of hearing impairment is a key component of DEIP. Family members need to talk about their feelings and fears regarding their child's disability with others who can provide empathic and objective feedback within an accepting, trustworthy environment. Counseling is an inherent, necessary function of the parent/DEIP advocate relationship so that desired family and child outcomes can be achieved (Schuyler and Rushmer 1987). Counseling is provided by a psychologist with the DEIP advocate in conjunction with the child's psychological/developmental evaluation. Typically, the focus on the child's hearing loss during the early months after identification has eclipsed the parents' view of their child's needs and abilities as a whole. Helping families gain a whole-child perspective is a goal of the developmental evaluation; helping families gain a whole-family perspective is a goal of family assessment by the program's family specialist, a counselor. Families gain insight into their own family system and their strengths, needs, goals, ways of problem solving, and coping with crisis. They learn about their relationships and support networks. Parents empowered with appreciation of their family's needs and abilities are better able to achieve balance and to cope effectively with stress related to hearing impairment.

The DEIP team has come to realize that families need, early in the intervention process, "a sense of community, a sense that others can understand or have experienced and survived what they are feeling" (Schuyler and Rushmer 1987, p. 147). During the early years of DEIP, on-going involvement in parent support groups was deferred until decisions regarding communication modality and consequent intervention program were made. When asked how the DEIP experience could be improved for future families, parents urged staff to provide more opportunities for mutual support by parents early: "I would make sure that you had a support group; none of you know how much that helped me." "I felt a need in the beginning to interact with other parents of deaf children and to see other young deaf children." "One of the best experiences, that I wish had been repeated several times through DEIP, was the parent nights during the Parent/Child Workshop week when we went out to dinner and got to just sit and ask other parents questions." Recent efforts to give parents routine access to a support group during DEIP have met with enthusiasm, reflected in attendance, participation, and feedback, from both "new" and "veteran" families who sensitively explore the issues, realizations, and decisions faced soon after identification.

A biweekly parent/toddler group provided as part of BTNRH's total communication parent/infant program has not only provided DEIP families with access to an on-going parent support group but served as a diagnostic placement for selected children as well. Participation in the children's group has given parents hope, appreciation for how communication competence develops, and a "lab" in which to hone their skills. Parents learn to promote conversational language and social skills through play with their own and other hearing-impaired children. Parents and professionals can address complex diagnostic questions such as the impact of signing on speech and language development, the impact of behavior problems on learning, or the impact of additional handicaps on overall functioning for some children in DEIP. Counseling, speech/language, occupational, and physical therapy services are integral components of the parent/toddler group experience. Diagnostic group experiences in other settings offering auditory/oral communication only have also been arranged when needed.

David Luterman (personal communication) has often advised, "If a parent program is designed to meet parent-identified needs, it will be effective." This premise has been a guiding principle in the design of a Family Sign Program that is available for appropriate DEIP families. The program focuses on helping families gain functional sign communication skills to promote successful interactions with their children. This has required inclusion of vocabulary and concepts necessary for daily interaction with young children (Luetke-Stahlman and Moeller 1990) and focus on interactions that are typical in family dyads (e.g., bedtime stories, table grace, and gaming rituals). Family members are asked to critique lesson approaches regularly and contribute topics, vocabulary, and skills. The open critique policy has led to parental "ownership" of the class. They are confident that the program is evolving for the primary purpose of meeting their needs. Their contributions make this goal possible. The program includes a sibling class, where sibs, neighborhood children, and cousins gain skills for interaction with the deaf child. A videotape "homework" program allows the families to extend their learning beyond class and involve family members who are unable to attend. The team has discovered that program success has been directly proportional to the instructor's responsiveness to suggestions from families about their needs.

PROJECT OUTCOMES

The Diagnostic Early Intervention Project has provided families with a systematic mechanism for discovering their child's primary needs and for gaining access to appropriate services. In the past, parents were often provided with a single point of view regarding their child's immediate needs following diagnosis and were not encouraged to consider alternatives. Parents participating in DEIP have been shown that an appropriate program must consider their child's unique needs. Parental participation in the ongoing discovery process allows them to make informed decisions based on an understanding of how their child functions.

Parents have reported a high level of comfort and satisfaction with the communication modality or program choice, once they have been through this process. This is in distinct contrast to the OPS district's experience prior to the implementation of DEIP. Prior to DEIP, the district was involved in several due process hearings regarding inappropriate placements. Nineteen of thirty-eight families who were provided with early intervention had to make a modality or placement change in the early elementary grades. Longitudinal follow-up on the DEIP participants indicates a striking stability in placements and modality choice; sixty-seven of seventy have successfully maintained the placement or modality recommended by the DEIP team. Undoubtedly, the positive shift in outcome has been cost-effective for the district and for families. Importantly, the authors believe that the approach has been pro-active, and has allowed for maximum use of the early intervention period for children and families.

Another important outcome of DEIP has been the early identification of multiple handicaps in participating children. Funding for DEIP has been structured so that neither the district nor BTNRH is tied to a predetermined battery of procedures. Rather, team members are free to explore areas of concern to identify possible undiagnosed problems that will affect the child's learning ability. These findings are considered jointly by team members in order to determine implications and provide input. The net effect of this is to collaborate with parents to obtain an integrated view of their child, rather than a file of separate reports that they must interpret. The approach also provides the clinical staff with broad expertise and experience necessary to recognize variety and range of handicaps typical in these children (Moeller, Coufal, and Hixson 1990).

ONGOING CHALLENGES AND FUTURE NEEDS

Team members have learned a great deal from families over the past eight years, but much is yet to be learned. The area that has been perhaps the most challenging to the team is that of dealing with families different than the professionals' own families. In some cases, professionals have had difficulty resisting biases or negative predictions about apparently "dysfunctional" families.

Ongoing challenges include working with needy families. Those whose basic needs for food, shelter, medical care, and safety are unmet, typically are involved with multiple service agencies. Sadly, social service agencies tend to focus narrowly on the single problem they are mandated and funded to ameliorate. Case workers frequently change. Addressing problems in a whole family context across agencies is challenging. The DEIP advocates' task of empowering such families can be a frustrating one.

Truly dysfunctional families—abusive or with untreated mental illness—do not or cannot act in the best interests of the child. Establishing collaborative partnerships with such families is challenging. Dovetailing intervention efforts with those of mental health professionals involved is critical. The DEIP advocate and team often face difficult problem analysis, decision making and consequent course of action, as they weigh commitment to family-centered intervention with responsibility for the child. Coping with limitations is often a painful process.

Improving the ability to provide culturally sensitive intervention is another area of ongoing growth for the DEIP team. Transition issues for children, families, and professionals also continue to challenge the DEIP team as it strives to gain insight into the conversations and activities necessary to ensure that transition is a process, not an event.

The DEIP team originally set out on a quest for a neat formula that would predict children's needs. Instead, team members gained a healthy respect for the dynamic nature of development—in families, children, and teams. Team members discovered that the DEIP process would always be a growing, evolutionary one. The program cannot be described as an end-product. Rather, it represents a developmental, dynamic process, in which team members continually re-examine beliefs, strategies, and outcomes. The team, itself, has been empowered by recognizing that its own developmental process is dynamic.

APPENDIX A   FOURTEEN FACTORS AND MEASUREMENT STRATEGIES

I.   Family Support/Strengths

   A. *Faces III:* (D. Olsen, J. Portner and Y.Lavee, Family Social Science, University of Minnesota, 290 McNeal Hall, St. Paul, MN 55108) A self-report, clinical rating scale based on the Circumplex Model of Family Systems, administered by a social worker.

   B. *Family Satisfaction Scale:* (D. Olsen and W. Marc, Family Social Science, University of Minnesota, 290 McNeal Hall, St. Paul, MN 55108) This scale is used by a social worker to assess the degree of satisfaction caregivers feel with their present situation.

   C. *CHIP:* Coping-Health Inventory for Parents: (H. McCubbin, M. McCubbin, R. Nevin, and E. Cauble, Family Stress Coping and Health Project, 1300 Linden Drive, University of Wisconsin-Madison, Madison, WI 53706)

Records that parents find helpful or not helpful to them in the management of family life when a member has a condition that requires continued care.

D. *Home Observation for Measurement of the Environment:* (B.M. Caldwell and R. H. Bradley, University of Arkansas, Little Rock, AR 72204) Assesses family dynamics, objects, and experiences available in homes.

E. *Family Needs Survey:* (D. Bailey and R. Simeonsson, Frank Porter Graham Child Development Center, University of North Carolina, Chapel Hill, NC 27599) This 35-item scale assesses family needs in the areas of support, information, financial resources, explaining to others, child care, and community support and services.

F. *Family Support Scale:* (Dunst, Trivette, and Deal 1988) This series of brief questionnaires helps identify parental support systems, needs, and perceived priorities.

II. **Parent/Child Interaction**

A. *Caregiver-Child Interactive Behaviors:* (Cole and Claire-Stokes 1984) This videotape analysis procedure allows for assessment of the caregiver/child dyad during free play.

B. *Hanen Early Language Stimulation Program:* (A. Manolsen, Hanen Early Language Resource Centre, 252 Bloor St., W., Room 4-126, Toronto, Ontario M5S 1V6) Coding materials from the intervention program, "It Takes Two to Talk," are used to document changes in parental communicative style resulting from parent-focused intervention.

III. **Parental Compliance/Preference**

Compliance and preference are measured indirectly through documentation in the following areas: (1) Attendance records; (2) Records indicating parental changes in targeted behaviors in response to individualized guidance; (3) Parental involvement in IEP process; and (4) Interviews related to communication modality preferences.

IV. **Etiological Factors**

Etiological factors are examined through a thorough medical/genetic test battery, completed under the direction of the team pediatrician.

V. **Developmental Status**

Developmental evaluations are completed to determine the level of the child's psychomotor/cognitive skills. Cautious interpretation of early developmental measures is exercised, given the lack of predictive validity of these types of measures. Developmental scales used cautiously by the team include the following.

A. *Bayley Scales:* (Bayley 1993) These are infant scales that measure development across several domains.

B. *INSITE Developmental Checklist:* Assessment of developmental skills for young multihandicapped sensory-impaired children. (E. Morgan and S. Watkins, SKI*HI Institute, Department of Communicative Disorders, Utah State University, Logan, Utah 84322) This checklist is used by parents and parent advisors to monitor development and set appropriate goals.

C. *Hawaii Early Learning Profile: Help . . . at Home:* (S. Parks, S. Furuno, K. O'Reilly, C. Hosaka, T. Inatsuka, and B. Zeisloft-Falbey, Vort Corporation, Palo Alto, CA 94306) This program contains a comprehensive collection of developmental activity sheets that are given to parents with children in the developmental age range of birth to 36 months.

D. *Minnesota Infant and Child Development Inventories:* (H. Ireton and E. Thwing, Behavior Science Systems, Box 1108, Minneapolis, MN 55458).

VI. **Medical Status**

In addition to the medical/genetic studies discussed above, children in the project receive regular pediatric visits. The pediatrician is responsible for coordinating medical aspects of the evaluation and reporting to the DEIP team.

VII. **Audiological Factors**

A. *Auditory Brainstem Response (ABR)* is completed on all neonates who graduate from the intensive care nursery. High-risk registries are used to assist early identification efforts.

B. *Pediatric Audiological Evaluation and ongoing Amplification Needs Assessments.* Loaner aids are provided during the period of evaluation, and the parent/child facilitator participates in the process of examining instrument efficacy.

C. Regular electroacoustic impedance studies are completed to monitor the middle ear system.

VIII. **Age of Identification/Amplification**

To monitor this factor, the team documents: (1) Dates/age of identification of the hearing loss; (2) Dates/age of fitting of amplification; and (3) Frequency and duration of daily hearing aid use through logs completed by the parent and clinician.

IX. **Documentation of Secondary Handicaps**

Additional handicapping conditions are identified through the following mechanisms: (1) multidisciplinary evaluations and staffings/case management; (2) developmental evaluations (described above); and (3) monitoring of learning rates.

X. Motor Development

If significant delays are observed in motor milestones, the psychological evaluation is augmented with OT/PT and vestibular evaluations. Speech physiology evaluations may be obtained when oral motor deficits are suspected.

XI. Interpersonal/Social Development

The play evaluation schemes are used to evaluate the child's schemes in relating to objects and persons in the environment, and the child's level of complexity of play skills. Tools include:

A. Assessing Linguistic Behaviors (Olswang et al.1987).

B. Play Scale (Westby 1988).

XII. Learning Rates in Communication

Daily intervention data, ongoing language sample analyses and limited pre-post standardized or criterion-referenced measures contribute to evaluation of learning rates. Communicative evaluation tools used include:

A. *Assessing Linguistic Behaviors* (referenced in item XI above).

B. *Sensorimotor Communication Profile* (C. George, Meyer Children's Rehabilitation Institute, 444 South 44th Street, Omaha, NE, 68131)

C. *Communication and Symbolic Behavior Scales* (A. Wetherby and B. Prizant, Special Press, Inc., 474 N. Lake Shore Drive, Ste. 3910, Chicago, IL 60611)

D. *MacArthur Communicative Development Inventory* (Infant and Toddler Scales used) (P. Dale and D. Thal, Center for Research in Language, UCSD, San Diego, CA 92093)

E. *SKI*HI Language Development Scales* (S. Tonelson, and S. Watkins. Project SKI*HI, Logan, UT)

XIII. Phonological Development

Phonological development is monitored using the categorization scheme developed by Dr. Carol Stoel-Gammon and incorporated in the *Assessing Linguistic Behaviors* scales (referenced above). Functional use of vocalizations is monitored using the Communicative Intention Inventory of Coggins and Carpenter, also a part of the ALB.

XIV. Auditory Learning

Formal audiological results are supplemented with naturalistic observations of the child's auditory responsiveness to the environment over time. Measures include the *Minimal Auditory Integration Scale* (Robbins 1991) and a team-constructed criterion referenced scale, *Functional Auditory Abilities*.

REFERENCES

Andrews, J., and Andrews, M. 1986. A family based systemic model for speech-language services. *Seminars in Speech and Language* 7(4):359–65.

Bailey, D. B., and Simeonsson, R. J. 1986. Design issues in family impact evaluations. In *Evaluating Early Intervention Programs for Severly Handicapped Children and Their Families*, eds. L. Bickman and D. L. Weatherford. Austin: PRO-ED.

Bailey, D. J. 1987. Collaborative goal setting with families: Resolving differences in values and priorities for service. *Topics in Early Childhood Education* 7(2):59–71.

Bayley, N. 1993. *Bayley Scales.* New York: The Psychological Corporation.

Cadman, D., Goldsmith, C., and Bashim, P. 1984. Values, preferences, and decisions in the care of children with developmental disabilities. *Developmental and Behavioral Pediatrics* 5(2):60–64.

Cole, E., and Claire-Stokes, J. 1984. Caregiver-child interaction behaviors: A videotape analysis procedure. *Volta Review* 86(4):200–16.

Downs, M. 1974. Deafness management quotient (DMQ). *Hearing and Speech News* 42:26–28.

Dunst, C. J. 1985. Rethinking early intervention. *Analysis and Intervention in Developmental Disabilities* 5:165–201.

Dunst, C. J., Trivett, C. M., and Deal, A. G. 1988. *Enabling and Empowering Families: Principles and Guidelines for Practice.* Cambridge, MA: Brookline Books.

Ensher, G. L. 1989. The first three years: Special education perspectives on assessment and intervention. *Topics in Language Disorders* 10(1):80–90.

Fitzgerald, M. T., and Fischer, R. M. 1987. A family involvement model for hearing-impaired infants. *Topics in Language Disorders* 7:1–19.

Geers, A., and Moog, J. 1987. Predicting spoken language acquisition of profoundly hearing-impaired children. *Journal of Speech and Hearing Disorders* 52:84–94.

Healy, A., Keesee, P. D., and Smith, B. S. 1985. *Early Services for Children with Special Needs: Transactions for Family Support.* Iowa City: University of Iowa Division of Developmental Disabilities.

Idol, L., Paolucci-Whitcomb, P., and Nevin, A. 1986. *Collaborative Consultation.* Rockville, MD: Aspen.

Kilburg, G. 1990. Family assessment: The family as a context for language learning. Short course at ASHA convention, November 1990, Seattle.

Luetke-Stahlman, B., and Moeller, M. P. 1990. Enhancing parents' use of signing exact English: Progress and retention. *American Annals of the Deaf* 135(5):371–79.

Luterman, D. 1991. *Counseling the Communicatively Disordered and Their Families*, 2nd Ed. Austin: PRO-ED.

Luterman, D. Personal communication.

McCubbin, H. I., and Thompson, A. I. 1987. *Family Assessment Inventories for Research and Practice.* Madison: University of Wisconsin-Madison.

Moeller, M. P., Coufal, K., and Hixson, P. 1990. The efficacy of speech-language intervention: Hearing impaired children. *Seminars in Speech and Language* 11(4):227–41.

Olswang, L., Stoel-Gammon, C., Coggins, T., and Carpenter, R. 1987. *Assessing Linguistic Behavior* (ALB). Seattle: University of Washington Press.

Robbins, A. 1991. Developing meaningful auditory integration in children with cochlear implants. *Volta Review* 91(7): 361–71.

Roush, J., and McWilliam, R. A. 1990. A new challenge for pediatric audiology: Public Law 99–457. *Journal of the American Academy of Audiology 1(4):196–208.*

Schuyler, V., and Rushmer, N. 1987. *Parent Infant Habilitation: A Comprehensive Approach to Working With Hearing-Impaired Infants and Toddlers and Their Families.* Portland: IHR Publications.

Schwartz, S. (ed.). 1987. *Choices in Deafness. (Foreword by S. Doctors.)* Kensington, MD: Woodbine House, Inc.

Segal, M. 1988. *In Time and With Love: Caring for the Special Needs Baby.* New York: New Market Press.

Siegel, G. 1975. The use of language tests. *Language, Speech & Hearing Services in the Schools* 4:211–17.

Simmons-Martin, A., and Rossi, K. 1990. *Parents and Teachers: Partners in Language Development.* Washington: A. G. Bell Association for the Deaf.

Simons, R. 1987. *After the Tears: Parents Talk About Raising a Child With a Disability.* San Diego: Harcourt Brace Jovanovich.

Sparks, S. N. 1989. Assessment and intervention with at-risk infants and toddlers: Guidelines for the speech-language pathologist. *Topics in Language Disorders* 10(1):43–56.

Trout, M., and Foley, G. 1989. Working with families of handicapped infants and toddlers. *Topics in Language Disorders* 10(1):57-67.

Winton, P. J. 1990. Promoting a normalizing approach to families: Integrating theory with practice. *Topics in Early Childhood Special Education* 10(2):90–103.

PART • IV

**Family-Centered
Early Intervention
*Implementation Models***

Chapter • 10

The Mama Lere Home
Vanderbilt University

Rebecca M. Fischer

The evolution of the Mama Lere Early Intervention Program, founded in 1966 with a demonstration grant from the Bureau of Education for the Handicapped, reflects the changes that have occurred in parent-infant training during the past 25 years (Fitzgerald and Bess 1982). The impetus for change has come from two primary sources: (1) changes in demographics of the population served and (2) new theoretical perspectives on language development in young children with disabilities.

As did many programs, the Mama Lere Program began as child-centered intervention. Following assessment, specific objectives in the areas of auditory training and amplification, speech, and language were selected and "taught" using parents as their childrens' primary teacher (Knox and McConnell 1968; Northcott 1972; Pollack 1970). The role of parents was to provide the children with experiences similar to those of any other child and to use language connected with objects and activities in the surrounding environment as a vehicle for stimulating communication development (McConnell 1974).

From this child-focused beginning, the program gradually moved toward a family-based model. Information on the impact of hearing impairment on the family system suggested that additional components should be incorporated into the early intervention program in order to meet family needs more completely (Breslau, Weitzman, and Messenger 1982; Luterman 1979; Moses 1985; Murphy

1979). The interactive roles of parent and infant continued to be documented (Clarke-Stewart and Apfel 1978; DePaulo and Bonvillian 1978; Lewis and Rosenblum 1974; Snow and Ferguson 1977), as well as the differences in interaction between parents of hearing and hearing-impaired children (Greenberg 1980; Greenstein et al. 1977; Meadow et al. 1981). Thus, it seemed appropriate to assimilate new theories on families and language development with earlier practices (Bill Wilkerson Hearing and Speech Center 1984; Fitzgerald and Fischer 1987).

As a result of developments over the past quarter-century, two premises have evolved to guide intervention with families of hearing-impaired children (Fitzgerald and Fischer 1987). The first is:

> The family is the social context in which the child grows and develops—emotionally, communicatively, and physically.

Providing a family with skills necessary to assist a child is one of the primary roles of a parent-infant specialist. A parent, however, is not only a "language facilitator," but has other roles and responsibilities as well. Often other circumstances impinge on a family and its members, including a hearing-impaired child. In order to provide a child with an environment conducive to learning communication skills, a clinician must first meet family needs, which will then enable parents to begin assisting the child.

I am reminded of a humbling experience that emphasizes the influence of outside events on families. Several years ago I worked with a young hearing-impaired child from a family of modest means. Although the child's parents had recently separated, the child had a supportive mother and grandmother who attended intervention sessions and seemed interested in and capable of learning strategies to help the child. In time, however, it became obvious that generalization to the home environment was minimal, especially with regard to consistent use of amplification. I became frustrated and was unable to understand the dichotomy between the adults' commitment and their lack of follow-through. One day, however, as I walked out to the car with the family, I noticed a large, perhaps 50 pound, sack of potatoes in the back of the car. I commented on it and the grandmother replied, matter of factly, "Well, that's what we're going to eat for the rest of the month." In that moment, the family's situation became clear to me: they had more urgent concerns than the child's hearing aid and language development, and, although they were truly interested in helping their child, resources were very limited.

It is this aspect of the family that we have come to recognize as a crucial component in early intervention and that leads us to the second premise of the program:

Each family possesses unique needs for economic, social, and emotional support, in addition to the usual information and guidance regarding the communication development of their child.

Family status is an important component of parent training, having an impact on the parents' ability to provide a rich communicative environment and on the child's capacity to derive benefit from such. Changes in family circumstances have demanded that we provide a wider variety of options for intervention, interact with other programs in offering supportive services, and increase our sensitivity to the needs of families outside the immediate demands of the hearing-impaired child. Certainly, passage of P.L. 99-457, Education of the Handicapped Act Amendments of 1986, suggests that the federal government recognizes the need for a national policy of access to services, not only for handicapped and at-risk children, but for their families as well.

SERVICE DELIVERY COMPONENTS

Four service delivery components enable staff members to implement a program that attempts to fulfill the two premises of parent-infant intervention (Fitzgerald and Fischer 1987). Through supportive counseling, information exchange, educational advocacy, and facilitation of parent-child communicative competence, the objective is to provide the family with the assistance needed to understand hearing loss and its impact on the child and family, communicate effectively with their child, and plan for their child's future. Recognizing that the latter two goals are shared by all parents, intervention seeks to "normalize" the relationship between parent and child and to "minimize" possible negative outcomes. By offering a variety of options, a clinician can individualize each implementation plan according to family, parent, and child needs (figure 1).

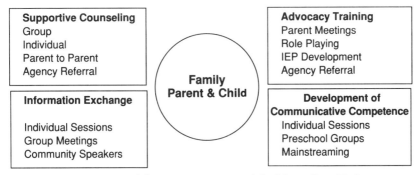

Figure 1.   Four service delivery components of the Mama Lere Early Intervention Program.

The need for supportive counseling occurs throughout intervention; during the first few months following diagnosis, however, this need often goes unacknowledged by parents. Thus, it falls on clinicians to listen carefully to parents and decipher the "true" questions or information being sought (Luterman 1979). To meet the personal preferences of parents from diverse backgrounds and experiences, individual and group counseling opportunities are offered. Individual counseling may occur during therapy sessions as a clinician and parent discuss issues pertinent to the family's circumstances. Parents of a child who has been recently diagnosed with a hearing impairment may also be paired with parents of an older hearing-impaired child who can offer unique insight and support. Small parent groups provide a third means of sharing experiences and "brainstorming" possible solutions to the daily challenges of raising a child with a hearing impairment. Opportunities to participate in activities and share experiences are also provided for siblings of the hearing-impaired child. Finally, if a clinician feels that a parent's emotional needs require the expertise of a professional counselor, a referral is made to a social worker, psychologist, or psychiatrist for in-depth therapy. Regardless of the options chosen by a parent, supportive counseling offers an opportunity to acknowledge emotions and feel empowered to manage short- and long-term challenges.

The feeling of empowerment is enhanced through exchange of information between parents and professionals. Information exchange is an important component of weekly therapy sessions and offers parents an opportunity to be active participants in the intervention process from the beginning. A clinician emphasizes that it is parents who are the "experts" on their children, while the clinician provides information related to those childrens' hearing impairment. Parents learn that, through information exchange, an individualized therapy program appropriate for parent and child is developed. Weekend and evening parent meetings also serve as learning formats. Here the focus is on offering families information on high-priority topics chosen by parents; for example, speech and language development, new advances in amplification, life as a hearing-impaired teenager and adult, and career choices. Outside speakers are incorporated into the second component in an effort to give parents different perspectives and additional resources for information and assistance.

The third component is educational advocacy in which parents learn to participate actively in monitoring and developing intervention plans for their child. Although the Mama Lere Early Intervention Program is a private preschool program, parents learn skills that enable them to work effectively with their child's home school district in securing appropriate educational services. The staff emphasizes a collaborative rather than an adversarial role with public school systems.

Through informative meetings, role playing, and participation in planning their child's intervention program at the parent-infant level, parents begin to understand their role and responsibility in the educational process. Parents acquire observational skills to assist them in monitoring their child's program, information on options available for their child (Nix 1977; Testut and Baldwin 1977), and knowledge of the multidisciplinary team approach for developing individualized education programs (IEPs). By working with a local agency, Effective Advocacy for Citizens with Handicaps, the Mama Lere staff provides parents with additional information and support as they work with school systems to secure an appropriate education for their child.

The final component of the program focuses on establishing, enhancing, and maintaining communication between a parent and child. It is important to note that the emphasis is on facilitating communicative competence of *both parent and child*. Each partner is recognized for his or her respective contribution to the interaction (Kretschmer and Kretschmer 1979). Regardless of the level at which a child is functioning, developing parental interactional skills is a priority of the therapy process. Thus, as a child continues to develop more sophisticated communication, the parent also learns how to modify interactive behaviors to reward and augment the child's skills effectively.

Through an intervention model involving three primary steps—assessment, identification of objectives, and implementation—the four service delivery components are integrated within a therapy program uniquely designed for each family (figure 2). By incorporating a model in which these three steps re-occur in a spiral fashion, changes in child and family status can be incorporated readily into therapy and a variety of implementation programs can be offered to meet the individual needs of participants.

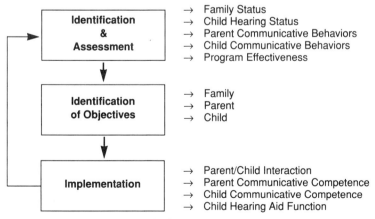

Figure 2.   Intervention model for the Mama Lere Program.

THE INTERVENTION MODEL

Because every family is unique, the intervention model serves as a framework for providing respective families with the supportive services required to help their hearing-impaired child (Fischer and Kenworthy 1988; Kenworthy and Fischer 1988). Rather than specify a curriculum for all families, clinicians choose from a number of resources and design a program that will best assist a particular family. Assessment and implementation tools are selected that enable the clinician to individualize each step of the intervention process.

Assessment

During the assessment phase, five questions guide the clinician in obtaining information necessary to begin providing appropriate supportive services for a family (table I).

Based on the premises of the Mama Lere Early Intervention Program, that is, the importance of the family to a child's continued development and the unique needs of each family, intervention first involves assessment of the family's status. Through interviews and an extensive history, strengths and needs are evaluated, and the impact of family circumstances on the child's and parents' development is analyzed. By first examining the family constellation, the clinician determines what initial services and support the family may require and plans accordingly. For many of the families served, financial assistance requires working with public and private agencies to secure funding for amplification and therapy.

Understanding the child's and parents' present level of ability enables the clinician to plan a program that addresses immediate needs for building communication between parent and child. Assessment involves analyzing the interaction between parent and child (Cole and St. Clair-Stokes 1984; Garrard 1991; Russo and Owens

Table I.   Questions To Guide the Assessment Process

1. What are the strengths and needs of the family?
2. At what level of ability are child and parent currently functioning?
3. What is the next stage or level in developing communication competence for parent and child?
4. Is rate of development adequate for parent and child goals?
5. What is the most effective intervention approach to adequately develop the communication skills of parent and child?
    —Supportive services
    —Program options
    —Communication methodology
    —Structured/unstructured approach
    —Elicitation strategies

1982) to determine how well parent input matches the child's current skills and supports the development of more complex communicative behaviors. The parent's ability to stimulate speech, language, and auditory skills is also assessed. Child behaviors are usually evaluated informally using clinician observations and parental reports to establish baseline data via observational checklists (Ling 1978; Northcott 1972). Information is supplemented with formal tests of language production and comprehension, speech, and auditory skills, as well as language/speech sampling procedures appropriate for the child's level of functioning. Other skill areas are screened (gross and fine motor, cognitive, oral-motor, self-help, and personal-social), followed by referrals for more in-depth evaluation if necessary.

To integrate assessment and implementation, it is necessary that the evaluation procedure assists the clinician in formulating future objectives for intervention. In general, the linkage between assessment and implementation tends to be rather weak, and few assessment/implementation packages meet the needs of the diverse populations served by the parent-infant specialist. Rather than incorporate a single assessment-implementation protocol, the Mama Lere Program uses an outline for developing communicative competence and selects evaluation procedures that examine the child's and parent's current communication abilities and help the clinician and parent develop future therapy goals, as specified in the outline.

Rate of development is an issue critical to evaluating the success of any intervention program, but it is rarely discussed. Some measure of progress can occur for almost any intervention program; however, it is clear from the data of older, hearing-impaired students (Trybus and Karchmer 1977) that one primary cause of the deficiencies of hearing-impaired learners compared to hearing learners is the difference in rate of development, specifically the "leveling off" of the learning curve. Unfortunately, there is little normative data on development of a hearing-impaired child at the parent-infant level. Yet, it is imperative that the clinician evaluate the intervention plan critically in order to determine whether the combination of parent support, child objectives, and implementation strategies are effectively moving both parent and child toward communicative competence. Some formal assessment instruments, such as The Grammatical Analysis of Elicited Language Tests (Moog and Geers 1979; Moog, Kozak, and Geers 1983), provide the clinician with normative data and can be used in combination with language development outlines (Bloom and Lahey 1978; Miller 1981) to determine whether the rate of progress is appropriate for accomplishment of long-term objectives.

The most effective intervention approach is one that allows both parent and child to develop communicative competence, recognizes their individual abilities and needs, and facilitates development in a timely manner. For implementation to be effective, a clinician must monitor family and child status, and be alert to changes that may dictate modifications in the intervention plan. Flexibility in designing effective programs is provided by assessing and modifying five major elements in the implementation plan.

1. Family support services include financial assistance from the private sector in the form of scholarships and fee reductions for therapy, and public assistance such as Supplemental Security Income. In addition, counseling programs mentioned previously also help families adjust to life changes. As family circumstances change, different support services may be required to allow the family to continue active involvement in their child's intervention.

2. A variety of program options also helps maximize the effectiveness of implementation plans for family participants. For example, in addition to individual weekly or twice-weekly parent-infant sessions, children may be enrolled in a preschool classroom for hearing-impaired children. Such placement may be predicated by knowledge that the child requires a more intensive program than can be provided by individual sessions. Alternatively, for working families who cannot find or afford adequate day care, a daily preschool program enables their children to continue to make gains in communication skills. Part- or full-time mainstreaming in a community school in combination with individual therapy or a group preschool class offers families a means of gradually integrating their children into schools of their choice.

3. Methodological decisions also have an impact on an intervention's effectiveness. In choosing a mode of communication, parent involvement is crucial. Parents are strongly encouraged to make the decision and are given support and information during the process. In the first months of therapy, parents are exposed to methodological issues via written materials, discussion with the parent-infant specialist, interaction with other parents, and observation. When a method has been chosen, it is presented as a *means to an end*—the objective being child communicative competence—rather than an end in itself. Thus, parents come to realize that communication methods can be modified to meet changes in the child and family system. Emphasis on methodology as a tool helps eliminate some of the emotional overtones surrounding this issue.

4. The therapist may decide to use either a structured or an unstructured approach to language learning, depending upon a number of factors. Regardless of the approach, the goal is to design an environment that enhances and supports the development of communication skills by the child. The amount of structure may be modified,

especially if there is a change in the child's hearing status. Modifications also may occur for short periods of time while a child is learning a specific communication skill that requires structuring situations that maximize the child's chances for success. It is important to note that the use of structure does not require that the parent become a "teacher of the hearing impaired"; rather, it challenges both parent and teacher to alter the environment and/or linguistic input, thus assisting the child to acquire new communication behaviors.

5. Specific elicitation techniques are effective intervention strategies if they match the child's level of functioning. Research examining language models suggests that no one model is superior; rather, conversational practices may be more or less useful depending upon the child's skills and language objectives (Yoder, Kaiser, and Alpert 1991) Thus, the aim of parent-infant intervention is to monitor and modify parental input in order to facilitate the development of more sophisticated linguistic behaviors on the part of the child.

As a result of the assessment process, clinician and parents evaluate the use of a number of intervention strategies. They continue to implement techniques that further the goal of communicative competence and to modify techniques to accelerate the process. Assessment becomes an ongoing, interactive procedure viewed as a valuable tool in and of itself in the intervention plan.

Identification of Objectives

Following assessment, objectives for the family, parent, and child are delineated. The process is a collaborative one between clinician and parent. In this manner, the parent has an investment in the intervention process and assumes the role of a partner with the parent-infant specialist. A number of resources (Bill Wilkerson Hearing and Speech Center 1984; Bloom and Lahey 1978; Garrard 1991; Hasenstab and Horner 1982; Northcott 1972; Miller 1981; Pollack 1970; Schuyler et al. 1985) are available to a clinician for selecting objectives toward building communicative competence.

Implementation

Following selection of short-term goals, the implementation process begins to build a foundation for communication between parent and child. Implementation is a three-step process focusing first on building interaction patterns between parent and child, next on assisting the parent in acquiring skills necessary to encourage elementary verbal/signed communication skills in the child, and finally on helping the child develop sophisticated linguistic behaviors. The ultimate objective is the establishment of communicative competence in both parent and child.

ESTABLISHING COMMUNICATIVE COMPETENCE

Building Interaction Patterns

In the process of adjusting to the hearing handicap, parents naturally are worried about their child's ability to communicate. These anxieties may be expressed as, "When will my child begin to talk/sign?" or "Will my child 'catch up' by the time she goes to kindergarten?" The parent's expression of concern early in the intervention process provides a clinician with the opportunity to direct the parent toward the goal of establishing effective and rewarding communication with his or her child. In fact, it is the "establishment of good communication patterns between parent and child," rather than the "development of speech and language skills" per se that is the primary focus of early intervention. Although the distinction may be subtle, it has important implications for the way in which therapy is implemented.

This approach acknowledges the primary role of the parent in helping the child develop a viable communication system and the importance of establishing a special rapport between parent and child so that *daily activities can serve as a basis for pleasant interactions and, consequently, language development*. Note that the interaction between parent and child is the precursor to, rather than the consequence of, language development.

Building parents' confidence in their ability to help their children develop language skills is achieved by establishing a foundation of general language stimulation techniques. Skills learned enable parents to engage in "conversations" with their hearing-impaired children that are positive and rewarding for both participants. As children develop more advanced forms of communication, parents then learn to stimulate specific language, speech, and auditory skills, always within the context of a dialog in which both partners—parent and child—have acquired basic interaction skills.

Observations of mothers and normally developing infants reveal that much communication occurs between mothers and nonverbal infants (Ainsworth and Bell 1974; Bateson 1975; Brazelton, Koslowski, and Main 1974), yet parents of hearing-impaired children typically ignore their children's efforts to communicate nonverbally by using gestures and nonvocal behaviors typical of much younger children. Because more sophisticated communicative behaviors have not developed, interactions between a parent and a hearing-impaired child can be anxious, frustrating, and demanding. Expectation of unrealistic behaviors may cause a parent to be unable to see how the child is communicating. Thus, one of the first goals in implementation is to develop good parental observation skills so the child's efforts to communicate are recognized, acknowledged, and rewarded. By coaching the parent and allowing him or her to observe the clinician interacting with the child, the parent-infant specialist helps the parent interpret and respond to child communication efforts using the surrounding environment and activities.

During initial sessions, identification of and response to child behaviors establishes turn-taking between parent and child. Turn-taking then serves as the foundation for development of communicative competence. The establishment of turn-taking at the prevocal level provides child and parent with a framework within which conversation and language learning occur. Although the parent must drive the system in the beginning and assume responsibility for creating conversations by fitting his or her responses between the child's communicative attempts, through many hours of conversations, the child learns to imitate and then to initiate verbalizations. The result is development of true interaction as both partners begin to share the responsibility for dialog.

Encouraging Elementary Child Verbal Skills

Once turn-taking skills are established, parental responses are modified to promote language development in the hearing-impaired child. Through *The Rules of Talking* (Bill Wilkerson Hearing and Speech Center 1979), parents learn to establish and promote enjoyable interaction by learning skills that move the parent and child from the preverbal to verbal levels (table II).

The parent first learns that establishing a climate for communication is important for helping the child develop language. The parent is encouraged to speak close to the child, at eye level, to promote attention and to vary voice quality to establish and maintain the child's attention. Parents learn that any activity is a language-learning opportunity if the child is interested. Thus, "following the child's lead" is a prerequisite for creating an environment in which the child is motivated to learn to communicate. Highly structured activities such as "peek-a-boo" and other games played by the parent and child enable the child to learn and anticipate his or her role in the interaction. Other less-structured activities such as dressing, feeding, and bathing offer the child opportunities to see how his or her behavior influences the parent. Everyday activities provide the child with many repetitions of language he or she will soon be learning.

Table II.   Rules of Talking

—Creating the Climate for Communication—
—Listening for a Child's Message—
—Making Talk Relevant—
—Encouraging a Child to Use Voice to Make Sounds—
—Helping a Child Understand Words—
—Talking When a Child Begins to Use Words—

Next, the parent learns to listen for the child's message. Observing the child, listening to the tone of voice, and using the surrounding environment help the parent interpret the child's meaning. The parent also learns to provide the child with an opportunity to participate in conversation by allowing the child to take a turn. The emphasis is on encouraging vocal or signed attempts at communication by the child. This may require the parent to pause in order to allow the child an opportunity to take a turn.

The parent also learns to make conversation relevant by talking about the "here and now" and focusing on the child's activities rather than the parent's interests. Just as the parent relies on context to interpret the child's message, so does the child depend on what he or she observes to begin to connect language with daily activities. The parent is also shown how to speak for the child much as parents of normally hearing children ask and answer their own questions.

The next group of skills act to enhance and develop child communicative efforts to include more sophisticated modes of interaction. At this point, the parent is shown techniques for encouraging a child to use voice to make sounds. The parent is first taught to stimulate the child to use his or her voice much as a parent of a normally hearing child would—by singing songs and simple rhymes, adding sounds to accompany nonvocal activities such as playing cars, and varying the sounds to which the child is exposed—in short, to create a vocal environment for the child. The parent learns to encourage the child to use voice to get the parent's attention and to react immediately when the child incorporates voice into communication, reinforcing the idea that "When I talk/sign, something happens!" Finally, development of nonvocal and vocal imitative behaviors helps reinforce turn-taking, establish behaviors necessary for babbling, and expand the child's vocal and language repertoire. By imitating the child's babbling and vocalizations and modifying the sounds, the parent provides the child with a model for later imitation of parent vocal communicative behaviors.

While expanding the child's expressive skills, the parent is affording opportunities for the child to demonstrate his or her understanding of words. The parent is encouraged to label objects accurately and to use short, simple sentences in order to maintain the child's interest and match his or her short attention span. Repetition and natural gesture also assist the child to comprehend the parent's message.

Finally, once the child begins to use words/signs, the processes of reward and expansion are important. The parent learns to reinforce the child's efforts, therefore encouraging more communication. Expansion skills are also critical to establish more complex language production. Adding new words, using more difficult sentence structures, and adding new information to the child's expressed ideas help the child understand that language learning is a process involving increasing levels of complexity.

At this point the parent, as accurate observer and reporter, has established basic turn-taking skills with the child, is comfortable and competent in communication with the child, and has developed skills to advance the child's communication abilities. The child, in turn, has learned the rules of conversation and interaction and is beginning to use vocal symbols to express early-developing pragmatic functions. Thus, both parent and child have a foundation of positive, effective interactions upon which advanced auditory, speech, and language skills can be learned.

Developing Complex Child Communication Skills

Development of communicative competence is accomplished by the family's participation in a variety of experiences through the four service delivery components described earlier (figure 1). Emphasis is on matching parent facilitative strategies and child communication behaviors so that the response of each conversational partner reinforces the other; simply stated, parent and child enjoy both the interaction and the advancement of the child's communication skills. Integration of audition, speech, and language is stressed so that each area is not "taught" as a subject but, rather, developed within the context of the interaction.

The importance of audition as input is emphasized regardless of the communication method employed to develop language skills. Child hearing and hearing aid function are evaluated regularly, and parents are skilled in monitoring the amplification system on a daily basis (Hanners and Sitton 1974) and using the Five Sound Test (Ling and Ling 1978) to note changes in hearing aid function and the child's speech detection abilities.

Auditory skill development begins by increasing parental awareness of the effects of environmental noise and distance on the ability of a child to process auditory input. Hierarchies developed by Erber (1979), Ling (1978), and Northcott (1972) serve as resources to the clinician in developing specific objectives. As mentioned earlier, the clinician's role is to integrate the objectives into activities that develop speech, language, and auditory skills as a unified whole. Games to increase the child's perception of environmental and voiced sounds and to recognize their presence and absence are developed to enhance the child's detection skills. Later the parent learns to help the child localize and attach meaning to environmental signals and voices. Discrimination of voice parameters such as pitch, duration, and intensity helps the child focus on voice input, which is critical for development of language comprehension and production.

Once a foundation of listening behaviors has been established, intervention focuses on using auditory input to assist the child in interpretation of incoming communication. Detection, discrimination, identification, and comprehension (Erber 1979) are developed by increasing the child's auditory memory for language input. The clinician also helps the parent use naturally occurring situations to systematically decrease the child's reliance on context, repetition, and exaggerated suprasegmental speech features (as appropriate according to the child's auditory function) to interpret incoming messages and enhance the child's ability to use segmental cues identifying phonemes. In this manner, the child's own ability rather than preconceived estimations based on the audiogram determines maximum auditory potential.

The Ling Speech Program (Ling 1976) and normative developmental data serve as a guide for the growth of child speech skills. By incorporating repetition and alternation of babbled syllables into imitation games and songs shared by parent and child, a generalization of skills from the phonetic to the phonologic level is facilitated. The clinician helps the parent understand the difference between speech and language, and the importance of integrating speech skills and expressive language to enhance child communication. The parent and child learn to use pitch and intensity changes to convey underlying emotions behind linguistic messages, for example, the use of a rising intonation for questions ("Ball?") or intensity changes for emphasis ("Sshh, the baby's sleeping!"). Early developing sounds such as /b/, /m/, and /h/ are incorporated into initially learned vocabulary such as the protoverb "bye-bye," possessive "mine," and the question form "what?" Thus, the child learns to use recently acquired phonemes in meaningful interaction, and the parent begins to see how speech and language are interdependent.

The development of language skills involves integrating form, content, and function in interactions between parent and child. At the same time, parent-infant language training is directed toward developing flexibility in both parent and child. Too often, parents and their hearing-impaired children become rigid and concrete in their interactive and language behaviors. Thus, a parent may focus on stimulating and reinforcing a child's use of single words to label objects, ignoring other important functions of language. To facilitate a child's understanding, the parent may continue to use familiar vocabulary and phrases, for example, "juice," "eggs," and "meat" to describe common beverages and food. Expanding the child's receptive and expressive language to include "grape juice," "*Diet Coke*," "*Gatorade*," "scrambled eggs," "fried eggs," "pork," and "beef" is important to demonstrate at a simple level the creative and generative properties of language.

Once basic turn-taking and reciprocity skills are developed, attention is focused on expanding pragmatic functions (Dore 1975; Halliday 1975) and learning conversational rules and dialog skills. The clinician helps the parent encourage the child to incorporate the imaginative, heuristic, informative, and practicing functions into his or her repertoire of more commonly used functions such as instrumental, regulatory, labeling, interactional, and personal. The child also learns dialog rules such as following parental utterances, asking and answering questions, initiating and maintaining conversational topics, and telling stories, all of which enable the child to become a more active participant in interactions with the parent.

Semantic development begins at the single-word level with a core lexicon of 25 to 35 words. Words chosen are those the parent feels are important for building communication skills of the child and that encompass a variety of semantic intentions such as existence and nonexistence ("ball" and "all gone"), recurrence ("more"), attribution ("big" and "hot"), possession ("mine"), action ("fall down" and "open"), and location ("under"). Again, the aim is the child's incorporation of a variety of semantic relations, not simply the development of "noun vocabulary" or "verbs." As the child's language becomes more complex, semantic roles are combined and sophisticated semantic relations evolve.

Syntactic development is emphasized only after the child demonstrates the ability to communicate simple ideas. Once firm pragmatic and semantic bases are established, attention turns to expanding noun phrases and verb phrases into simple adult declarative sentences, but always within the context of an interaction. Rather than learn how a prepositional phrase is formed using a series of unrelated pictures, the parent and child may read a book such as *Where Is Spot?* (Hill 1980) which offers opportunities to use prepositions within a story format. In acquiring new syntactic structures, the appropriate use of structure in conversation is of primary importance. While working to develop syntactic structures, pragmatically appropriate responses should not be sacrificed. For example, the question form, "What are you doing?" is often used to elicit the syntactic structure: I + am + verb + –ing ("I am watching TV"). In answering the question, "What are you doing?" the typical listener uses ellipsis to omit redundant information and replies, "Watching TV", instead of, "I am watching TV." Care must be taken to always elicit syntactic structures within conversation so that the child learns how syntactic and pragmatic skills interface with each other.

As the child progresses from prevocal to single-word and word combination stages, auditory, speech, and language development are integrated in a model that highlights the interaction between facilitative parent behaviors and emerging child behaviors (Fitzgerald and

Fischer 1987). Selected objectives in the areas of speech, language, and audition are chosen for the child and parent. As figure 3 shows, activities are designed to incorporate each skill area. In this manner, the goal of parent and child communicative competence, rather than the development of specific skills, is facilitated.

At the prelinguistic level, the development of infant babbling involves turn-taking (language pragmatics), phoneme imitation (speech), and listening to voice patterns (audition). A listening game requiring the infant to respond to a knock on the door or to a voice develops auditory awareness and reciprocity. Once the child reaches the single-word level, early developing speech sounds are incorporated into the core lexicon. An activity in which the child is asked to "Find the cow that goes 'Moo'" first requires the child to use available auditory cues to process the instruction. Then the child may be encouraged to imitate animal sounds using acquired speech skills. At the word combinations level, a short story such as "The Tortoise and the Hare" may combine the following child objectives: (1) answering simple questions about the characters and actions; (2) sequencing story events; (3) using the

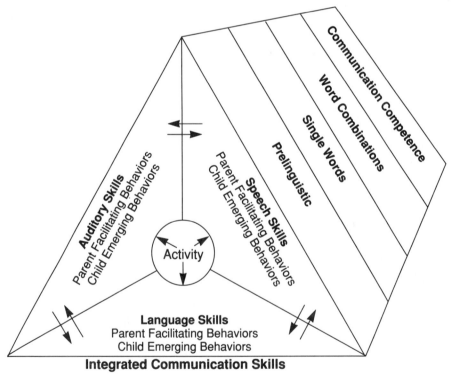

Figure 3. Model for developing parent/child communicative competence.

phoneme /t/ correctly in short phrases; and (4) discriminating three-word phrases. Integration and incorporation of objectives from each skill area help the parent see how language, speech, and audition combine to enhance communication development of the child. At the same time, the parent learns how to facilitate the development of skills from each area in a single activity.

SUMMARY AND CONCLUSION

The Mama Lere Early Intervention Program has evolved over the past twenty-five years from a child-based to a family-centered intervention program. Through the use of four service delivery components—supportive counseling, information exchange, parent advocacy training, and the development of parent and child communicative competence—programs are individualized to accommodate each family's strengths and needs. The intervention model incorporates assessment, identification of objectives, and implementation; it emphasizes periodic evaluation of program parameters to determine if rate of progress is acceptable and if modifications to increase program effectiveness are required. Throughout the intervention program, development of parent and child communicative competence—rather than specific auditory, speech, and language skills—is emphasized. By emphasizing the two premises upon which the Mama Lere Early Intervention Program is based, that is, the importance of families as the social context in which children develop and of meeting the unique needs of each family as a prerequisite for optimizing the child's development, the challenges presented by changes in families and children can be met. In this manner, the outcome of parent-infant training is not only a child who communicates, but also a family who understands, accepts, and shares all aspects of the family's life with their hearing-impaired child.

REFERENCES

Ainsworth, M. D., and Bell, S. M. 1974. Mother-infant interaction and the development of competence. In *The Growth of Competence*, eds. K. Connolly and J. Bruner. New York: Academic Press.

Bateson, M. C. 1975. Mother-infant exchanges: The epigenesis of conversational interaction. *Annals of the New York Academy of Sciences* 263:101–13.

Brazelton, R. B., Koslowski, B., and Main, M. 1974. The origins of reciprocity: The early mother-infant interaction. In *The Effect of the Infant on Its Caregiver*, eds. M. Lewis and L. A. Rosenblum. New York: John Wiley and Sons.

Bill Wilkerson Hearing and Speech Center. 1978. *Listening Skills Competencies*. Nashville, TN: The Bill Wilkerson Center.

Bill Wilkerson Hearing and Speech Center. 1979. *Rules of Talking*. Nashville, TN: Language Development Programs.

Bill Wilkerson Hearing and Speech Center. 1984. *Programming for Preschool*

Hearing-Impaired Children. Symposium presented at the Bill Wilkerson Hearing and Speech Center, Nashville, TN.

Bloom, L., and Lahey, M. 1978. *Language Development and Language Disorders.* New York: Wiley and Sons.

Breslau, N., Weitzman, M., and Messenger, K. 1982. Psychologic functioning of siblings of the disabled child. In *Annual Progress in Child Psychiatry and Child Development,* eds. S. Chess and A. Thomas. New York: Bruner/Mazel.

Clarke-Stewart, K. A., and Apfel, N. 1978. Evaluating parental effects on child development. *Review of Research in Education.* Vol. VI, Itasca, IL: Frank E. Peacock.

Cole, E., and St. Clair-Stokes, J. 1984. Caregiver-child interactive behavior: A videotape analysis procedure. *Volta Review* 86:200–17.

DePaulo, S. M., and Bonvillian, J. D. 1978. The effect on language development of the special characteristics of speech addressed to children. *Journal of Psycholinguistic Research* 1:189–211.

Dore, J. 1975. Holophrases, speech acts, and language universals. *Journal of Child Language* 2:21–40.

Erber, N. P. 1979. An approach to evaluating auditory speech perception ability. *Volta Review* 81:16–24.

Fischer, R. M., and Kenworthy, O. T. 1988. Intervention with preschool hearing-impaired children. In *Decision Making in Speech-Language Pathology,* eds. D. E. Yoder and R. D. Kent. Toronto: B.C. Decker.

Fitzgerald, M. T., and Bess, F. H. 1982. Parent/infant training for hearing-impaired children. *Monographs in Contemporary Audiology* 3(3):1–24.

Fitzgerald, M. T., and Fischer, R. M. 1987. A family involvement model for hearing-impaired infants. *Topics in Language Disorders.* 7(3):1–18.

Garrard, K. 1991. *Speech-Language Development: A Manual for Studying Children's Oral Language Skills.* Murfreesboro, TN: Middle Tennessee State University.

Greenberg, M. T. 1980. Social interaction between deaf preschoolers and their mothers: The effects of communication method and communication competence. *Developmental Psychology* 16:465–74.

Greenstein, J. M., Greenstein, B. B., McConville, K., and Stellini, L. 1977. *Mother-Infant Communication and Language Acquisition in Deaf Infants.* New York: Lexington School for the Deaf.

Halliday, M. 1975. *Learning How to Mean: Explorations in the Development of Language.* New York: Arnold.

Hanners, B. A., and Sitton, A. B. 1974. Ears to hear: A daily hearing aid monitoring program. *Volta Review* 76:530–36.

Hasenstab, M. S., and Horner, J. 1982. *Comprehensive Intervention with Hearing-Impaired Infants and Preschool Children.* Rockville, MD: Aspen Systems Corporation.

Hill, E. 1980. *Where Is Spot?* New York: Putnam Publishing Group.

Kenworthy, O. T., and Fischer, R. M. 1988. Assessment and the hearing-impaired child. In *Decision Making in Speech-Language Pathology,* eds. D. E. Yoder and R. D. Kent. Toronto: B.C. Decker.

Knox, L. L., and McConnell, F. 1968. Helping parents to help deaf infants. *Children* 15:183–87.

Kretschmer, R., and Kretschmer, L. 1979. The acquisition of linguistic and communicative competence: Parent-child interactions. *Volta Review* 81: 306–22.

Lewis, M., and Rosenblum, L. A. Eds. 1974. *The Effect of the Infant on its Caregiver.* New York: John Wiley and Sons.

Ling, A. 1978. *Schedules of Communication Development.* Washington, DC: The Alexander Graham Association for the Deaf.

Ling, D. 1976. *Speech and the Hearing-Impaired Child: Theory and Practice.* Washington, DC: The Alexander Graham Bell Association for the Deaf.

Ling, D., and Ling, A. H. 1978. *Aural Habilitation: Foundations of Verbal Learning in Hearing-Impaired Children.* Washington, DC: The Alexander Graham Bell Association for the Deaf.

Luterman, D. 1979. *Counseling Parents of Hearing-Impaired Children.* Boston: Little, Brown and Company.

McConnell, F. E. 1974. The parent teaching home: An early intervention program for hearing-impaired children. *Peabody Journal of Education* 51:162–70.

Meadow, K. P., Greenberg, M. T., Erting, C., and Carmichael, H. 1981. Interactions of deaf mothers and deaf preschool children: Comparisons with three other groups of deaf and hearing dyads. *American Annals of the Deaf* 126:454–68.

Miller, J. 1981. *Assessing Language Production in Children.* Baltimore, MD: University Park Press.

Moog, J. S., and Geers, A. E. 1979. *Grammatical Analysis of Elicited Language— Simple Sentence Level.* St Louis, MO: Central Institute for the Deaf.

Moog, J. S., Kozak, V. J., and Geers, A. E. 1983. *Grammatical Analysis of Elicited Language—Presentence Level.* St Louis, MO: Central Institute for the Deaf.

Moses, K. L. 1985. Dynamic intervention with families. In *Hearing-Impaired Children and Youth with Developmental Disabilities: An Interdisciplinary Foundation for Service.* Washington, DC: Gallaudet College Press.

Murphy, A. T. (Ed.) 1979. The families of hearing-impaired children. *Volta Review* 81(5):265–384.

Nix, G. (Ed.) 1977. *The Rights of Hearing-Impaired Children.* Washington, DC: The Alexander Graham Bell Association for the Deaf.

Northcott, W. H. 1972. *Curriculum Guide: Hearing-impaired Children—Birth to Three Years, and Their Parents.* Washington, DC: The Alexander Graham Bell Association for the Deaf.

Pollack, D. 1970. *Educational Audiology for the Limited Hearing Infant.* Springfield, IL: Charles C Thomas.

Russo, J. B., and Owens, R. E. 1982. The development of an objective observation tool for parent-child interaction. *Journal of Speech and Hearing Disorders* 47:165–73.

Schuyler, V. S., Rushmer, N., Arpan, R. K., Melum, A., Sowers, J., and Kennedy, N. 1985. *Parent-Infant Communication* (3rd ed.). Portland, OR: Infant Hearing Resource.

Snow, C. E., and Ferguson, C. A. (Eds.) 1977. *Talking to Children: Language Input and Acquisition.* Cambridge: Cambridge University Press.

Testut, E. W., and Baldwin, R. L. 1977. Educational Options. *Volta Review* 79:281–86.

Trybus, R. J., and Karchmer, M. A. 1977. School achievement scores of hearing impaired children: National data on achievement status and growth patterns. *American Annals of the Deaf* (122):62–69.

Yoder, P. J., Kaiser, A. P., and Alpert, C. 1991. An exploratory study of the interaction between language teaching methods and child characteristics. *Journal of Speech and Hearing Research* 34(1):155–67.

Chapter • 11

The V.I.P. Program
Clarke School for the Deaf

Janice C. Gatty

The Visiting Infant and Parent (V.I.P.) program, located at the Clarke School for the Deaf in Northampton, Massachusetts, is a short-term program of evaluation, intervention, and parent education for families with deaf and hard-of-hearing children from birth to five years of age. Families stay on campus for three and one half days in a suite of rooms in the building where the Parent-Infant and Integrated Preschool programs are located. During their stay, children participate in audiologic, psychologic, speech, and language evaluations. Parents observe all evaluations, and a substantial portion of their visit includes discussion of test results and the implications for their child's development. In addition, parents discuss their questions about deafness, observe classes for deaf students, eat meals in the dormitories, and meet with deaf adults. Parents leave with a better understanding of hearing loss, the effects it will likely have on the development of their child, and a list of recommendations for the next phase of intervention.

Families who come to the V.I.P. program are usually involved with long-term early intervention programs in their home communi-

The author gratefully acknowledges the staff at the Clarke School for the Deaf and, particularly, Holly Altman, Kathleen Casale, Dennis Gjerdingen, Jeanne Moriarty, Joy Munson, Joanne O'Connell, and Patricia Wood for their role in making the V.I.P. program a valuable and meaningful experience for families with young, hearing-impaired children.

ties. Often, programs in their home communities are not designed specifically for hearing-impaired children or they focus narrowly on one aspect of deafness, such as speech production. The V.I.P. program is an educational experience that attempts to deal with the whole child in the context of the family. It is designed to complement, not replace, other programs of early intervention. Although its setting, in an established oral school for the deaf, gives parents exposure to the oral capabilities of profoundly deaf children, recommendations for the child and family are always based on the results of evaluation, taking into account the parents' goals and expectations.

GOALS OF THE V.I.P. PROGRAM

The goal of the V.I.P. program is to provide families with the support, insight, and knowledge that will enable them to make informed decisions about their child's education. Families with young children (neonates to three years) are faced with decisions about how to make their home environments accessible to their child. After the age of three, parents need information about the effects of hearing loss on their child's development in order to make decisions about school placement.

Within this general goal are several specific objectives including evaluation, parental counseling, recommendations, and establishing confidence in the professionals. The first objective is *comprehensive evaluation*. Professionals and parents need reliable and valid information not only about a child's current performance levels but also about auditory, intellectual, social, and emotional abilities in order to make appropriate recommendations for intervention.

A second goal is *parental counseling*. Parents need full access to test results in a form they can use and understand. They need also to identify and discuss their own feelings regarding hearing loss before they can make appropriate decisions regarding their child's future intervention program (Luterman 1979, 1984).

A third goal is to provide parents with specific *recommendations*. Recommendations for intervention and educational programming are made on the basis of evaluation results, and are developed in collaboration with parents.

The last goal is to establish *confidence*. Managing a hearing-impaired child is an ongoing process that requires parents and professionals to use each other as resources. This reciprocity is based on mutual trust. Parents must perceive professionals as competent, thorough, and sincerely interested in them and their child. Professionals must perceive parents as seeking an understanding of their child, of his or her hearing impairment, and of themselves in relation to the challenges that deafness creates.

These goals are addressed in various ways depending upon the needs of individual children and their families.

HOW THE V.I.P. PROGRAM WORKS

The activities of the V.I.P. program vary from family to family depending on the individual needs of children and their families. Although the program always includes evaluation and counseling activities, the choice of activities and the extent to which these are child-centered or family-centered is determined by factors such as the age of the child, as well as the cause of and degree of the hearing loss. The needs of a family with a congenitally deaf 18-month-old, for example, are different from those of a family whose four-year-old child has suddenly lost hearing as a result of meningitis.

Family needs also differ depending upon the scope of services they are receiving in their home communities. The families who come to the V.I.P. program all are involved in some form of early intervention in their home communities; however, the particular type of program differs from family to family. For example, one family may receive intensive communication therapy in a hospital setting several times a week; another may be visited by an early intervention teacher in their home once a week; and still another may have employed a teacher of the deaf to work with the child. To accommodate these differences and to make the V.I.P. program meaningful to each family, several telephone calls are made to determine the family's needs, goals, and objectives prior to their involvement with the V.I.P. program. Previous records are also obtained as well as a survey questionnaire detailing referral questions and goals and expectations of their visit. All information is carefully reviewed by members of the V.I.P evaluation team. When the family arrives, parents and the coordinator review the schedule of activities and discuss goals and expectations for the week. Any adjustments or additions to the schedule are made at this time. All families participate in a core of evaluation and counseling activities.

Audiologic Evaluation

The first activity is audiological testing. There are two test sessions. Each is scheduled for two hours and involves an audiologist as well as a teacher of the deaf. The purpose is to assess unaided sensitivity, aided sensitivity, middle ear status, and the electroacoustic performance of the child's hearing aid(s). Results and recommendations are discussed with the parents.

Educational Evaluation

The second activity—educational evaluation—requires three sessions. A national survey of the tests used in early intervention programs for hearing-impaired individuals was made before the V.I.P. program was initiated. Most professionals expressed dissatisfaction with standardized instruments designed to test young deaf children. Even the best are limited in the amount of information they reveal about a child's performance. Our consultants agreed that diagnostic teaching and reporting may be more useful tools for evaluation. Because families are on campus for several days and evaluators observe them in a variety of settings, observation and diagnostic teaching are viewed as valid and reliable ways of measuring and describing communication competence, cognitive development, and social skills in natural settings.

There are, however, several advantages in using formal tests: they provide specific information in a short time; they compare a child's performance with that of a group of children; and the results are in a form that is easily understood by other professionals involved in the child's early intervention. We supplement informal observations with the following standardized instruments for educational evaluation.

1. Intellectual ability:
   The C.I.D. Performance Scale (previously known as the Randall's Island Performance Scale) (Geers and Lane 1984).
   Leiter International Performance Scale (Levine 1986)
   Kaufman Assessment Battery for Children (Kaufman and Kaufman 1983)
2. Fine motor development:
   Test of Visual-Motor Integration (Beery and Buktenica 1967)
3. Language development:
   Expressive One-Word Picture Vocabulary Test (Gardner 1979)
   Rhode Island Test of Language Structure (Engen and Engen 1983)
   Sentence Elicitation Task (Engen and Clarkson)
   S.E.C.S. (Scales of Early Communication Skills) (Moog and Geers 1975)
   G.A.E.L. (Grammatical Analysis of Elicited Language) (Moog, Kolzak, and Geers 1983)
   The T.A.G.S. (Teacher Analysis of Grammatical Structures) (Moog and Kolzak 1983)

The P.P.V.T. (Peabody Picture Vocabulary Test) (Dunn and
   Dunn 1981)
R.E.E.L. (Receptive-Expressive Emergent Language Scales
   (Bzoch and League 1970)
4. Speech:
      Goldman-Fristoe Test of Articulation (Goldman and Fristoe
         1969)
      Photo Articulation Test (Prendergast et al. 1984)
      Assessment of Phonological Processes-Revised (Hodson
         1986)
5. Social-emotional development:
      Meadow/Kendall Social-Emotional Assessment
         Inventories (Meadow 1983)
6. General development:
      Clarke Preschool Evaluation Scales (Boothroyd et al. 1979)

Not all instruments are used with all children. Decisions about
which tests to use are based on the child's level of development and
the diagnostic questions of interest.

In addition to formal testing, we make videotape recordings of
children interacting with their parents and with a teacher. Also, we
observe each child in one of two educational settings in the school.
One is a toddler group, made up of hearing-impaired children between the ages of 18 months and three years of age. The other is a
preschool class, which includes both hearing and hearing-impaired
children, three to five years of age.

Introduction to Deafness

The third set of activities is designed to give parents an introduction to
deafness. For many parents, their hearing-impaired child is the first
deaf person they have ever encountered. In the V.I.P. program we
introduce parents to older deaf students and to deaf adults. This is
done through observations of classes at all levels of the Clarke School
by dining with the students in the Clarke dormitory, through visits to
the homes of families in which the parents and sometimes the children
are deaf, and by including deaf adults in the parent meetings (Meadow-
Orlans 1987; Greenberg and Calderon 1984). In addition, parents discuss such topics as: interpretation of the audiogram, speech perception
in hearing-impaired children, use of hearing aids and FM systems,
cochlear implants, and behavioral management of children with oral
language delay.

Parent Counseling

The fourth activity is parent counseling. The agenda for individual
counseling is set largely by the parents themselves. We try to identify

specific questions before the parents arrive. In fact, a single issue or question may be the primary motivation for the family's visit. Examples of such questions might include the following.

What are the benefits and limitations of different modes of communication in terms of the growth and development of our child?

What is the most appropriate educational environment for my child at this time?

Will my child be able to participate in classrooms with hearing children?

What is the best type of amplification for my child at home and at school?

Is my child a candidate for a cochlear implant?

Sometimes V.I.P. parents also participate in weekly meetings with parents of local children enrolled in the toddler group or preschool class on campus.

Wrapping-up

At the end of the visit a final meeting includes all staff members who evaluated and observed the child. During the wrap-up meeting, each professional gives a report of the evaluation findings as well as less formal observations that support test results and may make evaluation information more meaningful to parents. The staff is experienced in sharing test results in lay terms supplemented by instructional aids designed to make information more meaningful to parents.

Specific recommendations are then made based on test results and parents' choice in regard to rearing and educating their child. Recommendations may be made directly to the parent or, with their approval, directly to a teacher, audiologist, or speech-language pathologist involved with the child at home. Sometimes a home teacher or representative from the child's school will attend the final meeting to facilitate implementation when the family returns to their local program.

After the visit, a comprehensive report is written by each evaluator reflecting background information, a description of the week's activities, test results, behavioral observations, and recommendations. When all the reports are completed they are collated and mailed to the parents with a summary report.

Schedule of Activities

The following are illustrative schedules for two families participating in the V.I.P. program. The first is for a child between birth and three years of age; the second is for a child between the ages of three and five. Each visit is preceded by telephone calls and a review of records and questionnaires so that the schedule reflects the self-identified needs of individual families.

For an Infant or Toddler

Monday Afternoon/Evening

1:30–3:00	Arrival and in-take
	The family arrives, gets settled in their quarters and meets with the coordinator of the program to review: developmental history of the child; goals, expectations, and questions to be addressed during the week; and schedule of the week's activities.
6:00	Dinner in the dormitory
(7:30)	In the case of late arrival, uncompleted interview, or specific questions related to daily routine at home, the coordinator may return to observe bed-time routine and continue discussion with the parents after the child has gone to bed.

Tuesday

8:45	Parents observe in the Preschool
9:30–11:30	Audiologic evaluation and interpretation
12:00	Lunch in guest suite
1:30–2:30	Psychologic evaluation
2:30–3:30	Coordinator meets with the family to discuss audiologic results from the morning and non-verbal cognitive abilities of the child.
6:00	Dinner in the dormitory
7:30	Family swim

Wednesday

8:45	Observation of a class in Lower School
9:30–11:30	Continuation of audiologic evaluation and dis-cussion of hearing aids.
12:00	Lunch in the dormitory
1:30–2:30	Speech and language evaluation

2:30–3:30	Meet with coordinator to discuss child's non-verbal and verbal communication skills as well as the role of hearing and cognitive development in development of communication skills.
3:30–4:00	Visit the Assistive Devices Center on campus.

Thursday

8:45–9:30	Observation of a class in Upper School
9:30–10:30	Videotape child playing with parents and professional. Completion of language or speech evaluation as necessary.
10:30–11:30	Meet with deaf adults
12:00	Lunch in the dormitory
1:30–3:30	Wrap-up meeting

For a Preschooler

Monday Afternoon/Evening

1:30–3:00	Arrival and in-take
	The family arrives, settles into their quarters and meets with the coordinator of the program to review: developmental history of the child; goals, expectations, and questions to be addressed during the week; specific questions regarding school placement, the schedule of the week's activities.
6:00	Dinner in the dormitory

Tuesday

8:45	Parents observe in Preschool
9:30-11:30	Audiologic evaluation and interpretation
12:00	Lunch in guest suite
1:30–2:30	Psychologic evaluation
2:30–3:30	Coordinator meets with the family to discuss interpretation of audiologic results from the morning and nonverbal cognitive abilities of the child.
6:00	Dinner in the dormitory
7:30	Family swim

Wednesday

8:45	Observation of a class in Lower School
9:30–11:30	Continuation of audiologic evaluation, and discussion of personal hearing aids and classroom amplification.
12:00	Lunch in the dormitory
1:30–2:30	Language evaluation
2:30–3:30	Meet with coordinator to discuss child's non-verbal and verbal communication skills as well as the role of hearing and cognition in development of communication skills.
3:30–4:00	Visit the Assistive Devices Center on campus.

Thursday

8:45–9:30	Observation of a class in Upper School
9:30–10:30	Speech evaluation and videotaping child in play situation with a teacher.
10:30–11:30	Parents meet with deaf adults while child is observed in the preschool classroom.
12:00	Lunch in the dormitory
1:30–3:30	Wrap-up meeting

GUIDING PRINCIPLES OF THE V.I.P. PROGRAM

Several principles guide our interactions with children and their parents: (1) we listen to parents; (2) we maintain professional honesty; (3) we make recommendations based on evaluation findings; and (4) we inform parents about deafness.

Listening to Parents

Listening to parents fosters the independence and confidence they need to make choices. Soon after their child's hearing loss is diagnosed, parents are faced with many decisions. Most parents of deaf children are not hearing-impaired themselves and have little or no personal experience with deafness. Hearing parents of hearing-impaired children often feel inadequate in making decisions that will affect the course of their children's lives. In addition, well-intentioned professionals, in an effort to help parents make the "right" decisions regarding communication, hearing aids, or educational programming, may actually undermine the parents' sense of autonomy and control. This is ultimately debilitating for parents and leaves them feeling powerless and incapable of taking charge of their own affairs.

In order to make responsible, well-informed decisions, parents of hearing-impaired children need emotional support and knowledge about the effects of deafness. Listening to parents, without judging what they say, validates their feelings of self-worth and contributes to a sense of self-esteem (Rogers 1961; Gordon 1970). Listening to parents sends a message that we, as professionals, have confidence in their ability to make decisions. Listening to parents provides them with the emotional support they need to proceed with confidence.

Professional Honesty

The second principle is to maintain professional honesty. Evaluation of deaf children requires professionals who have expertise in their specialty (e.g., audiology, speech, language, etc.), as well as breadth and depth of knowledge about children. It is difficult to imagine how professionals in a field where the majority of the children are not reaching their potential can purport to have all the answers. Professionals who behave as if they are all-knowing in their interactions with parents create unhealthy, dependent relationships that undermine the parents' confidence and their ability to take charge of their own lives. Professionals have an ethical responsibility to acknowledge strengths and limitations and then to interact with parents based on that self-knowledge.

Make Recommendations Based on Evaluation

Recommendations, whether related to hearing aids, communication methodology, or academic programming, are always based on the results of careful evaluation. Parents of children from birth to age three often seek recommendations about hearing aids and modes of communication that are best for their child's development. Recommendations for amplification are based on hearing test results and the developmental needs of the child. The concerns and preferences of parents are also considered because ultimately it is they who determine how and when hearing aids are used.

Advocating a particular method of communication is complicated by the social, political, and ethnocentric issues that have an impact on questions concerning communication and the deaf. The Clarke School is well known for its oral approach to educating deaf children. In general, parents visit Clarke either because they want more information about their child's potential for speaking and lipreading or because they are curious about oral education. Parents of very young children are often ambivalent about their choice of methodology. At 18 months of age toddlers are too neurologically immature to make predictions as to how they will function when they are 7 or 10 years old. As professionals we try to integrate the test results based on the child's performance, with the parental wishes about how their child is educated before recommending a methodological approach. All methods of educating deaf children are discussed openly.

Parents of hearing-impaired children three to five years old are usually concerned with preschool placement, with the provision of special services, or with appropriate amplification for a classroom setting. Examples of referral questions are as follows.

Can my child go to a preschool for hearing children or should we consider a special program for hearing-impaired children?
Should my child wear an FM system at school?
How often should my child receive communication therapy?
Can you help us identify educational and communication goals and objectives for my child's Individualized Education Program?

Again, recommendations are based on evaluation results together with consideration of the goals and expectations of the parents, and resources available to them.

Informing Parents about Deafness

The fourth principle is to inform parents about deafness. Parents have some knowledge of deafness before they visit Clarke. Many programs are child-centered, however, and experiences with audiologists, physicians, or home-visit teachers often take the form of a one-hour session in which professionals interact with the child for 45 to 50 minutes and speak to parents for 10 to 15 minutes. Parents' understanding of hearing loss may be incomplete or inaccurate. Anyone new to the field of deafness (as most of these parents are) needs time to synthesize and understand such concepts as: auditory and speech perception, language acquisition, speech production, and the relationship of language to cognition and social-emotional development. Every activity in the V.I.P. program is seen as a forum for broadening the parent's knowledge of deafness. It is important that parents perceive the professional as one who is continuing to refine his or her own understanding of the effects of hearing loss on development and, particularly, the effects of hearing loss on the development of their child as an individual.

WHAT MAKES THIS PROGRAM UNIQUE

We believe there are three unique features of the V.I.P. program: (1) integration of audiologic and educational components; (2) a global approach to evaluation; and (3) the complementary role that the program fulfills.

The program's most distinguishing feature is integration of audiologic and educational components. Many early intervention programs separate clinical and educational components because it is easier to administer them separately. In the V.I.P. program, the audiologist and teacher/counselor function as a team. Both are involved in evaluation and postevaluation counseling sessions. Audiologic test results are always interpreted in light of their educational implications.

Second, unlike many early intervention programs, which address only one aspect of deafness, the V.I.P. program addresses the *global needs* of children and their families. The success of this approach relies on professionals who are broadly trained with expertise in more than one area (Boothroyd 1982).

Third, the program is unique in that it is designed to complement other early intervention programs. We offer ourselves as a resource to parents, but are careful not to undermine their confidence in the professionals and programs from whom they receive ongoing support.

PARTICIPANTS IN THE V.I.P. PROGRAM

Seventy-six families with hearing-impaired children between birth and five years of age have participated in the Visiting Infant and Parent program since its inception in 1984.

Children and Adults

About half the families that have visited had children between birth and three years of age; and half had children between three and five years of age. All parents have had normal hearing. In general, we request that two adults attend the program to provide emotional support for each other as well as to share in child-care responsibilities. Usually, both parents come; although occasionally a grandparent, relative, friend, or only one parent will come. Parents may invite partners, extended family members, home teachers, or school representatives from their local communities to attend the wrap-up meeting at the end of the week.

Siblings

In general, we discourage parents from bringing hearing siblings to the V.I.P. program. The activities in the program focus on observing, evaluating, and interacting with the hearing-impaired child in the family. Deafness is clearly the topic of discussion and the hearing-impaired child is the center of attention. If the V.I.P. participant is the only child in the family who is deaf, he or she may have been a central concern to the parents and a focus of their attention since the hearing loss was diagnosed. Hearing siblings in such a family may feel neglected or excluded, and as a consequence, may need special attention from the parents. Unfortunately, the V.I.P. program cannot provide special activities for siblings and their feelings of isolation may be exacerbated. This topic is usually discussed during the initial telephone calls when parents arrange their visit. Most parents understand the difficulty of addressing the needs of hearing siblings during their visit and make alternate arrangements for the care of their other children. The exception is the hearing sibling who is an infant and very dependent upon the mother. In such cases, we insist that a second adult accompany the parent to help with childcare.

Parents Interested in an Oral Approach

The V.I.P. program attracts parents who are interested in using an oral approach with their children because it is located at the Clarke School for the Deaf, an oral school for the deaf established in 1867. Those most likely to come to the V.I.P. program are: (1) parents of children whose hearing loss is a result of meningitis; (2) parents of children whose hearing losses are progressive in nature; (3) parents who want to know more about oral educational programs for profoundly deaf children; and (4) parents who are using a unisensory approach with their children.

Children Who Have Had Meningitis. Ten (14%) of the children attending the V.I.P. program have had acquired hearing losses as a result of meningitis. Some were postlingually deafened and subsequently retained many spoken language skills. Others were prelingually deafened and, although they retained rudimentary language skills, they did not retain enough hearing to use auditory feedback to control their speech mechanism. Others suffered general regression in the areas of motor, speech, and language development. Parents who have already established an oral communication pattern with hearing children are more likely to want to continue that pattern, even if their child has lost a substantial amount of hearing.

Children with extensive damage to the inner ear as a result of meningitis and who demonstrate very limited, if any, benefit from conventional forms of amplification, may be candidates for cochlear implants. Preliminary research suggests that children who have lost their hearing from meningitis are more likely to benefit from the cochlear implant if the time between loss of hearing and implantation is minimized (N.I.H. Consensus Development Conference 1988). In addition, we know that children are more likely to use auditory information in acquiring spoken language skills if they receive the implant and rehabilitative therapy during the critical period for language acquisition, from birth to five years of age (Lenneberg 1967). Parents of children who are totally deaf as a result of meningitis and are exploring the possibility of a cochlear implant may come to the V.I.P. program to discuss this alternative and to assess baseline performance in the area of hearing, speech, language, and psychosocial development.

Children with Progressive Hearing Losses. Parents of children who lose their hearing gradually over a period of time are most likely to use an oral approach with their child. These children establish auditory-motor feedback early in their development and acquire spoken language primarily through the sense of hearing. Careful monitoring of hearing levels is critical for such children so that adjustments can be made in their amplification and environment as soon as a shift in hearing is detected. Parents may return to the campus periodically for audiologic evaluation, electroacoustic modifications in amplification, and counseling regarding the progression of the hearing loss.

Children with Profound Congenital Hearing Loss. Some parents come to the V.I.P. program having been told that their child is too deaf to speak. Although the audiogram may be an important factor in predicting the speech intelligibility of a deaf child (Boothroyd 1985), it has little to do with predicting the potential for cognitive, language, and social-emotional development, all of which contribute to the development of oral communication skills. Even today, 85% of the students at the Clarke School are profoundly, some totally, deaf. As in all educational institutions, there is a range in performance among students. Ninety percent of the graduates, however, leave Clarke to attend and to graduate from high schools for hearing students. Mainstreaming has been a long-term goal at the school for over 125 years. Clarke uses a global, multisensory approach to oral communication: the children wear hearing aids and use their residual hearing, in combination with lipreading to understand speech. Teachers use hearing, vision, and in some cases, touch, to help children learn to understand and produce speech. Classes are small and a high priority is placed on English language and academic skills in the curriculum. For some families, the V.I.P. program is a forum for observing a model oral program for deaf students. In some instances, observing school-aged hearing-impaired children at the school is helpful to parents who have had limited exposure to older deaf children.

Parents Who Use a Unisensory Approach. We also see children in the V.I.P. program whose families are using a unisensory auditory habilitative approach. Children using this approach are asked to rely exclusively on their residual hearing without the benefit of lipreading to learn spoken language. Advocates of unisensory methods believe that visual cues, such a lip movements, detract from the child's ability to learn to use his hearing. They believe children should be taught to rely on hearing as much as possible and usually cover their mouths while speaking to a hearing-impaired child (Pollack 1985; Schmid-Giovannini 1986). These methods are known as unisensory, acoupedic, or auditory-verbal methods.

Unisensory methods may be very beneficial for some hearing-impaired children depending upon auditory capabilities. This approach is not, however, suitable for all children. "The crucial thing is not how much information can be presented to the child," says Ling, "but how much of it can be perceived and in what way the child can learn to process it" (1984, p. 8). As a result, some children enrolled in unisensory programs fail to make adequate progress and parents become concerned. Parents of children using a unisensory approach are attracted to Clarke School because of the shared goal of successful oral communication. The purpose of these families' visit is usually to assess the appropriateness of the approach for a particular child, and to augment their knowledge of hearing loss and educational options.

RESULTS OF THE V.I.P. PROGRAM

We judge the success of our program by three criteria: (1) feedback from parents and school personnel who use the evaluation results and implement the recommendations; (2) referrals from professionals and parents who have participated in the program; and (3) ongoing contact with the families.

Based on follow-up survey questionnaires, we feel that our attempts to instill professional confidence and trust have been successful. Parents give high ratings to the evaluation and counseling sessions. In addition, they maintain contact after they leave campus. All report benefits from observing and interacting with older deaf students and particularly with parents. One parent reported that the V.I.P. program was the single most exciting, emotionally fulfilling experience she had had since before the diagnosis of her son's hearing loss.

Referrals for V.I.P. often come from families or professionals who have had direct contact with someone who participated in the program. Several families who attended the V.I.P. program also participate in the same support group for parents of hearing-impaired children located in more densely populated metropolitan areas.

The V.I.P. program is a model for *short-term* intervention. We provide parents with comprehensive baseline information on all aspects of development and recommendations for the next phase of intervention. Because of the age of the participants, and the powerful effects of maturation on growth at this age, re-evaluation within a year is almost always recommended. Re-evaluation does not necessarily need to be done at the Clarke School. It may be possible for such re-evaluations to be completed closer to home. In many cases, families return to Clarke for follow-up re-evaluation because of the trust and confidence they have in the staff.

HOW FOLLOW-UP SERVICES ARE PROVIDED

Once parents have completed the V.I.P. program and a relationship with the staff has been established, most families feel free to use us as a resource and to contact us by telephone, particularly if they are in the throes of a critical decision regarding their child's educational program.

Families may also return for a more formal, one-day visit that includes one or more evaluation. Often children return for a follow-up audiologic evaluation. Our audiologists are very experienced in working with profoundly hearing-impaired infants and toddlers and their families. They have developed techniques for testing children, making earmolds, adapting hearing aids, and explaining technical information in a manner that is particularly effective with young children and their families.

Comprehensive Educational Evaluations

Comprehensive Educational Evaluations (C.E.E.s) are conducted at the Clarke School in the same center that houses the V.I.P. program. Comprehensive Educational Evaluations are similar to the V.I.P. program except they are designed for children ages 5 to 20. Children and their families stay on campus for two days and are evaluated in the same areas: auditory, psychological, speech, and language development. In addition, children are tested in academic areas. Standardized tests are used more commonly in this program and more time is spent interacting directly with the child rather than with the family. Recommendations are focused on school placement and programming. Thirty-two percent of the families who come for V.I.P. programs return to participate in C.E.E. programs when the child is older.

The School

About one third of the children who participate in V.I.P. programs enter the Clarke School program at a later date. Many families arrange an adequate early intervention program in their home, as the success of an early intervention program relies heavily on the activities performed at home by the parents. Parents may also be able to develop an appropriate preschool program in their home community by sending their child to a small, structured, well-organized preschool program for hearing children and by addressing their child's special needs in individual tutorial sessions. Once children are ready to begin a more academically oriented program, however, resources in their home communities may be limited. At that time parents may consider a self-contained class or school for the deaf. A school such as the Clarke School becomes an option at that time. Although recruitment is not the purpose of the V.I.P. program, parents may return to Clarke because of the early support they received and the trust they have developed in the professionals there.

WHAT WE HAVE LEARNED

The V.I.P. program is a relatively new service compared with others provided at the school. It has been in operation since 1984 and 76 families have participated thus far. As a result of this experience, several changes have been made.

First, we have discovered that the program is a powerful emotional experience for the families involved. One parent said, "I thought I came here for my daughter; I guess I really needed to come for myself." For four days parents are immersed in a world of deafness without the distractions of their usual daily routines. By midweek the children are tired from all the adult attention and the parents are emotionally exhausted. One parent commented, "I don't know why I feel so tired; I haven't done any cooking or cleaning this week!" Parents are now encouraged to take a break by leaving the campus in the middle of the week for dinner or a drive. Parents also are encouraged to come with their spouse or with another emotionally supportive adult so that they have company in the evening.

Second, we have learned that we have to be flexible in scheduling the children's evaluations. Although the accommodations are very gracious and homelike, the children are in a strange place and eating different food on a different schedule that requires a period of adjustment. We have tried to schedule ample time at different periods during the day so that a child is rested and ready for evaluation sessions.

Finally, we have learned to take more time to identify parents' goals and expectations. If the parents' goals and expectations are realistic, then parents, children, and professionals readily complete the program with a sense of accomplishment and success. Unrealistic expectations can leave everyone feeling disappointed and dissatisfied. One mother asked if, by observing speech classes, she could learn enough to teach her daughter to speak.

HOW THE V.I.P. PROGRAM EVOLVED

The Clarke School is well known as a residential school that, since 1867, has provided oral education to school-age, hearing-impaired children (Marvelli 1973; Numbers 1974; Yale 1931). At a time when most schools for the deaf did not admit children until ten years of age, children as young as four and a half years old, from all over the world, came to live at and attend the Clarke school. In 1974, the Center for Audiological Services opened to provide audiologic management and educational services. Within this Center, a clinic provided audiologic services to people of all ages on an outpatient basis, a Parent-Infant program served hearing-impaired children between the ages of birth and three years, and an Integrated Preschool program served hearing and hearing-impaired children from three to five years. There was also a Mainstream program that provided support services to hearing-impaired children placed in schools for hearing children (Boothroyd, Gatty, and Poland 1978). The Center for Audiological Services was, in part, the result of mounting social and political pressures to serve handicapped children within their local communities (Boothroyd et al. 1977).

At the time of writing, the Center for Audiological Services continues to provide comprehensive, audiologic diagnostic, and management services, and dispenses hearing aids and assistive devices to hearing-impaired people of all ages. The Mainstreaming, Preschool, and Parent/Infant programs have expanded their services. Mainstreaming is now a self-contained department at the school and the Preschool and Parent/Infant programs are housed with the V.I.P. program in the Harriette Smith Short Center for Parents and Young Children at the Clarke School.

Problems

The provision of early intervention to hearing-impaired children in their own communities is accompanied by two serious problems. First, because deafness is a low incidence disability, there are not enough experts to staff large numbers of small local programs. This leaves both parents and children with inadequate professional resources.

Second, many of these programs focus on only one aspect of hearing impairment such as evaluation, methodology, parent counseling, or auditory training. Participation in such narrowly focused programs can leave parents uninformed, confused, and lacking in confidence, all of which ultimately work to the detriment of the child's development.

Problems also have been experienced at those schools for the deaf expected to serve only families in their local communities. Again, the low incidence of hearing loss limits the number of hearing-impaired children born in a given geographic region. Hence, it is economically inefficient to operate a comprehensive intervention program for only a few families.

Solution

As a solution to these problems, the Clarke School instituted the Visiting Infant and Parent program in the fall of 1984. This short-term, residential program provides services to families who are not within commuting distances of the Clarke School. While living in a private apartment within a larger building that houses the Preschool and Parent-Infant programs, parents receive much of the information about deafness that they will need in order to make decisions concerning the education of their child.

Funding

Parents usually pay for the V.I.P. program themselves. Many have insurance policies that reimburse them for the audiologic portion of the evaluations. This amounts to approximately half the cost of the V.I.P. program. Occasionally, if the child is over three years old, the local school system will fund the program. In addition, approximately one-third of the families participating in the V.I.P. program receive financial aid from the Clarke School.

Staffing

At present the V.I.P. program is staffed with several part-time professionals from the audiology clinic and Parent-Infant and Preschool programs. A full-time program would require one full-time teacher of the deaf who also has expertise in the areas of speech, language, and hearing assessment; child development, early childhood education, and parent counseling; one part-time (20%) audiologist; one part-time language evaluator (10%); one part-time speech pathologist (5%); one part-time psychologist (10%); and a support staff that includes a part-time (40%) secretary/coordinator, a part-time (10%) parent/professional, and several hearing-impaired adults to meet with V.I.P. participants.

FUTURE OF THE V.I.P. PROGRAM

The V.I.P. program has been successful in providing a much-needed service to a geographically distributed population of families with deaf children. It has several unique features, such as: (1) its global approach, (2) the integration of clinical and educational services, and (3) the operating premise that, through parent education and counseling, parents of deaf children can and will take charge of their lives and make informed decisions on behalf of their children.

Government agencies, in spite of good intentions and repeated efforts at structural and conceptual reorganization, have a long way to go in terms of providing programs that adequately address the developmental, educational, and social issues surrounding childhood deafness. All indications are that the need for this kind of program will remain, or continue to increase.

REFERENCES

Beery, K., and Buktenica, N. 1967. *Developmental Test of Visual-Motor Integration*. Chicago: Follett Publishing Company.

Boothroyd, A. 1982. *Hearing Impairments in Young Children*. New Jersey: Prentice Hall.

Boothroyd, A. 1985. Residual hearing and the problem of carry-over in the speech of the deaf. *ASHA Report #15*.

Boothroyd, A., Gatty, J., and Poland, N. 1978. Mainstreaming and the role of the special school. St. Louis, Missouri, paper presented at the A. G. Bell Association for the Deaf Convention.

Boothroyd, A., Gatty, J., Hoar, N., Kelly, K., and Poland, N. 1979. *The Clarke School for the Deaf Preschool Evaluation Scales*. Northampton, MA: The Clarke School for the Deaf.

Boothroyd, A., Gatty, J., Meagher, K., Wilson, D., and Wisner, J. 1977. Parent/Infant, integrated nursery and mainstream programs at the Clarke School for the Deaf. Los Angeles, A panel presentation at the meeting of the Convention of American Instructors of the Deaf.

Bzoch, K., and League, R. 1970. *Receptive-Expressive Emergent Language Scale*. Baltimore: University Park Press.

Dunn, L., and Dunn, L. 1981. *Peabody Picture Vocabulary Test*. Circle Pines, MN: American Guidance Service.

Engen, E., and Clarkson, A. *Sentence Elicitation Task*. Providence, RI: Rhode Island School for the Deaf.

Engen, E., and Engen, T. 1983. *Rhode Island Test of Language Structure*. Baltimore, MD: University Park Press.

Gardner, M. 1979. *Expressive One-word Picture Vocabulary Test*. Novato, CA: Academic Therapy Publications.

Geers, A., and Lane, H. 1984. *C.I.D. Preschool Performance Scale*. Chicago, IL: Stoelting Company.

Goldman, R., and Fristoe, M. 1969. *Goldman-Fristoe Test of Articulation*. Circle Pines, MN: American Guidance Service.

Gordon, T. 1970. *Parent Effectiveness Training: The No-lose Program for Raising Responsible Children.* New York: P. H. Wyden.

Greenberg, M., and Calderon, R. 1984. Early intervention: Outcomes and issues. *Topics in Early Childhood Special Education* 3:1–9.

Hodson, B. 1986. *The Assessment of Phonological Processes—Revised.* Austin, TX: PRO-ED.

Kaufman, A., and Kaufman, N. 1983. *Kaufman Assessment Battery for Children.* Circle Pines, MN: American Guidance Service.

Lenneberg, E. 1967. *Biological Foundations of Language.* New York: John Wiley and Sons.

Levine, M. 1986. *Leiter International Performance Scale: A Handbook.* Los Angeles, CA: Western Psychological Services.

Luterman, D. 1979. *Counseling Parents of Hearing-Impaired Children.* Boston: Little, Brown and Company.

Luterman, D. 1984. *Counseling Parents of Communicatively-Disordered Children.* Boston: Little, Brown and Company.

Ling, D. 1984. *Early Intervention for Hearing-Impaired Children: Oral Options.* San Diego: College Hill Press.

Marvelli, A. 1973. An historical examination and organizational analysis of the Smith College-Clarke School for the Deaf graduate teacher education program. Unpublished dissertation, University of Massachusetts.

Meadow-Orlans, K. 1987. Early intervention for hearing-impaired children. In *The Effectiveness of Early Intervention,* eds. M. Guralnick and F. Bennet. New York: Academic Press.

Meadow, K. 1983. *Meadow-Kendall Social-Emotional Assessment Inventory (SEAI) for Deaf and Hearing-Impaired Students.* Washington, DC: Gallaudet University Pre-College Programs.

Moog, J., and Geers, A. 1975. *Scales for Early Communication Skills for Hearing-Impaired Children.* St. Louis: Central Institute for the Deaf.

Moog, J., and Kolzak, V. 1983. *Teacher Assessment of Grammatical Structures* (Pre-sentence and simple sentence level). St. Louis: Central Institute for the Deaf.

Moog, J., Kolzak, V., and Geers, A. 1983. *Grammatical Analysis of Elicited Language* (Pre-sentence level). St. Louis: Central Institute for the Deaf.

Numbers, M. 1974. *My Words Fell on Deaf Ears.* Washington, DC: A. G. Bell Association for the Deaf.

National Institute of Health (N.I.H.) Consensus Development Conference. *Cochlear Implants,* May 2–4, 1988, Program and Abstracts.

Pollack, D. 1985. *Educational Audiology for the Limited-Hearing Infant and Preschool.* Springfield, IL: Charles C Thomas.

Prendergast, K., Dickey, S., Selmar, J., and Soder, A. 1984. *Photo Articulation Test.* Austin, TX: PRO-ED.

Rogers, C. 1961. *Becoming A Person.* Boston: Houghton-Mifflin Company.

Schmid-Giovannini, S. 1986. *Counsel and Guidance for Parents and Teachers of Hearing Impaired Children: Handbook 1, 0–2 Years of Age.* Zollikon, Switzerland: The International Counselling Centre for Parents of Hearing Impaired Children.

Yale, C. 1931. *Years of Building. Memoirs of a Pioneer in a Special Field of Education.* New York: Lincoln McVeagh The Dial Press.

Chapter • 12

SKI*HI

Applications for Home-Based Intervention

Thomas Clark

SKI*HI is a model program of the U.S. Office of Education's Handicapped Children's Early Education Program, now the Early Education Program for Children with Disabilities (EEPCD). SKI*HI has been funded for twenty years to develop, refine, and disseminate an exemplary model of early intervention services for young children with hearing impairments and their families. An original demonstration model was developed from 1972 to 1975 in Utah. This model was adopted and funded by the state of Utah as a service model and as the EEPCD-funded SKI*HI Outreach in 1975. The model has been adopted by approximately 250 agencies throughout the United States and Canada, serving approximately 4,000 infants, toddlers, and preschoolers annually. With twenty years of federal support and collaboration among hundreds of professionals, including experience with thousands of children and their families, SKI*HI has developed a state-of-the-art model of family-centered home-based programming.

The SKI*HI Model today has the basic components of the early childhood home-based program developed during the model demonstration grant period. With a basic philosophy and components as its core, and guided by experience as well as new concepts, the SKI*HI model has grown, expanded, and evolved into a dynamic model that continually is incorporating new philosophies and practices.

The first *Programming for Hearing Impaired Infants through Home Intervention, The SKI*HI Home Visit Curriculum* (Clark and Watkins) was published in 1972, the second edition in 1975, the third in 1977, and the fourth in 1985. The following developments in curriculum and material have supplemented and expanded the model to include: (1) development of the first state-wide computerized birth certificate hearing screening program; (2) use of a programmatic approach to language intervention; (3) use of family dynamics; (4) provision of bin-aural ear-level amplification; (5) incorporation of a transition program from home-based programming to a center-based model; and (6) implementation of speech development procedures.

GENERAL DESCRIPTION

The SKI*HI Model is a comprehensive, home-based support model for families of children with hearing impairments. SKI*HI home intervention services are delivered to the family and/or alternate locations with alternate caregivers, and parents usually receive these services at no cost (funding is provided by the sponsoring agency). An early intervention specialist we refer to as a "parent advisor" visits the home weekly to provide support, information, and intervention. Through these home visits, the parent advisor supports, models, and advises family members in the areas of parent-child communication, child development, hearing aid use, listening skills, speech, and language. Parents are directly involved in assessing their family needs, developing family/child goals, and selecting meaningful experiences and activities in which to practice stimulation skills. It is not the goal of the parent advisor to work directly with or to tutor the child. Rather, the parent advisor works with the child while modeling and teaching skills and activities for the parent to use in the home environment. This ecological model involves child and family in the natural surroundings in which they live. A goal of the SKI*HI agency and the parent advisor is to coordinate services with other agencies and professionals who are providing services to the child and family.

The SKI*HI model adheres to guidelines established by Part H of Public Law 99-457. The process for formally determining the most appropriate early intervention services and a home education program for a hearing-impaired child begins as soon as a child/family is referred to a SKI*HI agency. The SKI*HI agency ensures that federal guidelines are followed through a multidisciplinary assessment and a written IFSP or IEP.

To provide maximum services to children and families, the SKI*HI agency maintains a rigorous interagency coordination effort to ensure that multiple agency resources are available and coordinated. For example, the Utah Model SKI*HI Program coordinates services with the Utah Statewide Hearing Screening and Testing Program and with the Utah Health Department, also the state's lead agency under Part H. The SKI*HI Program participates in the Governor's Interagency Coordinating Council activities. It also coordinates services with the Utah Parent Center, State Office of Education, local education agencies (LEAS), hospitals, speech and hearing centers, the State Audiology Association, and the State Ear, Nose, and Throat Medical Association.

Through the IFSP/IEP process the team can work with a family to determine a child's developmental needs, which are then addressed through SKI*HI home intervention. The SKI*HI curriculum addresses communicative development, hearing, speech and auditory development, cognitive development, language development, social-emotional needs/development, self-help, and motor development. There are three main components to the SKI*HI curriculum: (1) direct service; (2) administrative services; and (3) supportive services. Each is described briefly here.

Direct Service Component

Direct service to families is the essence of the SKI*HI Model. Direct services are delivered by a parent advisor who makes weekly home visits of approximately one hour. The parent advisor develops a plan for each family and then reports on each visit. The *SKI*HI Manual* provides comprehensive guidelines for parent advisors, including information on determining parent readiness for formal SKI*HI intervention procedures. Strategies are provided to assist parents with participation in their child's early intervention program. Also included are strategies for providing emotional support to families. This unit contains information about family dynamics, the mourning process, the role of the parent advisor, assessing the impact of parent advisor in the home, and identifying and meeting family psycho-emotional needs. The parent advisor is given basic information on each topic and specific strategies for dealing with the issues.

Guidelines for conducting a home visit are also provided. This unit is a complete guide to planning, delivering, and reporting on a home visit. This information enables parent advisors to make preparations for the visit, deliver intervention procedures effectively, and assess parent and child progress to determine the effectiveness of the program.

The parent advisor also uses *Home-based Programming for Families of Handicapped Infants and Young Children*, SKI*HI Institute, Logan, Utah, 1989, to provide information, skills, and support to the family.

This provides resources in the following areas.

I. *Parent Management of Infants' Hearing Aids in the Home.* The Hearing Aid Program provides a tutorial designed to facilitate proper fitting of hearing aids and acceptance of amplification by the child. It also provides instructions to help parents understand the function of hearing aids, as well as their care and maintenance.

II. *Developing Communication with Child and Parent in the Home.* The Home Communication Program is a pragmatic approach to building a communicative system for the hearing-impaired child and family. The program helps parents to understand the importance of communication and its development. It also helps parents to develop essential communication skills and leads to the selection of an optimum language method for the hearing-impaired child and family. It consists of information lessons and skill lessons, and it provides instructions and guidelines for the parent advisor.

III. *A Program for Developing Auditory Skills in the Home.* This program provides a means of teaching the parent to facilitate the child's use of residual hearing so that he or she is able to derive meaning from vocalizations of others and to relate them to his or her own vocal productions. The Auditory Program consists of guidelines for developing the child's hearing through five phases.

IV. *Language/Communicative Methods for Families of Hearing-Impaired Children.* The home language program consists of four components designed to facilitate four communicative methods: (1) Total Communication/Manually Coded English; (2) Cued Speech; (3) Aural/Oral; and (4) American Sign Language.

    A. *Total Communication/Manually Coded English.* This program is based on interactive language development principles including turn-taking, reinforcement, expansion, and vocabulary development. Important aspects of this program include strategies unique to total communication use, especially the learning of Manually Coded English and its consistent and effective use in home situations.

    B. *Cued Speech.* This option is available for those children and families where this method is desired. A set of videotapes with accompanying instructions can be used to teach the family cued speech.

    C. *Aural/Oral Language Program.* This component integrates ten topics consisting of strategies and techniques for listening and language development. These topics include information and techniques to "tune in" the child, and to help parents develop a foundation of basic language stimulation principles and skills such as verbal conversational skills, being an active listener, and modeling, reinforcing and expanding language.

D. *American Sign Language.* This section in the Communication Program provides guidelines for families wishing to use ASL. For example, this section provides information on learning to use ASL and information on the cultural aspects of deafness. In addition, it demonstrates how to modify the total communication program for families electing to use ASL.

Administrative Component

The administrative component ensures early identification of children with hearing impairments and includes:

Screening. Birth certificate screening and maternal questionnaire high-risk hearing screening are the most commonly used screening systems. Hearing screening in intensive care newborn hospital units is also recommended. The agency conducting the hearing screening works directly with the parent-infant program to ensure immediate referral.

Public Awareness and Referral. This program includes a public awareness referral system and "sensitive" professional resource referral system.

Assessment. The assessment program includes a diagnostic evaluation to determine if a child has a hearing loss, and if so, the nature and degree of hearing impairment. When a child is medically and audiologically diagnosed with hearing impairment, the multidisciplinary team assesses the effects of the hearing loss in all areas of the child's development.

The family assessment consists of the Family Focused Interview developed at the Frank Porter Graham Child Development Center at the University of North Carolina, Chapel Hill (Winton 1988). This provides professionals with an on-going process for interacting with families in a collaborative spirit, to implement a family-focused intervention program that complies with P.L. 99-457.

Personnel. The program management component must provide personnel for a home-based, family-centered program. The personnel required for a parent-infant program will depend to a great extent on the size of the program. Regardless of size, however, it must have one or more parent advisor. An early childhood program in a school district may be limited to one person acting as parent advisor to children with a hearing impairment. In Utah, and in some other states that have adopted our model, the parent advisor is a professional who has early intervention/early childhood certification and who has completed the SKI*HI basic training program. The parent advisor may be a full-time or part-time employee. A complete parent-infant program includes: (1) a coordinator-supervisor; (2) parent advisors; (3) an audiologist/s team; (4) a counselor; and (5) a child development specialist.

Inservice. The administrative component has an active inservice training program for staff that includes topics related to adult learning strategies, child development, and family dynamics.

Interagency Cooperation. The interagency cooperation program works within community, school, and state structures that exist to provide services for hearing-impaired infants and their families. The program identifies these services, then attempts to form linkages to provide an optimal service plan to families without gaps or redundancy. Hearing screening, identification, diagnostic programming, and hearing aid fittings require use of state, regional, and local health, medical, and audiologic services. The parent-infant program uses and coordinates these services. Family support, psychological and emotional support, and child development services may or may not exist within the milieu of the community service pattern. If they do exist, the parent-infant program must make use of and coordinate these services. If they do not, the program provides these services as best it can.

Supervision. Large, well-organized parent-infant programs have a full-time coordinator who provides supervision services. Some large programs have a director and regional supervisors. It is critical to have supervision when parent advisors are scattered over a large area. Parent advisors receive regular visits and telephone calls from their supervisors. The following system has been used successfully.

1. New parent advisors receive on-site supervisory visits monthly for the first three months, every other month for the remainder of the first year, every three months for the second year, and twice per year thereafter.
2. Supervisory telephone calls are made once a month. A regular format and time for these calls is predetermined.
3. Periodic staff meetings provide a cost-effective supervisory tool.
4. Parent advisors use collegial supervision. The parent-infant program provides time and travel for one parent advisor to visit another. He or she then accompanies the fellow advisor on home visits, observing, discussing, and sharing ideas, procedures, and materials.

Evaluation. Program evaluation must not be confused with evaluation of the child's performance. Child-performance data assist in determining an individualized program for a child, whereas program evaluation measures the effectiveness of the program itself. Child-performance data are used collectively to evaluate the performance of the program. SKI*HI has developed a program evaluation system that includes child demographic and child assessment data. A national data system collects child data from SKI*HI adoption programs. Each participating agency then receives an annual evaluation report. This national data bank is available for research on parent-infant home programming.

Supportive Service Component

Some important services that cannot be delivered by the parent advisor are offered through the supportive service component. They include the following.

Clinical Services. Although a parent-infant program cannot provide direct medical services, it should provide coordination, information, and linkage with appropriate medical facilities. A large school district and/or large early intervention program can provide direct clinical support through its audiologists, physical and occupational therapists, and speech-language specialists. These services should be available to provide assistance to the child including support and information to the family and the parent advisors. Smaller programs unable to provide these services can provide the necessary information and linkages to these services.

Inservice. Provision of high quality early intervention requires supportive services that include inservice training to parent advisors. This training covers child behavior, child-parent relations, and specific child development processes.

Audiologic Services. The audiologist coordinates a team that includes a parent advisor and parents. The audiologist is involved in home-based fitting, management of the hearing aids and earmolds, and periodic audiologic testing.

Materials for Families. Access to a resource library through a home loan system facilitates parents' acceptance of the hearing loss and their ability to assist and enjoy their child. The SKI*HI Model has a program that provides a free library loan system for parents. The SKI*HI Institute has also developed a series of Total Communication videotapes that demonstrate how parents can sign with their child. Through local video rental agencies, the tapes are widely available to parents.

IMPLEMENTATION

Several states and large geographic regions in the United States use the complete SKI*HI Model as their comprehensive program of home-based services for infant, toddler, and preschool age children with hearing impairments. If an agency chooses to use the complete model, the following guidelines are provided.

Administration

The administration of a comprehensive family-centered home-based program will vary depending upon the number of families, geographic location, and other factors. The basic functions of the administrative component, however, always include child identification and assessment, personnel (parent advisor) management and supervision, training, and interagency cooperation. The manual, *The Management of Home-based Programs for Infant, Toddler, and Preschool Age Children with Disabilities* (Watkins 1989), provides information on all aspects of early home-based programming.

Curriculum Implementation

The direct service component is the most crucial aspect of the SKI*HI Model. The two major goals of the direct service component are (1) to prepare the child with hearing impairment to enter school ready to acquire school-related skills; and (2) to optimize family functioning for families with children who are hearing impaired. The SKI*HI direct service component can be used to accomplish these goals. The program is designed to identify a hearing-impaired child as soon after birth as possible and to implement a hearing aid and auditory development program promptly. It provides for maximum early treatment of the hearing disorder and optimal auditory development. Concurrently, a home-based communication program based on SKI*HI's *Developing Communication with Child and Parents in the Home* is implemented to coincide with the hearing aid and auditory skills programs.

SKI*HI Institute now has data on 3,759 children in SKI*HI Programs throughout the United States, comparing language development of children in a Total Communication approach to children in an aural/auditory approach. Our data have shown no statistical difference in their achievement.

Transition

When child and family are using a communication method they are comfortable with, when the child is appropriately fitted with hearing aids, and when the home environment is appropriately supported, a plan is developed to facilitate a smooth transition from the home-based environment to a center-based preschool. Carlberg (1989) describes a transition program that includes: (1) assessment; (2) parent involvement; (3) cooperative decision making; (4) program modification; (5) the child in transition; (6) the parents in transition; (7) the parent advisor in transition; and (8) the center-based teacher in transition.

SERVICE DELIVERY

With more than 250 adoptions of the SKI*HI Model, several service delivery methods have been developed to meet the needs of various agencies. The most common, but perhaps the most innovative, method is that of using part-time parent advisors. This permits a cost-effective model that can be applied in rural or urban settings, using a central or regional supervisor who manages the part-time parent advisors in the state or region. Local professionals including early childhood specialists, elementary school teachers, speech and hearing specialists, or teachers of the hearing impaired are recruited to serve local families. The parent advisors must take the SKI*HI Basic Training and complete a rigorous and comprehensive supervision and inservice program. The part-time parent advisor is then paid by the visit. The advantages of this delivery system are:

1. *It is cost effective.* The parent advisor is paid only for actual home visits and other services. The cost of serving a child for eleven months ranges from $1,000 to $2,000, depending upon the amount of service. In comparison, Singer and Raphael (1988) reported $7,577 to be the average cost to serve a child with disabilities for a nine-month period in a center-based school setting.
2. *It optimizes rural delivery of services.* A parent advisor is recruited from the local community or area where children live. Travel for the local parent advisor is limited. Utah, for example, has remote rural areas, but the average distance a parent advisor must drive per visit is less than fifteen miles. Few parent advisors drive more than twenty-five miles one way for a home visit. The parent advisor is part of the community where she or he serves and thus is well suited to provide interagency coordination and public awareness.
3. *It is flexible.* Because program managers cannot predict when or where families will enter the program, it is difficult to provide a full-time case load. There are generally too many or too few cases for a full-time worker. Using a parent advisor paid on an individual family basis makes flexibility possible, according to the size of the case load.

SKI*HI also can be implemented through the school district's early intervention/early childhood program. An early interventionist is trained in the SKI*HI Model and is given a case load of children. Virginia, Minnesota, Michigan and other states use this method. Some programs use a full-time teacher who provides a half-time preschool program and half-time home visit program. This model provides services for children ages birth to three years and children three through five years of age. It also facilitates a smooth transition from home to school. Full-time parent advisors are used in areas where there are enough children to warrant them. The full-time parent advisor has been used successfully throughout Texas in the Texas Day School for the Deaf Program.

The parent advisor, whether full-time or part-time, is the key to direct home-based services to families. Carlberg (1989) describes the process of selecting and hiring parent advisors. Noteboom (1989) gives details on the job description of parent advisors. Frick (1989) provides information on contracts and payment for parent advisors. Reese (1989) details a management and supervision plan for parent advisors.

EFFICACY

Data have been collected on children in SKI*HI programs since 1973 and a National Data Center has been established to which programs throughout the United States provide data. The U.S. Office of Special Education Programs supported a research project to study data on thousands of children.

A study of children who received SKI*HI treatment before twenty months of age compared them with ones who received treatment after thirty months of age. Children who received early treatment had significantly higher language skills than children who had later treatment (Clark 1979). The long-term effects of SKI*HI treatment have also been studied by Watkins (1987). Children who had completed the SKI*HI program and who were six through thirteen years of age were matched with children from three states who had not received treatment. Children who had early home-based intervention scored significantly better on receptive language, expressive language, communication, academic achievement, speech, social emotional adjustment, and several other measures.

Early identification and early treatment are essential to effective intervention with children who are hearing impaired. Data on children entering SKI*HI programs from 1979–1990 (N=3,801), show a median age of identification of seventeen months (table I). The median age of entry to a SKI*HI program is twenty months of age (N=4,016).

Table I.   Age of Identification and Program-Placement Age for SKI*HI, 1979–1990

	Mean (months)	Median (months)	Standard deviation	n
Age at identification	18.8	17	12.2	3,801
Program start age	25.7	20	13.4	4,016

The median age of fitting hearing aids is 22 months for 3,036 children (table II). These data indicate that by the time children enter school at six years of age they will have a developmental level of more than four years and hearing aid use for more than four years. These children enter school ready to acquire school-related skills. The home/family environment has been optimized to help the child develop communicative, linguistic, and interactive skills that have prepared him or her for school facilitated by early hearing aid fittings and auditory training.

Children who have had SKI*HI intervention come from programs throughout the United States. The demographics of an average of 4,000 SKI*HI children are compared to National Demographic Status data on 46,666 children in table III.

SKI*HI data on infants, toddlers, and preschool-age children with hearing impairments can be compared to the national demographics of children with hearing loss. As shown in table III, the demographic data on the SKI*HI population differ somewhat from national and demographic data.

The efficacy of the SKI*HI Model is demonstrated by the achievement of children who have had SKI*HI intervention. A study was conducted to gain validation of the SKI*HI Model by the U.S. Department of Education, Program Effectiveness Panel (Strong and Clark 1990). Receptive and expressive language development were measured using the SKI*HI Language Development Scale. Intervention developmental rate was compared with pretest scores. The predicted mean scores indicated what the children would have scored as a result of maturation alone (Sheehan 1979). The difference between the mean pre- and posttest scores were examined to determine if the differences were statistically significant. The standards were computed to determine the magnitude of the pre- to posttest gains. A proportional change index (PCI) was computed for each child as follows: The Rate of Development During Intervention equals gain between pre- and posttest. The Rate of Development Prior to Intervention equals pretest score divided by

Table II.   Age of Hearing Aid Fit for SKI*HI Overall, 1979–1990

	Mean	Median	Standard deviation	n
Age at hearing aid fit	23.1	22	12.1	3,036

Table III.   Demographic Comparisons of 1986–89 SKI*HI Children with Gallaudet University's 1989–90 Annual Survey of Hearing–Impaired Children and Youth Overall

	Gallaudet 1989–90 (%)	SKI*HI 1986–89 (%)
Gender		
Male	53.9	51.6
Female	45.8	44.2
Unreported	0.3	4.2
Cause of hearing loss		
Maternal rubella and cytomegalovirus	8.3	6.8
Birth trauma	4.6	3.9
Pregnancy complication	6.0	3.1
Heredity	24.9	19.6
Premature	8.8	6.5
Defects at birth	7.9	7.8
Meningitis	16.9	29.5
High fever or infection	9.2	5.7
Otitis media	6.8	7.1
Other	6.6	10.2
Communication method		
Aural/oral	38.6	36.2
Sign, etc.	61.4	63.8
Ethnic background		
Caucasian	63.4	72.3
Black	17.0	16.0
Hispanic	13.6	8.6
American Indian	0.7	1.4
Oriental	3.3	0.7
Other	2.0	1.0
Hearing loss level		
Normal	7.9	2.0
Mild	9.1	8.2
Moderate	11.9	20.7
Severe	31.2	43.4
Profound	39.9	25.7

Totals may not equal 100 because of rounding.

chronological age. The PCI equals Rate of Development During Intervention over the Rate of Development Prior to Intervention. Children whose rates of development were slower during intervention than at pretest receive PCIs of less than 1.0. Children whose rates of development were accelerated during intervention received a PCI greater than 1.0. Table IV shows the PCIs for SKI*HI children.

The overall PCI on receptive language was 1.76, while the PCI on expressive language was 1.79. If these children had experienced no change in the rate of development after intervention began, the PCI

Table IV. Median Proportional Change Indices (PCIs) for SKI*HI Children Overall, 1979–1990

LDS* Receptive SKI*HI overall	LDS Expressive SKI*HI overall
1.76	1.79
(n=2,632)	(n=2,628)

* SKI*HI Language Development Scale.

would have been 1.0. However, the average child receiving SKI*HI intervention scored about 1.75. These children developed at about a 75% higher rate after SKI*HI treatment than before treatment.

Another way to look at language development is to examine the actual monthly growth of the child's language. Table V displays pre- and posttest scores. Data on about 2,600 children with hearing impairment, birth to five years, who received SKI*HI services show one month of language gain for every month of treatment. In contrast, Moores (1987) notes that school-age children with hearing impairments have traditionally gained less than two months of academic achievement for every school year.

CONCLUSION

The SKI*HI Model is based on the following tenets.

1. Language and communication development begin at birth and occur primarily in the home environment as the child interacts with family members. Therefore, an effective intervention program for children with hearing impairments should begin as soon after birth as possible, it should be provided in the home, and be family centered.

2. Identification and intervention should begin as early as possible. Thus, the service delivery model must include a hearing screening

Table V. Mean Actual Pre- and Posttest Scores and Predicted Language Development Scale Posttest Scores for SKI*HI Children Overall, 1979–1990

	LDS Receptive SKI*HI Overall	LDS Expressive SKI*HI Overall
Mean actual		
Pretest:	16.05 months	14.78 months
Posttest:	28.24 months	26.14 months
Gain	12.19 months	11.36 months
SMD (Standardized Mean Difference)		
Pre to Post:	1.08	1.06
n	2,637	2,635

Note: Associated mean score differences were statistically significant, $p \leq .001$. Average treatment time = 12 months.

and identification system, as well as a team approach to hearing aid selection and fitting.

3. A planned auditory program is necessary for the child to develop his or her auditory potential. Parents need teaching and assistance in understanding and managing hearing aids and in facilitating use of residual hearing.

4. The child is a dynamic partner in a two-way communication system. Thus, a pragmatic language approach is preferred. While the hearing-impaired child is still very young, the parents need a model to show them how to develop a pragmatic communicative system with that child.

5. Some hearing-impaired children need a visual supplement to develop an effective communicative/language system. Thus, the parent-infant program should provide both an auditory-oral and a signing approach; however the program must avoid biasing the parents toward one communicative method. Rather, it should assist parents in choosing the preferred approach for each child and family.

6. The parent-infant program should assist in providing the necessary resources *in the home* to make the program effective for the family. This includes a hearing aid trial and loaner system, earmolds, library materials, and for those interested, a system for learning signing skills.

Experience with thousands of children has provided evidence that children who are deaf or severely hearing impaired develop little language if they are left without home-based intervention. With an appropriate home-based program, it has been our experience that they can gain a month of development for every month in the program. This emphasizes the critical need for early identification and early home-based programs. The longer the child remains unidentified and unserved, the further behind the child becomes and the more difficult it is to overcome the delay.

The SKI*HI Model represents a planned, systematic approach to meeting educational and developmental needs. The challenge is to prepare children to enter school ready to acquire school-related skills. Over a twenty year period, a model demonstration program has been developed, refined, and replicated throughout the United States and Canada. A complete curriculum and an array of materials are available for implementing this model. Efficacy data on more than 4,000 children provide strong evidence that the model works.

REFERENCES

Carlberg, K. 1989. Selecting and hiring parent advisors. In *Management of Home-Based Programs for Infants, Toddlers, and Preschool Age Handicapped Children*, ed. S. Watkins. Logan, UT: HOPE, Inc.

Clark T. 1979. Language development through home intervention for infant hearing impaired children. Ph.D. dissertation, University of North Carolina, Chapel Hill.

Clark, T., and Watkins, S. 1985. *The SKI*HI Model-Programming for Hearing Impaired Infants Through Home Intervention: Home Visit Curriculum.* 4th ed. Logan, UT: HOPE, Inc.

Frick, C. 1989. Contracts and payment for parent advisors. In *Management of Home-Based Programs for Infants, Toddlers, and Preschool Age Handicapped Children*, ed. S. Watkins. Logan, UT: HOPE, Inc.

Moores, D. F. 1987. *Educating the Deaf: Psychology, Principles, and Practices.* Boston: Houghton Mifflin Company.

Noteboom, F. 1989. Job description of parent advisor. In *Management of Home-Based Programs for Infants, Toddlers, and Preschool Age Handicapped Children*, ed. S. Watkins. Logan, UT: HOPE, Inc.

Reese, E. 1989. Management of parent advisors: Supervision. In *Management of Home-Based Programs for Infants, Toddlers, and Preschool Age Handicapped Children*, ed. S. Watkins. Logan, UT: HOPE, Inc.

Sheehan, R. 1979. Mild to moderately handicapped preschoolers: How do you select assessment instruments? In *Perspectives on Measurements: A Collection of Readings for Educators of Young Handicapped Children*, ed. T. Black. Chapel Hill, NC: Technical Assistance Development Center.

Singer, J. D., and Raphael, E. S. 1988. Per pupil expenditures for special education. Final Report for Grant Number G00 8630147. Washington, DC: Office of Special Educaton, United States Department of Education.

Strong, C., and Clark, T. 1990. Evidence of program effectiveness, project SKI*HI outreach. Recertification Statement. Washington, DC: Office of Special Education, United States Department of Education.

Watkins, S. 1987. Long-term effects of home intervention with hearing impaired children. *American Annals of the Deaf* 132(4):267–71.

Watkins, S. (Ed.). 1989. Training new parent advisors. *Management of Home-Based Programs for Infants, Toddlers, and Preschool Age Handicapped Children.* Logan, UT: HOPE, Inc.

Winton, P. 1988. The family-focused interview: An assessment measure and goal-setting mechanism. In *Family Assessment in Early Intervention*, eds. D. Bailey and R. Simeonsson. Columbus, OH: Merrill Publishing Co.

Chapter • 13

ECHI
The University of Washington, Seattle

Marie Thompson

The Early Childhood Home Instruction Program for Hearing-Impaired Infants and Their Families (ECHI), currently in its 22nd year of operation at the University of Washington, serves approximately 65 birth to three year old hearing-impaired children and their families each year. In accordance with state law, any child with a bilateral sensorineural hearing loss of at least 20 dB whose family wishes to participate may do so. ECHI also offers assistance to families of children with conductive loss associated with other problems such as Treacher-Collins syndrome. The average age of referral is 20 months.

The family has been the primary focus throughout the program's existence. Families in ECHI, as in the rest of the country, have changed. Although many consist of mother, father, and one, two, or three children, we also serve single parents (mostly mothers), adolescent single mothers, grandparents, and "partners." Most of our families live in rural areas and many live in poverty, thus requiring support from many different state agencies. For most of our families, home visits are the only feasible way to provide services specifically designed for hearing-impaired infants and toddlers. Our efforts are directed toward helping members of any family to better understand their child's special needs and to learn how to use appropriate strategies during daily child care routines. Although parent facilitators use the child as a model to demonstrate techniques and procedures to family members, most "teaching" is parent centered. Working directly with the child at home or in a play group, the teacher or therapist *cannot* take the place of the family's knowledgeable and active involvement in providing ongoing learning experiences for their child. Parents need to feel that they are a respected, integral part of their child's early education. The education we provide, therefore, must be carried out in collaboration with parents and other family members. For this reason ECHI uses a "family systems" approach. This means that we view the child as one part of the total family unit and address the needs of the child within that family structure. It is important to recognize that a family systems approach is not used to label a family as "good" or "bad" but rather to allow professionals to identify where and how a family is functioning and in what way the professionals can best meet their needs.

ECHI is supported partly by state funds and partly by private contributions. There is a director who donates her time; three full-time paid staff members—the coordinator/supervisor, audiologist, and administrative assistant; part-time counselors; a part-time preschool teacher; and 15 parent facilitators who live in the general area of the families they serve and are paid hourly wages, plus mileage. The program provides services to approximately 65 families year round at a cost of approximately $4,200 per family.

The director, coordinator, and audiologist meet for three to four hours every two weeks to discuss families, the program, contacts with the community, workshops for both parents and parent facilitators, and other issues or concerns. Additional group meetings with the counselor and preschool teacher are arranged as needed. Individual meetings among staff occur regularly. The ECHI Advisory Board is composed of parents, grandparents, staff, and professionals from the community. The Board meets five times each year to discuss the program, budgets, and fund-raising issues.

The coordinator and audiologist train and supervise the parent facilitators and visit families on a regular basis. The coordinator assesses each child every six months and, with the parent facilitator and family, reviews the individualized family service plan (IFSP) every six months and makes modifications as needed. She also does all intake interviews, documentation, and writes all final reports. The audiologist establishes, implements, and reviews all auditory teaching goals and objectives. The counselors maintain contact with all families as needed. All staff maintain contact (both in person and by telephone) with agencies, schools, and community individuals and groups.

Parent facilitators live throughout western Washington as do the families. By living in relatively close proximity to their client families, they can assist better in emergencies and can provide more information to the parents about local services. Most of the parent facilitators have master's degrees either in early childhood special education or speech and hearing sciences. Several are mothers of hearing-impaired children who were previously involved in ECHI when their children were first identified and have received additional training. These mothers are among the best of our parent facilitators and, of course, easily gain the trust of other parents.

THE EARLY INTERVENTION PROCESS

Most referrals are made by audiologists, but a few are made by psychologists, nurses, and pediatricians. As soon as a referral is made, the coordinator telephones the parent(s), discusses the program, and determines if they would like to schedule a visit. If so, arrangements are made for a date and time convenient for the parent(s). The coordinator meets with each family in their home, answers any questions they have, describes the program, and enrolls the family. The family selects a schedule for weekly visits on a day and at a time most likely to involve all family members, including siblings. After receiving permission from the family, the child's home school district is contacted, as well as the referring audiologist, the child's primary care physician, and any other community programs involved with the child. Arrangements are made for sharing information about the child's process.

During the first few visits, the family is given the *Birth to Three Curriculum* (Thompson, Atcheson, and Pious 1985); a sign book; and a list of books, articles, and videotapes that are available to them through the ECHI lending library. A parent survey is completed, the child is assessed, and the IFSP is developed in collaboration with the family. The parent survey is what is referred to in P.L. 99-457 as a "Needs Assessment." Many parents were offended by the terminology and the implication that they were "needy" and not "good" parents. Therefore, the term *parent survey* and the survey itself were developed in collaboration with many parents. After the assessment process is completed and family goals and objectives are developed, the coordinator and audiologist make visits to ensure that all staff members are introduced to the family and get to know all family members.

Each week the ECHI parent facilitator makes a home visit to work on the established goals and objectives. The coordinator and audiologist continue to make periodic visits. Staff members also visit other programs the child is attending, such as centers for developmentally delayed children and day-care centers. Discussions about future school placement, the transition from ECHI to school, and visits to schools begin when the child turns two.

For families who live close to the University or for those able to provide their own transportation, play group activities are available three mornings a week for the hearing-impaired children and their siblings. Parent support groups and sign language classes are available for parents, friends, and relatives.

ASSESSMENT

Child Assessment, Initial and Ongoing

In accordance with P.L. 99-457, assessment is conducted by a multidisciplinary team in collaboration with the family. We employ a two-level method of gathering data. The first level involves gathering assessment information from other professionals who have seen the child. The second level involves using our own assessment battery, which establishes a developmental baseline to help parents and professionals identify strengths and needs in establishing beginning goals and objectives. Standardized tests designed especially for hearing-impaired infants and toddlers are not available. Even if they were, the results might not be as useful as longitudinal data collected on an individual child through a battery composed of a variety of measures (Thompson et al. 1987).

We use a test battery composed of both published scales and checklists and those we have developed over the years. These are summarized in table I.[1]

The first three measures in table I are used when the child enters the program, every six months while the child is enrolled, and before he or she leaves the program. The next four are used weekly. The weekly home visit report is used by the parent facilitator and parent(s) to monitor progress. Copies of this weekly report are sent to the coordinator each month so she can review the child's and family's progress; if there are problems, she can make suggestions for changing the intervention.

Table I.   List of Scales and Checklists

HOME (Caldwell and Bradley 1979)
Rockford Infant Development Scales (Project RHISE 1979)
SKI*HI Language Development Scales (Tonnelson and Watkins 1979)
Communicative Intention Inventory (Coggins and Carpenter 1981)
Auditory Training Checklist (ECHI)
Speech Production Checklist (ECHI)
Cognitive Checklist (ECHI)
Weekly Home Visit Report (ECHI)

[1]All forms and checklists developed through ECHI are available by writing to the program.

General Development

In order to obtain information about gross motor, fine motor, personal-social, and self-help skills, we use the Rockford Infant Developmental Scales (RIDES). RIDES is a checklist of more than 300 developmentally significant behaviors from birth to four years of age that informally assesses developmental functions. The checklist of behaviors represents the most commonly cited descriptors of normal development found in the professional literature. RIDES is a product of Project RHISE (Children's Development Center, Rockford, Illinois) and was field tested by personnel from the U.S. Department of Education. The resultant scales provide those assessing a child with advantages not available previously, such as: (1) skills at three-month intervals; (2) more items within each skill and age level; and (3) a 0–3 scoring choice that enables the observer/tester to identify emerging skills as well as those nonexistent or fully achieved. Data can be collected by observing the child, engaging the child in an activity, or asking the parent for information. If a hearing-impaired child has no problems other than hearing loss, results of the RIDES in the four domains covered should be consistent with the progress of normally developing children who have hearing. If one or more skill areas are below developmental expectations, it suggests that the child may have problems beyond the hearing loss.

Language/Communication

In order to obtain in-depth and longitudinal information about a child's communication and language development, we currently use a modified version of the Communicative Intention Inventory (Coggins and Carpenter 1981), an observational tool designed to classify use of language in young children, which may be gestural or gestural and vocal. In addition, we use the SKI*HI Language Development Scale (LDS) (Tonnelson and Watkins 1979), which was developed for use with hearing-impaired infants and young children. The LDS developers used 19 other developmental scales, many of which were norm-referenced and have demonstrated reliability and validity. Unlike many assessment tools for children with normal hearing, the LDS does not unduly emphasize auditory items. Expressively, children are given credit for sign, vocal, and verbal responses. They are also given credit for comprehension of signed input. The LDS covers an age range of birth to five years, with the language skills listed in two-month intervals for birth to two years, four-month intervals for two to four years; and six-month intervals for the five-year-olds. We have found it to be very helpful and easy to use. Parents appreciate it because it is easy to understand and provides them with a broad perspective about where their child is functioning developmentally—earlier skills, current skills, and future directions.

Cognitive Development

Whenever possible, ECHI obtains information regarding cognitive development from a developmental psychologist with knowledge about young hearing-impaired children. Because such a professional is not always available, we often must include our own cognitive assessment. A complete analysis can be obtained with *Assessment in Infancy* by Uzgiris and Hunt (1975). In the ECHI program, we use an abbreviated version that we refer to as the cognitive skills checklist. This checklist evaluates Piagetian-type behaviors from 7 through 26 months and enhances our overall knowledge about each child.

Although the mental scale of the Bayley Scales of Infant Development is often used throughout the United States to assess the cognitive functioning of children from birth to three years, this instrument may not be appropriate for hearing-impaired infants and toddlers. At least 31 items on the mental scale are auditory, and 20 items are vocal/verbal; if they are included in the total score, they can make a cognitively normal hearing-impaired infant seem to be mentally retarded. Thus, results of the Bayley in reference to the infant's cognitive ability must be interpreted cautiously, and additional testing should be provided to corroborate their validity.

Audition

It is most important for those who work with a very young hearing-impaired child to realize that the results of initial audiologic assessment do not necessarily provide threshold levels regarding usable hearing. After a child has received a consistent program of auditory training with appropriate amplification, audiologic test results may be quite different. Therefore, it is important to (1) begin a program of auditory training immediately; and (2) avoid labeling a child as deaf when he or she is initially unresponsive to sound. Normal infants respond because from birth they are inundated with a variety of sounds that they are able to hear and that gradually become meaningful to them. Hearing-impaired infants do not receive the same input; sound is either absent, attenuated, or distorted. Initially, therefore, sound is not meaningful to many of these infants and they must learn the discriminations that normal-hearing infants already understand and respond to. It is often a long process and parents can become discouraged; however, the importance of the initial stages of auditory stimulation cannot be over-emphasized. In our program, we maintain close contact with the family's audiologist for ongoing testing while working consistently to assist the child in maximizing his or her residual hearing.

Because awareness of and localization to sound are critical, we provide opportunities for infants and toddlers to learn these skills as soon as possible. It often takes a relatively *long* period of time and much patience before we can begin to obtain satisfactory, accurate behavioral responses to sound. In order to teach a young hearing-impaired child the skill of localizing to sound, we encourage the child to *look at* and *feel* the object that is making the noise in order to help the child know what is creating the sound and what we want him or her to do. Later, visual and tactile cues are eliminated and we can use auditory stimuli alone. When children are responsive to sound, we assess their ability to discriminate, first between noisemakers, environmental, and animal sounds, then speech sounds. We pay particular attention to ensure that the auditory skills we are teaching are commensurate with each child's cognitive and language level because the child's comprehension of the task can influence his or her response. We have found it much easier to teach the task and responses we want by using gross sounds first, then speech sounds related to interesting objects and familiar people. We use an auditory skill sequence with accompanying activities that we have developed. Our auditory checklist assists in keeping track of progress in this area.

Speech Production

Speech production is assessed using a modification of Ling's (1988) phonetic and phonologic levels of development. Because most children entering ECHI have no real "speech," our first step in assessment is at the phonetic level to determine if the infant or toddler is vocalizing, using different vocal patterns, or will vocalize imitatively and "on command."

If the child is not vocalizing or cannot be encouraged to imitate vocalizations, we start intervention at that stage. As children learn to vocalize, we can continue to assess and encourage production of suprasegmentals as well as different patterns, and eventually look for achievements at the phonologic level where they begin to connect speech sounds with linguistic meaning and eventually produce "real words." We use the Speech Production Checklist we have developed in the initial assessment process to monitor progress.

Weekly Monitoring

The weekly home visit report is an integral part of the ECHI program. It enables us to keep track of the number of visits a family receives while they are in the program, what objectives have been established and completed, as well as information about new language, speech, hearing aids, communication, and how the family is doing. A minimum of three objectives are written for each home visit and space is provided to present the *reason* for each objective. This forces parent facilitators to think about *why* they are going to ask parents to work toward that objective and carry out a new activity during the following week. When parents understand *why* they are performing certain activities, they are much more likely to pursue these activities consistently. The three objectives might include one for auditory training, one for language/communication, and one for speech. On some visits, one or two objectives might be devoted to responding to parent or sibling needs, and only one to the needs of the hearing-impaired child. On some occasions, family needs take precedence over objectives that address only the needs of the child.

Family Assessment

Public Law 99-457 states that the initial and ongoing assessment process must include the child's family and family needs in a variety of areas, such as: the information they want; support systems; finances; or community services needed. In keeping with our philosophy that parents are members of the team, parents helped us develop a form that allows us to obtain necessary information. The resulting form is titled "Parent Survey" rather than "Needs Assessment." Originally, each item in the "Needs Assessment" started with the statement, "I need," and as one mother put it, by the time she was finished, she felt totally inadequate. Eliminating the "I need" for each statement and inserting "I would like" once, at the very beginning, was a major positive change. An additional change was made by replacing "I need or do not need help" with "I would like or do not want help." This change makes the parents feel less "needy" and provides them with "a sense of control" because they are making a statement about what they want. A review of the survey and its contents also provides a clear understanding about the importance of including many disciplines and community services to assist families with finances, counseling, medical services, and respite care. To assist parents in making these connections, ECHI's counselors, coordinator, and audiologist maintain contact with professionals and service groups in the communities where families are located and help families learn about and obtain the services they want.

Public Law 99-457 states that the family-needs assessment must be completed as soon as the family is identified and enrolled in a program. However, it has been our experience that parents of an infant or toddler whose hearing impairment has just been identified are often in a state of shock, attempting to cope with new stresses and emotions, and have not yet sorted out these things in their own minds. Thus, they may not yet be able to identify and prioritize what they need or want. Some parents may have been mismanaged by professionals and are not ready to trust new ones. It is advisable, therefore, to allow parents to have some time to rebound, to identify their priorities, and to develop trust for the person who will be helping them complete the survey of needs. After some time has passed, parents will be far more at ease, have more accurate insights, and will be able to provide more precise information about the assistance they would like. In the meantime, initial services and information can still be provided.

Public Law 99-457 states that each family served must be included in the development of an Individualized Family Service Plan (IFSP). The plan is developed after child and family assessments are completed, and includes the results of the assessment as well as a description of services to be provided to both the child and family. However, there is a need for constant monitoring of both the child and family because families are dynamic and services must change as family needs change. Therefore, dates are recorded for a review of objectives and services so that changes can be made as needed. In ECHI, reassessment occurs every six months.

Because the family assessment and needs are multifaceted, the services provided must come from many sources. In ECHI, all staff members are involved in identifying community services available to the family and assisting the family in obtaining them. These services range from financial help to physical therapy to locating a day-care center or putting parents in touch with deaf adults in the community. With so many professionals involved, it is imperative that everyone stay in touch so the family does not feel fragmented. According to P.L. 99-457, coordination of people and services is accomplished by the Family Service Coordinator. The needs and the number of people involved vary with each family and so does the identity of the family resource coordinator. Although the ECHI coordinator is usually the person responsible for coordination, occasionally another professional assumes that responsibility. For example, a nurse practitioner is the family resource coordinator for one of the children in our program who has several problems in addition to hearing loss. It is her responsibility to convene the entire group, which often includes ten professionals, the grandparents, and the single mother, to coordinate the various *child* goals and objectives of the IFSP, and to assemble and distribute all the information concerning this child and her family.

If a family participates in ECHI and their child also attends a center for developmentally delayed children, the ECHI coordinator visits the center at the time of the IFSP review and family/child needs are identified and responses worked out cooperatively. In this case, there are Co-Family Service Coordinators. Although these are only two examples, it should be clear that flexibility and cooperation are essential.

INTERVENTION

Although ECHI is primarily a home-based program, it also has a center-based component located at the University of Washington. There are numerous reasons for developing and using a home-based intervention program for very young hearing-impaired children. One of the major reasons is to help parents learn how to use the home environment most effectively.

Home Visits

ECHI staff, particularly the parent facilitators, work with the child and the entire family rather than provide only child-focused therapy. An initial goal is to help the family understand hearing loss, hearing testing, audiograms, hearing aids, and how all these affect the child's communication and language development. As family members become ready, the parent facilitator helps them to use objects and the natural experiences around the home for ongoing auditory, speech, and language training. These are, as much as possible, integrated into the family's routine activities so that they do not interfere, but rather occur naturally. Parents and siblings are not encouraged to become "teachers" per se but to provide an environment that will stimulate the hearing-impaired child's learning. We try to expand on the natural skills of families to make sure the child is provided with input that is appropriate and consistent.

Figure 1.   Professionals and family preparing for the transitioning process. Research shows that moving from birth-to-three programs into schools is a traumatic time for parents.

Figure 2. Parent facilitator and family work on "language through play."

If the child is ill, the parent facilitator usually visits with the family instead of conducting a regular intervention visit. Unless parents request that this not occur, this type of visit enables the family and parent facilitator to discuss adult issues without interruption and it is usually welcomed by parents. Parent facilitators also visit the child's other caregivers in day care, other centers, or hospitals, in order to share information and provide greater continuity of services to both child and family.

When children are hospitalized, members of the staff as well as parent facilitators make visits as often as possible. Although the child may be too ill to enjoy the visit, the parents find this kind of support invaluable and have often remarked about how much it helped them through a traumatic situation.

Because we serve annually approximately 65 families residing throughout western Washington, we are able to offer an adjunct center-based program only for those who live in the greater Seattle area. Therefore, all goals and objectives for individual families and children are developed at home and are carried out by the parent facilitator.

The Adjunct Center-based Program

The center-based portion of the program offers opportunities not available at home. Parents meet other parents of hearing-impaired children as well as deaf adults. If desired, they can become involved in sign classes and support groups. The young children see and play with other hearing-impaired children; they see them wearing hearing aids like their own and learning to communicate and use language. Hearing siblings also participate. This not only provides good models for the hearing-impaired children, but also offers an opportunity for the hearing siblings to participate in fun and exciting activities, to be "special" too, and to feel more a part of the early intervention program. This is important because siblings often feel that the hearing-impaired child receives all the attention and that they are left out.

Our play group is organized around concepts. Concepts provide an organizational scheme that permits us to develop activities and language that are appropriate to and of interest to various age levels, both for hearing and hearing-impaired children. For example, one concept might be farm animals. Children can play with toy animals, build a farm, look at picture books, sing farm songs, learn nursery rhymes, and visit a farm. Language is centered around this concept and learned through many activities.

Using the concept approach can keep group activities motivating and allows for work on individual needs at the same time. We are fortunate to have a large, well-lit room with many windows and an outdoor playcourt. The children can enjoy riding bikes, swinging, and sliding, as well as feeding the ducks and geese that come to visit.

The room itself is organized into "interest areas" so that children can move from puzzles to blocks to a "home area," a book area

Figure 3. Center-based adjunct program showing a group language activity, involving graduate students from Early Childhood Special Education and Speech and Hearing Sciences as well as the physical therapist who works with the hearing-impaired toddler with gross motor problems.

with pillows, and so forth. Adults follow each child, providing appropriate language and assistance, if necessary. Mirrors, a place for a child's coat, and placemats with the child's photograph are used to help each child achieve a sense of self. Group time helps children learn to sit still and attend as well as to share items to touch, smell, taste, and listen to. Parents are welcome to participate in the group activities, or they can choose to attend a parent class, have coffee with other parents, or have some quiet time for themselves. Although we feel that it is important to offer programs to parents, it is even more important for them to feel free to choose what is best for them at any given time.

The play group also provides an excellent, natural learning environment for language, social, and cognitive growth because new, creative experiences can be provided (such as water play, painting, and other messy activities that may not be welcome in all homes) with peers who also have a hearing loss, wear hearing aids, and need to learn to interact. Walks to find leaves and play in the snow, picnics, or trips to visit the zoo and other favorite places can also provide further enriching experiences for both the child, siblings, and parent(s).

Parent group activities occur while the children are in the play group and vary with the desires of the parents. Often parents want someone to talk to them about behavior problems, nutrition, middle ear problems, the State School for the Deaf, and other topics. These sessions are alternated with sign language classes taught by deaf adults, parents, or others when these resources are not available.

In order to provide other families who cannot attend the center program with contacts and information, we hold approximately four Saturday workshops each year as well as one or two evening meetings. The Saturday and evening meetings provide a time for newer parents to meet and talk to deaf adults, parents of older deaf children, and the older children themselves. These times also provide an opportunity for parents, grandparents, and other members of the various families to get to know each other better. Parents and other family members come from all over western Washington to attend.

We maintain an extensive library, which is available to all parents. Each family receives a library list and may obtain books, videotapes, or audiotapes about normal development, positive behavior management, deafness, families, what stimulates positive social/emotional development, and signing.

Counselor

Part of any system's design is knowing that boundaries exist and recognizing what and where they are. Although the ECHI parent facilitators are skilled in such areas as auditory stimulation, hearing aids, communication, and language, they are usually not qualified to respond to depression, feelings of guilt, marital disputes, and other personal or psychological problems; these latter represent boundaries for their particular professional expertise and should not be crossed. Because emotional issues are usually prevalent in hearing family members of hearing-impaired children, we believe it is essential to have, as an integral part of the program, a counselor, or counselors, who are trained to respond appropriately to these issues in the program.

Curriculum

Most hearing parents of children whose hearing loss is newly identified need information—all kinds of information. A curriculum, written in nontechnical language, can provide both information about the auditory system and hearing loss and guidelines for working naturally with the child in such areas as language, auditory training, and speech. The curriculum we use includes basic information, is very easy to follow, and provides a nice beginning for developing a partnership between parents and parent trainer. Each parent and parent trainer has a copy; they can read and discuss information together and develop shared experiences.

Communication

In early interactions between normal-hearing mothers and infants, mothers look and smile at and talk to their infants as if the infant is a true communicative partner. Parents also expect some sort of response such as gazing or smiling back. Very young children communicate intentionally by pointing, gesturing, or indicating in some nonvocal way what they want or need. We feel that it is important to help parents identify the communicative intentions of their young hearing-impaired children. We assist parents in recognizing and rewarding communicative attempts, accompanying this recognition with appropriate language such as, "Oh, you want your bottle. Here it is." Reinforcing these early attempts encourages the continuation of communicative interaction and assists in building self-esteem.

For example, after the parent facilitator has discussed and demonstrated what communication is, he or she might watch the parent(s) and child play and each would identify times when the child was making an attempt at communication. After discussing this, the parent facilitator might ask the parent(s) to do the following during the next week, until the next home visit.

1. Write down the ways you believe your child is communicating, and what that communication might mean.
2. Star the most frequent attempts.

Language

It is widely recognized that children receive language input over a long period of time before expressing language. Therefore, in ECHI we work with parents to help them develop understanding and patience related to their expectations for the first words or signs expressed by their child. We encourage parents to continue using the normal conversational language they used before identification of the hearing loss or with their other children. Language used with hearing-impaired infants, as for those with normal hearing, should relate to objects and activities within their environment that are important to them. Language surrounding such activities as changing diapers, preparing a bottle, fixing dinner, taking a bath, and looking at books can be easy and enjoyable because it accompanies actions that occur as part of regular household routines.

By using the same type of language as do parents of normal-hearing children, by working on communication skills, and training the auditory system, we have found that our children follow the same patterns of language development as do normal-hearing children.

Auditory Training

It has been our experience that very young children, newly identified as having a hearing loss, must be taught that sound is important and needs to be attended to. Hearing aid use is also a critical part of the auditory training process. Parents need to learn how to put hearing aids on their child, take them off, and maintain them, and then eventually teach their children to assume these responsibilities. We place the hearing aids on the child for short periods initially, and then gradually increase the amount of time they wear them over the first few weeks until they are eventually wearing them willingly full time. This process allows the child to adjust gradually to the newness of the aid and earmold as well as to new "loud" sounds. We provide all parents and parent facilitators with battery and hearing aid testers and encourage them to check the hearing aid and batteries as part of the daily routine. The children are always encouraged to watch the process and, as soon as they are able, are shown how to check their batteries—a basic part of auditory training.

Auditory training also involves teaching each child to use his or her residual hearing. Auditory training begins, with most of our children, at the awareness level. Our parents learn how to call attention to sounds both in the home and in the various places they may go, such as parks, the zoo, and other's homes. Feeling and listening at the same time is helpful when a child is first beginning to listen. An activity that parents and child usually enjoy is listening to a noisy dryer.

> Let your child feel the top of the clothes dryer when it is on. Stop the dryer and put tennis shoes or other clunky objects in. Listen. You can point out other "dryer sounds" to your child as appropriate (e.g., a garment with metal buttons clanking).

As each child is ready, auditory training proceeds from awareness, to localization, to discrimination of gross sounds and finally to speech sounds.

Depending upon the child's age when the hearing loss is identified, the quality of residual hearing, and parent involvement, some young hearing-impaired children are able to perform fine discrimination tasks and learn to speak before leaving ECHI and entering school at age three. Others may not even be able to perform gross discrimination tasks. There is a wide range in skill acquisition.

In the ECHI program, teaching parents about speech and assisting the hearing-impaired infants and toddlers to learn to produce speech is based upon the approach developed by Ling (1976, 1988), which emphasizes a systematic, rationally organized process that views speech acquisition as developmental, with normal sequential stages. Informal strategies are used to encourage parents and others to employ playful techniques making sure the interactions are enjoyable for the child so that vocalizations will continue and evolve into spoken communication. Parents and other caregivers learn to imitate their child's vocalizations and to elicit changes in vocal patterns. Typical adult-child activities are used, such as looking at picture books and making animal and transportation sounds, saying/signing nursery rhymes, singing repetitive verses, and making sounds with objects as they play. During this time, parents learn how to assist the child in developing control over duration, pitch, and intensity of vocalizations. The next stage includes producing vowels, dipthongs, and finally consonant vowel combinations on command. As children begin to use certain vocal combinations consistently to communicate, these attempts are reinforced by the adult responding appropriately to the *intent* of the communication so that speech itself is not the focus. As Ling (1988) suggests, criticisms of *how* children produce speech can discourage further attempts at communication. Therefore, it is important to praise and encourage, not correct. Correct adult models of the attempted "words" can be provided without discouraging the child. Thus, if a child vocalizes /ba/ and indicates that she wants her bottle, the adult can expand the utterance and model the word by responding with, "Oh, you want your *bottle.*"

In ECHI we use a total communication approach that emphasizes a variety of ways to express needs, wants, and feelings. Because we stress the use of hearing aids, auditory training, and speech production, we feel that we offer parents what is basically an oral program with sign. This includes:

—using hearing aids
—lip reading
—auditory training
—training speech production
      —with infants and toddlers (playing with and imitating sounds)
      —encouraging vocalizations
      —providing good, consistent speech models
      —reinforcing the use of consistent sound patterns to represent
        an object or action
—verbal language
—sign language (signing Exact English)

Thus, children always wear their hearing aids, which are kept in good working condition, and auditory training is emphasized. Auditory training objectives and activities are an integral part of the program. Professionals and parents use verbal language accompanied by sign so that an appropriate model is always provided. Parents are encouraged to continue to use verbal input, read books to their children, and use smiles and frowns appropriately to accompany the verbal input. As soon as they feel ready, parents and parent facilitator select the names of objects or people that are important to the infant or toddler and learn the accompanying signs. Parents then continue to provide verbal input but use the verbal, plus sign, of the word they are learning. For example, if bottle is the target word, it would be the only word signed in a "conversation" between mother and child.

> Here's your *bottle.* Your *bottle* is warm. Umm, it tastes good. You finished your *bottle*—let's put it in the sink.

Because most caregivers may have other children and certainly have many tasks to complete during each day, and because language is best learned in a natural context, it is important to find ways for caregivers (parents and others) to "teach" language "on the run." White and his colleagues (1973) sum this up nicely.

> . . . when the child confronts an interesting or difficult situation, he often turns to his mother for help. . . . These *10 to 30 second* interchanges are usually oriented around the child's interest of the moment rather than toward some need or interest of the mother. . . .
> These mothers very rarely spend 5, 10, or 20 minutes teaching their one-

or two-year olds, but they get an enormous amount of teaching in "on the fly".... (pp. 243–44)

Learning to sign is often difficult for parents (Swisher and Thompson 1985). However, if they do learn to sign, consistently accompanied by verbal language, their children will not be deprived of language while they are learning to use their residual hearing. Some professionals and parents believe that if a child learns sign, he or she will not learn speech. Lowenbraun and Thompson (1988) reviewed 15 years of research and found no support for this belief. We have never found this to be a problem in ECHI because so much emphasis is placed upon auditory input and vocal production.

Transition

The transition process must be a part of any early intervention program. Although most of our children enter a school program at three years of age, there are some who at two-and-one-half years need consistent interaction with peers and are ready for a daily school program. Whatever the child's age, this can be a very traumatic time—especially for the parents—and it is helpful if information and materials are provided for them ahead of time. The ECHI staff maintains contact with the "home" school districts of our students; we alert the district when a child enters ECHI and again at least six months before the child makes the transition to the district's program.

A year before the child will enter school, the parent facilitator provides the parents with a transition packet that includes a checklist of what to look for in a good program,[1] a sample IEP, and information about P.L. 94-142 and parent/child rights. At the same time, parents are informed about the usual school assessment process, which often differs significantly from what they are accustomed to, and how assessment results may be very different. In the school assessment process, three-year-olds are usually tested by strangers in a strange room using standardized tests that the children have never seen. In ECHI, developmental measures have been used longitudinally over several years by professionals and parents; thus, our children do not have test-taking skills, such as pointing to a picture on command. All of these factors may result in poor test performance and results that can be devastating to parents who have watched their child grow and progress. It helps if they are prepared for this possibility and know that they should (1) take a professional who knows their child to the assessment, (2) request further testing, (3) request placement and

---

[1]Information available from Marie Thompson.

observation before further testing, and (4) not sign the IEP until they are satisfied with test results, placement, and program. In ECHI, during the year before the child enters school, we provide parents with verbal and written information, and accompany them on visits to schools so that they can become acquainted with the school's personnel, policies, and environment. Even with prior planning, unfortunate incidences do occur; but at least the parents are prepared for these possibilities and know they have support from the ECHI staff.

As part of the transition process, we perform a final assessment and forward a lengthy and detailed final report to the school district(s). This report summarizes the child's progress over time and provides information about his or her current functioning, including specific speech sounds or words and language the child is using. We have received compliments from both physicians and school district personnel for this report. Copies of all assessment data are included as well. We have found that each school district has its own entry-level form and that, if we place our data onto their form, it helps both the school district and the family.

We also try to impress upon parents that they are always welcome to telephone with questions or just to talk. Reminder letters restating our continued interest are sent six months after each family has "graduated." We also extend invitations to graduates to attend the play groups, especially during the summer when school programs are closed, and to join us during the Saturday and evening events. This transition period is often difficult and support may be needed until parents feel welcome and comfortable in the new school environment.

PERSONNEL PREPARATION

Preservice Education

ECHI provides a unique preservice experience for students obtaining graduate degrees in both early childhood special education and speech and hearing sciences.

Speech and Hearing Sciences. Students who are obtaining Master's degrees in speech and hearing sciences may obtain ASHA hours for aural rehabilitation by participating in the ECHI playgroup. Both speech/language pathology and audiology majors participate and learn to work with students from other disciplines as well as with the hearing-impaired children and their families. Each student receives a four hour orientation, which includes information about communication, language, hearing aids, and auditory training as they relate to the birth to three hearing-impaired population, as well as specific infor-

Figure 4. ECHI audiologist works with a hearing-impaired toddler and graduate student from speech and hearing sciences in order to teach about hearing aid "checks."

mation about each child. A rationale is provided for the physical arrangement of the classroom and the cognitive orientation of the curriculum. All students participate in all the activities of the center program so that they begin to have a more thorough understanding of this young population. In addition, each student must reach specific speech, language, and auditory training competencies developed by the ECHI staff.

Doctoral-level students in speech and hearing sciences may also participate in the same activities with young hearing-impaired children and their families. In addition, they may also elect independent studies to learn more about this population and seek the participation of children and/or families in their dissertation research.

Early Childhood Special Education. All course work specific to this Master's degree includes information about young hearing-impaired children and their families. All students have the opportunity to include ECHI as part of their practicum experience and most do. Those students who are in the early childhood hearing-impaired track, must take the additional course work relating to hearing-impaired and include ECHI as their birth to three practicum (practicum with three-five year olds is provided in the schools). In addition to working in the play group, these students must also work with the ECHI families in the home. These students must master all the competencies required of the other early childhood students plus those required of the speech and hearing students and special ones designed for learning to work in a home-based program.

Other Disciplines. Students from other disciplines, such as nursing, social work, educational psychology, and occupational/physical therapy, participate in the center-based portion of the ECHI program. These students spend anywhere from three months to one year in ECHI in order to develop a better understanding about how to interact and "teach" very young hearing-impaired children and their families. They participate in all aspects of the play group—leading group time, serving snacks, and taking the children to the playground, on walks, and field trips.

Inservice Education

Parent Facilitators. Key to the success of any early intervention program are those who provide the ongoing service to parents. In ECHI, these people are called parent facilitators. Most of these individuals have a master's degree in speech/language, audiology, or education of hearing-impaired children. A few are parents who were formerly involved in ECHI with their children. Because most university training programs that relate to hearing impairment do not train people to work with the birth-to-three population and their families, almost all parent facilitators need additional special training. Thus, ECHI provides ongoing inservice training in such areas as: early childhood development, early speech and language acquisition, auditory training for infants and toddlers, family systems, the interdisciplinary process, and how to work with families in their homes. We have found that the typical one-day workshop is not sufficient. Rather, appropriate training is an ongoing process of reading, observing others, and, each year, four or five daylong workshops with follow-up. These activities are accompanied by continuous one-to-one supervision and training by the coordinator and audiologist. Parent facilitators must stay informed about new information content areas such as language development, and changes in federal and state laws, so that they can pass this information along to parents. They also must know about the school districts where their families live so that they can help provide a smooth transition when the child enters school. Parent facilitators play a critical part in the lives of these families. Their understanding of the problems the families face and the knowledge they can impart are key to helping the family experience success in interactions with their hearing-impaired child.

Other professionals. ECHI staff members provide training to numerous other service providers in Washington and other states. The training ranges from working with individuals regarding specific content areas, to running workshops for large numbers of professionals who are interested in learning more about young hearing-impaired children and their families. Staff members consistently provide training to professionals in both eastern and western Washington and, through Outreach projects, have trained professionals in Alaska, Colorado, Idaho, Oregon, and Florida.

SUMMARY

In summary, ECHI provides year-round service to approximately 65 young, hearing-impaired children and their families. These services include:

—Involving the entire family
—Developing of an IFSP in collaboration with each family. This includes individual input from parents about their specific "needs" or desires
—Assessing and consistently monitoring growth and change for both the child and family
—Identifying and implementing modifications in the IFSP as appropriate
—Providing content information and activities to assist the family and hearing-impaired child in all areas of development by ECHI staff
—Providing a lending library to supplement learning
—Providing a support system for the family through the program itself and through interaction with other parents and deaf adults
—Providing a curriculum to each family, written in nontechnical language
—Helping to empower parents through education and support so that they will become knowledgeable and can be advocates for themselves and their child
—Assisting families in identifying and finding other resources (agencies, individuals, materials, etc.)
—Assisting families in understanding and using other agencies
—Providing counseling services by appropriately trained professionals
—Assisting the family in making the transition into school
—Promoting a team approach, both within the program itself and with other individuals and agencies
—Promoting contact with the deaf community
—Providing consistent supervision and inservice training for staff
—Providing preservice training for graduate students specializing in early childhood, speech and hearing, social work, nursing, educational psychology, and occupational/physical therapy

REFERENCES

Bayley, N. 1969. Bayley scales of infant development. CA: Psychological Corp.

Bloom, L., and Lahey, M. 1978. *Language Development and Language Disorders.* New York: John Wiley & Sons.

Caldwell, B., and Bradley, R. 1979. *Home Observation for the Measurement of the Environment.* Little Rock, Arkansas: University of Arkansas Press.

Coggins, T. and Carpenter, R. 1981. The communicative intention inventory: A system for observing and coding children's early intentional communication. *Applied Psycholingustics* 2:235–52.

Ling, D. 1976. *Speech and the Hearing-Impaired Child.* Washington, DC: A. G. Bell Association.

Ling. D. 1988. *Foundations of Spoken Language for Hearing Impaired Children.* Washington, DC: A. G. Bell Association.

Lowenbraun, S., and Thompson, M. D. 1988. Environments and strategies for learning and teaching. In *Handbook of Special Education: Research and Practice, Volume 3: Low Incidence Conditions,* eds. M. C. Wang, M. C. Reynold, and H. J. Walberg. New York: Pergamon Press.

Project RHISE. 1979. *Manual for Administration of the Rockford Infant Developmental Evaluation Scales (RIDES).* Bensenville, IL: Scholastic Testing Service.

Swisher, M. V., and Thompson, M. D. 1985. Mothers learning simultaneous communication: The dimensions of the task. *American Annals of the Deaf* 7:212–17.

Thompson, M. D., Atcheson, J., and Pious, C. 1985. *Birth to Three Curriculum.* Seattle, WA: University of Washington Press.

Thompson, M. D., Biro P., Vethivelu, S., Pious, C., and Hatfield, N. 1987. *Birth to Three Curriculum for Parents, Parent Trainers, and Teachers of Very Young Hearing-Impaired Children.* Seattle, WA: University of Washington Press.

Tonelson, S., and Watkins, S. 1979. *The Instruction Manual for the SKI*HI Language Developmental Scale.* Logan, UT: Project SKI*HI.

Uzgiris, I. C. and Hunt, J. 1975. *Assessment in Infancy: Ordinal Scales of Psychological Development.* Urbana, IL: University of Illinois Press.

White, B., Watts, J., and Barnett, I., 1973. *Experience and Environment: Major Influences on the Development of the Young Child. Vol. 1.* Englewood, NJ: Prentice-Hall.

Chapter • 14

Infant Hearing Resource
Portland, OR

Nancy Rushmer and Valerie Schuyler

Infant Hearing Resource was founded in 1971 as a private, non-profit agency to serve families and their young children (birth to four years) with hearing loss. The agency's mission is to provide family-centered services to infants and toddlers with impaired hearing, to increase the knowledge and skills of professionals serving these populations, and to promote attitudes and procedures throughout the state that will lead to the identification of infants with hearing loss within the first months of life.

Founded by the authors of this chapter, who are educators of hearing-impaired persons, and by Brian and Peggy Casey, parents of two deaf children, Infant Hearing Resource (IHR) is now a department of the Porland Center for Hearing and Speech.

Family-centered habilitation for infants and toddlers with hearing loss is the core service provided at Infant Hearing Resource. Two additional areas of focus are the training of early intervention professionals and early identification activities. Each of these three priority areas is described herein.

FAMILY-CENTERED HABILITATION SERVICES AT IHR

Habilitation activities include individual and group sessions at the agency, home visits, and audiologic services. Families enrolled at

Infant Hearing Resource are served by an interdisciplinary staff of infant-family specialists from the fields of education of hearing-impaired persons, audiology, speech-language pathology, and early childhood education. The services of a family counselor and the multi-disciplinary diagnostic clinics of the Child Development Rehabilitation Center at Oregon Health Sciences University are also utilized by families. Deaf adults work with child and parent groups, serve on the board of directors, and collaborate on the production of training materials.

Philosophic Bases of IHR's Services to Families

IHR services to families are grounded in four tenets, which describe our beliefs about *when* intervention is most effective, *who* is responsible for the child enrolled for services, *who* should deliver early intervention, and *how* intervention is delivered most effectively.

Tenet #1: The early months and years in the life of a child with hearing loss comprise the most critical period in the entire educational process for him or her. There are strong implications from studies of children with early conductive hearing loss that the first year of life is a "critical period" in the acquisition of both listening and language skills (Gunnarson and Finitzo 1991). During this first year, the infant's central nervous system is developing in response to sensory input from the environment, by way of peripheral structures. *When hearing loss prevents sound stimulation from being transmitted adequately to the central nervous system, physiological responses are altered.* Thus, a child with hearing loss who is fitted with hearing aids during the first year of life has an enormous advantage over the child, also hearing impaired from birth, who does not get a hearing aid until three to four years of age. In the latter case, the child will never achieve maximum potential to utilize sound in his or her environment because the critical period for development of the central nervous system related to processing sound has passed and cannot be re-activated.

Human beings have a similar "critical period" for language learning. Ninety percent of children with hearing loss are born to parents with normal hearing and are exposed to an auditory language system—speech. If hearing loss prevents their acquiring language during their early years, they will have missed the period during which their brain is programmed to learn language. The 10% of hearing-impaired children born to deaf parents who use a visual mode of communication—sign language—from the time of the child's birth do not suffer this same language deprivation. This fact likely contributes to their greater degree of academic success when they are compared as a group with hearing-impaired children of normally hearing parents. Leonard (1991, p. 44) states, ". . . by the end of their 1st year, children know a great deal about the language spoken around them. Evidence of this sort is sobering for those of us who are responsible for the identification of communicative problems in children. Each month that passes in the child's 1st year could well represent a possible opportunity to remove or apply some external factor, or to foster some compensatory skill."

Unidentified hearing loss has an impact on areas of development in addition to audition and language. Parent-child bonding, social-emotional development, and cognitive development, all of which provide the foundation for later educational achievement, are adversely affected by late identification of hearing loss (Schuyler and Rushmer 1987; Elssmann, Matkin, and Sabo 1987).

Tenet #2: Families retain responsibility for their child, utilizing our service as one of many sources of information, support, feedback, and guidance. In order to determine how best to help their child, family members must be able to rely on professionals to serve as resources for information and developmental techniques that are most appropriate to their needs. IHR specialists support parents, extended family, and siblings as they participate in initial activities carried out during the family's individualized sessions: the survey of each member's needs, interests, and expectations; the multidisciplinary infant assessments and subsequent habilitation plans and, decisions regarding time, place, and types of services as well as (and perhaps most important) the type of communication method to be used with the baby.

Families are offered all the information and resources to which staff have access, including materials written for parents, the agency library, parents of older hearing-impaired children, families in which all members have hearing loss, and other services in the community. Some families are eager to utilize all the literature, guidance, and suggestions offered. Others find only certain aspects of the curriculum pertinent to their situations and needs.

Tenet #3: Professionals must have specialized information and skills to meet the specific needs of infants and toddlers with impaired hearing and their families. The quality and appropriateness of the input received during the first years of life by a child with hearing loss have a significant effect on the child's development. This significance requires that we look at who is providing this input through early intervention services. IHR specialists have identified over 200 competencies specific to the roles and tasks of a qualified infant-family specialist. These competencies include three discrete sets of skills and knowledge not historically included in university programs training communication disorders professionals. These are: (1) skills and knowledge related to infant and toddler development; (2) skills and knowledge related to family systems, family counseling, and techniques of working in partnership with adults; and (3) skills and knowledge related to hearing impairment, hearing testing, and management of amplification in infants and toddlers.

Too often professionals without specialized training find themselves working with families of infants and toddlers with hearing loss. This occurs because there are limited opportunities for the training needed and because some administrative decisions are still based on the belief that not much happens in infancy, therefore, just about anyone can do the work. This kind of decision making has serious implications for a child's future. If the family is not served by professionals with the highest levels of skill in a variety of areas during the first years of life, the young child's subsequent delays in learning can be irreversible. Major areas of knowledge and skills required by the infant-family specialist are shown in table I.

Technical skills and academic knowledge will be useless to the parent-infant specialist in the absence of good interpersonal communication skills and the ability to build positive relationships. Because of

Table I. Knowledge and Skills Needed by Infant-Family Specialists for Hearing-Impaired Infants and Toddlers

Knowledge	Skills
Normal infant/toddler auditory behaviors	Keen ability to detect signs of hearing in hearing-impaired children (birth to four years) in order to promote auditory/verbal and auditory/vocal learning.
Complete understanding of audiogram; characteristics of amplification systems; acoustics of speech in order to meet auditory/verbal goals	Ability to manage process of trial hearing aid use and to use equipment to test electroacoustic function of aids.
	Proficiency with standardized assessment tools to evaluate infant/toddler development in motor, cognitive, socioemotional, hearing, language, and self-help
	Promoting infant/toddler cognitive development
Infant/toddler development	Use of communication strategies that promote prelinguistic communication development[b]
Visual communication strategies used effectively by Deaf parents with their hearing-impaired infant[a]	Guiding parents in process of promoting sequential prelinguistic communication and symbolic language in infants/toddlers
Strategies for working with hearing-impaired infants with other special needs	Communicate use of visual communication strategies effectively to normally hearing parents of infants with hearing loss
Awareness and understanding of Deaf community and culture	Competence in vocal/speech development techniques unique to the young child with hearing loss
	Use of play as a primary learning milieu and an innate sense of playfulness and enjoyment of infants/toddlers

Signed communication if offered to families or if
    Deaf parents are enrolled with their infants
Design and instruction of sign classes for families
Support of and consultation with parents who are
    "nonelective" students
Support family's assessment of their strengths and
    needs
Support family's drafting of their Individualized
    Family Service Plan (IFSP)
Effective "interactional approach" to intervention
    with families[c]
Counseling parents and interacting comfortably
    with family members
Facilitating a family support group of selecting an
    appropriate facilitator
Accommodating to diverse cultural practices and
    a variety of family styles and values
Interdisciplinary team skills
Case management skills

[a]Exaggerated size of signs, referent object brought into the conversational space, repetition of signs and movement within a sign, positive facial expression most of the time (Kantor 1982; Launer 1982; Harris et al. 1989).

[b]Use of "motherese/fatherese" and nondirective language, responding to the child's intent, and turn-taking with the baby.

[c]Use of listening, observing, modeling, and joint problem solving (Bromwich 1978).

Figure 1.　Family-centered intervention is illustrated here as all members of the family are learning to promote acquisition of listening and communication skills.

the elements of counseling involved, personal characteristics desirable in counselors are among those sought in professionals who will work well with families and their infants. Some of these essential characteristics include personal comfort with their own and with others' expressions of strong feelings including sadness, guilt, depression, and anger. The ability to relate to families with warmth, empathy, respect, and positive regard is also important. The ability to use active listening skills and reflect back to parents what they are hearing promotes good parent-professional collaboration. And finally, the specialist must be able to relinquish control of the habilitation process and replace the traditional role of "teacher," "therapist," or "intervention manager" with that of "consultant and resource."

Realistically, programs may not have access to individuals possessing all these competencies and characteristics. Then, it is essential that the team that serves families possess these skills collectively in order that the needs of the infant and family be met.

Tenet #4: The efficacy of early intervention is directly related to the effectiveness of the partnership between parents and skilled professionals. Comprehensive services can be delivered only by specialists competent in infant-family habilitation and in establishing collaborative relationships with families. Effective intervention strategies are based on relationships: the professional with the family; and the family with their infant. The quality of the *parent-professional* relationship will determine its effectiveness in supporting optimal *parent-child* interaction.

The values, dreams, life goals, beliefs, information, and personalities of family members influence the character of their partnership with professionals. The partnerships are as diverse as the families and professionals that comprise them. Goal-oriented professionals entering the family system must be prepared to respond to a variety of cultural practices, belief systems, and lifestyles. It is natural for well-intended professionals to want to initiate a plan of action as soon as possible, to focus on the goal of the child's acquisition of listening and language skills. However, failure to spend adequate time learning the family's values and their goals for their child is a mistake. What is needed at the outset of habilitation is a focus on each family member's feelings, thoughts, and actions, and careful attention to what they say will help them at any given moment. This will be different for every family and for each family member. And it will change from visit to visit.

The effective parent-professional relationship is a collaboration between peers, each with valuable elements to contribute and each needing to learn from the other. Effective partnerships come from sharing goals, knowledge, and questions. Partners who are working together will show their mutual trust and respect for the other's competencies and individuality and their enjoyment of the working partnership. Their joint problem solving incorporates playfulness and delight in and respect for the child.

The parent-specialist partnership evolves as parents are able to express concerns, questions, and feelings in an accepting and understanding environment. They begin to see their roles as consumers and managers of their infants' learning progress, and that of the specialist as resource, consultant, and counselor.

Comprehensive Programming for Families

IHR is dedicated to providing comprehensive and appropriate services to families. Our program components have varied over the years, depending on current staff and financial resources. A comprehensive program at IHR includes the following.

1. Focus on and adaptation to individual families, including fathers, mothers, siblings, and extended family members.
2. Habilitation based on a curriculum of sequential objectives for infants and parents, *Parent-Infant Communication.*
3. Activities that serve the family's expressed needs to learn information and skills at a rate and depth comfortable to them so they can assume responsibility for the management of their child's acquisition of skills.
4. Skilled attention to emotional needs of family members as an integral part of all interactions in the intervention process.
5. A family support group.
6. Activities specifically for siblings in addition to their involvement in all aspects of the habilitation program for the child with hearing loss.
7. Sign language class, if appropriate to the approach used.
8. Introduction to and involvement with the Deaf community.
9. Case management and coordination of multidisciplinary services.
10. Other support services needed/requested by the family.

Family Goals Set the Course. Throughout the habilitation process at IHR, specialists support the family's action that will advance them toward their goals for their baby. However, during the first months of enrollment, families do not always know what to hope for, plan for, or expect. In the rapidly changing maelstrom of beliefs about "the right" communication method and culture for children with hearing loss, parents unfamiliar with hearing loss can be caught in the middle of heated controversies. It is important that parents are given unbiased information about all their options and are respected and supported by professionals as they make difficult decisions.

Parents bring their own values to the decision-making process. These values determine their unique goals for themselves and for their baby. The specialist's responsibility is to uncover and respect the unique values that will guide each family's response to and participation in services.

The more specialists and parents talk about the family's goals for themselves, their child with hearing loss, and other family members, the better insight the specialist will have into what is important to a particular family. Although all families articulate their own goals in their own words, some goals are more universal than others. Some of the goals generated by families at IHR include: (1) developing a sense of self confidence and competence in interacting with their child; (2) acquiring feelings of comfort with the child's hearing loss on the part of all family members; (3) helping the child make optimal use of his or her residual hearing; (4) helping the child acquire linguistic competency (whether in signs, speech, or both) that leads to good communication skills and academic achievement; (5) helping the child acquire intelligible speech; (6) promoting the child's acquisition of appropriate social skills, emotional well-being, and positive self-esteem; and (7) laying groundwork that will enable the child to be motivated to learn, acquire career/work skills, and achieve economic independence.

In some cases, a family's goals may seem to be in direct opposition to the specialist's values and goals. It is not always easy for the academically oriented specialist to set aside personal values and support the family whose only wish for their child seems to be that he or she be "happy," especially when the family's perception is that the happiness will derive from having few limits set on the child's behaviors or no apparent goals for communication and/or eventual academic achievement. Although it is the specialist's responsibility to present other points of view gently to family members, he or she may need support from colleagues in remembering that families retain responsibility for their children and for the goals and dreams they have for those children.

Focus on Infant-Family Interaction. Prior to diagnosis, a baby's impaired hearing may have changed the parent-child relationship in at least two significant ways.

1. The infant is not able to respond to the parents' nurturing vocalizations and speech in ways the parents expect. Failing to get a response from the baby, parents may be confused, may not feel reinforcement, and may reduce their communication and interaction. Parents generally do not recognize that their baby is primarily a visual communicator and would respond if they used different communication strategies. Once they learn that their baby does not hear, they may feel helpless to communicate with the baby and further reduce the interaction.

2. Following the diagnosis of hearing loss, parents generally experience a range of strong emotions. As they work through these feelings, the process of attachment can be interrupted. Loving, nurturing, and joyous interactions with their baby are difficult when parents are hurting.

The period following diagnosis can be characterized by confusion, frightening emotions, and seemingly impossible choices. It may be difficult for family members to interact with the infant with hearing loss in ways that are necessary for the infant's optimal growth. Yet the ways in which family members and caregivers interact with the infant have far-reaching implications for the child's later learning. Supporting the maintenance of a nurturing, positive relationship between the infant and family members is the focus for the specialist during the early months of a family's participation in the IHR habilitation program.

Support for Parents and Caregivers. Communication is central to our interactions with family members. We seek professional staff with good interpersonal communication skills and we encourage on-going training and growth in this area. The early intervention program can be a logical source of emotional support for families because it may be the family's first, and perhaps only, professional contact following diagnosis of their child's hearing loss. Regular contacts with a specialist can promote trust that is essential to a therapeutic environment characterized by open and effective communication. The infant-family specialist needs to be able to listen, attend, and respond to the emotional needs of family members.

We believe that although a specialist is not a full-fledged counselor, he or she can learn to use basic counseling techniques that allow and encourage parents and other family members to discuss, explore, and accept their feelings about their child. A specialist will be effective as a counselor only to the extent that he or she is able to create an environment in which family members feel accepted, appreciated, and valued by the specialist. We believe strongly that a specialist is not responsible for solving a family's problems or for making family members feel better. A specialist's responsibility is to interact with family members in ways that encourage them to explore and accept their own feelings and to make the necessary decisions regarding their child. IHR staff is encouraged to participate in on-going training in interpersonal communication and counseling skills.

The final responsibility of a specialist regarding the counseling function is to refer a family to a licensed counselor when their needs exceed those the specialist can deal with and/or when a family member has concerns that fall outside the realm of habilitation.

Family Decision Making and Agency Values. When a young child is diagnosed with a hearing impairment, the family has some decisions to make right away. In many cases, family members feel ill-prepared to make decisions that may have lasting implications for their child. Two areas in which families must make choices related to their family values and goals for their child involve the selection of communication mode(s) and the use of hearing aids. IHR specialists give families as much information as they can to help families make informed choices in both of these areas.

The IHR curriculum for families is designed to assist them to help their child develop communication and language skills *based on the language used in the home*. A family enrolled in the program can choose either an auditory-verbal approach or the use of Signed English with an auditory-verbal emphasis as communication modes with their infant. Families who elect to use an auditory-verbal approach are exposed to developmental techniques based on teaching a heard and spoken language. Families who speak English and choose Total Communication as their communication mode with their children learn Signed English enhanced by features of American Sign Language (ASL), with extensive orientation to visual communication strategies. Auditory-verbal development is also emphasized in the Total Communication approach. Deaf parents who enroll at IHR generally use ASL at home, increasing the amount of English syntax and grammar as the babies get older. They come to IHR to learn to provide their babies with auditory input and speech stimulation. Families electing to teach ASL as the childrens' only language during the first years (omitting most spoken language) do not choose to enroll in the IHR program.

Communication/Language System. How do parents make an initial decision regarding communication approach to use with their child? They must decide whether to use sign language or not. If a system of signing is selected, should it be one based on English or on ASL? Regardless of reassurance to the contrary, many parents fear that their initial decision about communication methodology is irreversible. This can be a time of tremendous anxiety for them.

Unfortunately, neither research data nor experience clearly points us in one direction over another in terms of what is the "best" communication approach for *every* child and his or her family. The family members' ultimate goals for their child will influence the choices they make. The approaches used at IHR are based on our understandings and beliefs, which continue to evolve over the years as we continue to learn from families, children, and advances in the field. We believe—and tell parents—that decisions made for children with hearing loss in their first years of life must promote their abilities to have choices later in life. We want to provide children with tools that allow them the most expansive opportunities during the course of their lives. We believe these tools to be: (1) the sense of well-being and positive self-esteem that grows from a warm, nurturing relationship with their families; (2) an effective and complete communication system that allows childrens' language and cognitive abilities to grow at a rate commensurate with their ages and needs; (3) access to the most appropriate amplification and auditory-vocal foundations of spoken language, which will allow them to develop their auditory-verbal capabilities; and (4) contact with deaf adults who use ASL and with those who use spoken language.

Agency values and philosophy determine a specialist's role during a family's initial decision making. Specialists provide a family with all available information and resources related to each option and direct the family to individuals who use and/or advocate different options. They clearly outline agency values and services and support the family members in whatever choices they make.

Use of Hearing Aids. As discussed earlier, research on sensory deprivation related to critical periods of auditory development provides us with evidence that appropriate amplification and consistent auditory-vocal exposure must begin as early as possible in order to take advantage of the brain's ability to learn to process sound. *It is our belief that early decisions made for children should promote opportunities for full development of all capabilities rather than narrow the options available later in life.* For this reason hearing aids are used with all babies at IHR. As children mature they will eventually make their own choices regarding use of amplification, speech, and sign language.

Major Program Components for the Child. Faced with the challenge of contributing positively to a family's interactions with the baby, a professional must understand which elements of those interactions are affected by hearing loss and the appropriate programming content to address them. Family members will be involved in a multi-faceted program that incorporates on-going assessment across all areas of development: motor, cognitive, hearing, language, social-emotional, and self-help.

Parents work with a specialist and a pediatric audiologist in hearing aid evaluation, serial supervised trial aid usage, and recommendation of aids for purchase. They discuss with the specialists the elements of what will be a meaningful and accessible communication system for their child, given his or her particular characteristics. Family members become intimately familiar with a sequential curriculum of auditory, prelinguistic, and receptive and expressive language development, and learn to determine when their baby has accomplished target objectives and is ready to move to the next objective. Finally, family members learn to incorporate all developmental goals into individual and group intervention and into the daily routine of home activities.

Description of Habilitation Model at IHR

Habilitation activities for IHR families occur at three sites: the agency, the families' homes, and the audiologic suite. When a family enrolls at IHR, its members are assigned an infant-family specialist with whom they will work during individual sessions, audiological evaluations, and home visits throughout their one to three years of enrollment. Family participation consists of two individual sessions and one group session per week, weekly sign language classes, one session in the family's home each month, and audiological evaluations as needed. Families able to participate in the full program at IHR attend four activities a week. If a child with hearing loss is enrolled in a child care center, a specialist may work with the child care staff in place of the monthly visit in the home.

Individual Sessions. When IHR was founded, the decision was made to provide most services at the agency rather than in the home for practical reasons. In a small, nonprofit agency, heavily dependent on private funding to support services, paying for the time it takes specialists to travel to families' homes several times a week is not possible because some families live 40 to 60 miles away. We have discovered that agency-based sessions have many advantages: access to equipment such as a hearing aid analyzer and audiometers, access to educational toys, availability of written materials for parents that address a current concern, interaction with other families, a respite from home responsibilities and distractions, and immediate access to other specialists to help with issues and concern raised by parents.

However, a monthly visit in each family's home is an integral part of the service for families. This setting has several advantages: it avoids the stress for parents of travel and of "getting the kids dressed and out of the house"; the familiar home atmosphere can facilitate discussion and sharing of concerns or questions; the caregiver has the opportunity to interact more naturally with the infant, who is also likely to exhibit more typical behaviors; the specialist gains valuable (and perhaps more realistic) information about the demands and pressures on the caregivers and also about family interests, needs, and activities.

Most families meet with their specialist for two 50-minute individual sessions each week. One or both parents, a regular caregiver other than the parents, or an adult member of the extended family accompanies the child to sessions. Some families bring several members to sessions, with siblings attending as they are able. During habilitation sessions, parents and specialist work together to assess the learning needs of the child and other family members and to select teaching objectives. They identify activities appropriate to the child's developmental levels that can be used to teach targeted objectives and involve the child in these activities.

There is no set pattern of activities during every individual habilitation session. Although there are always several learning activities planned for the 50-minute period, needs or questions expressed by parents upon arrival at the agency take precedence over planned activities. Often the reading of nonverbal clues alerts a specialist to the need to inquire, "How are things going?" Given this opening, parents can opt to bring up concerns they have, knowing that discussion of their feelings related to their child is considered an important part of the habilitation process.

During initial sessions, families provide information about the interests, concerns, and needs that form the foundation of their learning plan and objectives. Most families elect to follow the core curriculum used at IHR, *Parent-Infant Communication*. This curriculum provides skills and information objectives for both parents and infants related to the development of auditory function, prelinguistic communication, and receptive and expressive language.

It is a fact of life that dozens of variables affect the pace at which each family acquires the information and skills they want. The job of the specialist is to support families in the learning process and to offer new information and skill objectives when previous objectives are met.

Families of infants with special needs in addition to hearing loss (about one-third of our enrollment) select either a parent or a specialist to function as service coordinators. A case manager coordinates interactions and collaboration with service providers in other agencies and monitors the need for joint meetings of these providers when families have concerns about services/information they are receiving or when input from all professionals working with the family is needed for decision making.

Group Sessions. Each week all enrolled families come to the agency to participate in child and parent groups in addition to their individual sessions. Most families also elect to attend weekly evening sign language classes.

Child Groups. Infants and toddlers enrolled for habilitation are grouped by age or developmental levels for play/learning activities once each week while the parent group is meeting. Preschool age siblings may also attend these groups. Activities planned for the child groups incorporate objectives from the following areas of child development: cognition, audition, receptive and expressive language, perceptual and fine motor control, self-help, and socialization. Self-help and socialization activities promote children's development of self-confidence and appropriate assertiveness, acceptance of responsibility, turn taking, sharing, following directions, and different types of play. Preschool teachers who work with graduates of this program report that this group experience produces children with much higher readiness for preschool learning activities than that of children with no prior group experience.

Parent Groups. The primary purpose of the parent groups is to provide an opportunity for parents to share concerns with other parents, to gain information regarding child development, and to explore questions and feelings associated with being the parent of a child with hearing loss. During the past 23 years, IHR staff has tried a variety of formats for group sessions for parents and caregivers. The present system, which seems to be meeting parents' needs, is a weekly support/information group, the focus of which is determined by the families attending. A specialist trained and experienced in counseling and support group facilitation leads the group, with assistance from three different co-facilitators during the year. Early in the year, a family therapist spends about two months as co-facilitator, followed by a deaf adult, who is also a parent. Both of these experts can help parents and caregivers learn more about both the joys and the emotional, physical, and financial stresses that are part and parcel of raising a child with hearing loss. Finally, as enrolled families are preparing to make the transition from IHR to public preschool programs, a parent of an older child with hearing loss, usually a graduate of IHR, co-facilitates the group so she or he can provide information on "life after IHR."

Sign Language Classes. IHR offers three nine-week sessions of sign language classes for parents and extended family members of enrolled children with whom signed English is used. Because sign class is held in the evening, it is the only opportunity some family members have to participate in one of the habilitation activities offered to families. Sign classes are designed with this in mind: they provide an opportunity for participants to get to know one another and to talk among themselves about their common concerns as well as provide them with a congenial environment in which to learn the beginning elements of a signed English system. The vocabulary taught is relevant to infants and toddlers. Elements of ASL are incorporated into the instructional approach. In some years we are fortunate to have deaf adults instruct in the sign language classes.

In the beginning class, parents, other family members, friends, and neighbors who attend are encouraged to use "whatever works" in building communication bridges with children. Pantomime games are presented to promote thinking about how the body is used to communicate nonverbally. Families are introduced to those visual communication strategies that deaf parents use to communicate effectively with their babies. They learn that perfection in signing is not necessary to help a child learn. They are reminded that babies learn best through repeated exposure to short, simple language related to what they are attending to.

Not all families are able to attend the evening sign classes. They are encouraged to take another class in the community, use sign language videotapes from IHR's library, and include sign language practice in their individual sessions.

Special Groups

Sessions for fathers. In the "ideal" parent-infant program, both parents would be able to attend all the individual and group sessions that are offered to their family. For close to 50% of families enrolled at IHR, the father attends many or most sessions. Fathers who are able to attend their family's individual habilitation sessions have the opportunity to discuss their ideas and concerns with a specialist on an ongoing basis. Fathers who attend sign language classes get to know both the sign language instructor and other class participants with whom they can talk about issues.

But there are families in which one parent, generally the father, is not able to attend any of the sessions. Fathers who can attend neither regular habilitation sessions with their child nor sign language classes are usually at a disadvantage in their understanding of their child's hearing loss and its effect on themselves, their child, and their family. Some fathers are uncertain about what is happening during the habilitation process. If the father and mother have a well-established pattern of clear and frequent communication, this disadvantage may be diminished. However, if communication between the parents is limited, the father can come to feel more and more estranged both from the child and from the mother who may, in turn, grow to resent her unshared responsibility for meeting the child's needs.

Specialists at IHR want to provide some service for these fathers. The ideal would be to hold frequent sessions that address the needs of fathers and to arrange home visits for each family around the fathers' schedules on evenings and weekends. Our agency is not able to offer regular services during these times. Instead, we plan at least one meeting each year for fathers only. When polled, the majority of fathers have requested that meetings of this kind be held on Saturday mornings.

A group of fathers (and grandfathers, uncles, and supportive neighbors) in attendance at a Saturday morning meeting may be composed of men whose emotional states and understanding of hearing loss vary widely. For this reason the fathers' meetings that IHR has offered have been led, in the past, by a male psychologist or social worker familiar with deafness and the effects a child with hearing loss has on the family. A male sign language interpreter is also employed. The objective of these meetings has been to give fathers an opportunity to talk about their own situations and feelings they have related to their child. It is important, therefore, that the individual who leads the fathers' meetings be a highly skilled counselor who can elicit discussion and comments from the fathers present. Because many of the fathers are not familiar with each other, disclosing feelings can be a scary proposition. Fathers have responded positively to those counselors who have a comfortable, down-to-earth manner and who use colloquial language and humor with ease to set the tone of camaraderie and man-to-man exchange as opposed to a professional-to-client interaction.

Sessions for extended family members. Members of the extended family are almost always involved to varying degrees in the habilitation process. In some cases, grandparents are the primary caregiver for a child and are the focus of intervention. In some cases, grandparents retain their traditional position on the sidelines. In either event, grandparents—even those living half-way across the country—may still figure prominently in day-to-day decisions that are made by a child's parents or caregivers. Sometimes input from extended family members is supportive of and helpful to parents. At other times relatives or close friends may contribute to the level of stress parents are experiencing by offering advice and "solutions" that are in opposition to what parents hear from professionals. Diagnosis of hearing loss in a grandchild is devastating for many grandparents who experience pain and sorrow not only for the baby who has impaired hearing, but for their own grown child who is grieving because of the baby's disability.

Grandparents, aunts and uncles, and close family friends can be an important source of support for parents who are raising a child with hearing loss. Sometimes, feeling inadequate because they lack information about hearing loss and its effect on the child, relatives and friends pull away from parents at the very time parents need support the most. An agency serving families and their infants with hearing loss can provide a valuable service by offering informational sessions specifically for their extended families and close friends, with parents attending too, if they wish.

IHR has held two types of Saturday morning meetings—informational and therapeutic—for extended families and friends. The first type incorporates three to four 20- to 30-minute minisessions covering topics such as: Types and Causes of Hearing Loss, What Hearing Aids Can and Cannot Do, Services Offered to Families at IHR, The Effect of Hearing Loss on a Child and His Family, and What It's Like to Grow Up Hearing Impaired. The second type of Saturday meeting for extended families has been led by a skilled counselor who is knowledgeable about hearing loss in children and with deaf culture. This type of group is more of a family therapy/support group. A counselor talks about feelings that members of the extended family may experience when they learn of the child's hearing loss. In the safety of these groups, some family members have voiced, for the first time, concerns, feelings, and needs which have been too frightening to express within the family without the assistance of a facilitator. They receive answers to their questions, guidance and support from one another, and the affirmation that they are not alone in their feelings.

Audiologic Activities of Habilitation. The third site in which IHR habilitation activities occur is the audiological suite. Audiologic services are an essential part of the habilitation process for a child. A child's ability to develop a well-functioning auditory input and processing system is dependent on placement and use of the most appropriate amplification system as early as possible. The time invested in gaining information about a child's auditory abilities will enable the child to learn about his or her world through sound.

The Audiologic Team. The pediatric audiology program at IHR is a cooperative effort in which a staff pediatric audiologist, an infant-family specialist, and a family work as equal members of a team throughout the diagnostic, training, and hearing aid evaluation and selection processes. This team approach combines audiologic and medical findings with the specialist's and family's observations of the child's auditory behaviors to gain as complete a picture as possible of the child's auditory capabilities.

This approach differs from a traditional approach to auditory assessment and hearing aid evaluation in three primary ways: (1) the audiologist must *relinquish traditional control* of problem-solving and decision-making tasks that occur in the diagnostic process; (2) the infant-family specialist must *acquire additional expertise* in procedures of auditory assessment and hearing aid evaluation; and (3) parents must *take responsibility* for observing and reporting their child's auditory behaviors, first while the child is unaided and then while he or she is wearing different amplification systems on a trial basis. The auditory evaluation process continues throughout a family's enrollment at IHR, which ranges from one to three years.

The team approach to audiologic services used at IHR requires that specialists, whether they be trained as teachers of hearing-impaired persons, speech-language pathologists, or early childhood special educators, acquire and use skills from the field of pediatric audiology in addition to those skills acquired in their traditional training programs. Knowledge and skills on the following topics are essential to effective participation on the team: (1) maturation of auditory skills in a normal infant; (2) measurement of hearing in infants and young children including: (a) purposes, methods, and limitations of hearing screening; (b) clinical hearing assessment procedures appropriate to infants and young children (visual reinforcement audiometry, play audiometry); and (c) physiological auditory assessment (impedance audiometry and auditory brainstem response testing); (3) acoustic parameters of speech; and (4) effects of hearing loss and of the acoustic environment on reception of sound, including speech.

Because enhancing the infant's optimal use of amplified sound is a critical element of every session, infant-family specialists are further required to have thorough knowledge of and experience with hearing aids, including electroacoustical characteristics of hearing aids, hearing aid coupling systems, relationship of electro- and psycho-acoustical measures, conventional hearing aid selection procedures and considerations, hearing aid selection for infants and young children, and hearing aid use, care, and maintenance.

Trial use of amplification.   At first glance it might seem that the only information an audiologist and specialist need in order to recommend appropriate aids for immediate purchase for an infant is an accurate audiogram, medical clearance for hearing aid use, and hearing aids whose specifications seem to match a child's needs for amplification. Many audiologists do recommend hearing aids for purchase for an infant on the basis of this information. Another approach is to use a system of trial amplification in which several sets of loaner hearing aids are worn by a child over a one-to-two year period before the most appropriate set is recommended for purchase. Extensive practice with this later approach has reinforced its use at IHR.

Audiograms give an audiologist and specialist information about a child's hearing thresholds at octave or half-octave intervals. Hearing aid analyzers supply information about the amount of gain provided by a hearing aid at similar intervals. Neither of these sources gives an audiologist information about a child's hearing thresholds or the performance of the hearing aid between these intervals, nor does an audiologist gain any information about the subjective aspects of the sound a child receives.

The object of amplification is to raise a child's aided auditory thresholds to within a range that he or she can both perceive and discriminate speech without exceeding his or her tolerance level. The audiologist and specialist must consider variables in three areas when selecting appropriate amplification to meet this objective. These areas are: (1) the child; (2) characteristics of the child's hearing loss and residual hearing; and (3) specifications of hearing aids available for trial use.

Although infants cannot verbally state their preference for one amplification system over another, they do provide many nonverbal behavioral clues that the careful observer can use to determine which amplification system is providing an infant with the most usable auditory information. Some of a child's behaviors associated with an amplification system that is providing effective and useful sound are: increased response to sound, increased amount and variety of vocalization, willingness to wear aids for longer periods of time, protest when aids are removed, and request (nonverbally) for placement of aids. Parents and siblings who have been trained to look for these behaviors and who have observed their child demonstrating these behaviors with one set of trial-use aids are very quick to notice if these behaviors are reversed or absent when another set of trial-use aids is placed. Conversely, if a parent has observed few of these behaviors in a child, a marked increase in these behaviors, or acquisition of new behaviors, when a new set of aids is used is an exciting development that parents are eager to report.

It may be that a child's acquisition of new auditory skills just happens to coincide with the placement of a different set of trial-use aids. If the question of maturation versus the effects of the new aids is raised, there is no reason not to reinstate use of the first set of aids (after the new auditory skills are established) then observe the child to see if the new behaviors are maintained and acquisition of further skills occurs.

Each child is observed and tested with an average of two to five different models of aids before a recommendation for purchase is made. Recommendation of hearing aids for purchase generally occurs after two years of enrollment at IHR. By that time, the audiological team has had an opportunity to ascertain that the child's hearing loss is stable, as opposed to progressive, and has observed the child wearing a number of amplification systems. All members of the team are comfortable that the amplification system purchased is the most effective system available.

OTHER MAJOR ACTIVITIES OF IHR
Training of Professionals

A second major set of activities at IHR is directed to increasing the number of personnel with comprehensive training in serving infants and toddlers with hearing loss and their families. The IHR staff works toward this goal in two ways: publishing materials for professionals working in the field and developing and providing training to professionals.

Publications. Infant Hearing Resource staff members (1985) wrote *Parent-Infant Communication*, a curriculum of sequential auditory, prelinguistic language, and symbolic language development objectives for infants, birth to four years, and information and skills for family members. They also have written *Parent-Infant Habilitation*, a textbook that delineates the "hows" of working with families of young children with hearing loss. This text is used in several university training programs, and, like *Parent-Infant Communication*, is used by educators in the United States and abroad. The IHR staff collaborated with film maker Susan Shadburne on the production of *Turn Around*, an award-winning documentary videotape on family-centered habilitation.

Infant Hearing Resource has recently produced two series of training modules for use in inservice and preservice training of early intervention personnel. Each series contains training modules—Training Outlines and Videotapes—on topics essential to early intervention. The *Early Intervention Series I* (Infant Hearing Resource 1993) contains seven modules and the *Trainer's Handbook*. It is designed for trainers of personnel working with families of deaf and hard-of-hearing infants and toddlers. The *Early Intervention Series II* (Infant Hearing Resouce 1994) is geared to trainers of early intervention special education personnel. It contains four modules and *Trainer's Tips*. Topics covered in both series are: Play-Based Learning, Supporting Emotional Needs of Family Members, Promoting Early Communication: Prelinguistic Communication, and Public Law 99-457 and the Basics of Family-Centered Intervention. Additional topics in the *Early Intervention Series I* are Promoting Early Communication II: The Role of the Family, Promoting Speech Development, and Team Approach to Audiologic Assessment.

Preservice Training Activities. Surveys of professionals serving infants and toddlers with hearing loss and their families (Roush, Harrison, and Palsha 1991; Infant Hearing Resource 1989), indicate that most were not specifically trained to meet the unique needs of these populations. In response to the need for trained personnel, IHR was funded by the U.S. Department of Education between 1976 and 1992 to provide preservice training of Infant-Family Specialists: Hearing Impaired. Each year up to six trainees, with bachelor's or master's degree in education of the hearing impaired, audiology, speech-language pathology, or early childhood special education, come from across the United States for the eight-month training program. Training includes course work in pediatric audiology, family counseling, adult training techniques, infant and toddler development, infant-family habilitation, and case coordination-interagency cooperation. Trainees spend eight months in intensive, supervised practicum with enrolled families. These professionals become integral members of the habilitation team, enriching the services to families with their own experiences and background.

Graduates of training have earned up to 34 credits through Lewis & Clark College and are qualified for certification as a Parent-Infant

Specialist: Hearing Impaired through the Council on Education of the Deaf. Many have taken additional course work at Lewis & Clark College and earned master's degrees. Graduates have worked or are presently working in early intervention programs in 24 states.

Blending family-centered habilitation with professional training. Carrying out effective professional training through a daily practicum with families requires careful planning, orientation, and open discussion with all team members. In practicum, a family's needs, interests, and goals take priority over trainees' needs. Trainees might prefer to be "set loose" to practice skills in a "sink or swim" manner with little supervisory intervention, as they may have done during student teaching or clinical practicum while earning prior professional degrees. In the IHR training program, however, trainees work alongside the specialist as a member of the interdisciplinary team. We hope that, having experienced first hand a model in which family needs take priority, trainees will be more likely to use it in their future work.

Inservice Training Activities. The Infant Hearing Resource staff has intensified and expanded its inservice training activities in response to P.L. 99-457, which mandates and/or supports services to children with disabilities ages three to five and birth to two years. Most university programs training professionals in communication disorders cannot devote the time necessary to prepare professionals sufficiently to specialize in infants with hearing loss and their families. For that reason, professionals must obtain further training to become qualified to work with infants and adults. Not all professionals can avail themselves of a year-long training program, yet they are presently serving or want to serve infants and toddlers with hearing loss and their families.

IHR has developed resources for inservice training to address the needs of these on-the-job educators. The *Trainer's Handbook* contains 200 plus competencies identified by IHR as being required by the infant-family specialist. A professional can measure his or her knowledge and skills against the list of competencies and identify those areas in which he or she needs additional training. He or she can then seek sources of information and skills, such as course work at local institutions of higher education (e.g., in pediatric audiology, family counseling); local professions with specialized training who are willing to be mentors; workshops, conferences, and summer institutes; relevant texts and journals; other infant-family programs; and videotapes produced by infant-family programs.

The Early Intervention Series I and *II* are resources for university faculty delivering preservice training to students and for supervisors and administrators responsible for providing inservice training to their staff. The modules in both series detail learning objectives and outline content of workshops/courses on topics relevant to working with families in early intervention programs. Information on adult training techniques and evaluation of workshop/course effectiveness is also included. The IHR staff is also available to travel to a site to offer training through workshops or seminars on a variety of topics. One of the most productive formats for these on-site training sessions involves IHR staff members observing sessions with families and meeting with infant-family educators after the sessions to offer consultation and feedback and to exchange techniques.

Early Identification Activities

Former Surgeon General C. Everett Koop, M.D., (1989) stated:

> If it is to be effective, early intervention with children who are deaf should begin before the child's first birthday. Unfortunately, we are not doing a very good job of detecting infant deafness in the United States. A recent report to Congress and the President by the Commission on Education of the Deaf pointed out that the average age at which profoundly deaf children in the country are identified is $2\frac{1}{2}$ years. In contrast, the average at which such children are identified in Israel and Great Britain is 7 to 9 months. . . . (p. 53)

An August 1991, press release from the Joint Committee on Early Identification of Hearing Loss (comprised of The American Academy of Otolaryngology—Head and Neck Surgery, Inc. and the Alexander Graham Bell Association for the Deaf) confirmed that for the 4,000 children born annually in the United States with a significant hearing loss, the average age at which identification occurs is $2\frac{1}{2}$ years.

The third major set of activities carried out at IHR relate to the early identification of infants with hearing loss. These activities have been a significant part of the mission of IHR for the past 20 years. Our efforts, focused in the Portland metropolitan area, have included presentations and workshops for medical personnel on the importance of early identification of infants with hearing loss, a public service announcement run on local television channels alerting parents to the need to check their baby's hearing, and frequent talks to service organizations in the community. Data compiled by the Oregon Newborn Hearing Registry (personal communication, November 1990) show that the mean age of confirmation of hearing loss in the Portland metropolitan area while almost seven months earlier than the mean age of confirmation in the state as a whole, is still a dismally late 23.8 months. Obviously, there is work still to be done.

The IHR staff is currently working on the development and dissemination of a *Community Early Identification Campaign* that can be used by agencies and organizations nationwide to address the need for *identification of infants with impaired hearing within the first year of life.* Goals of the project are: (1) to lower the age, nationwide, at which infants with hearing loss are identified so that they can be enrolled in an appropriate, family-centered early intervention program in their first year of life; and (2) to develop, for national dissemination, a model community campaign of early identification activities to educate personnel who serve infants and toddlers and to promote action leading to audiological testing of infants at risk for hearing loss/deafness and to identify infants whose hearing is impaired.

IHR staff is currently engaged in first phase activities of this project and is developing activities and funding for the second phase.

CONCLUSION

All early identification efforts, family-centered habilitation, and professional training activities conducted at Infant Hearing Resource, Portland Center for Hearing & Speech are colored by the non-profit environment in which they are carried out. The intensive and individualized services to families must be subsidized by fund raising activities of the staff and Board of Directors. Other activities must be funded by local and/or national grants. Our freedom to develop and carry out innovative services is balanced by the perpetual challenge of funding our on-going services to families and the community.

REFERENCES

Bromwich, R. 1978. *Working with Parents and Infants.* Austin: PRO-ED, Inc.

Elssmann, S. F., Matkin, N. D., and Sabo, M. P. 1987. Early identification of congenital sensorineural hearing impairment. *The Hearing Journal* (87): 18–22.

Gunnarson, A. D., and Finitzo, T. 1991. Conductive hearing loss during infancy: Effects on later auditory brain stem electrophysiology. *Journal of Speech and Hearing Research* 34:1207–1215.

Harris, M., Clibbens, J., Chasin, J., and Tibbitts, R. 1989. The social context of early sign language development. *First Language* 9:81–97.

Infant Hearing Resource Staff. 1985. *Parent-Infant Communication. A Program of Clinical and Home Training for Parents and Hearing-Impaired Infants.* Portland, OR: Portland Center for Hearing & Speech.

Infant Hearing Resource. 1989. Unpublished survey of educators in five western states. Portland, OR.

Infant Hearing Resource. 1993. *Early Intervention Training Personnel Series I: Materials for Serving Families of Deaf and Hard of Hearing Infants and Young Children.* Portland, OR: Portland Center for Hearing & Speech.

Infant Hearing Resource. 1994. *Early Intervention Series II: Materials for Training*

Early Intervention Special Education Personnel. Portland, OR: Portland Center for Hearing & Speech.

Kantor, R. 1982. Communicative interaction: Mother modification and child acquisition of American Sign Language. *Sign Language Studies* 36:233–82.

Koop, C. E. 1989. Let's talk. *American Speech-Language-Hearing Association* 31:53.

Launer, P. 1982. Early signs of motherhood: Motherese in ASL. Paper presented at American Speech-Language-Hearing Association Convention, Toronto, Ontario, Canada.

Leonard, L. B. 1991. New trends in the study of early language acquisition. *American Speech-Language-Hearing Association* 33:43–44.

Roush, J., Harrison, M., and Palsha, S. 1991. Family-centered early intervention: The perceptions of professionals. *American Annals of the Deaf* 136(4): 360–66.

Schuyler, V., and Rushmer, N. 1897. *Parent-Infant Habilitation. A Comprehensive Approach to Working With Hearing-Impaired Infants and Toddlers and Their Parents*. Portland,OR: Portland Center for Hearing & Speech.

Chapter • 15

The Thayer Lindsley Family-Centered Nursery
Emerson College

David Luterman

I began working at Emerson College both as an academician teaching undergraduate and graduate courses in audiology and as a clinician in the speech and hearing center associated with the college program. After a few years, I realized that a traditional clinical audiology practice was not for me. In 1965, while casting about for another way to relate to the field, I started—with incredible naïveté—a parent-centered nursery program. (I think at times one must leap into the professional void. If one waits to be fully qualified to do something, it is probably too late. A growing professional is always operating on the margins of competency, or incompetency, as the case may be.) It had occurred to me quite early in my professional life that parents of deaf children were not treated well—least of all by me. I knew then that parents needed more help than I could give them in the short-term audiologic counseling sessions I was accustomed to, and also more help than they were able to get from the child-centered programs available to them in the local schools for the deaf. So I conceived a program that was to be a transition for parents as they moved from the diagnosis of their child's hearing loss to entrance into the educational establishment: I wanted to bridge the gap.

Parents of newly diagnosed hearing-impaired children were invited to enroll in the program for an academic year before moving on

This chapter was prepared with the help of Polly Meltzer and Julie Rubin Goldberg. Their generous support is acknowledged.

to a program for the deaf. They were required to come with their child two mornings a week (later increased to three). We insisted that the parents must attend, and that merely "dropping off" the child would not be acceptable. "Parents" were loosely defined to be any primary caregiver. Over the years we have had nannies, grandparents, and aunts bring the child. Occasionally, families have been able to arrange for fathers and mothers to alternate attendance, although most of the time it has been the mothers who have participated.

The nursery room is equipped with a large one-way mirror and observation room. Adjacent to the nursery are two small therapy rooms, also equipped with one-way mirrors and observation rooms. A typical nursery group consists of eight hearing-impaired children between the ages of 18 months and 3 years, and one or two nonhearing-impaired children. There are three components to the program: nursery, individual therapy sessions, and the parent/caregiver support group.

NURSERY

One of the many premises upon which the program was founded is that we need to take care of human needs before we can take care of "special" needs. I had met too many "successful" deaf adults who had good oral skills but were unhappy human beings with a limited capacity for joy; I counted them as failures. I did not want to repeat the mistakes of the past, and I wanted to be sure that we treated the children as children first. I hired a nursery teacher who was not a teacher of the deaf. Her task was to keep the staff focused on developmental issues and to remind us that these were *children* who happened to have a hearing loss. To that end, we also put a hearing child in the nursery (the first one was my third-born child). The primary reason for doing this was not to provide language stimulation for the deaf children, but to remind all staff and parents what the developmental issues are for a two year old. It often seems that there is no creature more deaf on the face of this earth than a two year old whether he or she has a hearing problem or not. At every age parents continually confuse developmental issues with deafness issues. In my experience, parents invariably give the child too much credit for being deaf and, therefore, do not discipline the child appropriately. Expectations for the child's behavior are too low, which I think is the biggest obstacle to deaf children realizing their full potential. Low expectations by parents and teachers limit the child severely, because people, especially children, have a way of conforming to the expectations of others.

In our program we have never altered the basic notions of keeping the parents as our first responsibility and staying continually focused on the human needs of parents and children.

Parents are required, in the first few months of the program, to watch the children in the nursery as they interact with our staff and students. The nursery staff is comprised of the teacher and three graduate students majoring in speech-language pathology. The staff tries to model effective intervention strategies as well as good speech-language, within an informal, spontaneous play environment. In the nursery classroom, language is always used in a manner that will give meaning to a child's activities and will fortify the goals of the individual therapy sessions. With an eye toward future years of schooling, some structure is introduced in the form of a daily story hour, snack-time, and activities planned by the students. A great deal of the learning, however, is accomplished in one-to-one play situations made possible by the number of adults available in the classroom. Our goal is to model for the parents those activities they can engage in at home. One of the rules we have is that no equipment can be purchased for the nursery that is not within monetary budgets of most parents. In the same vein, we do not demonstrate any exotic techniques for parents to use. It is far more useful to show them how an ordinary daily activity, such as having a snack, can become a valuable language-speech learning experience.

After a while (usually six to eight weeks) the parents rotate through the nursery. Because there is a surplus of adults at that point, one student usually observes while the parents work with the remaining nursery staff. We are careful not to let this be seen by the parents as "helping out," but rather as part of their learning experience. We believe there are three routes to learning: you can listen, you can see, or your can do. All three are needed, but the most effective learning is by doing. Keeping parents as passive observers is not enough—they must participate actively in the early intervention process.

THERAPY

Each morning every child receives a twenty-minute individual speech and language intervention session. This is a more structured, formal session directed to the child's specific language needs. The therapy is provided by second-year graduate students under the supervision of a teacher/clinician. In some years the supervisor has been a teacher of the deaf. More recently it has been a rehabilitative audiologist. Here again the parents first observe and then gradually take over the session with the interventionist, either in the room or observing through the one-way mirror. Toward the end of the academic year, the parents are the primary interventionists. After each session there is a conference to discuss the goals of therapy and what will be happening next. The children are given speech and language tests periodically to determine their progress. Because of the young age of the children, most testing is done through informal evaluation. Parents periodically fill out a speech-language questionnaire for their child and are encouraged to share the child's communication attempts at home with the therapist. In this way, communication goals and the therapy program are determined together by therapists and parents.

Some years we have started parents in therapy by having them teach a child other than their own. Usually the first session with their own child is a disaster; the parent is nervous and wants so badly for the child to perform well that the tension is communicated to the child. Children seldom respond well when we really want them to. In a similar vein, the child has been having so much fun "playing" with the interventionist that he or she does not want the parent to intrude. The child often resents the parent's being there, and doesn't mind letting him or her know it.

By having parents start with another child, the initial therapy sessions are often more successful. It also permits them to look more objectively at what the child is doing, because they tend to look at their own child with bias. We do not always mix the children and parents in this manner, but we always encourage parents to observe another child in therapy.

During the posttherapy conferences, we always try to accent the positive and look at what the parent did well. It is not necessary to tell people what went wrong; they usually know that quite well. We do this in the group session as well, almost never criticizing parents (or students for that matter), but modeling good intervention strategies and supporting the learner at every juncture.

SUPPORT GROUP

One morning a week the parents are required to attend a group session with me as the facilitator. I remember vividly that first session of the first nursery group, and my sitting at the head of the table looking at the anxious, grief-stricken faces of the parents and wondering what in the world I was doing there. I knew I only had a few of the time-worn speeches that had served me well in the short-term contact that typically occurs between audiologists and parents, but I knew they would not serve for the long-term commitment of a support group. An academic year was composed of two fifteen week semesters and each group session was ninety minutes in length. I couldn't fake it for that long, so I had all the parents introduce themselves and tell how they had decided to get involved in the nursery. When everyone had finished, I told them that I didn't know what was supposed to happen in the group, but I hoped that they would be comfortable there. (Actually I was hoping I would be comfortable there). A long silence followed as everybody looked around at everybody else. The actual length of silence was probably only thirty seconds, but it felt like hours. Then the parents began to talk to each other; their stories had triggered similar memories in each other. The talk soon became a torrent—I realized, that first day listening to the parents, how lonely they were and that all I needed to do was to bring them together in a safe environment and they would do all the work.

In time, I found that the support group became the one place where parents felt they could be understood, where their experiences could be shared. I now know that there is no greater gift that professionals can give to parents than other parents. To do this, professionals must be willing to put aside their set speeches and be willing to listen. Parents will teach you much.

There are certain topics that constantly recur in all groups and, although every group is unique, similar themes run through all of them. At first, parents need to tell their stories. These emerge in the first few sessions. There is usually a great deal of affect in these first few sessions as parents recall the grief and pain of the diagnostic process. One parent's tears usually trigger a like response in other parents. What they are establishing is their credibility. Issues around methodology and hearing aids occupy a considerable amount of time. The dominant emotions in the early stages are fear and grief. Guilt usually emerges somewhat later, as the group develops more trust.

Family issues usually emerge within the first few sessions. Parents invariably are concerned about their marriages, the hearing siblings, and the grandparents. I have found that, after the first few sessions, there are few new topics, the parents merely recycle the ones that emerged early in the life of the group. When a topic re-emerges, parents who were silent the first time contribute and parents who talked the first time now may add details.[1]

A typical group is composed of the eight parents (usually mothers), two or three graduate students, and the two or three parents of the hearing children. After the first few sessions, I do not allow a new parent in to a group. A group rapidly becomes cohesive and develops its own history. When you add a new member, it forces the group to go back to square one. Everyone has to tell his or her story again and trust has to be developed anew. Also, the parents move fairly quickly past the initial grief reaction and they resist being taken back to the uncomfortable place they were by the new parent, who is now openly grieving. They are sympathetic to the pain but unwilling to again expose their own pain. Consequently, the group tends to be static for

---

[1]For more details on parent feelings and issues in raising a deaf child, please refer to *When Your Child is Deaf: A Guide for Parents*, by David Luterman with Mark Ross. This book is published by York Press, Inc.

several sessions until the new member can be assimilated. It is always a setback to have a new member join an ongoing group.

Because our program is based on a two-academic semester model, we refashion the group for the second semester. Parents who applied during the first semester are seen individually and are allowed to enter the group during the second semester. The first-semester college students are replaced by new students. The second semester starts with a reconstituted group that needs to establish its own rules and history.

Parents are not forced to participate in a group. At the outset it is just assumed that they will. If a parent decides he or she does not want a group experience (most are fearful at first), he or she can observe the individual and group sessions instead.

The group usually becomes the focal point of the program for parents. It is the one place where they can share their feelings and experiences and be understood. The group gives them a feeling of universality. They also get an opportunity within the group to help others, a process that enhances their self-esteem. By using a nondirective strategy (I never give them a topic), I create vacuums that parents must fill. Eventually, they realize that they know more than they thought and are also more competent than they thought. A group is a powerful vehicle for promoting the growth of parents. I could not conceive of a program without it.

SPECIAL FEATURES

Other features of the program also make it valuable to the families we serve. Some of these features we started at the beginning, whereas others have been added over the years.

Deafness is very much a family affair and programs have to afford options for the whole family to participate. We have evolved several.

Saturday Nursery

Once each semester we hold nursery on a Saturday to allow participation of family members who might otherwise not be able to attend. Usually it is the fathers who attend, but the extended family of aunts, uncles, and grandparents are also included. This gives them all a chance to see the child in the nursery and in their individual sessions, and to talk with the staff. While the staff invariably grumbles about giving up a Saturday, it is generally acknowledged afterward that these sessions are very worthwhile.

Grandparents' Day

One of the Saturdays, usually in the spring, we designate as Grandparents' Day. We ask the parents to make a special effort to get the grandparents to attend because, in addition to observing the group and individual sessions, we try to form a Grandparent Group. The grandparents have a unique perspective on the child's deafness and its effects on the family. For them it is a double hit; not only are they grieving for their grandchild but for their child's pain as well. Grandparents usually get locked into denial and often resent receiving information second hand from their adult children. Frequently, there is a lot of tension within the family created by the grandparent's denial and the lack of communication between parent and grandparent. Grandparents are frequently seen as a burden rather than an asset. Grandparents are also incredibly lonely—they rarely have the opportunity to talk to other grandparents of deaf youngsters.

It is hard to assemble a grandparent group. They usually live away from their children or spend several months of the year in warmer climates. Many are too infirm to travel to our center. Whenever we've had a large percentage of grandparents living in the vicinity of the nursery, we've had a parent/grandparent evening meeting. At these times I have used a fish bowl design very effectively. In this design, the grandparents are in the center of the circle while the parents are on the outside. (Only people on the inside can talk.) I start the session with a question such as "What is it like to be the grandparent of a deaf child?" After 45 minutes of discussion, the groups reverse with grandparents on the outside and the parents on the inside. I start the parents' discussion with a parallel question of "What is it like to be the parent of a deaf child?" Afterward, we form a large circle and everyone discusses the experience. This design mandates listening; it is sometimes much easier to hear someone other than your own child or your parent. I have also found this design useful in groups consisting of husband/wife or parent/professional dyads.

Sibling Day

All siblings are affected by the presence of a deaf child in the family, and they, too, need professional attention. We always allow siblings to come to nursery with their parent (we do not provide day care but, if the parent is willing to supervise the child, sibling attendance is encouraged). We also set aside separate days specifically for siblings. These are held during school vacation times that do not coincide with the college vacation. On sibling day, the hearing child participates in nursery and individual sessions. We answer all their questions and usually test the sibling's hearing to give them a chance to experience and better understand these procedures.

Because the deaf children in our program are so young (birth to three years), the siblings are usually also quite young. Rarely do we find a family with hearing adolescents. Because of this we have not had a sibling group session, although we would certainly be open to one. Siblings need a chance to talk with other siblings, in much the same way as the adults need each other.

Evening Meetings

Evening meetings are held for spouses who cannot attend during the day. This is usually the father, but occasionally the group includes a mother or two. These groups meet infrequently and seldom develop the cohesiveness we find in the weekly day group. We usually hold only one or two evening meetings a semester. A fathers-only group is rarely emotional in the overt way that a mothers' group is. The men usually prefer to stick with the nuts and bolts of deafness, although some groups are surprisingly open and forthcoming. There is a subtle chemistry of groups that the leader has no control over—groups must be taken as they come.

We always give the parents their choice of the format and the frequency of evening meetings. They can be fathers-only groups or husband/wife groups. In husband/wife groups there is usually more restraint because neither spouse wants to pay a heavy price for what is said in public. For a few heady years, we were flush with money and were able to take parents away for a weekend without children. Within the confines of a limited time and space, the groups developed a great deal of intimacy. The fish bowl design was very powerful. Those husband/wife groups became the most powerful groups we have had. (During the past several years I have been facilitating parent learning vacations for other programs. I also find them to be the most powerful group sessions I do. When people are out of their traditional environments and roles, they are apt to risk more.)

Day Off

Several times each semester we give the parents a day off. We tell them to leave the child and to do something for themselves. This sends an important message to the parents that they need to take time for themselves. One of our themes is that happy parents produce happy kids. Taking time for themselves periodically enables them to be able to give quality time to their children. I often tell parents that when I travel by air, the stewardess reminds me that if I am accompanied by a child and the oxygen mask should fall down, I should put the mask on my face first, then the child's. As nurturers/providers we need to take care of ourselves first in order to be able to take care of our children. The periodic day-off conveys to the parents our programmatic support for that notion.

Infant Program

During the first decade or two of the program, we rarely saw a child under 18 months of age. We are now getting referrals for many children under one year of age. I think there is an increased awareness of deafness as a diagnostic possibility on the part of the medical profession. This has occurred as angry parents have gone back to pediatricians and apprised them of their errors. There is also an increased use of auditory brainstem testing in our geographic area and deaf children are identified sooner. It is now mandatory in our state for hearing testing to be provided for all newborns in intensive care units.

On the day that the support group meets, the parents of newly identified infants come as well. We provide care for the children while their parents participate in the support group. The infants and their parents are seen once a week for individual sessions with a rehabilitative audiologist and a graduate student. As the infants mature, they are able to participate in the nursery, and the parents enter the regular program.

Content Acquisition

On the days when parents observe in the nursery, we also offer miniseminars. The past few years we have offered a signing class for those parents who wish to attend. Occasionally, the audiologist will meet with parents to discuss testing procedures or hearing aids. The nursery school teacher may also meet with parents to discuss topics such as discipline or toilet training. All topics emerge from parent interest—we rarely impose a topic, but ask the parents what interests them.

Occasionally, I do lecture on specific topics in the parent support groups, but that invariably arises spontaneously from parental concern. Moreover, I have a book collection that I circulate among the parents. I prefer that they work a bit to get the information that they need. The groups themselves become highly informative as parents share with one another information they have acquired. The information is much more valuable to parents when they have learned it for themselves. It also boosts their self-esteem enormously when they are able to supply information to others.

Admission Procedures

From the outset, we have been interested in seeing only those families who choose us. Choice, when made freely, always involves a greater commitment. To that end we developed a passive admissions procedure. We do not accept a third-party referral; parents must call us. I encourage them to come and see the program in action. Then I explain that it is a parent-centered program and the emphasis is on them (they usually don't hear this). I give them an application form and the name and telephone numbers of parents who are either currently enrolled in the program or were recently enrolled. I also give them a directory of other programs in the area and urge them to consider other options. I never follow up on the initial visit. If the parent does not send in the application, I assume that he or she found another one more suitable. We have never denied admission to any parent who wished to attend our program.

As a consequence of our admission policy, we have tended to deal with middle-class or upwardly mobile parents who are already actively involved in their child's education. It is a self-selecting group. Over the years we have had a low drop-out rate. Most families complete the program and many are reluctant to leave. We recognize that a parent-centered program is not for everyone—communities and facilities must offer a variety of program options without valuing any one program more than others. Parents will select what is best for them if we allow them to make choices. It is my firm belief that if a program tries to do everything for everybody, it will invariably either fail or doom itself to mediocrity.

SPECIAL ISSUES

Early intervention programs must address the following issues.

Methodology

In our program, parents are given a choice of methodology. We believe that no method will be effective unless the parents themselves choose it. The only way this will happen is if they make the choice and commit themselves to it. In the very early stages, parents often will not have a clear idea of what methods they prefer. If an infant has a profound loss and the parents cannot decide, we will suggest an auditory/oral approach with supplementary use of signs. For children with significant residual hearing, we will always start a child using an auditory/oral approach.

The methodology issue is discussed at length in the support group. The program affords parents ample opportunity to look at their child objectively (or as objectively as any parent can) in the observation room while our staff interacts with him or her. They also have a chance to compare their child's progress with others. They can request a change of method at any point.

Our philosophy of methodology is that if a particular approach works well for one child and family, it is good for them but not necessarily appropriate for others. At all times we try to fit the method to the child, rather than the child to the method. We often tell parents that the child will "tell" us how he or she wants to learn, because some children are more verbal and others more gestural by nature. We offer the parents the option of auditory/oral, cued speech, and total communication. To date, we have had no parents request that we use American Sign Language exclusively, without emphasizing hearing aids and speech. If a family should express a desire to use ASL exclusively, we would refer them to another program. Although ASL deserves recognition as an appropriate language for deaf adults, I cannot, in good conscience, offer ASL as an option for very young deaf children. Try as I might, I still see deafness as a disability that can be minimized by the appropriate use of technology, consistent methodology, and good parent education. I do not see ASL as a feasible option for most hearing parents primarily because they do not become so competent in ASL that it becomes the "mother tongue." I also feel strongly that the goal of early intervention should be to give the child as many choices as possible, and then to respect the choices eventually made: ASL, by limiting the use of hearing aids and oral communication, is, in my view, a very restrictive option. As professionals we need to have clear limits on what we will do, and although I have broad areas of accommodation, there are times I refuse to accommodate because to do so would compromise my own core values.

We hold an evening meeting in the spring semester in which parents get a chance to meet deaf adults. In the early years of the program the deaf panel was selected almost randomly. Unfortunately, we usually had at least one angry deaf adult who would lecture the parents on the virtues of ASL and signing. He or she would invariably upset the parents who had opted for an auditory/oral route and cause unnecessary guilt in all of the parents. During the last several years we have had panels consisting of graduates from our program accompanied by their parents. I select the panel carefully so that there are children who have elected an oral route and others who have opted to sign. I also try to pick mainstreamed children as well as children who have been educated in schools for the deaf. The parents of the children are there to add a much needed parental perspective. This meeting is always well attended and is very successful in promoting a thoughtful consideration of the methodology issues.

Deaf Parents

On rare occasions we have had deaf parents of deaf children attend the nursery. Generally, this has not been successful. Deaf parents respond very differently to having a deaf child than do hearing parents (Halpern 1989). They do not seem to have a grief reaction. One father said to me, "I'm glad my child is deaf. I wouldn't know how to raise a hearing child."

The major difficulty I encountered with deaf parents was in the support group. The presence of a deaf mother restricted the hearing mothers, making it difficult for them to voice their dismay at their child's deafness. Every time they did the deaf mother would say, in effect, "Deafness isn't so bad, look at me." The parents would look at her, and what they saw was an adult with barely intelligible speech who had to rely on an interpreter. But they could not express their pain openly—it would not be considered "polite"—and at that time, I lacked the skills needed to elicit their feelings.

In the early stages of coping, parents move from denial to resistance. In resistance, they bolster themselves with the belief that their child will be a special case—a super-oral adult who can pass for hearing. In this early stage, most parents are not ready to meet a non-oral deaf adult. Programs have to be sensitive to this and it is very difficult to work with a mixed group of parents. This also means one should not rush to provide deaf adults for parents to meet; later they will be better prepared to meet them, as they should.

I have worked with a group of deaf parents of deaf children; however, this group had very little emotion and it remained problem focused. Its members wanted specific information on child rearing and availability of assistance. Because they had already come to terms with their own deafness, they felt no need to discuss methodology or feelings. I do not sign and all communication was conducted through an interpreter. I was very uncomfortable using an interpreter, as I was missing the nuances of communication so necessary to facilitate growth and learning. Perhaps a facilitator who was a fluent signer could have done more.

I know now that if we have a deaf parent in a group with hearing parents, I will have to confront the whole group on how they are feeling about the deaf parent. This would be uncomfortable for everyone, but it would be necessary in order to encourage the kind of openness a group needs to function properly.

Funding

Funding is a chronic problem. The first several years of the nursery were fully supported by a U.S. Office of Education Demonstration Grant. There were no fees for the parents. In subsequent years, the program was fully supported by the college for training purposes and as a community outreach facility (it was good public relations). When the college could no longer support the program entirely, we instituted a fee scaled to ability to pay, but no one is ever denied service for financial reasons. The fee, if paid in full, would still not cover the full cost of the program and, while we are still subsidized in part by the college, there is a sizable funding gap that must be filled each year.

This gap is filled by philanthropy; both private and corporate alumni and friends of the college have been donors. There have been years when I was sure we would not be able to continue, and then an angel appeared. Somehow we survive from one year to the next. If a program fills a need, then clients and donors always find their way to its door.

The parents we deal with are so motivated to learn about deafness and to work with their children, that now the fee is irrelevant.

Parents with fewer financial resources are also quite motivated, but they are often so distracted by other life issues that they have little energy or resources to devote to early intervention.

Keeping Focused

The hardest thing to do in the program is to keep the focus on parents. It is easy to get seduced by children. They are so appealing that professionals often tend to put children as the center of their attention. In order for a parent-centered program to work, the focus must be on parents. The degree of parent work is inversely proportional to the amount of program time available for the children. If there is limited time for contact with the child, then almost all professional attention must be directed to the parents; if the professionals have a great deal of time with the child, then they can afford to reduce parent involvement.

We encourage focus on parents by asking our staff to write "lesson plans" for the parents rather than for the children. Everyone must see children as the raw material from which parents can learn. It is difficult for a staff member to sit in the observation room and watch a mother fumble through a communicative interaction with "her child." Professionals must lose their fear of parents (the students are always much more fearful of parent evaluations then they are of their supervisors). It is hard to encourage them to talk with parents after nursery sessions. It usually takes an entire semester for them to become relaxed around parents.

Parents themselves do not always appreciate the parent-centeredness of the program, preferring to keep the child in the forefront. There is a strong tendency on the part of parents to "let the professional do it." It is so much easier to sit back and watch rather than actually do, a tendency born out of parental insecurities. Our aim is to empower parents and thus build their self-esteem. They often prefer not to participate at this level. We are flexible and loving, but firm in our insistence that all parents participate directly in the early intervention process.

PROGRAM COORDINATION

In order to be successful it is absolutely essential that all the program elements be coordinated. For example, we coordinate individual sessions and the nursery by having a "goal box." Graduate student clinicians write out their goals for the children and leave them in the box in the nursery. The nursery staff reviews these objectives weekly and each member works on each child's goals during the spontaneous play that the nursery provides.

The entire staff meets weekly, usually after a parent support group meeting, to discuss each family. Graduate students participate in the support group and report on what happened that day so that everyone knows what is occurring at the parent level. The children are also reviewed by nursery staff and therapists.

Staff

The staff is the most critical aspect of the program. A program such as ours cannot succeed unless all staff members share the basic family-centered philosophy of the program. This is not to say that there are never disagreements, but the core philosophy must be in harmony. Each program has its own "culture" and everyone must agree with it in order for there to be consistency within the program.

In selecting staff, I am not impressed by titles or curriculum vitae. I want people who are vital and interested in others but willing to take risks and who care deeply about what they are doing. Over the years, I have hired speech-language pathologists, audiologists, nursery school teachers, parents, and an assortment of people with unusual backgrounds. Some have not worked out well and have left quickly. For our type of program, the key to staff selection is to identify people who are nurturing but not smothering. In effect, what happens within the program is that the staff becomes parents to the parents; we try to model effective intervention strategies by how we interact with family members. Therefore, it is essential for us to select only staff members capable of being nurturing human beings.

Staff and program culture are much more important than facilities. Our nursery is a remodeled garage that was built before insulation was considered important. Consequently, we all freeze during the winters and swelter during the summers, yet we are consistently able to turn out successful groups of parents and children.

We have made several attempts to try to evaluate the results of the program. One cannot design a rigorous scientific study to compare graduates of this program with graduates of child-centered programs in the area because the families are so different. I do know from a recent survey we did to commemorate the 25th anniversary of the program that there are many parents who are very grateful for having had a chance to participate in the program.
Over the years I have learned the following:

If you take good care of the parents, the children turn out fine.
You cannot go any faster than the parent is ready to go and you can't save children from their parents.
Parents are smart and will choose well for themselves, if given the chance. They are the only ones with the full picture.
There are no intervention techniques more powerful than those that serve to build parental self-esteem.

If you treat everyone in the program with loving respect, they will grow.
Never pity the parents; empathize with their pain and arm yourself
with the knowledge that if you allow them to struggle, they will
emerge with increased strength. Deafness is a powerful teacher
for everyone.

REFERENCES

Halpern, K. 1989. Hearing and deaf parents reactions to deafness. Unpublished Masters Thesis, Emerson College, Boston, MA.

Luterman, D. 1990. Audiological counseling and the diagnostic process. *Asha* 32:35–37.

Luterman, D., with Ross, M. 1991. *When Your Child is Deaf: A Guide for Parents.* Parkton, MD: York Press, Inc.

PART • **V**

Preparing for the Future

Chapter • 16

Preparation of Early Intervention Personnel

Barbara Bodner-Johnson

Over the last several years, a number of significant events have converged in a way that predicts a better future for infants and young children who are hearing impaired, and their families. Research on the development of young children has demonstrated that this development is mediated by the mutual effects of both nature and nurture; results from landmark empirical studies have extended our knowledge of the complex and transactional nature of the developmental process and have clearly pointed to the potential benefits of early intervention (Broman, Nichols, and Kennedy 1975; Werner, Biermin, and French 1971). Bronfenbrenner (1979, 1986), Garbarino (1990), and others have sought explanations for a child's behavior and development both within the individual child and beyond, in the child's social environment; their ecological perspective on developmental risk has directed attention to the child's interactions with family and friends, and with people in the child's neighborhood and school. The Infant and Toddler Program (Part H) of the Individuals with Disabilities Education Act, formerly known and still referred to as P.L. 99-457, marked a turning point in opportunity for developmentally vulnerable young children. This legislation, first passed in 1986, calls for statewide, comprehensive, coordinated, multidisciplinary, interagency programs of early intervention services for young children with disabilities and their families (*Federal Register* 1989). Furthermore, the provisions of P.L. 99-457 relating to the development of personnel standards and systems require that states work to ensure both the availability and the highest quality in all personnel. Finally, in 1986, a Commission was established by the Congress of the United States for the first time in history to study the quality of education for deaf persons (*Toward Equality: Education of the Deaf* 1988). Among the recommendations of the Commission to the President and Congress was the following:

> The Department of Education should require . . . the establishment of program and personnel standards that specifically address the educational and psychological needs of families with young children who are deaf. Individuals working with young deaf children and their families should be professionally trained in the area of deafness and early intervention (p. 99).

There is substantial reason for professionals and advocates seeking early intervention services for infants and toddlers who are hearing impaired to see both the unique opportunities and the enormous challenges in these events. The Commission's recommendations reflect established theoretical and empirically derived knowledge. Furthermore, they indicate the conditions necessary to make a better future for hearing-impaired children by ensuring that professionals working in early intervention are adequately prepared in the areas of deafness and family-centered early intervention.

Personnel qualified to serve infants and young children who are hearing impaired—as well as those at risk and with other disabilities—are in short supply. Weiner and Koppelman (1987) predicted that P.L. 99-457 would further intensify the qualified personnel supply-and-demand problem. Meisels et al. (1988) suggest that the shortage of qualified personnel is one of the most serious obstacles facing states in implementing services for infants and toddlers with disabilities. In a national survey of early childhood intervention policies, Meisels et al. (1988) found that nearly every state reported a severe shortage of both special educators and pediatric specialists. A majority also reported insufficient programs to prepare personnel to work with children who have special needs from birth through age six. Furthermore, these shortages are predicted to continue into the future.

Currently, few preservice or inservice preparation programs are available for entry-level personnel specializing in early intervention for hearing-impaired children and their families. The purpose of this chapter is to recommend the scope and specific content for comprehensive preparation in this area. At a time when the identification of hearing-impaired children under three years of age is increasing (Schildroth, Rawlings, and Allen 1989) and when P.L. 99-457 is being fully implemented, the national need for highly qualified early intervention professionals in the field of hearing impairment is also increasing.

ISSUES IN EARLY INTERVENTION PERSONNEL PREPARATION

Early Childhood Special Education: A Unique Field

Writing in 1849 for the *American Annals of the Deaf* on "Home Education for the Deaf and Dumb," Ayres (1849) suggested that:

> Education, to be complete, must begin and end at home. The foundation must be laid in the plastic mold of infancy; in the thoughts, principles and habits, with which the child opens upon life; and over the structure built up by many hands must be thrown, for its final completeness, the grace and refining influence of home (p. 12).

The recognition of the significance of the early years and of the home environment has a long history in the field of educating deaf children. Early home-based, child-centered education programs such as the John Tracy Clinic Correspondence Course (1968) focused primarily on communication and language development, and made a significant contribution to current efforts in the early intervention field.

Early childhood special education has since defined a broader set of values and philosophies, and has documented diverse models of effective service delivery (McCollum et al. 1989; Peterson 1987). Defining the unique contributions of this field, Bailey, Palsha, and Huntington (1990) propose that the primary mission of the early childhood special educator is:

> . . . to ensure that environments for handicapped infants and preschoolers facilitate children's development of social, motor, communication, self-help, cognitive, and behavioral skills, and enhance children's self-concept, sense of competence and control, and independence (p. 49).

Furthermore, in order for early childhood special educators to carry out their mission, Bailey, Palsha, and Huntington (1990) identify the following tasks: (1) conduct screening and child-find programs; (2) assess children's developmental competence; (3) plan and provide developmental intervention; (4) coordinate interdisciplinary services; (5) integrate and implement interdisciplinary team recommendations; (6) assess family needs and strengths; (7) plan and implement family support services or training; (8) coordinate services from multiple agencies; (9) evaluate program implementation and effectiveness of overall services for children and families; (10) be an advocate for children and families; (11) consult with other professionals, families, and caregivers; and (12) work effectively as a team member.

It is essential that universities and colleges coordinate with programs offering direct services to families for the design of their preparation programs. The competencies targeted in curricular content and the procedures used to carry out the course and field work should reflect and model the unique mission and roles of the early childhood special education professional.

Professional Credentials

When P.L. 99-457 was passed in 1986, states varied widely in their requirements for credentials needed for working as early childhood special educators (Smith and Powers 1987). Differences ranged from states having no certification standards and requiring no credential for the birth through age five range, to those requiring varying forms of a state credential for some portion of that age range.

As universities and colleges develop programs for educators as well as for other personnel working with hearing-impaired infants and toddlers and their families, two problems emerge: (1) some preparation programs may be driven by state certification requirements that do not reflect what is known about young children with disabilities (including hearing impairment) or about best practice in early intervention, and (2) degree and internship requirements in the preparation programs in some states may not permit certification in other states due to an absence of uniform certification standards (McCollum et al. 1989).

There are two sources of assistance for states seeking to establish certification guidelines for early childhood special educators to work either in noncategorical programs or with deaf children and their families: the recommendations for certification developed by the Division of Early Childhood (DEC), Council for Exceptional Children (McCollum et al. 1989) and the Council on Education of the Deaf (CED) requirements for certification for the parent-infant education specialization (Council on Education of the Deaf 1984). The DEC recommendations are compatible with those of CED. Together, these documents offer essential guidelines for universities and colleges when developing preparation programs for early intervention personnel for hearing-impaired children and their families. Each document represents the position of its respective profession based on best practice and research. A plea is made by McCollum et al. (1989) that state agencies, universities, and local early intervention programs coordinate their efforts so that a cohesive approach to preparation, personnel standards development, and certification emerges.

SOURCES OF CONTENT

The knowledge base for course and fieldwork for entry-level personnel preparation in early intervention, and the process by which the curricular content is delivered emanate from: (1) the purposes of early intervention; (2) the infancy period as primary service target; (3) the family-centered mandate of P.L. 99-457; (4) the multidisciplinary team-based service delivery requirements; (5) the level of maturity and professional judgment needed; and (6) the implications drawn from the literature on teacher education.

Purposes of Early Intervention

The overall goal of early intervention is to promote optimal development of the child and to support and enhance the quality of life for children and their families (Fewell and Vadasy 1987). Greenberg, Calderon, and Kusche (1984) argue that although early childhood hearing impairment may be considered in terms of the psychological and sociological impact, the overriding communicative delay and/or deprivation should be the major focus of early intervention. They propose further that, whether a program advocates use of American Sign Language, an English-based sign system, an oral/auditory approach, or some combination thereof— "the development of mutually satisfying communication between deaf children and their caregivers is crucial to help overcome the effects of deafness on communication and language" (p. 607).

More than 91% of hearing-impaired children are born to hearing parents (Rawlings and Jensema 1977) and most of these families have little contact or familiarity with hearing impairment or the deaf community in their area (Liben 1978). In addition, most hearing-impaired children today go to school in their neighborhood or district in their home communities without access to large numbers of hearing-impaired children and adults typically available in residential schools (Moores 1987). It is of paramount importance that early intervention with hearing-impaired children focus on the child's home environment and on developing family and community relationships, including both the family's home community and the deaf community whenever possible.

In her analysis of early intervention programs for hearing-impaired children and their families, Meadow-Orlans (1987) identified a number of key predictors of success for this population. Based on clinical experiences as well as studies of different early intervention programs, Meadow-Orlans suggests the following as hallmarks of excellence in early intervention programs.

1. A strong emphasis on parent counseling in groups and sessions for mothers and fathers, singly and together.

2. On-site capabilities to test hearing aids routinely and to provide new ear molds as required.

3. A strong commitment to development of speech and oral skills within a natural interactional approach with parent involvement.

4. Inclusion of sign language as a program component for all parents and children with the view that sign language is a helpful communicative adjunct for all hearing-impaired children and a necessary tool for language acquisition in severely and profoundly hearing-impaired children.

5. Matching family language needs and program capabilities so

that both hearing-impaired and hearing parents' communication needs are met with staff competence in a variety of sign systems.

6.   Presence of hearing-impaired adults as program staff or as resources.

Coursework for early intervention personnel should cover infant development, multidisciplinary assessment, the impact of hearing impairment on development and assessment practice, and curriculum and instructional strategies appropriate for birth to three-year-old children who are hearing impaired. Parent-child interaction and the visual, auditory, and oral aspects of communication must be emphasized. Specified levels of proficiency should be required in American Sign Language (ASL) as well as in English-based sign communication systems and cued speech. Coursework and practicum opportunities should be offered in counseling and should include instruction and practice in consulting with parents, other family members, and caregivers. Opportunities to observe and participate in individual and group parent-professional meetings and to work with professionals and parents who are hearing impaired should be integrated into courses and fieldwork.

Early Intervention versus Preschool

There is strong consensus that program needs of infants and toddlers differ from those of older preschool-aged children, and that these differences should be reflected in the preparation of personnel for early intervention (e.g., Bricker and Slentz 1989). In their survey of preservice training programs in early childhood special education, 89% agreed that working with infants and their families requires different knowledge and skills from working with the 3 to 5 age group. Bricker and Slentz (1989) specify their reasons for supporting distinct training for the birth to two-year-old population: (1) the knowledge base differs because development in the infant and toddler period is different; (2) instructional practice for infants and toddlers incorporates one-on-one, play-oriented strategies and child-initiated interactions with an adult and includes providing families with information and support related to promoting the child's development; (3) the setting where early intervention occurs is likely to be the child's home, a day care center, a hospital, or clinic versus the more traditional classroom; and (4) during the first two to three years of a child's intervention program, significantly more teamwork is required among professionals in acquiring appropriate medical, allied health, educational, and social services for the child and family.

Because the age of the population being served is such an important factor in planning personnel preparation programs, distinctions in course and practicum emphases must be clearly made between the birth to two or three and the three to five age groups. Although personnel may, in fact, be knowledgeable about both age groups and the line between differences at age two or three may not always be distinct, significant differences in roles and in perceived needs of professionals working in each setting indicate that having information only about the 3- to 5-year period is insufficient when working with infants and toddlers (Bricker and Slentz 1989; McCollum 1987).

Family-Centered Early Intervention

The provisions of P.L. 99-457 require that parents of eligible infants and toddlers play a central and collaborative role in directing and monitoring their child's early intervention program. The law recognizes the primacy of the family and mandates that services "be developed jointly by the family and appropriate qualified personnel involved in the provision of early intervention services" (*Federal Register* 1989, p. 26320). Thus, the law expects that parents will become full partners with professionals in facilitating their child's development.

A commitment to parent involvement in early childhood education and special education is not new (e.g., Turnbull and Turnbull 1990); however, what is new is the nature of the parent-professional relationship that ensues if the service mandates of the law are upheld. Mutually determined family goals as well as child goals must be included in a written Individualized Family Service Plan (IFSP) so that "services necessary to enhance the development of the child and the capacity of the family to meet the special needs of the child" (*Federal Register* 1989, p. 26320) are provided. With the family's agreement, the content of the IFSP should include information on the family's concerns, priorities, and resources related to enhancing the child's development. Furthermore, provisions require that at age three, the program must provide activities for parents that prepare them for their child's transition to preschool.

The new roles and responsibilities of parents have implications for the knowledge and skills expected of early intervention professionals and, therefore, have an impact on the design of preservice and inservice programs preparing these professionals. Specifically, early intervention personnel must have knowledge and skills related to the family as a social system, family dynamics and functions, and how families develop. They must have comprehensive information about the impact of hearing impairment and other disabilities on these aspects of the family. Moreover, these professionals must be prepared to assist parents in developing the resources and strategies required to cope with the diverse situations they encounter relative to the needs of their hearing-impaired child. One such resource, especially helpful to parents of children with disabilities, is access to an informal social support network (Crnic, Friedrich, and Greenberg 1983; Kazak and Marvin 1984). Early intervention professionals must recognize that support from established networks of friends and relatives, as well as support from other parents of hearing-impaired children, contribute to the family's well-being and should be considered integral to the early intervention program. Training in identifying family priorities, resources, and concerns related to the child and in developing workable, mutually agreed-upon family goals is needed in both preservice and inservice professional preparation. Early interventionists need opportunities to develop advocacy skills, to acquire knowledge regarding adult development and strategies for facilitating adult learning, to work with families and communities different from their own, and to develop skills to communicate effectively with parents not only about their children, but on other sensitive issues that have an impact on their child's development.

It is incumbent on professional preparation programs to embed a family-centered perspective throughout the curriculum and to provide opportunities for trainees to develop relationships with families having diverse backgrounds, priorities, and resources. When developing a professional preparation program in early intervention for hearing-impaired children, parents should participate in the planning process and should continue to serve in an advisory role to the program. As much as possible, direct participation of parents and other family members in teaching and supervision should be built into the program design.

Interdisciplinary, Team-Based Service Delivery

Public Law 99-457 specifies that early intervention services must be provided by qualified personnel, including: audiologists, nurses, nutritionists, occupational therapists, physical therapists, physicians, psychologists, social workers, special educators, speech and language pathologists, and other relevant personnel such as vision specialists, paraprofessionals (e.g., respite service providers), and parent-to-parent support personnel. Services specified under "early intervention" include: audiology, service coordination, family training, counseling and home visits, health services, medical services for diagnostic or evaluative purposes, vision services, nursing, nutrition, occupational therapy, physical therapy, psychological services, social work, special instruction, speech-language pathology, transportation, and other types of services such as provision of respite and other family support services. As appropriate, the regulations state service providers in each area are responsible for: consulting with each other and representatives of community agencies, training each other, and participating in the interdisciplinary team assessment of the child and family and the development of integrated goals in the IFSP (*Federal Register* 1989).

Clearly, disciplines overlap in serving eligible birth to three-year-old children under P.L. 99-457 and an integrated rather than discipline-specific approach to program development and delivery is required. This follows from the nature of the-infant-as-learner and the interrelatedness of the developmental domains during the early period (McCollum and Thorp 1988).

What emerges as the primary implication for preparation programs is the need to provide courses and fieldwork that offer interdisciplinary perspectives. Integrated opportunities should be provided for students from different disciplines (e.g., audiology, education, counseling) to participate in the same classes and practicum settings so that they may develop team skills and acquire interdisciplinary content. Additionally, preparation programs should offer study and field opportunities relevant to understanding local, state, and federal policies to ensure services that are comprehensive, consistent, and in the best interests of children and families (Bricker and Slentz 1989).

Maturity and Professional Judgment

Bricker and Slentz (1989) have identified an important problem regarding curriculum and practicum experiences needed in early intervention preparation and the level of maturity and professional judgment required. They suggest that structure and administrative supervision in the school-age environment offer a level of support and predictability that is often unavailable in the early intervention setting. Early intervention services to the child and family are often provided in the home, in a day care setting, or in a community center where no particular structure exists and where support services are not readily available. Often the early interventionist alone must interpret situations, make decisions, and generate solutions to questions and problems. Thus, the need to manage emotional situations and difficulties related to the child's hearing impairment, as well as health questions, or family problems becomes a serious concern for professional preparation. In addition to information, parents often require high levels of emotional support. The service provider must have the background and experience needed to understand difficult situations and the good judgment to refer the parents to other professionals when appropriate.

While current direct service providers have acquired valuable experience with infants and families, preservice students typically enter early intervention preparation with limited practical experience with families, infants, and other professionals. In their field work they most often have little practice in making substantive program decisions with families and have little chance to explore and understand the reasons for doing things in particular ways. The inexperienced early interventionist is in a vulnerable position—and so are the families and children they serve—if they leave their preparation programs without the appropriate experience to complement the abilities and knowledge needed to deal with these problems. Bricker and Slentz (1989), based on their synthesis of the literature, recommend that personnel preparation programs provide extensive supervised practicum in delivering services to young children and their families. These experiences should be multidisciplinary and team based in nature; they should involve child assessment and collaborative goal setting with families, program planning and implementation; and they should occur in a variety of settings (e.g., hospitals, schools, homes) and cultural situations.

Related to the issues of maturity and professional judgment, McCollum and McCartan (1988) and others (e.g., Zeichner and Liston 1987; Kennedy 1990) indicate the importance of including reflection and problem solving in teacher education in order to develop independence and flexibility in early intervention practice. McCollum and McCartan (1988) propose that the early interventionist's awareness of conflicting views regarding approaches and models, and the ability "to use a wide range of knowledge, to generate hypotheses, and to reflect on the outcomes may not only be desirable, but necessary as the only way students can be adequately prepared for the heterogeneous populations and roles encountered by early childhood special education teachers" (p. 283).

Research in Teacher Education

Although literature on the preparation of early childhood special education teachers is sparse, university and college faculty interested in designing programs to prepare early intervention specialists to work with hearing-impaired infants and their families can find a wealth of resources in the teacher education literature. McCollum and McCartan (1988) suggest that the comprehensive body of research available in the area of regular education can offer useful guidance in program development. From discussions of research in regular teacher education (Katz and Raths 1985; Lanier 1986; McCollum and McCartan 1988) and from the even broader perspective of professional education (Kennedy 1990), a number of implications can be drawn for personnel preparation in early intervention for hearing-impaired children and their families.

For example, greater coherence in teacher education is achieved when programs attend to the two main goals of professional education. These goals are: (a) to provide as much of the codified knowledge as possible so that graduates have content related to the maximum possible variety of situations they encounter; and (b) to enhance independent thought and analysis so that graduates have the reasoning skills and strategies for analyzing and interpreting new situations.

In addition, ways should be found in teacher education for socializing students to collegial and mutually supportive professional relationships that provide greater access to professional development and encourage an expanded, more flexible perspective related to teaching.

In designing programs for professional preparation in early intervention, the following points need to be discussed and resolved before appropriate training opportunities can be made available: student knowledge and experience backgrounds; availability and expertise of faculty; availability of practicum sites and families; relationships to community agencies, parent groups and the deaf community; traditional university practices that support discipline-specific program design; and faculty willingness to accommodate parents as colleagues. Activities within courses and fieldwork should be interrelated and coordinated as well as closely supervised so that students can apply their theoretical knowledge in practical situations, e.g., translating knowledge and techniques of collaborative goal-setting into identifying family priorities, resources, and concerns. The linkage of classroom and field work and the type and variety of field placements are critical. Students should have opportunities to participate in decision making with parents and professionals regarding the child and family; they should be required to generate and evaluate goals and to plan and implement individual IFSPs. Moreover, students should be expected to examine their decisions with their peers, cooperating teachers and university supervisors in order to promote self-analysis and understanding of outcomes.

Lanier (1986) suggests two approaches to promoting collegiality and mutuality of support among students: (1) moving through the preparation program as cohorts rather than as individuals and, (2) engaging in joint planning and reflection. Mechanisms should be developed that allow faculty to teach as a team across disciplines (e.g., infant development, deafness and audiology, or education, deafness and counseling) so that classes, perhaps cohorts of students from various disciplines, can be formed.

CONTENT AREAS AND PROCESS COMPONENTS[1]

Content Areas

The specific knowledge areas recommended in table I integrate content from infancy (birth to three years) and hearing impairment, and focus preparation on the needs of very young children who are hearing impaired and their families. The content and related process components of early intervention preparation derive from the purposes of early intervention for hearing-impaired children, the need to work with families and professionals from different disciplines and to achieve maturity

---

[1]Because it is impossible to know how to separate my own ideas from those of colleagues with whom I have worked for years in the Department of Education at Gallaudet University, I want to give credit to the Department's teacher preparation programs for many of the specific content and procedural recommendations presented here.

Table I. Recommended Content Areas for Early Intervention Personnel Preparation

General Education*	Deafness	Infancy/Families	Deafness/Infancy
Life-span human development and learning	Introductory audiology	Cognitive, affective, language, psychomotor development from birth to three	Impact of deafness on development: birth to three
Survey of exceptionalities	Introduction to deafness: education	Atypical development: birth to three, integrating all domains of development and environmental, biological, and medical factors	Language acquisition and cognition
Foundations of education	Language structure: English and ASL	Family systems, dynamics, development, and functions	Families with young deaf children
Educational psychology	Speech development	Adult development and learning	Support, collaboration, counseling, consultation, education, and advocacy for parents/caregivers and families
Curriculum and instruction: general and early childhood, all domains of development	Auditory habilitation	Interdisciplinary assessment of the young child and identification of family resources, concerns, and priorities	Pediatric audiology and oral habilitation
Language development	Social/cultural diversity: communities and families	Physical, vision, and medical management including health management	Research in early childhood with emphasis on special education and deafness
	Proficiency in ASL	Environmental and behavior management	Interdisciplinary assessment: deaf/birth to three; identification of family resources, priorities, and concerns
	Knowledge/skill in a variety of communication systems including fingerspelling, cued speech, manually coded English	Development and organization of environments, activities and materials for early intervention	Curriculum and instruction: deaf/birth to three, all areas of development
			Interdisciplinary and interagency team-based program planning and service delivery coordination
			Intervention strategies and application of research-based knowledge and best practice
			Program development, leadership, and administration

*Prerequisite to professional preparation

and professional judgment, and from the recommendations from research on teacher education.

Moreover, the content areas related to the roles in which early intervention personnel are expected to function in order to provide comprehensive services (Klein and Campbell 1990). These general roles of developmental specialist, parent consultant, and team member broadly focus the responsibilities of early intervention personnel and incorporate the twelve specific roles cited earlier and developed by Bailey, Palsha, and Huntington (1990). For hearing-impaired children and their parents, the overriding problem that crosses all roles is that of facilitating mutually satisfying parent-child interactions.

Regarding field experience, the Division of Early Childhood (DEC) (McCollum et al. 1989) and the Council on Education of the Deaf (CED 1984) suggest two types: practicum and student teaching/internship, to total from 300 to 400 clock hours. DEC recommends that practicum experiences occur in multiple settings, either as part of specialized coursework or separately, but concurrent with content related to development and methods. Practicum and student teaching/internship experiences in the field work sequence should be developmental; that is, initial directed observation and participation should lead to supervised clinical practice and, finally, in student teaching/internship, responsibility for all professional duties should be assumed (see table II).

Graduates of early intervention preparation programs in the area of hearing impairment should be expected to demonstrate proficiency

Table II. Recommended Field Experience

Supervised Field Work	Coordinated Activities	Guided Observation/Participation
Early intervention programs that vary in philosophy, communication method, and setting and offer a range of services to families of various cultures Programs for infants/toddlers with hearing impairment and for children with other disabilities Major responsibilities for assessment, planning, and intervention; working with families; supervising paraprofessionals; and participating on an interdisciplinary team	Activities with families and hearing-impaired infants and toddlers to foster family/preprofessional relationship	Family/parent group meetings Interdisciplinary team meetings of professionals, both hearing and hearing impaired in family/parent group meetings, including early interventionists, psychologists, and counselors Seminars in which students and faculty discuss issues and concerns related to concurrent field work and examine decisions made in programming with families and children and varying rationales and perspectives related to those decisions

in ASL and in English-based sign systems. Students should take sign communication courses throughout their program of studies; specific courses and course sequences should be determined by the instructor, individual student, and advisor.

The curriculum of coursework and field experience recommended in table I is based on graduate-level work in the context of both preservice and inservice systems of training. There is consensus in the literature that both undergraduate training as prerequisite knowledge and the breadth and depth of knowledge plus experience associated with graduate work are essential for gaining competence in each of the roles of the early interventionist (Bricker and Slentz 1989; Klein and Campbell 1990). To support the interdisciplinary team approach to early intervention, applicants with undergraduate backgrounds in regular and special education, early childhood education, social work, psychology, and other clinical fields may be admitted to preparation programs. If applicants who are not teacher certified wish to seek teacher certification at the completion of the master's program, their preparation program should include general education prerequisite courses. Specific courses and other prerequisites, such as experience with young children or sign communication ability, should be identified on the basis of state certification requirements and program outcome expectations. The list of content areas under the heading, "General Education," in table I includes typical minimum requirements. In addition, these general education content areas satisfy CED prerequisites for provisional certification (CED 1984).

The recommendations in table I represent content areas rather than courses. If 2 to 3 credit hours of coursework are provided for each content area, the preparation program will satisfy CED requirements for professional certification for the parent-infant specialization (CED 1984) and DEC recommendations for the continuing professional certificate in early childhood special education if the graduate has the requisite 2 to 3 years work experience (McCollum et al. 1989). Without the work experience, graduates are eligible for CED provisional and the beginning professional certification recommended by DEC.

State personnel planning agencies working with universities should seek ways to provide comprehensive in-depth early intervention content through preservice preparation and inservice programs. While the preservice preparation process typically includes comprehensive preparation by taking the student through a set scope and sequence of courses and field work, the same goals may be realized through an inservice process that systematically builds on a current worker's existing experience and knowledge (McCollum and Bailey 1991). Where inservice programs recognize competency and provide individually designed programs of study targeted to need, the field's current investment in valuable personnel is preserved. Both preservice and inservice education strategies are necessary in early intervention personnel preparation if states are to provide the highest quality practitioners.

Process Components

Course content and field experiences recommended for graduate-level study in early intervention for hearing-impaired children and their families should be developed within a family-centered, interdisciplinary, interagency framework. This is in accordance with current views regarding "best practice" in early childhood development, and with the services required under P.L. 99-457. To achieve that orientation, certain curriculum development and instructional strategies must occur in both preservice and inservice training programs. These strategies are process components that determine how the knowledge and skill will be delivered. Many have been highlighted earlier:

1. Specific goals, objectives, and requirements for courses and field work experiences should be developed together so that the scope and sequence of each course's content and material are integrated and are consistent across disciplines in the early intervention curriculum.

2. Each of the early intervention specialization courses and practica should have an identified family-centered emphasis in the knowledge and skills it develops. This focus should be clearly specified in course and practicum objectives.

3. Each of the specialization courses should be linked to applied experiences (e.g., an assignment or project) in the field so that theoretical course content is incorporated into practice.

4. Early in the preparation program, during the first practicum, students should be "partnered" with individual families. The supervised partnership should be long term (2 to 3 semesters) and should involve sequentially developed consulting, planning, and intervention activities in the context of a developing family preprofessional relationship.

5. A parent advisor should be a member of the faculty team involved in the preparation program. As a professional staff member, the parent advisor should provide input to course and practicum development, should co-teach and participate in classes, and should co-direct and co-supervise field work activities (Bohlin 1989; McGonigel, Kaufmann, and Johnson 1991). The parent advisor should be a parent of a hearing-impaired child, knowledgeable and involved in local school and community early intervention services, and have the ability to teach and advise graduate level students.

6. Specialization courses should be team taught by faculty across disciplines whenever feasible (McGonigel, Kaufmann, and Johnson 1991). For example, pediatric audiology could be taught by an audiologist and educator of hearing-impaired children/early childhood educator team; the families course could have an educator-counselor-parent team.

7.   Courses should be dual-listed across academic departments to enable students from different disciplines (e.g., audiology, counseling, social work) to enroll in the same courses. Teams of students can then be coordinated and coursework developed to promote an interdisciplinary perspective and to foster the ability of the individual to make unique and discipline-specific contributions within a consultation model.

8.   For student teaching/internship, cooperating teachers should be sought (or trained) whose instructional methods and processes for guiding the student's development include positive problem solving and reflection and are, therefore, congruent with the student's preparation program.

CONCLUDING REMARKS

This chapter has examined the scope of graduate-level preservice or inservice preparation in early intervention for hearing-impaired children and their families. Specific content for the necessary knowledge and field experiences has been outlined, and several organization and process strategies for delivering the curriculum have been described. The recommendations are guided by the requirements of P.L. 99-457, satisfy the certification guidelines of the two professional organizations most related to the field (DEC and CED), and are responsive to the 1988 Report from the Commission on the Education of the Deaf. However, they still do not guarantee eligibility for state certification because of the tremendous variability in state certification requirements. Each state has the important tasks of developing early intervention personnel licensure or certification standards and the structure of personnel development to support the standards (McCollum and Bailey 1991). One goal of any university program should be to prepare individuals who are able and eager to assume leadership roles in directing the future of early intervention for infants and toddlers with hearing impairments and their families. At a time in our society when "culture" is used to describe the habits of big business, as well as ethnic groups and other communities of people, it is time to address "the culture of the early intervention profession." The field, although in a developmental period, is clearly not in its infancy and "ways of living" or habits of the profession are accumulating. A cultural perspective might better enable us to identify and understand those unique habits and, thus, to transmit them.

Comprehensive preparation of early intervention specialists is a challenge for the university as well as for federal, state, and local agencies developing personnel systems. The national need for early intervention services is pressing and availability of highest quality personnel has not kept pace. The recommendations made in this chapter for preservice and inservice training are made with the belief and optimism about what can and must be done to ensure a better future for children with hearing impairments and their families.

REFERENCES

Ayres, J. A. 1849. Home education for the deaf and dumb. *American Annals of the Deaf* 2:176–87.

Bailey, D., Palsha, S. A., and Huntington, G. S. 1990. Preservice preparation of special educators to serve infants with handicaps and their families: Current status and training needs. *Journal of Early Intervention* 14:43–54.

Bohlin, J. K. 1989. Teaching and learning: My first year as an advisor at Wheelock College. *Zero to Three* 10:12–15.

Bricker, D., and Slentz, K. 1989. Personnel preparation: Handicapped infants. In *Handbook of Special Education: Research and Practice*, Vol. III, eds. M. C. Wang, M. C. Reynolds, and H. J. Walberg. New York: Pergamon Books.

Broman, S. H., Nichols, P. L., and Kennedy, W. A. 1975. *Preschool IQ: Prenatal and Early Developmental Correlates*. Hillsdale, NJ: Lawrence Erlbaum and Associates.

Bronfenbrenner, U. 1979. *The Ecology of Human Development: Experiments by Nature and Design*. Cambridge: Harvard University Press.

Bronfenbrenner, U. 1986. Ecology of the family as a context for human development research perspectives. *Developmental Psychology* 22:723–42.

Council on Education of the Deaf. 1984. *Standards for the Certification of Professionals Involved in the Education of Hearing Impaired Children and Youth*. Washington, DC: Council on Education of the Deaf.

Crnic, K. A., Friedrich, W. N., and Greenberg, M. T. 1983. Adaptation of families with mentally retarded children: A model of stress, coping, and family ecology. *American Journal of Mental Deficiency* 88:125–38.

Federal Register. 1989. U.S. Department of Education (34 CFR Part 303) Early Intervention Program for Infants and Toddlers with Handicaps: Final Regulations. Washington, DC: U.S. Government Printing Office.

Fewell, R., and Vadasy, P. 1987. Measurement issues in studies of efficacy. *Topics in Early Childhood Special Education* 7:85–96.

Garbarino, J. 1990. The human ecology of early risk. In *Handbook of Early Childhood Education*, eds. S. J. Meisels and J. P. Shonkoff. New York: Cambridge University Press.

Greenberg, M. T., Calderon, R., and Kusche, C. 1984. Early intervention using simultaneous communication with deaf infants: The effect on communication development. *Child Development* 55:607–16.

John Tracy Clinic. 1968. *Correspondence Course for Parents of Preschool Deaf Children*. Los Angeles, CA: John Tracy Clinic.

Katz, L. G., and Raths, J. D. 1985. A framework for research on teacher education programs. *Journal of Teacher Education* 5:9–15.

Kazak, A. E., and Marvin, R. S. 1984. Differences, difficulties and adaptation: Stress and social networks in families with a handicapped child. *Family Relations* 33:67–77.

Kennedy, M. M. 1990. Choosing a goal for professional education. In *Handbook of Research on Teacher Education*, ed. W. R. Houston. New York: Macmillan.

Klein, N. K., and Campbell, P. 1990. Preparing professionals to serve at-risk and disabled infants, toddlers, and preschoolers. In *Handbook of Early Childhood Education*, eds. S. J. Meisels and J. P. Shonkoff. New York: Cambridge University Press.

Lanier, J. E. 1986. Research on teacher education. In *Handbook of Research on Teaching*, 3rd ed., ed. M. C. Wittrock. New York: Macmillan.

Liben, L. S. 1978. The development of deaf children: An overview of issues. In *Deaf Children: Developmental Perspectives*, ed. L. S. Liben. New York: Academic Press.

McCollum, J. A. 1987. Early interventionists in infant and early childhood programs: A comparison of preservice training needs. *Topics in Early Childhood Special Education* 7:24–35.

McCollum, J., and Bailey, D. 1991. Developing comprehensive personnel systems: Issues and alternatives. *Journal of Early Intervention* 15:57–65.

McCollum, J., and McCartan, K. 1988. Research in teacher education: Issues and future directions for early childhood special education. In *Early Intervention for Infants and Children with Handicaps*, eds. S. L. Odom and M. B. Karnes. Baltimore: Paul H. Brookes Publishing.

McCollum, J., and Thorp, E. 1988. Training of infant specialists: A look to the future. *Infants and Young Children* 1:55–65.

McCollum, J., McLean, M., McCartan, K., and Kaiser, C. 1989. Recommendations for certification of early childhood special educators. *Journal of Early Intervention* 13:195–211.

McGonigel, M., Kaufmann, R., and Johnson, B. 1991. (Eds.). *Guidelines and Recommended Practices for the Individualized Family Service Plan* (2nd ed.). Washington, DC: ACCH.

Meadow-Orlans, K. P. 1987. An analysis of the effectiveness of early intervention programs for hearing-impaired children. In *The Effectiveness of Early Intervention for At-Risk and Handicapped Children*, eds. M. J. Guralnick and F. Bennett. New York: Academic Press.

Meisels, S. J., Harbin G., Modigliani, K., and Olson, K. 1988. Formulating optimal state early intervention policies. *Exceptional Children* 55:159–65.

Moores, D. M. 1987. *Educating the Deaf: Psychology, Principles, and Practices*, 3rd ed. Boston: Houghton Mifflin.

Peterson, N. L. 1987. *Early Intervention for Handicapped and At-Risk Children: An Introduction to Early Childhood Special Education*. Denver, CO: Love.

Rawlings, B., and Jensema, C. 1977. *Two Studies of the Families of Hearing Impaired Children*, Series R, No. 5. Washington, DC: Gallaudet College, Office of Demographic Studies.

Schildroth, A. N., Rawlings, B. W., and Allen, T. E. 1989. Hearing-impaired children under age 6: A demographic analysis. *American Annals of the Deaf* 134:63–69.

Smith, B., and Powers, C. 1987. Issues related to developing state certification policies. *Topics in Early Childhood Special Education* 7:12–23.

Toward Equality: Education of the Deaf. 1988. A Report to the President and the Congress of the United States. The Commission on Education of the Deaf. Washington, DC: U.S. Government Printing Office.

Turnbull, A. P., and Turnbull, H. R. 1990. *Families, Professionals, and Exceptionality: A Special Partnership*, Second edition. Columbus, OH: Merrill.

Weiner, R., and Koppelman, J. 1987. From *Birth to 5: Serving the Youngest Handicapped Children*. Alexandria, VA: Capitol Publications.

Werner, E. E., Biermin, J. M., and French, F. E. 1971. *The Children of Kauai.* Honolulu: University of Hawaii.

Zeichner, K. M., and Liston, D. P. 1987. Teaching student teachers to reflect. *Harvard Educational Review* 57:23–48.

Chapter • 17

Strengthening Family–
Professional Relations
Advice from Parents

Jackson Roush

Every family with a deaf or hard-of-hearing child has a story to tell. In the early stages it is often one of shock and bewilderment. But for many families there eventually comes a sense of personal growth and insight. In every family's story there are highs and lows, successes and failures. Some of the frustrations seem to be part of the inevitable struggle facing families with young, special-needs children. But others seem to be the direct result of experiences with professionals. Indeed, as families share their experiences it is clear that parent–professional relationships have an enormous impact on a family's outlook and attitude.

For this chapter we invited families to share some of their personal observations and experiences. They were asked to respond, via a letter of invitation, to the following questions:

> What do you think professionals need to know about working with and communicating with the parents of young, recently identified deaf and hard-of-hearing children?
>
> How could we improve the education of these individuals?
>
> In your experience with professionals, what was especially helpful?
>
> What was frustrating or problematic?

Parents were advised that their comments could pertain to any professional discipline (parent–infant specialists, audiologists, physicians, programs administrators, or any other professional group).

These families were referred to us by professional colleagues in several states across the United States. Although we did not attempt a formal sampling procedure, the families were from a variety of income levels and ethnic backgrounds, with children of various ages attending early intervention programs with a broad range of philosophical orientations. Their written comments were edited only for length and when reference was made to specific people or places. Although the parent contributors were not given a specific format, their comments seemed to fall within a limited number of categories: experiences surrounding the initial diagnosis; experiences with supportive and nonsupportive professionals; conflicts with schools and other institutions; and methodological issues.

EXPERIENCES SURROUNDING THE INITIAL DIAGNOSIS

Parents have remarkable recall of the events surrounding the initial diagnosis of hearing loss. Parents often remember in vivid detail the clinician who delivered this information and the manner in which it was imparted. Unfortunately, this is often among the most painful events experienced by parents, as illustrated in the following.

> When our daughter lost her hearing from pneumococcal meningitis at one year of age, my husband and I were emotionally devastated. We had been so hopeful that the behavioral response test that had been given to her shortly after her illness was inconclusive. But when the results of the auditory evoked response test confirmed that our child was deaf—probably profoundly deaf, I could not believe what I was hearing. My memory of what followed blurs, as did my vision from the rush of tears I could not stop. I felt my world crumbling around me. I know I couldn't absorb much of what was being said, but I also know it was technical and aloof—not compassionate. I don't think many professionals (particularly audiologists) realize, or want to address, how devastating the news they are conveying can be. A "bedside manner" could be so comforting to parents at a time like this—and so few professionals with whom I have come in contact have it.

Another parent remembers this event with similar emotions.

> I can remember how devastated I was—there was anger, the "why us?", "Why my child?"; the guilt "What did I do to cause this?", "No wonder he didn't respond to my yelling—he couldn't hear." There was also a long grieving process for us—that even now five years later will resurface at times.

For many parents the initial diagnosis is accompanied by a profound sense of personal loss and disillusionment.

> There are a handful of things in my life that I know will never leave my memory. The first is the birth of our son and all of the hopes and dreams that accompanied his entrance into this world. The second is the day all

of those dreams were shattered in that thirty-minute office visit. Our son's pediatrician was on vacation, consequently her associate explained the impairment. I know that she answered my questions, but to this day the only question I remember asking was what about school? She said that he would need to go to a special school throughout his education. The last shred of reality faded and my husband and I were faced with rebuilding our lives. Telling our family and friends was very difficult because although they felt our pain and loss to an extent, it was too big to grasp. The reactions and comments were so mixed it was unbelievable. The two most commonly heard responses were, "Modern medicine is constantly making new advances that in a few years, who knows?" And, "Why can't they just operate." The most painful comment, though well intended, was, "There are so many other handicaps that he could have had, thank God it is just his hearing." I always wanted to reply back that as parents we don't want him to have any handicaps, selfish as that may sound.

Fathers, too, can be devastated by the diagnosis of deafness, especially when delivered in a manner perceived as harsh and unsympathetic.

I have always considered myself to be this tough guy who could handle any situation. Instead, I broke down and cried, not knowing what to do. In our case, my wife and I did not have time to get over the "shock" of learning of our son's handicap. The way the options were presented to us seemed to be in a cold, uncaring way.

Still, some parents may view the naive comments of well-meaning friends and relatives as an opportunity to impart information and a deeper understanding.

Well-meaning friends, relatives and even strangers who knew nothing of deafness would say things with the best of intentions, yet very difficult for parents to hear, such as "it could have been worse," "it was meant to be," or "are you sure?" The number of times we have stood by and watched someone try to prove to us that our son can really hear, that he was just being "stubborn" is unbelievable yet understandable given that hearing impairment is such an "invisible" handicap. We learned, rather than be hurt or upset by insensitive comments, to view those interactions as an opportunity to teach someone about deafness and other handicaps in general.

The process leading up to a definitive diagnosis may result in a protracted period of mental anguish for parents.

When our son was about 18 months old, I remember approaching our pediatrician about our concern that he wasn't talking yet. She assured us that many kids are delayed in some way or another and that it was nothing to worry about. She performed a rudimentary test on him in her office with tuning forks and concluded that there was nothing wrong with him, but suggested that we could have him tested at the local university if we wished. Unfortunately for us, the university was closed for six weeks. Not knowing where else to turn, we waited for what seemed at the time to be an eternity to get an appointment.

Many parents are unaware of the nature of hearing loss. This mother recalls the pain of observing her child's first behavioral hearing test.

> Despite the fact that I realized people can have different degrees of visual impairment and therefore need varying prescriptions for their glasses, I knew so little about hearing impairment that I was under the delusion that either a person is, or is not, deaf. After we first suspected our son had a hearing problem, we tested him constantly while waiting for his first audiogram appointment—clapping our hands behind his back, dropping things on the floor, slamming doors, etc. Every time he reacted, no doubt to feeling the books drop and the doors slam, we convinced ourselves that he was fine, never realizing that he could be partially deaf. So, when we finally had him tested in the soundproof room at the university, and our teeth were rattling in our heads before he heard a sound, the shock was total and complete.

As if the initial shock of being informed of the child's deafness is not enough, some parents report further frustration due to lack of information regarding the hearing loss and steps to be taken to proceed.

> I remember the instantaneous feeling of guilt. Having been sick during my third month of pregnancy, I immediately connected that with my son's diagnosis. The audiologist who tested him was unwilling to tell us anything, feeling that was our pediatrician's responsibility, although the results of the test were obvious even to us. The audiologist was distinctly uncomfortable when I asked him whether the illness during my pregnancy could have caused the problem. Obviously, he couldn't have known, and therefore couldn't honestly answer *yes* or *no*, but by his discomfort I understood he couldn't rule out the possibility. We left his office knowing nothing except that our son was deaf. We were devastated, overwhelmed, terrified, and at a loss as to what to do next and where and what kinds of help to get for him.

In contrast to the experiences reported above, some families had positive experiences surrounding the initial diagnosis.

> We knew that our first child was not hearing normally, but the pediatrician had assured us that his hearing loss was probably temporary and correctable. We were stunned when the audiologist told us that our son had a severe-to-profound hearing impairment, which was neither temporary nor correctable, but the manner in which the audiologist communicated the diagnosis helped us. She was matter-of-fact, but compassionate, and unhurried. She did not overwhelm us or use the word "deaf." She knew all the difficulties ahead, but also knew that we should learn these gradually, one day at a time. We did know from this first meeting that one of the most important tasks was to fit our son with hearing aids as quickly as possible and see that he wore them consistently. We learned, too, that he needed to begin speech therapy as soon as possible.

The following comments reveal the importance of considering the parents emotional state apart from the specific needs of the child.

> I will never forget my initial contact with one particular individual. I had been networking with other parents of deaf children and his name had

come up several times. I called him at home one evening and described the terrible turn of events that had left our daughter without hearing. I fully expected him to say, as many others have, "How is she doing?" Instead, he very sincerely asked, "And how are *you* doing?" I burst into tears and described my emotional ordeal. In essence, his tone gave me permission to cry. I was allowed to acknowledge my loss openly. I felt my burden being lifted by his empathy. Over the course of the next two years, I relied on him and his staff for guidance, information and education for my child. Through it all, he was always willing to help me confront my feelings head on, and for that I will always be grateful.

Many parents report that the audiologist's focus on ability rather than disability helped them to maintain a more positive and constructive attitude during the early stages.

Our lifeline over the next few years was our contact with one particular [professional] individual. From her we learned to concentrate not on what was lost, but what was possible. We learned how to make the most of our son's hearing, how to teach him to listen, where to buy hearing aids, and how to get financial assistance. She was an invaluable resource and friend. To her credit, she never made light of the seriousness of the problem; she simply concentrated on the solution.

PROFESSIONAL BIAS

While each professional is influenced by his or her education and experiences, some parents feel professionals were not objective in their recommendations regarding early intervention. Professional bias was noted by several parents as a serious obstacle during the early stages of identification and program planning.

When our daughter was diagnosed, we encountered several biased professionals. The issue of how to teach deaf children language has become quite a passionate one, and thus, one would expect someone in the field to have an opinion. However, it is unfair to parents of a newly diagnosed child not to be presented with all options in a clear, thorough and unbiased manner.

Many parents expressed concern and even anger toward professionals they perceived as overtly biased.

As parents of a handicapped child, we feel we have the right to have access to all information regarding the education of our child. The final decisions of whether or not to use sign language, or whether or not to place our child in a residential school, ultimately rest with us. While the support and information supplied by professionals was very valuable to us, it was incomplete due to the "oral bias" built into the educational system in our area.

Comments regarding professional bias cut across lines of methodology, and all other categories.

> The city where our daughter was diagnosed is heavily biased towards ASL and against cochlear implants in children. As a parent of a highly successful auditory-verbal cochlear implant child, I find this reprehensible. She is a happy, well-adjusted hearing child because we actively pursued all options. However, in the early years, we were told that auditory-verbal therapy was full of "extremists."

In contrast, parents who were served by professionals they perceived as objective and unbiased gave parents a sense of empowerment and self-confidence.

> There seemed to be a rapid turnover in teachers for our hearing impaired son. Then all of a sudden, the substitute from heaven was upon us. She had this amazing way of making me feel like I was actually doing something good for my child. After I held out 10 minutes for a vocalization from my son she told me, "I wish we could clone you." I think she sincerely felt that a mother who is with her child 24 hours a day could have some influence. It sounds so simple, but in 2 years she was the first to encourage me. It rejuvenated me and I worked twice as hard with a newly found confidence toward the goals we had set. The feeling that I might be doing more harm than good had vanished.

Most parents want guidance in the options they choose.

> It was very frustrating when our daughter was first diagnosed to know what to do with this child who all of a sudden was "hearing impaired." We tried to read as much as we could to gain a better understanding of what this child was going to need. With the help of audiologists and an itinerant teacher we decided to give it some time with the hearing aids and see how she would respond. It was always a guessing game. Was she improving and progressing enough? The itinerant teacher thought so, but we kept having our doubts. Things just didn't feel comfortable after a while—feeling more doubtful about her auditory and speech skills gradually improving. Was the oral way the best choice for her now? We were fortunate to get to work with a clinician who helped guide us objectively two different times in our daughter's toddler and preschool years. I say helped guide because that's what she did. She did not tell us what to do or say, "I think this is the best for your daughter and your family." No, she laid out all the options for us and let us choose ourselves what was best for our daughter and family. I felt so good about that because it was more comfortable and easier for us to accept.

Another parent reports a similar, collaborative relationship although her comments reflect the enormous influence that professionals can have on parents at this stage.

> The professionals were guiding us along a course of action. We probably would have followed wherever they had taken us. Early on, we were walking "by faith and not by sight." We could not immediately see the results. Soon, however, we did start to see results. Our son made slow, but steady progress. The speech therapists and preschool teachers celebrated each small step with us.

Parents are particularly appreciative when professionals recognize that each child is an individual with his or her own strengths and needs, apart from hearing loss, per se.

> We've mostly had good experiences with professionals dealing with our daughter. I've appreciated the professionals that have understood that each child has individual needs and that not all children whether hearing impaired or not, are the same.

The following series of comments, from parents whose children range in age from toddlers through elementary age, underscores the importance of a supportive, nonjudgmental approach and a willingness to alter the level of parent participation and decision making as families become better informed and more "self-directed."

> We've tried to listen to advice as fairly as possible and have also appreciated those professionals who do not side with one specific method of communication that they most agree with, but the ones who believe that they are all good ways and that the individual needs of the child depend on which method to "go for."

ða.

> When we were in the early stages of information gathering, we found it extremely frustrating to feel like we were constantly caught in the middle of an on-going battle between opposing points of view. I am grateful for the program we attended because of its unbiased willingness to adopt a teaching style compatible with parents' wishes, no matter what they were. As a result, families utilizing different modes of communicating with their children were brought together in a noncombative environment. If we sought information on an alternative method, it was gladly provided and we never felt pressured to adopt a new approach. Although we were quite sure we wanted to pursue oralism with our daughter, we were allowed to experiment with Signed English and Cued Speech. We finally chose a cochlear implant for our child.

ða.

> Working with people from our early intervention program was very rewarding. The parent–infant advocate I worked with was a tremendous help. She explained things so that I was able to understand everything; all the technical jargon, the different types of hearing impairments, and my "stupid" questions. She arranged all our appointments to fit my schedule. The most valuable person I've come in contact with was that first parent–infant advocate because she made everything come into perspective and was my voice at IFSP meetings.

ða.

> The best piece of advice I got was from a speech pathologist who told me that my child would be a success in whatever "mode" we chose because we (the parents) were so committed to helping this child reach full potential. And if we changed along the way, we wouldn't have lost anything. We would have gained something from every experience. And five years later I see that this is still true. I can tell by looking at the progress we have made.

ða.

> It was our son's first sign language teacher who taught us that he was a normal little boy first, and hearing-impaired second. She viewed her students as normal children using a foreign language, not as handicapped children trying to be normal. It was through her, two years after he was

discovered to be deaf, that we finally met a deaf adult. The importance of this cannot be overemphasized. Deaf children do grow up to be deaf adults. Our son thought that he would be hearing when he grew up because all the adults he knew were hearing. And, we learned that trying to make him into a hearing person wasn't necessarily in his best interest. Sign language became so important to us that we have moved twice to different states searching for better schools and peer groups.

CONFLICT WITH SCHOOL PERSONNEL

Among the most frequently cited sources of frustration were clashes with local educational agencies and school systems. In many cases, parents perceived school personnel to be adversarial rather than supportive.

> Most program administrators are extremely biased toward the methodology of aiding and educating deaf children espoused by their particular program. It is understandable that they should endorse their own program methods, but not, I think, to the exclusion of alternatives.

A lack of agreement among professionals, although inevitable, presents an especially frustrating situation for parents of young children.

> What has been frustrating (outside of money) when we first entered this world of hearing impairments, was to find out that the professionals couldn't agree on how to treat it. Aids vs. no aids, ASL, Signed English, Oral, Cued Speech, residential schools, mainstream. There were tough choices I had to make and I had no expertise at all. I not only found differences in where in the USA you were from, but from within our state as well.

In some cases, a fellow parent or other advocate can provide a helpful bridge between the family and the early intervention program.

> The decisions and options I'm talking about were that of choosing what type of communication was best for our daughter. With the outcome of the first evaluation we felt comfortable with staying with oral communication; but 14 months later at the second evaluation we made the decision to begin total communication for our daughter and to change the educational placement. This brought about a struggle with our school district to get them to see what was best for our child now. We did not get the approval for the placement we wanted for our daughter, but went ahead with what we knew was best for us. Later in the summer, we had a mediation conference to see if we all could come to an agreement. At that time another parent had agreed to come to our meeting to help support us. She was a very knowledgeable person about the needs of deaf children and had gone through meetings like this for her daughter. She added such valuable support for us at that early stage. It was so hard to know all the things we needed the services to ask for and to not feel threatened. It was hard not to take the rejections personally and to know what to say. This mother and a preschool consultant were there thinking for us. It was wonderful to have their support.

Parents also express concern that the limited contact professionals have with the child may lead to misinterpretation and erroneous conclusions.

> I feel sometimes professionals can draw wrong conclusions about the child if they don't know them or are evaluating them in an environment that is new or strange to the child. We had an opportunity when our daughter was first diagnosed to go to a week-long workshop for parents of newly diagnosed deaf children and for the deaf children, too. It was a week-long session for both with testing and evaluations done on the children. The team was made up of professionals we did not know and I really felt that they reached the wrong conclusions about our daughter because she was not acting like herself in the new and strange environment and being left by us during the day at her age.

Even a single event can be permanently etched in a parent's memory.

> I only remember being discouraged by a professional one time. She reminded me several times in one session that my son was language delayed. I was painfully aware of that anyway, and I went home really low.

And even a supportive environment can cause divisiveness within the family if all interested family members are not involved to the extent they desire.

> I must admit I was somewhat apprehensive at first; after all, this lady was going to steer my son in an educational direction I knew nothing about. What if she was terrible at what she did? How would I know? Could I really ask for credentials? We were fortunate to have one of the best, a therapist that was understanding to our son's needs, as well as our needs. She became a support figure for my wife, especially when the "bad" days came around. I believe that this relationship was critical to the success of the initial therapy. However, I felt somewhat left out of this relationship. I was at work when the sessions took place, and I relied on what my wife had learned during the day for use in communicating and working with my son. Now, after several years, I play a highly active role with the communication learning experiences of our son, but feel I abandoned my wife during the early years. I suggest coming up with alternative learning methods which allow the spouse to become more involved with the sessions and intervention up front.

ADVICE FOR PROFESSIONALS

The following commentaries offer "advice for professionals" on a variety of topics regarding assessment and early intervention.

> I suggest that dealing with the parents' feelings, helping them to cope and understand the tragedy first, would allow the parents and professionals to build a firm base to start a relationship with.

> ૐ

> Every parent may not choose the path that we have, but they should have help in achieving a good understanding of all methodologies and the commitments entailed, as well as the long-term benefits/disadvantages for their child of each method.

&a

Professionals working with parents of young recently identified children with hearing loss, initially need to acknowledge the parent's grief and sense of loss. Supportive listening is the first step in establishing a rapport. It sounds so simple, yet acting like you care is crucial.

&a

Another thing that I've appreciated over these few years and which has made me feel so good is to have professionals, audiologists, speech-language pathologists, deaf educators and clinicians tell me what a good job I'm doing with our daughter. Compliments and praise really help us parents to keep pushing on for our deaf kids.

&a

Professionals must understand that this [the hearing loss] will have a major impact on everything the family does—where we live, work, go to school, vacation, and how we can afford it. Most of my life has now been planned around my child's ears. Professionals need to know that the family will go to you for more than just your expertise. . . . We need your help in dealing with this because we don't know who to ask. Most of us parents have never had contact with a deaf person.

&a

I can remember that when my three-year-old son was diagnosed as moderately-severely hearing impaired, I focused on all the things he wouldn't be able to do—but with the help of others, I was able to see what he would be able to do. He might not be able to serve his country in the military, but he could grow up and be a doctor, or a lawyer or even a politician. (I think most of them are really deaf anyway!)

&a

Professionals should offer as much information as possible—and much of it will need to be repeated. Handouts, books, groups in the community have been extremely helpful. When parents of a very young baby/child are told their child is deaf, it may be difficult for them to understand the long-term benefits of using hearing aids, speech therapy, etc. Frequent contact and explanations are important. Any resources you know of, offer them. The financial aspects of this is overwhelming. Most of us do not qualify for public aid and our insurance does not cover things such as hearing aids and molds.

&a

The people who were most helpful were the ones who took the time (in my case, the speech pathologist and audiologists) to find out how we were doing. They were not only interested in the children, but in how was my job, my marriage, my emotional well-being. Even on busy days when I had to walk in without an appointment to get a letter signed or a hearing aid fixed, they were always available. I think that's the key—these people were always available when I needed them. Looking back these professionals helped guide me through the most difficult period of my life, (I refer to them as my "dark years") and I will be forever grateful.

&a

The most helpful thing our pediatrician did for us is put us into contact with another family with a hearing impaired child. They welcomed us into their home and gently let us acclimate ourselves to the new world we were entering. They provided us with names of audiologists, schools, and organizations, that was invaluable. Meeting their son who was so animated and so vocal gave us the strength we needed to continue down our new path.

৯

I've also appreciated the respect I have been shown by professionals; the way they've asked for my opinions and have listened to me. I feel like parents know their children the best and professionals need to listen to what the parents are saying.

৯

I would like to mention that functions we attended for the hearing impaired, such as family picnics, allowed us to put things into perspective. What I mean by this is that we were able to see older children that had impairment, and were overcoming them in their own way. On the other hand, we saw children that had handicaps more severe than our son, or that were not responding to therapy as well as our son. In a way, this allowed us to see our son's progress. It also gave us an avenue to meet parents who have children with similar handicaps.

৯

I feel the first thing a professional can do in working with parents is to give them all the facts. In the beginning most parents don't understand some of the terms the audiologist uses. They need things explained thoroughly when they are over the initial shock and ready to comprehend it or whenever they have a question. Parents can't possibly make educated decisions about their child's future if they don't fully understand their child's hearing loss and what it means.

৯

One of the strongest messages that I could give to professionals is that we are dealing with people here, people who are new to this whole experience, whose lives have often been suddenly turned upside-down, people who are going to live with the consequences of professional advice for a long time. People though don't get very many days off from a challenge they never dreamed of facing in their lives. People though may need to grieve before they can move past denial to action.

৯

Another thing that parents desperately need is encouragement! When I really started to realize how important encouragement could be was when I finally started to get some from my child's teacher. I had been working extremely hard with my son from the time he was diagnosed almost two years earlier. During that time my feeling of inadequacy about being the mother of a child with a birth defect which I knew very little about had only been reinforced by the professionals we worked with.

৯

The last thing I would like to mention is the need for educating pediatricians. It took me three months to convince our pediatrician that my son may not be able to hear. It's incredible how many parents have the same story or worse. Since the hearing impaired child has a much better chance at success if his parents know he needs special education at an early age, why do pediatricians avoid hearing tests? My opinion is that if a parent has any feeling that their child may not be hearing properly that is reason enough for a hearing test.

Not surprisingly, much of the "advice for parents" revolved around issues related to "methodology," especially those related to the use of sign language.

Parents should not only be told about all options from ASL to auditory-verbal therapy and everything in between, but should also be able to see happy successful children and their parents in all options.

ра

Professionals should be well versed in the different educational options regardless of their particular discipline or philosophy. I think they have an obligation to present all options to parents, and then guide and support them in the decision-making process. This is a tricky area and can be problematic for parents if the professional fails to provide enough information, is very biased, or does not encourage parents to be active in making decisions for their child.

ра

I think professionals need to be aware of the range of educational options available today. Not to sell any particular methodology, but to help parents make informed choices. My experience is that professionals often stay within a comfort zone of discussing technology or providing educational information that gives the impression that only one method works. For children with profound hearing losses, educational strategies are probably the most important factor—all the technology in the world won't "fix" the child.

ра

Despite all the information we received from our professional contact, the one thing not then mentioned was sign language. Because we lived at that time in an "oral state," all hearing-impaired children were educated only by the oral method. Sign language was taught only to multihandicapped children and children who had failed in the "oral" educational system. When we talked to this person about the possibility of using sign language, we were strongly discouraged, as she felt we would be robbing our son of his chance to learn how to speak and be "normal." While we understood her point of view, we were not willing to let him become an "oral failure." Our primary concern was to communicate with him in any and all ways possible and as soon as possible.

ра

It is exactly one year since we learned of our son's impairment, and our lives are truly richer for it. We gain our strength through this child, who is like any other healthy normal two year old. We visited one school and were so saddened when we learned that they only encouraged the moderately hearing-impaired children to speak, and the profound children were expected only to sign. Our main goal is to give our son self-esteem to empower him against this limited thinking. We always tell him where we are going and what we are doing, leaving nothing to chance. I know that he can understand everything because we have a strong communication level. Concepts may take longer to explain, but the results are so rewarding. We have come to realize that our son will be able to accomplish anything he sets out to do, and that no one should limit him to his results on an audiogram.

ʚ

Having a degree in pediatrics, otolaryngology, or audiology does not make one an expert on deaf education. If you don't have current, accurate information on the subject, please don't offer opinions that you heard in school 15 years ago to help parents make educational choices. It's only human to want to relieve another's pain, but direct them to accurate sources of unbiased information instead.

ʚ

Take time to assess the mental state of the parents when giving them advice and information. It's OK to repeat things from an earlier session. Shock, grief, or denial can feel a lot like being hit in the head with a baseball bat, so don't assume that the parents are playing with a full deck on a given day. Perhaps having them tell you what they understood would help.

ʚ

Professionals need to know more about grief. I'm not suggesting that they become therapists, but they need to know that a parent in one of the stages of grief—shock, anger, denial—is really not playing with a full deck all the time. The first days and weeks after the diagnosis, I was walking around in a fog much of the time. It doesn't hurt to repeat things on subsequent visits, or to check out how clearly someone is functioning.

ʚ

Some families eventually gain new insights from their experiences in parenting a child with a hearing loss.

I try to remind myself when times get tough and I get depressed and feel totally "fed-up" with dealing with deafness. I look at my friends and their normal hearing children and say, "Why our daughter? Why us?" I then try to renew myself with this thought: that God chose this child for us and He knows and has confidence in us that we can handle it! Our lives have been enriched by our experience with this child.

CONCLUSION

These parent commentaries represent a broad spectrum of methodological and philosophical views. But despite the respondents' diversity, certain recurring themes emerge from their shared experiences.

   1.   The early stages of identification are among the most stressful some parents will experience in their entire lives. Families want professionals to provide facts and information, but also to consider the affective domain. A sincere, caring attitude from professionals, even if they don't know all the answers, is noticed and appreciated. This is particularly important during the early stages of identification and in-

tervention. Consideration of the parents' emotional state apart from the specific needs of the child, is especially appreciated.

2. Early on, many parents want the "right choices" presented to them; but eventually, most want to make their own decisions. They must depend on professionals, however, to provide honest, unbiased information, delivered at a level appropriate to their knowledge and experience. Most families seek professionals who will support and encourage them along the path of their own choosing.

3. Families want flexibility in methodology and placement decisions. What may be the "right decision" at a given point in time may change later on. Families want to be supported in the options they choose, and not made to feel "locked in" to these important decisions.

4. Families need to be praised and supported for what they are able to do, and not "judged" for what they are unable to do.

5. Parents want and need the support of other parents. Many families report an emotional "turning point" when they connected with a supportive group of other parents.

6. Professionals should consider the impact of hearing loss on the entire family. Parents are particularly appreciative when professionals seek creative ways to encourage the participation of all family members rather than designating a given individual, usually the mother, as the family expert and decision maker.

7. In many families, having a child with a hearing loss is an experience that eventually enriches their lives despite the difficulties encountered. Regardless of what placement decisions or methodological options a family may choose, professionals must impart a sense of hope for the future, with an emphasis on *ability* rather than *disability*!

Index

"T" (telecoil) option on personal
hearing aid, 68-69
Turnbull, A., 7, 115
Turnbull, H., 7

Underamplification, 72
Unisensory mode of communication,
228-29
University of Washington. *See* Early
Childhood Home Instruction
Program for Hearing-Impaired
Infants and Their Families
(ECHI)

Vanderbilt University. *See* Mama
Lere Early Intervention Program
Verbal skills, 205-7
Videotapes, 174; to observe child's

development, 146; of oral and
signed language samples, 148
The Visiting Infant and Parent
(V.I.P.) program at Clarke
School for the Deaf, 215-16, 217-
23; changes in the, 231-32; evolution of, 232-33; follow-up services and, 230-31; goals of, 216-
17; informing parents about
deafness and, 219, 225; participation in, 226-29; principles of, 223-
25; results of, 229-30; unique features of, 225-26
Visual Reinforcement Audiometry
(VRA), 57-59

Whistling from hearing aid, 66
Winton, P., 27, 30